W9-DDH-896

TEMPERAMENT AS A REGULATOR OF BEHAVIOR

After Fifty Years of Research

TEMPERAMENT AS A REGULATOR OF BEHAVIOR

After Fifty Years of Research

JAN STRELAU

Warsaw School of Social Psychology
Warsaw, Poland

Foreword by Robert Plomin

ELIOT WERNER PUBLICATIONS, INC.
CLINTON CORNERS, NEW YORK

Library of Congress Cataloging-in-Publication Data

Strelau, Jan.
Temperament as a regulator of behavior: after fifty years of research / Jan Strelau.
p. cm.
Includes bibliographical references and index.
ISBN 0-9752738-9-2
1. Temperament. 2. Individual differences. 3. Personality. I. Title.
BF798.S664 2007
155.2'62—dc22

2007018347

ISBN-10: 0-9752738-9-2
ISBN-13: 978-0-9752738-9-0

Copyright © 2008 Eliot Werner Publications, Inc.
PO Box 268, Clinton Corners, New York 12514
http://www.eliotwerner.com

Printed in the United States of America

I dedicate this book to all my collaborators, students, and disciples whose research has contributed to the origin and empirical verification of the Regulative Theory of Temperament

Foreword

I feel honored to write a foreword to this book that summarizes fifty years of temperament research by Jan Strelau and his colleagues at the Warsaw School of Social Psychology. Strelau has had a vision of temperament as rooted in the nervous system and has pursued that vision for the past half-century. As a pampered Western psychologist, I am humbled by the scientific progress Strelau made during the first two decades of his career despite the deprivation and brutality of the post-World War II Stalinist period in Poland, which is briefly described in the introduction to this book (a more extended account appears in his 1995 autobiography).

Most other theories of temperament are essentially a collection of personality traits selected on the basis of some criterion such as appearance in infancy, stability during childhood, heritability, or merely — as in the case of the so-called Big Five personality theory — lexical frequency of adjectives. Strelau's Regulative Theory of Temperament (RTT) of the Warsaw group is a theory in the deeper explanatory sense of the word "theory" in that it was derived initially from the core elements of functional properties of the nervous system described by Pavlov: strength of excitation, strength of inhibition, and mobility of the central nervous system. As a good theory should, the RTT developed to encompass other work on the functional nervous system, such as strength of excitation in terms of arousal and arousability as investigated by Jeffrey Gray and the concept of optimal level of arousal as described by Donald Hebb.

The primary emphasis of the RTT is on the biological basis of temperament, specifically the nervous system, and on the functional impact of temperament in the sense of its regulatory role on the energetic and temporal aspects of behavior rather than the specific content of behavior. A hallmark of a good theory is that it goes beyond what is known to make novel and testable predictions and the RTT gets good marks here too — for example, suggesting the neonatal emergence of temperament, the stability of temperament, the universality of temperament across species, its evolutionary origins, its heritability, and the importance of temperament as a regulator of behavior in difficult situations.

The RTT is not just a nice theory. Strelau's work has led to an innovative and carefully constructed questionnaire called the Formal Characteristics of Behavior–Temperament Inventory, which is derived from the RTT and has been translated into many languages. He has also followed the RTT where it leads—for example, into cross-cultural comparisons, genetics, disease, stress, and even staff burnout and trauma, including fascinating research following the 1997 Flood of the Century in Poland.

This book is much more than a historical review of the RTT. It presents data that shows the reader why and how the theory evolved and leads to an updated version of the theory in the form of ten propositions. Although Strelau's early search for physiological correlations of nervous system properties was disappointing and led to his subsequent focus on the behavioral level of analysis, he has bequeathed a theory that cries out for neuroscience research using modern techniques of neuroimaging.

Psychology can be a faddish field, not really solving problems but tiring of them and then running after a new fad. What I admire most is the systematic nature of Strelau's fifty-year research program. This book demonstrates the value of such long-term dedication to a systematic program of research.

Robert Plomin
Institute of Psychiatry
King's College London
London, United Kingdom

Contents

Introduction

I t took a long time to decide how to write the introduction to a book that summarizes fifty years of research. When I was still a student, I conducted several experiments—quite apart from my studies to fulfill the requirements for my master's degree—on conditioned reflex activity in the Pavlovian sense, and soon after I received my diploma in psychology in 1958, I published my first scientific paper in the journal *Psychologia Wychowawcza*. But before I introduce the main themes of this book, I would like to briefly describe the circumstances and conditions in which I matured as a pupil, student, and researcher.

I attended high school and university during the post-World War II Stalinist period. It was during this period, which lasted until 1956, that the Polish people—mainly former Home Army soldiers and their families and members of the prewar intelligentsia—were most severely mistreated. Many Poles were sentenced to death or long-term incarceration. These were the years of the most brutal activity of Security Police functionaries who, by means of blackmail, threat of loss of work or even life, or other methods, organized networks of secret agents, denunciators, and collaborators. Because of these crude manipulations, they managed to gain almost complete control of society—its opinions, attitudes, behaviors, and activities.

I mention this to familiarize Polish students and the younger generation, as well as scientists from the West, with the specific nature of the times in which my generation studied and conducted research. Drawing on my own experience, I described these times at length in my autobiography (Strelau, 1995a), published in a small edition (five hundred copies) in *The History of Polish Psychology in Autobiographies* edited by Teresa Rzepa.

In addition to my own experiences between my adolescence and the 1960s (which, compared with those of my psychologist peers, were quite dramatic), the conditions in which we studied and conducted research for at least twenty years after the end of World War II were extremely difficult. In the first half of the 1950s, the training of psychologists was largely based on Soviet literature and the dominant theory was so-called Pavlovism. A large portion of academic classes was devoted to Marxist-Leninist philosophy. For many years people had no access to English-language literature, and in the fifties people who violated the ban and read such literature risked serious political consequences. Polish universities suffered a drastic shortage of Western psychological journals that was not alleviated until the 1990s.

1

In Poland—as in the entire socialist bloc—not only were researchers cut off from scientific information, but many were also physically isolated from the West because they were forbidden to travel abroad. To illustrate this, let me give an example from my own experience, paradoxical as it may seem from our perspective today.

In 1963 the Seventeenth International Congress of Psychologists was held in Washington, D.C. On this occasion the American Psychological Association (APA) awarded a special scholarship to one young distinguished researcher from each socialist country (and perhaps also from Third World countries). The Polish Psychological Association decided that I was to be the beneficiary of this award. The APA agreed to defray all the costs of participating in the congress and also to pay for a three-month training period in either the United States or Canada. The congress organizers sent me a round-trip airline ticket and a letter saying that I had been granted a three-month scientific scholarship at the University of Alberta in Edmonton (Canada) with the outstanding neuropsychologist, Mortimer Mishkin. A few days before I was due to leave for Canada, however, I received an official letter from the Ministry of Higher Education saying that I had been refused permission for this journey. And that was the end of my "first visit" to North America. It was only eight years later, when I was already 40 years old, that I was allowed to travel to the West for the first time. I went to the United States for one year in 1971 thanks to a scholarship granted by the IREX Foundation. I spent most of my time with Jerry Hirsch and Raymond Cattell at University of Illinois in Champaign-Urbana and Richard Lazarus and Read Tuddenham at the University of California in Berkeley.

For psychologists, as for representatives of other scientific disciplines, the doors to the West did not open—and even then only a little—until the 1960s and 1970s. Because the Polish zloty was not exchangeable for foreign currency until the early nineties, researchers who attended scientific meetings abroad (conferences, congresses, etc.) had very little disposable money—just enough to eat at fast food outlets such as McDonald's. This meant that they were often confronted with embarrassing situations. For example, knowing that in most Western countries individuals pay for themselves, if someone invited me to dinner or lunch, I had to make up a story that I had a stomach ache, had some urgent work to do, was indisposed, or had already eaten, because the money I had would have barely been enough for that one meal or even not enough for that. Until the early 1990s, Polish citizens were not allowed to have credit cards. This too led to considerable discomfort during foreign visits, especially to the United States, because hotel receptionists demanded that guests show their credit card (not their passport) even if the organizers or host institution were paying. Many researchers (including me) who traveled abroad as scholars or visiting professors had credit cards issued in the host country and then held on to these cards illegally when they returned home and used them on future foreign trips.

In the face of these limited or even impossible (in the early years of my research career) contacts with Western psychologists, I compensated for this shortage by means of intensive contacts with Soviet psychologists. This was all the easier since my original scientific interest had been Ivan Pavlov's typology of the nervous system (NS), an important research focus at the Institute of Psychology at the Academy of Educational Sciences in Moscow and the College of Education in Perm (Ural). This way I came to know the most distinguished Russian researchers of individual differences, Boris Teplov and Vladimir Nebylitsyn (Moscow) and Vulf Merlin (Perm).

My six-month scholarship at the Laboratory of Individual Differences at the Moscow Institute in 1966 (my first foreign visit) also facilitated my first personal contacts with Western psychologists. At the Eighteenth International Congress of Psychology, which took place in Moscow during my stay in that city, I met Hans Eysenck and his most outstanding student, Jeffrey Gray. Both researchers had a very significant impact on my own temperament research and I maintained regular contact with them, first by letter and then personally. Eysenck and I became close friends through the International Society for the Study of Individual Differences, which he founded; we also coedited a book, *Personality Dimensions and Arousal* (Strelau & Eysenck, 1987). Jeffrey Gray, one of the world's leading neuropsychologists, wrote the foreword to my book *Temperament, Personality, Activity* (Strelau, 1983). This book was published in Polish in 1985 and in Chinese two years later. (Incidentally another distinguished personality researcher, Lawrence Pervin of Rutgers University, "smuggled" the manuscript of the book to Academic Press in London. These were the days of martial law in Poland when all correspondence was strictly controlled and I could not possibly send the manuscript abroad.) It is due largely to this book, which has the largest number of citations of all publications by Polish psychologists, that I entered the circle of leading temperament researchers.

As for me, the window on world science and research did not open widely until my first visit to the West—a one-year stay in the United States during the 1971–72 academic year. I shall not give a detailed account here of the many scientific contacts that I made during that visit and nourished in various ways later. I just want to say that during my stay in the United States, I collected hundreds of reprints of articles on temperament and individual differences as well as many books with which I was generously presented. These reprints, together with many more that American and European psychologists later sent me by mail, originated my reprint library— which now has almost six thousand items. At a time when such literature was totally lacking in Polish libraries, this private collection (which I computerized and classified according to my scientific interests) allowed my collaborators, graduate and postgraduate students, and me to keep up to date with the latest achievements in our discipline. I am deeply indebted to all those Western psychologists who supported us in the days of profound deprivation in the sphere of scientific information.

Beginning in the first half of the 1970s, I have been invited to numerous symposia, conferences, congresses, and lectures and have been able to reciprocate to my foreign counterparts. I have done so largely by inviting significant foreign psychologists to symposia and conferences in Poland, which my colleagues and I were among the first to organize in our country. We organized the International Conference on Temperament and Personality in 1974 and the International Conference on Temperament, Need for Stimulation, and Activity in 1979. These conferences were attended by—among others—Stella Chess, Alexander Thomas, Irvin Sarason, Robert Thayer, Marvin Zuckerman, and Kirby Gilliland (United States); Joseph Royce and Robert Hare (Canada); Anthony Gale (United Kingdom); Risto Näätänen (Finland); Wolfgang Schönpflug (West Germany); and Ko Orlebeke and Jan Feij (the Netherlands). Many researchers from former socialist countries also attended these conferences.

For both my collaborators and graduate students and for Eastern European participants, this was the only opportunity to meet renowned Western psychologists personally. The proceedings of these conferences were published in a two-volume work, *The Biological Bases of Personality and Behavior* (Strelau, Farley, & Gale, 1985, 1986). The articles published in this collection were also a good opportunity to familiarize Western researchers with our efforts. Another such occasion was the International Stress and Anxiety Conference (the occasion of Hans Eysenck's first visit to Poland) that my friend Charles Spielberger and I organized in 1983. The twelfth volume of the Stress and Anxiety series (Spielberger, Sarason, & Strelau, 1989), based on the conference proceedings, was yet another good opportunity to present our scientific achievements. After that we organized several other international symposia and workshops—for example, the Third European Conference on Personality (Gdańsk, 1986) and the Seventh Meeting of the International Society for the Study of Individual Differences (Warsaw, 1995).

When Poland began its political and economic transformation at the beginning of the 1990s (the first country in the socialist bloc to do so), we gained full civil liberties and the economy began to follow free market principles. The scientific community adopted the system of competitive grants, an innovation from which young postdoctoral fellows greatly benefited; previously their research activity had depended almost entirely on heads of departments (chairs) and directors of institutes. In short, as far as conditions of research are concerned, we began to function much as Western researchers do—particularly when Poland became a member of the European Union. The main difference between Western researchers and us, however, is budgets. Resources allocated for research in Poland are the lowest in the European Union and academic salaries are several times lower than the salaries of their American and Western European peers.

As I noted above, it was in such evolving political, economic, and social conditions that my own research activity of more than a half-century—reflected very briefly and selectively in this book—developed.

The chapters in this book illustrate the evolution of my scientific interests and the stages of research that I conducted with my colleagues and students, beginning with the experimental study of basic properties of the nervous system, which—according to Pavlov's physiological conceptualization—combine into the four classical temperaments: the sanguine, choleric, phlegmatic, and melancholic types. This explains why the titles of the first two chapters in a book devoted entirely to the study of temperament accentuate the NS properties that underlie Pavolov's typology. Research on the physiological and behavioral correlates of these properties (chapter 1) led me to believe that one cannot diagnose temperament by focusing on the specific physiological mechanisms that underlie these correlates, in the same way that we make inferences about temperament based on the overall characteristics of behavior; this diagnosis is specific, depending on the correlate we study (physiological, behavioral). Following the Russian psychophysiologists, I called this phenomenon trait partiality.

Disappointed with the search for physiological correlates of NS properties, I shifted my attention to the psychometric assessment of these properties—which, in line with Pavlov's approach, I interpreted in behavioral terms (cf. chapter 2). The difference between my approach and Pavlov's is that whereas Pavlov characterized the NS properties he identified in terms of conditioned-reflex activity, I focused on the behavioral indicators of the basic NS properties. It became clear to me that the questionnaire presented in this chapter (known as the Temperament Questionnaire in Poland and the Strelau Temperament Inventory abroad) cannot possibly assess properties of the nervous system. What it can do is measure temperament traits based on hypothetical NS properties postulated by Pavlov, on the assumption that these properties provide the physiological basis for temperament.

Influenced by Pavlov himself, and above all by my mentor and the founder of the Warsaw School of Psychology, Tadeusz Tomaszewski, and also by Eysenck, Gray, and other researchers who drew on the biological concept of arousal in their theories of temperament and personality, I began to think of temperament in functional terms and to conceive its role as a regulator and codeterminant of human behavior. This regulation has largely to do with the energetic and temporal aspects of behavior in situations varying in intensity of stimulation of the behavior itself and the environment. This thinking led to the conceptualization of the Regulative Theory of Temperament (RTT). This theory, and the first studies conducted by my colleagues, students, and me within the RTT paradigm, will be discussed in chapter 3.

The stages of research that I discuss in the first three chapters have been presented comprehensively in two of my books (cf. Strelau 1969, 1983) and I often refer to them in these chapters. The main reason why I return briefly to these early stages of my work here is to show readers the road that led me to develop the Regulative Theory of Temperament. Readers interested largely in the RTT itself and the research projects conducted within the RTT paradigm can skip these chapters and go directly to chapter 4.

Beginning with chapter 4, this volume is organized in such a way as to show the various paths leading to the empirical testing of the RTT against the backdrop of the theory itself. This explains why there are so many tables showing our findings. I have included these tables mainly because I want to avoid unconvincing cliches and to draw instead on tangible data that either confirm or falsify our hypotheses or our more intuitive predictions. Readers less inclined to figures and statistical data may skip some of the tables (especially the larger ones) and still grasp the main themes of the book.

The research presented in chapter 3 led to the revision of the basic outline of the RTT and to the development of the updated version of the theory as it is presented in chapter 4 in the form of ten theorems (propositions). Some of these are assumptions only — for example, the idea that not all temperament researchers share the notion that temperament traits are largely expressed in the formal characteristics of behavior. Most of the propositions, however, can be verified and hence the subsequent chapters are devoted to their empirical testing.

In order to put the functional role of temperament as it is conceived in the RTT to empirical test, we had to construct a psychometric instrument that would allow us to measure temperament traits as they are defined in the tested theory. Hence my colleagues and I began to study the structure of temperament and, drawing from a large body of empirical data, we constructed an inventory known as the Formal Characteristics of Behavior–Temperament Inventory, which now has many different language versions. This tool is presented in depth in chapter 5. As reflected in the subsequent chapters, we have been using it in nearly all our empirical work since the 1990s.

In our studies of the functional significance of temperament, we paid particular attention to RTT Propositions 9 and 10, which say that the regulative function of temperament is mainly to moderate the energetic and temporal value of behaviors and situations in which individuals find themselves, and that the role of temperament is most conspicuous when individuals are in extreme situations or conditions generally described as difficult. This explains why we launched a series of studies of the role of temperament as a moderator of stressors, the psychological consequences of the state of stress, and its role as a risk factor for somatic disease (cf. chapter 6).

The Flood of the Century, which hit Poland in 1997, presented us with a new challenge. If we were right and the role of temperament shows up most vividly in extreme situations and behaviors, then it was to be expected that temperament traits would affect human responses to this catastrophe and (above all) the psychological consequences of the trauma. Thanks to a grant that we received from the Scientific Research Committee for a project called Men and Women in the Face of Disaster, not only were we able to study the victims of the Flood of the Century, but we were also able to glean new ideas from this study for the larger studies presented in chapter 7. This chapter begins with an account of the construction of a psychometric instrument measuring the symptoms of post-traumatic stress disorders (when we began our studies, there was no appropriate tool in Poland with which to measure these symptoms). The rich data presented in this chapter confirmed beyond doubt that temperament traits play a functional role, especially with respect to the psychological consequences of exposure to extreme stressors. Depending on their specific nature, they may either predict disorders or act as a protective buffer against these disorders.

When Alois Angleitner—my friend from the University of Bielefeld (Germany)—and I were still involved in the study of the structure and assessment of Pavlovian temperament traits, we concluded that if we wanted to demonstrate the biological origins of temperament traits, we would have to attest first and foremost that individual differences in these traits are largely genetically determined. Therefore my colleagues and I launched a series of twin studies (comparison of monozygotic and dizygotic twins reared together), which confirmed our predictions in both the German and Polish samples. We applied this approach, later extended to family studies, another method used by behavior geneticists, to the RTT framework. Chapter 8 shows how individual differences in RTT traits depend on genetic factors to a considerable extent. It also demonstrates that these factors greatly account for the correlations we found between temperament traits and such aspects of stress as stressors (but only in the form of challenges), the psychological consequences of the state of stress, and coping styles.

This chapter also shows that as far as the genetic foundations of the RTT are concerned, my followers took a giant step forward and began a series of studies based on the molecular genetic paradigm. This paradigm answers different questions than the ones addressed by behavior genetics. For example, the methods used by molecular geneticists help to identify polymorphisms in the genes that are responsible for neurotransmitters (transporters and receptors)—which, we think, are the biochemical mechanisms of our postulated temperament traits. Although this work is still in an inchoate stage, the results that we have already obtained suggest that the biochemical mechanisms underlying RTT traits are genetically determined.

In the postscript I point out what we have managed to achieve over these many years and also what—contrary perhaps to our expectations—we have not managed to achieve and what still needs to be done. I also draw attention to the specific nature of our research methodology and try to show how this methodology differs from the pursuits of temperament researchers who represent other approaches or theories.

The scientific advances presented in this book would not have come about in this form and scope without my own research activity, but I must stress that it is certainly a joint effort. Hence the frequent use of the words "we," "our," "team," and so forth. I sometimes find it difficult to identify the original source of this or that idea or research project and if I have overlooked somebody or failed to express due appreciation, please forgive me.

Many of my collaborators and students made particularly significant contributions to the origination and development of the Regulative Theory of Temperament. I must mention my very first students and colleagues of many years, Andrzej Eliasz and Tatiana Klonowicz, both of whom—Eliasz mainly on a theoretical level and Klonowicz mainly on an empirical level—contributed to the preliminary outline of the Regulative Theory of Temperament and applied the first empirical data supporting this theory of temperament. For more than a dozen years, the persons who have contributed most to the empirical testing of the RTT are Bogdan Zawadzki and Włodzimierz Oniszczenko. Zawadzki, with whom I have coauthored the largest number of works, has given the RTT its present psychometric and methodological shape, whereas Oniszczenko has done a remarkable job in the field of genetic studies of temperament. Both were among the first readers of the manuscript of this book (Zawadzki read the whole book and Oniszczenko read chapter 8) and I wish to thank them for their insightful comments and critical suggestions. My very first reader, Magdalena Kaczmarek—who has worked closely with me for the last five years—shared her many critical comments and greatly assisted me in the preparation of the manuscript. I wish to thank her very much for everything she has done. I would also like to express my gratitude to Jerzy Brzesiński and Wiesław Łukaszewski, whose reviews of the manuscript convinced me that writing this book was well worth the effort.

My thanks also go to Gdańsk Psychological Publishers (GWP) for publishing this book in the original Polish. I do not exaggerate when I say that Anna Świtajska, director of this publishing house, helped to inspire this book. Many years ago Anna asked me to write a book that could be published by GWP and I agreed. She often repeated her request and I must say that my unfulfilled promise bothered me so much that I was finally motivated to "get down to work" and write the book. At this point I would like to thank Małgorzata Jaworska for her extremely meticulous and subtle language editing. She is one of the best editors I have known and I have known many. GWP was kind enough to limit the copyright of my book only to the Polish edition. Helena Grzegołowska-Klarkowska, my former doctoral student, was generous in translating the Polish version into English. I wish to express my most cordial thanks for the excellent job she has done.

Because I was always short of time due to the many academic duties to be fulfilled during the last few years, I owe much to the Warsaw School of Social Psychology, where I assumed the position of research professor in 1997. My good friend and also the rector of the school, Andrzej Eliasz, ensured that I could concentrate on my research.

During the final step in preparing the manuscript for the English edition of the book, my assistant Martina Gustak was very helpful on a number of levels (checking references, securing copyright permissions, compiling the index, etc.). Finally, I wish to express my most cordial thanks to Eliot Werner, who has undertaken the risk to publish the English version; he also undertook the effort to make a final, thorough editing of the manuscript. Our frequent correspondence, going beyond matters related to the book, has given me the feeling that I have gained a new friend.

We habitually thank our nearest and dearest for creating an atmosphere conducive to research. Here I would like to thank my wife Krystyna, who for fifty years has shared my successes and failures, encouraged me in my scientific and administrative endeavors, and helped me to realize my research goals.

Chapter 1

Experiments on the diagnosis of the basic properties of the nervous system as Pavlov understood them: The forerunners of the Regulative Theory of Temperament

I van Pavlov's (1928) theory of higher nervous activity was a compulsory subject during my freshman and sophomore years at Warsaw University. The part of this theory that particularly interested me was his typology of the properties of the nervous system (NS). It was in these properties that Pavlov, who won the Nobel Prize for his discoveries in the physiology of digestion, hoped to find the physiological bases of the four universally familiar types of temperament distinguished by Hippocrates-Galen.

1.1
Pavlov's typology as the starting point for my own studies of temperament

Observations of the behavior of dogs in experiments on classical conditioning, which Pavlov and his collaborators conducted in a so-called "silence tower," led him to conclude that individual differences are clearly manifested in the speed and exactness with which conditioned reflexes develop. Individual differences can also be found in the effectiveness, strength, duration, and facility with which these reflexes can be changed and in how animals behaved in the experimental chamber.

Pavlov (1928) formulated the following hypothesis. Specific properties of the central nervous system (CNS) are responsible for the individual differences in conditioning or, more generally, in the dogs' behavior. These properties are strength, mobility, and equilibrium of the nervous processes—excitation and inhibition. Particular configurations of these properties result in the type of nervous system. These types are discussed in detail elsewhere (see Gray, 1964; Mangan, 1982). I have also

9

described Pavlov's theory of CNS properties in my own publications (Strelau, 1983, 1998) and I shall refer to these works here.

Pavlov believed that strength of the nervous system was the most important NS property. He also distinguished between strength of excitation and strength of inhibition. Strength is important because unusual, exceptional events and intensive stimuli are often present in the individual's environment. Strength of excitation simply means the capacity of the nerve cells to work, their efficiency. It manifests itself mainly in the capacity to endure prolonged or brief but intensive excitation without going into a state of protective inhibition.[1] Strength of excitation can be assessed by registering reactions of responses to strong, long-lasting, or frequently repeated stimuli. Pavlov used the concepts strength of the nervous system and strength of excitation interchangeably and viewed them as a CNS trait (not an ongoing state). As expected, *ceteris paribus*, strength of the nervous system (trait) and intensity of the excitation process (state) are negatively correlated: the stronger the nervous system, the more resistant it is to intensive stimulation, the smaller the excitation understood as a transient state.

Pavlov also distinguished strength of inhibition—or to be more precise, strength of the nervous system with respect to inhibition—and attributed trait status to it as well. Pavlov did not tell us what to understand by strength of inhibition, however. When he talked about strength of inhibition, he meant conditioned inhibition as opposed to unconditioned inhibition, one of whose specific forms is protective inhibition. Strength of inhibition manifests itself in the effectiveness of the individual's functioning with respect to all possible forms of conditioned inhibition that is learned and acquired (i.e., extinction, delay, and differentiation of reactions to particular stimuli). Pavlov's ideas concerning strength of inhibition lacked clarity and were confusing and therefore his students and followers were reluctant to study this CNS property. Strength of inhibition was usually measured for one reason only: in order to determine the equilibrium (balance) between strength of excitation and strength of inhibition.

In his analysis of the nature of the equilibrium of the nervous processes, Pavlov adopted the functional point of view, much as he did with respect to the remaining CNS properties. He said that people and animals often have to inhibit certain excitations in order to respond to new environmental stimuli (Pavlov, 1938, p. 652). This is one of the reasons why equilibrium or balance of the strength of the

---

[1] According to Pavlov, protective (transmarginal) inhibition is a form of unconditioned inhibition whose purpose is to protect the central nervous system against overload. Pavlov (1928) said that strength and efficiency of the conditioned reflexes are a function of the intensity of the stimulus (the "rule of strength"). When the intensity of the stimulus exceeds the capacity (efficiency) of the central nervous system, the "rule of strength" no longer holds because protective inhibition sets in.

two nervous processes is so important. In other words, equilibrium of the nervous processes is defined by the ratio of strength of excitation to strength of inhibition.

The last property to be included in Pavlov's typology was mobility of the nervous processes. Mobility means "the capacity to give way, to give priority to one stimulus before another, excitation before inhibition, or vice-versa, as demanded by external circumstances" (Pavlov, 1938, p. 652). Mobility is manifested in the speed with which a given reaction to a stimulus is inhibited in order to give way to a reaction to another stimulus if need be. The environment is incessantly changing and therefore if individuals are to adjust adequately, their nervous processes must keep up with these changes.

Different configurations of these NS properties determine the type of nervous system, also referred to by Pavlov as the type of higher nervous activity. By taking strength of the nervous processes as his point of departure, Pavlov distinguished the strong and weak types of the CNS. Equilibrium (balance) between strength of excitation and strength of inhibition was the basis for the next division (but only of strong types) into the balanced type and unbalanced type. The unbalanced CNS type comes in one form only and is characterized by dominance of excitation over inhibition. The next criterion for Pavlov's typology was mobility of the nervous processes. He distinguished the mobile type of nervous system and the slow type of nervous system. Combining these three properties, which also differ in intensity, allows us to distinguish many more types than Pavlov suggested. Pavlov was adamant, however, that the four types of nervous system that he distinguished are equivalent to the four classical types of temperament proposed by Hippocrates and Galen (see Figure 1.1). He also argued that the types of nervous system determined on the basis of animal studies can be transferred to the human population.

> These types of nervous system are, when existing in people, what we call temperaments. Temperament is the most general peculiarity of every person, the most basic essentiality of his nervous system, and the type of nervous system colours all the activity of the individual. (Pavlov, 1928, p. 376)

In my own research, which directly referred to Pavlov's typology, I did not focus on Pavlov's four types of nervous system but on the underlying properties—or to be more precise, on the diagnosis of the basic NS properties as Pavlov understood them.

1.2
Receptor-determined specificity of the diagnosis of mobility of the nervous processes

In my master's thesis, which was published in two papers (Strelau, 1958, 1960), I focused on the diagnosis of mobility of the nervous processes. Mobility is the property that distinguishes the sanguine individual from the phlegmatic individ-

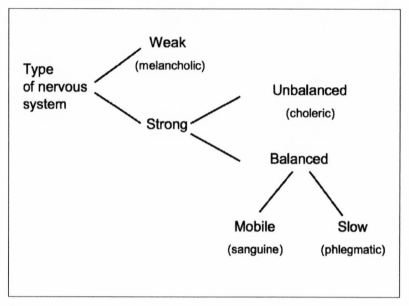

Figure 1.1. Pavlov's typology of the nervous system and its relationship with the Hippocrates-Galen typology of temperaments.

ual. The sanguine person has highly mobile nervous processes; the phlegmatic person's nervous processes lack this mobility (see Figure 1.1).

In this research several methods were applied, including the classical method of diagnosis of mobility of the nervous processes called "alteration of the signal value of stimuli"[2] (for a detailed description of this method, see Strelau, 1983). I demonstrated that the diagnosis of mobility of the nervous processes differs depending on the type of stimulus used to condition or alter the signal value of the stimulus (visual vs. auditory). The visual stimuli differed in color (a blue or green lamp) and the auditory stimuli differed in frequency (120 Hz or 1200 Hz).

---

[2] Alteration involves elaborating a positive and inhibitory conditioned reflex by associating a neutral stimulus (e.g., a sound whose frequency is 500 Hz) with an unconditioned stimulus. A second neutral stimulus (e.g., a sound whose frequency is 3000 Hz) is not reinforced by an unconditioned stimulus. Once a positive reaction to the reinforced sound and lack (inhibition) of reaction to the sound that was not reinforced have been elaborated, the experimental procedure is altered. The former inhibitory stimulus is now associated with the unconditioned stimulus and the stimulus that formerly evoked a conditioned reflex is now exposed without reinforcement (i.e., the conditioned response is extinguished). In this way the signal value of the two conditioned stimuli is altered. The fewer expositions of the stimuli that must be alternated in order to change their signal value, the greater the mobility of the individual's nervous processes.

The registered reaction was electrodermal activity (EDA) and the unconditioned stimulus was a benign electric shock (24 V). I must point out that before the late 1970s, the ethics of psychological research were largely ignored and laboratory experiments using electric shocks—which are unthinkable today—were standard procedure.

I concluded from my findings that alteration of the signal value of a pair of stimuli is quicker when visual stimuli are used than when auditory stimuli are used. On the basis of this finding, I hypothesized that mobility of the nervous processes is greater in those areas of the brain that are responsible for processing visual information than in those areas of the brain that are responsible for processing auditory information. I also concluded that the diagnosis of mobility based on visual stimuli is positively correlated (0.62) with the analogous diagnosis of mobility based on auditory stimuli.

As early as the 1940s and fifties, Russian researchers found that the diagnosis of the type of nervous system in animals (dogs, monkeys, mice) depends on the modality of the conditioned stimuli adopted in the conditioned reflex procedure (for a more detailed account, see Strelau, 1969). The studies demonstrating that the diagnosis of the strength of nervous processes in human beings depends on the type of stimuli (visual or auditory) were conducted by Vladimir Nebylitsyn (1957). He diagnosed strength of excitation using a method known as extinction with reinforcement[3] and alteration of the absolute visual and auditory sensory threshold in response to caffeine. Nebylitsyn found that the diagnosis of strength of excitation formulated on the basis of the two different stimulus modalities was consistent in 72 percent of the cases and inconsistent in 28 percent of the cases. These results were later to be confirmed in other studies conducted in the laboratory of Boris Teplov, the leading investigator of individual differences in the USSR (see Strelau, 1983; Teplov, 1985). Nebylitsyn, Teplov's most renowned disciple, concluded that there are both general NS properties and partial NS properties—that is, properties determined by the specific nature of the different analyzers (here the visual and auditory analyzers).

---

[3] In general, extinction with reinforcement works as follows. Once the conditioned reflex has been elaborated, its intensity is measured. The conditioned and unconditioned stimuli are exposed simultaneously and repeatedly and then the intensity of the conditioned response is measured once again. Reduction or disappearance of the conditioned response after these stimuli have been exposed, compared with the intensity of the conditioned response before these stimuli were exposed, is a sign of protective inhibition and the concomitant reduction of the capacity (efficiency) of the nervous system. If, on the other hand, the intensity of the conditioned response remains unchanged or even increases following exposition of the two stimuli, this is a sign of large capacity (efficiency) of the nerve cells—that is, a strong nervous system. For a detailed account of this method, see Strelau (1983).

1.3
Specificity of the diagnosis of strength of excitation and mobility of the nervous processes as determined by the modality of the unconditioned stimuli adopted in the conditioning process

In my next set of studies, conducted as part of the research for my doctoral dissertation, I focused on the diagnosis of type of nervous system depending on the modality of the unconditioned stimuli adopted in the conditioning process. I concentrated on those unconditioned stimuli that elevate EDA. The basic NS properties—strength of excitation, strength of inhibition, and mobility of the nervous processes—were diagnosed on the basis of speed of elaboration of positive and inhibitory conditioned reflexes and the speed of alteration of the signal value of a pair of stimuli. These indicators were also used in Pavlov's laboratory (Pavlov, 1938; for a description, see Strelau, 1983). Speed of elaboration of positive conditioned reflexes was the indicator of strength of excitation and speed of elaboration of inhibitory reflexes was the indicator of strength of inhibition. Mobility of the nervous processes was diagnosed on the basis of the speed of alteration of the signal value of a pair of stimuli. The unconditioned stimuli for EDA were an electric shock (400 V/0.1 mA), a thermal stimulus (65°C) exposed on the surface of the palm, and a powerful voluntary contraction of the muscles of the right hand evoked by pressing the correct button where the driving force was 10 kg. This last stimulus had already been used as an unconditioned reinforcement for EDA in Wulf Merlin's (1958) laboratory. Differently colored lamps served as the conditioned stimuli. The findings confirmed the hypothesis that specificity of the unconditioned reinforcements adopted in the conditioning process is a source of inconsistency in the diagnosis of the basic NS properties. Only 5.6 percent of the subjects received fully consistent diagnoses of their type based on all three unconditioned stimuli. Consistency for two out of three unconditioned stimuli was found in 50 percent of the subjects and the remaining 44.4 percent showed no consistency regardless of their diagnosis of basic NS properties.

These findings, which I have presented in several publications (Strelau, 1964, 1969, 1972a), led me to conclude that this variety of diagnoses of the basic properties of the nervous system is determined by the physiological strength (intensity) of the unconditioned stimuli. In this study three independent measures of the physiological strength were applied: EDA magnitude, latency following the exposition of unconditioned stimuli, and subjective ratings of the unpleasantness of these stimuli for the subjects.

Employing these measures, I found a correlation between speed of conditioning and the physiological strength of the stimuli. Since speed of conditioning was the basis for diagnosing type of nervous system, I concluded that the diagnosis of type of nervous system using the conditioned response method depends on the physiological strength of the unconditioned stimuli. The physiological strength of the three modalities of unconditioned stimuli applied in the experiment was individually specific and subject to considerable individual differences. In other words, for some individuals electric shock may be a more powerful stimulus than heat (and vice-versa) and these differences are probably partly determined by individual experience with the various categories of stimuli.

To the best of my knowledge, no human studies had previously been conducted demonstrating the specificity of the classical conditioning process depending on the modality of the unconditioned stimuli, at least in the research on basic CNS properties conducted within the Pavlovian research paradigm. In other words, partiality of nervous system properties depends not only on the kind of conditioned stimuli used, but also on the quality of the reinforcement applied in the conditioning procedure.

1.4
Specificity of the diagnosis of strength of excitation as determined by the kind of reaction measured

In the years that followed, I undertook a number of investigations focusing on diagnosis of strength of excitation, the NS property that Pavlov believed to be most important in the individual's adjustment to environmental demands. Pavlov expressed this conviction in his characterization of the melancholic, the temperament type whose excitation process is weak. Because the weak type of the CNS (melancholic) is so inefficient, the remaining NS properties (strength of inhibition, mobility, and equilibrium of the nervous process) are no longer important and the weak type is more or less handicapped (Pavlov, 1938, p. 669). It must be pointed out that this characterization of the weak type is based on research on dogs that was conducted in Pavlov's laboratory. Experiments conducted on children and adults in the second half of the twentieth century (see Strelau, 1998) suggest that as long as the environment makes provisions for the individual's temperament traits, the individual can adjust to that environment and function normally regardless of his or her temperament.

The relationship between diagnosis of NS properties (here strength of excitation) and modality of conditioned stimuli (e.g., auditory or visual) has been confirmed repeatedly. My own studies of the relationship between diagnosis of nervous system properties and type of unconditioned stimuli adopted in the conditioning procedure confirmed that this specificity exists and that it depends on the modality of the unconditioned stimulus. In order to determine whether the partiality of NS properties can also be found in reactions (responses) to be measured, I conducted another series of experiments specifically addressed to this problem;

the common denominator of these experiments was that they all focused on diagnosis of strength of excitation. I shall outline three of these experiments very briefly. Readers who would like to learn more about them are referred to other publications where the procedures and findings are reported more comprehensively (Strelau, 1969, 1972a, 1983).

The purpose of the first experiment was to determine whether the diagnosis of strength of excitation would differ depending on the type of activity (physical or mental) used to formulate the diagnosis. Since the research on diagnosis of NS properties using different modalities of conditioned and unconditioned stimuli demonstrated that the diagnosis is indeed specific and differs depending on the manipulated variables, I once again hypothesized that the diagnoses would differ depending on the type of reaction measured.

I used simple reaction time (RT) to measure physical activity, whereas to measure mental activity, a modified version of the Kraepelin test—a measure based on simple arithmetic problems—was applied. The subject must do 495 sums, each of which consists of five randomly selected, two-digit numbers. For the RT indicator, strength of excitation was measured using a simple procedure proposed by L. A. Kopytova (1963). This measure is based on the assumption that the long series of frequently repeated stimuli will lead to fatigue of the nerve cells (reduced efficiency) and therefore the RTs will increase. The underlying mechanism, as in the method of extinction with reinforcement, is protective inhibition.

In the experiment subjects were shown 240 visual stimuli (a green lamp) at 5–7 second intervals and RTs were measured. The indicator of strength of excitation was the change of the reaction time in response to repeated stimulus exposition. After Kopytowa, I assumed that longer RTs in the final stage of the experiment compared with the initial stage were a sign of low strength (weakness) of the excitation process. If the RTs did not change in response to repeated stimulus exposure or if they actually shortened, I assumed that this was a sign of strength of the excitation process.[4] A similar criterion was adopted for the Kraepelin test. Since the effectiveness of performance on arithmetic tests is measured both in terms of the number of completed sums in a given period of time and the number of errors committed, I calculated one indicator of mental effectiveness: the total number of completed sums minus the number of sums containing errors. Subjects took the Kraepelin test for eighty minutes and marked the last completed sum every five minutes. As with the RT experiment, the indicator of strength of excitation was the comparison of the effectiveness of the Kraepelin test in the initial and final stages. An essential decrease in effectiveness of the Kraepelin test in the final stage compared with the initial stage was a sign of weakness of the excita-

---

[4] Because the indicators of strength of excitation were complex in both this and the other experiments, I will not discuss them here. Details of these studies are available in Strelau (1969, 1983).

tion process, as in the RT experiment. If there was no difference between the outcomes of the initial and final phases or if effectiveness improved, it was assumed that this was a sign of strength of the excitation process.

The results of this experiment confirmed my hypothesis. Since two criteria of reduced effectiveness were adopted—lengthening the reaction time in the conditioned reflex experiment and reduced effectiveness in the Kraepelin test—four correlation coefficients were calculated. They were in the -0.06 to -0.38 range but only the latter coefficient was sufficiently close to be significant ($p < 0.07$). These findings unequivocally support the hypothesis that diagnosis of strength of the nervous system would differ depending on the type of reaction. However, the fact that all four correlation coefficients are negative suggests a certain tendency: wherever the RT increases in response to repeated stimulation, there also seems to be a drop in effectiveness due to prolonged mental effort.

The purpose of this experiment was to discover if the diagnosis of strength of excitation depends on the kind of effector (reaction). In the RT experiment, where the reaction consisted of pressing a button, there is no doubt about the effector. There is less clarity in the Kraepelin experiment, however. How entitled are we to speak of effectors when the activity is mental? While it is true that the final phase of the activity is realized by means of the muscular effector, effectiveness of subjects' effort (i.e., the speed and accuracy with which they do the sums) is not determined by this effector. The discrepancy in the diagnosis of strength of excitation may also be determined by the fact that the criterion in the RT experiment was the time needed to perform, whereas the criterion in the Kraepelin test experiment was effectiveness measured in terms of both performance time and performance accuracy. The two tasks also differed in many other ways (see Strelau, 1969) that could have affected the discrepancy in the diagnosis of strength of excitation.

Because of the methodological confusion in the first experiment, I conducted yet another experiment. This time strength of excitation was diagnosed on the basis of two different reactions, bioelectrical brain activity and the photochemical reflex.[5] In both these settings, I adopted the same indicator of strength of excitation (i.e., extinction with reinforcement), the same type of reinforcement (a light stimulus), and the same type of conditioned stimulus (an auditory stimulus). It was Nebylitsyn (1972) who introduced the method of extinction with reinforcement to the electroencephalogram (EEG) and Valentina Rozhdestvenskaya (1955) was the first to apply

---

[5] The photochemical reflex consists of changes in visual sensitivity in response to a light stimulus. An adequate number of associations of an unconditioned stimulus (light) and a neutral stimulus (e.g., a sound of a particular frequency) leads to the elaboration of a conditioned response. This is because the visual sensitivity is reduced in response to the isolated action of the conditioned stimulus.

it to research based on the photochemical reflex. I conducted this study, which is very briefly presented below, at Boris Teplov's laboratory in Moscow in 1966. Vladimir Nebylitsyn was director of the laboratory at the time.

As far as the experiment using the EEG technique is concerned, I registered alpha waves and their depression (appearance of beta waves) in response to a light stimulus (colored reproductions projected onto a screen). As in Nebylitsyn's (1966) study, this stimulus was treated as the unconditioned one. The conditioned stimulus was a sound whose frequency was 1000 Hz. Once the conditioned reflex to the sound stimulus was consolidated, as manifested in depression of the alpha rhythm in response to the sound alone, the extinction with reinforcement procedure began. This procedure involved combining a light stimulus with a sound stimulus in forty expositions (in 10–11 second intervals). Comparing the intensity of the conditioned response before and after the extinction with reinforcement procedure enabled me to diagnose strength of excitation. Bioelectrical brain activity was registered using bipolar leads: temporal-occipital from the left and right hemispheres.

The photochemical reflex was measured by means of an adaptometer, which was used to expose the subject in complete darkness to a circle and a square of increasing brightness in order to determine the sensitivity threshold. The light stimulus (which, in this case, had the status of an unconditioned stimulus) was projected onto a white screen placed in front of the subject. This stimulus elevated the sensitivity threshold considerably. In order to elaborate the conditioned reflex, a sound (frequency 500 Hz) was combined with the light stimulus. The extinction with reinforcement procedure, adopted after Rozhdestvenskaya, consisted of exposing the light stimuli and sound stimuli ten times at one-minute intervals. Once again, comparing the magnitude of the sensitivity threshold before and after the extinction with reinforcement procedure allowed me to diagnose strength of excitation.

The outcome of this experiment supported my initial hypothesis. The diagnosis of strength of excitation, formulated on the basis of the extinction with reinforcement procedure adapted to the EEG, did not correlate with the analogous diagnosis based on the photochemical reflex (-0.14; ns). This lack of correlation between the two measures of strength of excitation may actually be attributed to the fact that in both cases we were dealing with dramatically different reactions (exactly as we intended). It is possible, however, that the lack of correlation between the two measures of strength of excitation is caused by other factors. For example, when two independent measures of strength of excitation based on the photochemical reflex were compared, taken within a one-day interval, I found that the measures were not very reliable. The correlation coefficient was only 0.42 ($p < 0.05$). The reliability of EEG measures is far greater, however. In another study (Strelau, 1969) in which I compared the outcomes of extinction with reinforcement based on simultaneous registration from the left and right hemispheres, I found that two independent measures were highly correlated (0.82; $p < 0.01$), suggesting that this method is reliable.

Another doubtful element of the presented experiment was the use of colored slides as the unconditioned stimuli for the EEG response because some researchers have attributed the depression of the alpha rhythm in response to such stimuli to the orienting reflex (e.g., Anokhin, 1978; Sokolov, 1963). It must also be noted that as far as the photochemical reflex is concerned, the pupils of the eye are the effector; when we focus on bioelectrical brain rhythms, however, we are in fact measuring reactions in the middle part of the conditioned reflex arc. However, the term "effector" as it is understood is reserved for the descending path—that is, the end part of the arc. Finally, I must mention that individual differences in the speed of restitution of the sensitivity threshold—and visual sensitivity after the light stimulus has been switched off—create unequal conditions for the diagnosis of strength of excitation in different individuals, as pointed out by L. A. Shvarts (1965). Because of the doubts raised by this experiment, which have been discussed in detail elsewhere (Strelau, 1969), I conducted another experiment that I will now outline briefly.

In contrast to the previous experiment, which focused on involuntary movements, the third experiment devoted to diagnosis of strength of excitation focused on voluntary movements. The critiques of the two earlier experiments were the point of departure for this experiment, which allows us to resolve the question of whether diagnosis of strength of the human nervous system depends unequivocally on the type of effector (reaction).

The basic indicator of strength of excitation in this study was the change in motor reaction time in response to the multiple repetition of stimuli. A modified version of Kopytova's (1963) test was applied (see the first experiment). All the Ural psychologists working under Merlin, one of the most distinguished investigators of temperament among Russian psychologists, used this test to measure strength of excitation (see Merlin, 1973, 1986). In addition to the classic setting where RT is measured on the basis of the speed of response (pressing the response key with the right finger), RT was also measured less conventionally by means of a vocal response. In this way, by using an identical stimulus (sound) and an identical indicator of strength of excitation (the dynamics of motor RT in response to multiple repetition of stimuli), this CNS property was determined on the basis of two different motor reactions, each of which involves a different effector (reaction). Any differences in the outcomes of this experiment, designed to diagnose strength of excitation, can now be attributed to specificity of the effector (reaction) because this seems to be the only variable in this experiment.

The subjects performed two tasks. In the first task, they were to press the reaction key as quickly as possible with their right index finger (all the subjects were right handed) as soon as they heard the sound stimulus (a sound of 70 db intensity and 1000 Hz frequency). This was a classic measure of simple RT. In the second task, subjects were to respond as quickly as possible by saying "paf" (a semantically neutral sound in Polish) into the microphone as soon as they heard the sound. The distance of the microphone from the subject's mouth was the same for every subject. Of the 240 stimuli that were exposed, in 120 cases subjects responded with their hand and in the remaining 120 cases they responded with their voice. The two tasks were presented alternately, after every ten expositions of the sound stimulus at 5–7 second intervals. Half the subjects responded vocally to the first ten stimuli and the other half responded with their index finger. The other half responded in the reverse order.

The results of this experiment confirmed the hypothesis that the diagnosis of strength of excitation based on identical indicators of this NS property would differ depending on the motor reaction—either movement of the right index finger or saying "paf." The near-zero correlation coefficient (–0.03; *ns*) proves that the two measures, differing only in type of motor reaction, are completely unrelated.

1.5
Studies of partiality of nervous system properties diagnosed in the laboratory: Summary and conclusions

My research on the partiality of nervous system properties, which I conducted for more than ten years, demonstrates that differences in the diagnosis of NS properties are determined (among other things) by the following variables:

- Modality of the conditioned stimuli applied in the conditioning procedure (sound or light).

- Modality of the unconditioned stimuli (although this conclusion is limited to the elaboration of conditioned reflexes in EDA).

- Type of reaction on whose basis strength of excitation is determined (this pattern was found both for involuntary reactions [EEG and photochemical reflex] and voluntary reactions [mental activity and motor reactions]).

When interpreting the results of these studies (Strelau, 1969), I formulated four hypotheses.

First, there are only general properties of the central nervous system, as Pavlov postulated when he spoke of the physiological basis of temperament or when he actually identified his types of nervous system (various configurations of strength, mobility, and equilibrium of the nervous processes) with types of temperament. Partial CNS properties are artifacts. Divergence in the diagnosis of basic CNS properties is caused by other variables—for example, the physical intensity of the stimuli; the meaning attributed to the stimuli (conditioned and unconditioned), which is different for different individuals; current level of arousal; motivation; and so forth.

Second, there are both general CNS properties and independent partial properties that apply to various parts of the CNS. Hence the differences in the diagnosis of basic CNS properties depending on the degree to which the stimuli are applied and the reactions are registered involve parts of the CNS that are specific for these stimuli and these reactions. When discussing the problem of partial CNS properties in the context of general properties, Teplov (1956) said that partial properties are the physiological basis for special abilities, whereas general properties are the physiological basis for temperament (also as Pavlov postulated). The most important issue here, however, is how we can imply general CNS properties if the outcomes of research on the diagnosis of these properties are so inconsistent and dependent on the controlled variables.

The third and most radical hypothesis says that there are only specific CNS properties, partial to different neural centers. Hence every diagnosis of CNS properties is partial. The question in this case is to what extent we can say that the cortical and subcortical centers that underlie these partial properties are "atomized." Can we—as Nebylitsyn's studies suggested—talk about strength of excitation typical for the visual analyzer, meaning that it is the same in the whole cortical area related to the perception of visual stimuli, or should we stretch our atomization hypothesis further? For example, Rozhdestvenskaya concluded on the basis of her research that the characterization of strength of excitation is specific for the neural centers responsible for diurnal and nocturnal vision (Rozhdestvenskaya, Golubeva, & Yermolayeva-Tomina, 1969).

The fourth hypothesis, similar to the previous one, states that there are only specific CNS properties for the various neural centers. This hypothesis differs from the previous one in that it assumes the existence of dominant centers that are important for individual adaptation. Vatsuro (1945) had already made this suggestion on the basis of his studies on dogs and monkeys, which revealed that different analyzers have their own specific dynamics of nervous processes. This hypothesis says that the more perfect the functional properties of an analyzer (i.e., the greater the strength or mobility of the nervous processes in those parts of the brain), the greater the role that analyzer will play in the individual's adjustment to the environment.

A similar hypothesis, called the mass density principle (Jerison, 1982), has been formulated in the context of studies on the evolution of intelligence. "When the functional areas of the brain are mapped, there are both interspecific and intraspecific variations and disproportionalities in the maps that reflect the importance of the functions in the life of the animal" (Jerison, 1982, p. 781). According to this principle, the part of the brain that is responsible for a particular function reflects the amount of information that must be processed in order to perform that function. For example, in rodents the parts of the brain that are responsible for audition and olfaction—the dominant senses in these animals—are extremely well developed. In birds, meanwhile, large portions of the brain are responsible for balance and sight. It is highly probable that there are individual differences with respect to the dominant areas in human beings and if this is indeed so, it could help to account for partiality. Psychology has long been familiar with typologies that distinguish between visualizers and audiles depending on which of the two senses, vision or audition, play the dominant role (Strelau, 1969).

In subsequent years I have begun to approach partiality in the research on basic CNS properties from the perspective of studies conducted within the personality paradigm, based on the concept of traits. Practically all existing studies have confirmed that the diagnoses of personality traits (including temperament) in the laboratory setting, particularly when psychophysiological measures are involved, are inconsistent if different variables (stimuli, responses, indicators) are used in consecutive experimental sessions to diagnose a particular trait. For example, Hartshorne and May (1928) conducted a famous experiment on honesty and found that the diagnosis of this trait differed depending on the experimental setting. On the basis of this study and several studies of his own, which confirmed the finding that the personality traits will be diagnosed differently depending on the adopted variables, Walter Mischel (1968) initiated a critique of the trait theory approach to personality. Raymond Cattell (Cattell & Warburton, 1967) withdrew more than four hundred experimental tests that he had previously used to diagnose personality because the findings failed to give a consistent picture of the diagnosed traits. Jerome Kagan (1994) confronted similar obstacles when he tried to diagnose the inhibited temperament using various psychophysiological indicators and was forced to adopt a global index of this personality trait. Finally, in the most complex laboratory study of personality diagnosis ever conducted, Jochen Fahrenberg (1987, 1992) used both questionnaires and a wide array of psychophysiological measures (over a dozen) to assess neuroticism. On the basis of his studies, he arrived at a similar conclusion.

> Psychophysiological research on physiological correlates of the established emotionality (neuroticism) trait dimension has come to a standstill. Findings of questionnaire studies generally support the postulated psychophysiological relationship, but research that employs objectively measured physiological parameters in large-scale, methodologically well-controlled and replicated investigations has not substantiated these hypotheses. (Fahrenberg, 1987, p. 117)

In my own review of the research on the physiological correlates of sensation seeking, neuroticism, and extraversion, I arrived at the following conclusion: the assessments of these traits depending on the physiological indicators adopted (e.g., EDA vs. EEG measures) and the types of stimuli exposed to induce psychophysiological responses (e.g., visual vs. auditory)—on the basis of which implications could be drawn regarding these traits—are largely divergent (Strelau, 1991).

As we see, laboratory studies in general and psychophysiological studies in particular (which, almost without exception, have been conducted on CNS traits in animals and human beings since Pavlov's days) have usually led to inconsistent diagnoses of these traits. There are probably two reasons for this.

First, the physiological mechanism underlying a given temperament or personality trait is usually complex. The interaction between the various elements (components) of this mechanism codetermines the general tendency toward this or that behavior (i.e., trait). If so, then the results of the laboratory experiment in which we control one of these elements by means of the correlate (indicator) of a given trait need not correlate—and usually do not correlate—with the outcomes of studies in which other elements of the mechanisms are controlled, on the assumption that they are indicators (correlates) of the same trait.

Second, as Seymour Epstein (1979, 1984) convincingly demonstrated based on many of his own investigations and his analysis of the results of investigations conducted in other laboratories, temporal and cross-situational consistency (and the latter type of consistency is the main focus in the studies presented in this chapter) is a function of the aggregation of the various measures. By aggregating behaviors and reactions registered in many situations, each of which contributes a little to the total variance, it is possible to reach a highly reliable and valid assessment of the trait. Here trait is understood as "a generalized tendency to behave in particular ways, manifested in various tendency-consistent situations" (Strelau, 2006, p. 27). In the laboratory we usually measure what we are measuring once, over a short period of time, focusing on a single reaction or behavior; the setting is compulsory and new for the subject. If we examine Table 1.1, we can see that this situation greatly reduces the chances that traits will show up—and CNS properties have the status of traits. The variance of behaviors or reactions measured in the laboratory is determined not only by the controlled variables, but also by the situation (mood, motivation, current level of arousal, etc.) that is difficult or even impossible for the experimenter to control. Under these circumstances the individual's typical trait does not have much of a chance to show up.

These circumstances are probably one of the reasons why personality psychologists who describe personality structure in terms of traits or factors with trait status (see Strelau, 2006) usually resort to questionnaire techniques based on self-description (see, e.g., Cattell, 1965; Costa and McCrae, 1985; Eysenck, 1970) or, when young children are studied, rating scales[6] (see, e.g., Carey & McDevitt, 1978; Rotbart, 1981; see also Strelau, 1998). Questionnaires in the form of rating scales have also become popular in adult studies. Since rating scales are a quali-

---

[6] Rating means assessment by another person. In child studies the rating is usually done by parents, educators, or teachers; in adolescent and adult studies, it is done by peers, partners/spouses, or friends and acquaintances. Questionnaires used to assess traits in children were originally constructed as rating scales, whereas questionnaires used to assess traits in adults were originally constructed in the form of self-descriptions. When used as rating scales, the questionnaire items or questions are formulated in the third-person singular. This provides two fully equivalent measures of the same reactions or behaviors.

Table 1.1 Conditions under which environment or trait explain the variance of behavior

| | Best-explained variance of behavior | |
Condition	Environment	Trait
Frequency of behavior observation	Single observation	Multiple observations
Duration of behavior observation	Short	Long
Level of behavior diversity	Single acts of behavior	Multiple and wide spectrum of behavior
Possibility to express behavior	Limited	Free/unlimited
Possibility to choose situations	None	Unlimited
Possibility to create situations	None	Exists
Acquaintance with situation	New	Known
Type of situation	Experiment	Natural situation

Note. From *Psychologia różnic indywidualnych* [Psychology of Individual Differences] by J. Strelau, 2006, p. 30. Copyright 2006 by Wydawnictwo Naukowe Scholar. Reprinted with permission.

tatively distinct way of measuring the same traits, they are used as a validation criterion for psychometric instruments (e.g., Costa & McCrae, 1988; Ostendorf & Angleitner, 1994).

Questionnaires or inventories (I shall use the two terms interchangeably) have many shortcomings (for example, scales measure imprecisely and rarely enable cause-effect reasoning), but they also have many assets. One of their strong points is that the process of aggregation is usually embedded in the construction of the scale. "The separate items of personality (including temperament) inventories refer to various behaviors and various situations that take place at various times, and hence enable us to draw inferences about the traits they are supposed to measure" (Strelau, 2006, p. 38).

Disappointment with psychophysiological studies that do not allow the investigator to measure traits—understood as a general tendency toward specific behaviors—led my collaborators and me to abandon the psychophysiological method and focus instead on questionnaire studies of the basic Pavlovian CNS traits, and on the role of these temperament traits in the process of the individual's adaptation to environmental demands.

Chapter 2

Diagnosis of the basic properties of the nervous system by means of questionnaires

Before I began to assess the basic properties of the nervous system (as Pavlov understood them) by means of questionnaires, I tried observation—the method frequently used by Russian psychologists, particularly in the 1950s (see, e.g., Chudnovsky, 1963; Gorbacheva, 1954; Leites, 1956). Russian psychologists also resorted to interviews, mainly for clinical purposes (see, e.g., Birman, 1951; Ilina & Paley, 1958; and in Poland, Cytawa, 1959).

At this point, however, we must ask a fundamental question. How can we assess biological phenomena relating to the functioning of the central nervous system (CNS), including strength, mobility, and equilibrium of the nervous processes—that is, constructs to which Pavlov referred in his typology of the nervous system—by means of observation, interviews, or paper-and-pencil tests (to which questionnaires belong)?

The answer to this question, whose more expanded version I suggested more than thirty years ago (Strelau, 1969; see also Strelau, 1983), is as pertinent today as it was then. Pavlov was most concerned with the objective study of the activity of the cerebral hemispheres in dogs. According to his classical (Pavlovian) conditioning procedure, this involves identifying the relationships between external events (stimuli exposed in experimental settings) and various kinds of responses (in Pavlov's laboratory the response most commonly studied was salivation as a conditioned response to anticipated food). Hence Pavlov used the term "behavior" as a synonym for "higher nervous activity" in the title of one of his most important works: *Twenty-Five Years of Objective Study of the Higher Nervous Activity (Behaviour) of Animals* (Pavlov, 1928, 1938). This is a telling fact; it confirms the opinion that "physiology of the higher nervous processes," as Pavlov understood it, is actually a study of behavior. If this fact were not previously acknowledged, the reason probably lies in Pavlov's rejection of John Watson's classical behaviorism in which all behavior is reduced to stimulus-response relationships.

Physiology in studies of the type of nervous system, or its various properties whose combinations result in the different types, means that by interpreting specific behaviors and reactions that we associate with temperament traits, we are in fact referring to a hypothetical physiological mechanism—that is, a specific configuration of strength of excitation (SE), strength of inhibition (SI), and mobility of the nervous processes (MNP). These constructs are explanatory concepts referring to the functions of the central nervous system. As Gray (1972) pointed out, Pavlov's theory of higher nervous activity is about the functioning of the brain (conceptual nervous system) because Pavlov did not actually study the nervous processes underlying behavior. For example, when Pavlov defined strength of excitation, he characterized it in terms of the capacity of the nerve cells to work rather than in terms of the amount of "excitatory substance" in the neurone. He also drew inferences about the capacity of the nerve cells to work (their endurance) on the basis of the magnitude of the conditioned reflex; that is, he referred to the relationship between intensity of the conditioned stimulus and magnitude (intensity) of the conditioned response to that stimulus.

In other words, we can say that Pavlov's typology of the nervous system is about the basic properties of the nervous system understood in terms of behaviors and responses, and these in turn are the object of investigation of psychologists who measure them using the methods appropriate for their discipline (e.g., observation and questionnaires). If when we study temperament (a psychological concept) we talk about the basic properties of the nervous system (strength, equilibrium, and mobility of the nervous processes), what we mean is that the phenomenon we call temperament is determined by a hypothetical physiological mechanism that Pavlov and his followers associate with the processes and properties of the central nervous system.

2.1
Observation as a method for diagnosing the basic properties of the nervous system

After more than a decade of psychophysiological research on the Pavlovian CNS properties, which convinced me that the experimental method does not allow us to make inferences about properties understood as general tendencies toward specific behaviors or reactions (see section 1.5), I launched a new series of investigations whose purpose was to diagnose the basic CNS properties on the basis of behavior in natural settings.

In the first phase of this research, I applied the observational method. In order to assess the basic CNS properties, I used an observational chart based on a four-point rating scale. This method and the procedure for assessing the basic CNS properties based on the chart have been presented elsewhere (Strelau, 1965a, 1969). The observational chart, which has 75 items referring to various kinds of behavior and various situations, is a standard research program. This instrument allows us to diagnose strength of excitation, strength of inhibition, and mobility of the nervous processes and each property is assessed on the basis of 25 items. Here is a sample of the items.

Strength of excitation:

- Is the individual able to engage in one activity for a long period of time?
- Does the individual willingly undertake responsible work?
- Is the individual able to study (work) for a long time without a break?

Strength of inhibition:

- Is the individual able to control himself or herself when the situation demands it?
- Does the individual easily refrain from forbidden activities?
- Does the individual act thoughtfully in situations that require thoughtful consideration of the "pros and cons"?

Mobility of the nervous processes:

- Does the individual easily move from one activity to another?
- Does the individual easily adjust to a new daily routine?
- Does the individual easily adjust to new environments and new settings (e.g., change of residence, a new class, a new workplace)?

According to Pavlov, equilibrium of the nervous processes is determined by comparing the outcomes for strength of excitation and strength of inhibition. The situations and behaviors identifying the levels of the different properties were selected by analyzing other methods for diagnosing type of nervous system in human beings reported in the literature (see Strelau, 1969, 1983), and also by analyzing the concepts of basic CNS properties as Pavlov (1938) understood them.

2.2
The first attempt to construct a questionnaire to measure Pavlovian temperament

The observational chart, which we used to observe 41 men and women for three months, proved to be very laborious and impractical. Therefore, taking the chart as my point of departure, I made my first attempt to construct a questionnaire to assess temperament. Because this questionnaire enabled me to measure observable behaviors and reactions rather than CNS properties, I called it the Temperament Questionnaire (TQ). This questionnaire diagnoses temperament as understood by Pavlov. Recall Pavlov's claim that hypothetical CNS properties (i.e., strength of excitation, strength of inhibition, and their equilibrium) are the physiological mechanism of temperament and that various configurations of these three properties make up the type of nervous system.

The first stage of construction of the TQ, as well as its reliability and validity, have been presented elsewhere (Strelau, 1969, 1972b). The experimental version of the Temperament Questionnaire based on a three-point rating scale (Yes, No, ?) initially had 150 items, or 50 items per scale—Strength of Excitation, Strength of Inhibition, and Mobility of the Nervous Processes. According to Pavlov, equilibrium of the nervous processes is determined by calculating the ratio of strength of excitation to strength of inhibition. If the outcome is > 1, this means that strength of excitation is higher than strength of inhibition; if it is < 1, this means that strength of inhibition is higher than strength of excitation. The reason why the questionnaire has 150 items is that two equivalent questions were formulated for every item of the observational chart. This was done to facilitate the estimation of split-half reliability (according to Rulon's rtt formula). The split-half reliability coefficient for two separate testings was high and fell within the 0.72 (MNP) to 0.93 range (SI).

The validity of this experimental version of the TQ was assessed twice by comparing the results of this inventory with the results of the observational chart. Observation of the subjects' behavior by means of the observational chart lasted three months and therefore only a small group could be studied—14 subjects in the first sample (aged 18–30) and 27 subjects in the second sample (aged 17–42). Because the samples were small and the age ranges were limited, one should evaluate the validity outcomes for the TQ, which ranged from $r = 0.49$ to $r = 0.84$ (with one exception: the coefficient for SI was 0.17, ns), with great caution.

2.3
The Temperament Questionnaire that was used in psychological research and practice for about twenty years

The second version of the Temperament Questionnaire, which we used in our research from 1972 until the early 1990s (and even into the second half of the 1990s; see, e.g., Jachnis, 1996; Nosarzewski, 1997), was revised largely on the basis of item analysis. The number of items was reduced to 134: 44 in scale SE, 44 in scale SI, and 46 in scale MNP. This version of the TQ has been discussed at length elsewhere (Strelau, 1983) and therefore I shall outline only its most important features here.

Since the Pavlovian constructs of strength, mobility, and equilibrium of the nervous processes are explanatory concepts that refer to the functions of the central nervous system and are inferred on the basis of behavior and responses, the TQ scales are characterized in psychological terms. The items in the SE scale refer to Pavlov's idea that strength of excitation is simply the capacity of the nerve cells to work and is manifested in the capacity of the nervous system to endure prolonged or brief but intensive excitation without going into a state of protective inhibition. In his laboratory Pavlov measured SE in terms of resistance to intense, prolonged, or repeated stimulation (Pavlov, 1938). In the TQ four categories of items serve as indicators of strength of excitation:

- Willingness to perform (act) in highly stimulating settings.
- Continuing to perform under intense stimulation.
- Lack of emotional dysfunction in stressful situations (overload).
- Lack of obvious changes in the effectiveness (efficiency) of performance under intense or prolonged stimulation.

As far as the SI scale is concerned, it refers to the functional efficiency of the nervous system with respect to conditioned inhibition (as opposed to unconditioned inhibition). Strength of inhibition is manifested above all in how long the nerve cells can endure continual inhibition. According to Pavlov (1938), individuals who have a weak inhibition process cannot endure long-term conditioned inhibition, as manifested in disruption of activity or even neurosis. In the SI scale, this conception of strength of inhibition is reflected in items relating to three categories:

- The ability to refrain from various kinds of reaction (motor, verbal, emotional) adequately to the situation.
- The ability to delay (postpone) particular actions if necessary.
- The ability to interrupt a performed activity if necessary.

When Pavlov characterized mobility of the nervous processes—the last property to be included in his typology of the nervous system—he referred to the speed with which the nervous processes caught up with changes in the environment. "Because the environment surrounding the organism is constantly, and often intensively and unexpectedly, changing, both processes must, so to speak, catch up with these changes, and therefore should be highly mobile" (Pavlov, 1938, p. 652).

At the behavioral level, mobility as Pavlov understood it is manifested in the capacity to react swiftly and adequately to changing conditions and the items of the MNP scale were selected to meet this criterion.

In other words, Pavlov's theory of higher nervous activity and his defining accounts of the basic properties of the nervous system—strength of excitation, strength of inhibition, and mobility of the nervous processes—were the criterion against which items for the Temperament Questionnaire were selected. Unlike the majority of personality questionnaires, including those that measure temperament, the TQ scales are not based on factor analysis because they are directly inferred from Pavlov's (1928, 1938) theory.

2.4
The Strelau Temperament Inventory in research outside Poland

The Temperament Questionnaire in the format presented above was published in English (Strelau, 1972b, 1983) and achieved an unexpectedly high level of popularity. It probably owes its renown to the fact that it is the only questionnaire that measures the basic properties of the nervous system or, to put it another way, temperament traits as Pavlov understood them. In English-language versions of the Temperament Questionnaire, it is known as the Strelau Temperament Inventory (STI; Carlier, 1985; Daum & Schugens, 1986; Stelmack, Kruidenier, & Anthony, 1985). The STI was also translated into Chinese, Flemish, French, Hindu, Spanish, Japanese, Korean, German, Russian, Slovakian, and Italian. Most of these translations were made from the English version. When I constructed this questionnaire, largely for my own use and that of my collaborators and students, I was not psychometrically sophisticated because my main research interests concentrated on the psychophysiological correlates of temperament.

Two decades of research in which the TQ/STI was used to measure temperament traits confirmed the inventory's applicability to various populations and settings, especially those that required involvement of considerable resources of the subjects and exposed them to considerable stress. This will be discussed more thoroughly in chapter 3.

However, the empirical data gathered in numerous laboratories also showed that the STI has many shortcomings. Most of them have to do with itemmetric and psychometric characteristics. For example, studies using the English version of the STI revealed that a number of items do not fit its scales well. Of the 134 items, more than twenty do not meet the criterion for level of difficulty (Paisey & Mangan, 1980; Stelmack, Kruidenier, & Anthony, 1985); and in the German version of the STI, over 40 percent of the items correlate with their own scales at levels lower than 0.20 (Daum & Schugens, 1986). Factor analyses of four different versions of the STI—the Australian (Paisey & Mangan, 1980), French (Carlier, 1985), Canadian (Stelmack, Kruidenier, & Anthony, 1985), and Dutch (Van Heck, 1987)—yielded inconsistent solutions, partly because different factor analyses were used. Regardless of the names and number of factors obtained (from four to seven), however, all the factor analyses came up with a factor largely encompassing items from the Strength of Inhibition scale and another factor largely encompassing items from both the Strength of Excitation and Mobility of the Nervous Processes scales.

Strelau, Angleitner, and Ruch (1990) performed a meta-analysis of the psychometric characteristics of the TQ/STI gleaned from 35 studies conducted during a period of about twenty years (from 1969 to 1988) by means of the Polish, English, and German versions of the questionnaire. The number of respondents per study ranged from 22 to 312 and their age ranged from 16 to 55. Both males and females were tested. Depending on the psychometric characteristics, which were the focus of attention, the number of meta-analysed studies ranged from three to 21.

The average reliability of the TQ/STI measured either by means of the Cronbach alpha coefficient (five studies) or the split-half method was 0.78 for the SE scale, 0.78 for the SI scale, and 0.68 for the MNP scale. If we consider that a scale's reliability increases as the number of items in that scales increases, we can say that the reliability of the TQ/STI scales—each of which has more than forty items—is unsatisfactory.

In seventeen studies conducted on the Polish, English, and German versions, we obtained data on the correlation between the different scales. The mean correlation coefficients for the respective pairs of scales were as follows: SE – SI = 0.43; SE – MNP = 0.56; SI – MNP = 0.23. These correlations suggest that the TQ/STI scales are not orthogonal and this conclusion was one of the main sources of critique of the questionnaire (see Carlier, 1985; Stelmack, Kruidenier, & Anthony, 1985). However, if we remember that Pavlov himself believed that only the strong nervous system types (in psychological terms the sanguine and choleric types) have high mobility of the nervous processes, whereas the weak type (the melancholic type) has low levels of all three CNS properties including mobility, then the findings of the meta-analysis of the TQ/STI studies are not surprising. Russian researchers who used experimental measures of the basic CNS properties in both animal (e.g., Fedorov, 1961; Krasusky, 1971) and human studies (see Nebylitsyn, 1976; Turovskaya, 1963) found that strength of excitation correlated positively with mobility of the nervous processes. Troshikhin, Moldavskaya, and Kolchenko (1978) presented the most convincing findings illustrating the relationship between strength of excitation and mobility of the nervous processes. In a study of 225 individuals aged 5–24, they distinguished seven age groups and found that in each group mobility of the nervous processes correlated positively (from 0.51 to 0.83) with strength of excitation. Mobility of the nervous processes was measured by means of the method known as alteration of the signal value of a pair of stimuli (see chapter 1, note 2) and strength of excitation was measured by means of the method developed by Kopytova and described in section 1.4.

2.5
The Pavlovian temperament constructs and selected personality traits

Personality researchers, especially those who explained their constructs in terms of speed of elaboration of conditioned reflexes or level of CNS arousal (activation), naturally made references to Pavlov's theory of higher nervous processes. In one of his works, Hans Eysenck (1965) wrote that two major theories combine classical conditioning and personality. One theory, proposed by Kenneth Spence and Janet Taylor (1951), deals with the relationship between an individual's ability to produce the classical conditioned response and anxiety. The other, Eysenck's own theory of extraversion-introversion, draws on the Pavlovian constructs of cortical excitation and inhibition and speed of classical (Pavlovian) conditioning.

According to Spence (1956), conditioning to harmful stimuli or pain is faster in individuals with high drive potential (high anxiety) than in individuals with low drive potential (low anxiety). In Spence's laboratory the indicator of anxiety was speed of elaboration of the blinking reflex to a puff of air on the eyeball. Pavlov (1938) frequently found in his studies of dogs that anxiety responses are typical of dogs belonging to the weak type of nervous system (with weak excitation and inhibition).

Parallel to the research conducted at the Iowa School founded by Kenneth Spence, Eysenck (1957, 1970) adapted the classical conditioned reflex paradigm to his studies of extraversion. In the early phase of his investigations, he hypothesized that conditioning would be less effective in extraverts who are more sensitive (susceptible) to inhibition than introverts. This hypothesis, which Eysenck (1967) was later to refine in terms of arousal theory, remained basically intact; the only new aspect was the interpretation. Conditioned reflexes are elaborated more quickly in introverts than extraverts because introverts have a higher level of cortical arousal (activation). In Pavlov's laboratory conditioning effectiveness was one of the basic indicators of strength of excitation, although the research suggested that conditioning is more effective in strong types (with strong excitation and inhibition) than in weak types (the melancholic). If we remember that Eysenck (1972) associated extraversion with the strong nervous system type, then we arrive at contradictory conclusions. This contradiction seems to be artifactual, however, because it follows from the fact that the relationship between stimulus intensity and intensity of the conditioned reaction is curvilinear (it has the shape of an inverted U). In Pavlov's laboratory, when strong unconditioned and conditioned stimuli were applied to the weak type, the animals responded with so-called protective inhibition (see chapter 1, note 1), which leads to reduced conditioning effectiveness. However, in Eysenck's laboratory (and also in Spence's laboratory where the main conditioned reflex was blinking), the unconditioned and conditioned stimuli were much weaker and did not lead to protective inhibition. This explains why conditioning was more effective in introverts than extraverts (who are resistant to protective inhibition).

Marvin Zuckerman also cited Pavlov's theory of higher nervous activity when he presented his theory of sensation seeking. Among other things, he suggested that "[t]he sanguine dog, characterizable as a strong nervous system type with mobile processes, may be equated with high-sensation seekers" (1979, p. 38). Zuckerman assumed that if we characterize sensation seekers as individuals with a strong type of nervous system, we should expect them to have a high sensitivity threshold for various stimulus modalities and high tolerance for intensive stimulation. And vice-versa, individuals who are sensation avoiders should be sensitive to stimuli that lack intensity and should not tolerate intensive stimulation because they are susceptible to protective inhibition. Zuckerman tested his hypotheses on the relationships between his theory of sensation seeking and Pavlov's typology in the laboratory. Most of his experiments focused on the orienting response measured in terms of electrodermal activity, and also in terms of the intensity of evoked potentials in response to visual and auditory stimuli (Zuckerman, 1979, 1994).

The findings reported from the laboratories of Spence, Eysenck, and Zuckerman on the relationship between the dimensions of personality that they postulated—which have the status of temperament traits on the one hand, and the Pavlovian properties of the nervous system on the other—were by no means unequivocal. Presumably one reason for these inconsistencies was that the Western researchers used questionnaires to measure their temperament constructs, whereas the measurements of CNS properties under laboratory conditions show discrepancy between different indicators of those properties (the so-called partiality phenomenon; see chapter 1). The Temperament Questionnaire/Strelau Temperament Inventory was the only psychometric instrument that measured the Pavlovian nervous system properties, which explains why this inventory became so popular outside Poland. The TQ/STI made it possible to compare personality traits (including temperament) and CNS properties at the same level of measurement— that is, by means of the questionnaire method. Results obtained in this way may be considered as measures of validity of the TQ/STI on the one hand, and on the other they allow us to examine the relationships between psychometrically measured CNS properties and the temperament traits for which the authors sought affinity with Pavlov's theory of higher nervous processes from a new perspective.

I am not familiar with all the studies that have compared the traits postulated by Spence, Eysenck, and Zuckerman with the Pavlovian constructs. Strelau, Angleitner, and Ruch (1990) performed their meta-analysis of findings illustrating the relationships between these traits and CNS properties on the basis of 35 studies (see section 2.4). These studies are limited to the Polish, American, and

German versions of the TQ/STI. The Eysenckian personality traits included in the meta-analyses were measured on the basis of four different questionnaires: the Maudsley Personality Inventory, Eysenck Personality Inventory (EPI), Eysenck Personality Questionnaire (EPQ), and Eysenck Personality Questionnaire–Revised. Sensation seeking was measured with the Sensation Seeking Scale (versions SSS-IV and SSS-V). Anxiety was measured on the basis of the Manifest Anxiety Scale, the State-Trait Anxiety Inventory, and the Cattell Anxiety Scale.[1] Table 2.1 summarizes the patterns that emerged from the analyses.

As we can see, strength of excitation correlates positively with extraversion and selected SSS scales. This pattern corresponds to these scales' theoretical rationale (Eysenck, 1970; Zuckerman, 1979). The SE scale correlates negatively with neuroticism and anxiety, in accordance with Pavlov's (1938) opinion that the weak type is an anxious type. In addition, one of the defining components of the SE scale—lack of emotional disorder under conditions of stress (overload)—is directly related to anxiety and neuroticism.

The SI scale clearly correlates negatively with psychoticism and disinhibition. If we remember that strength of inhibition—one of whose defining components is the ability to refrain from various reactions adequately to the current situation—is related to behavior control, then this finding is to be expected.

Mobility of the nervous processes, which is manifested in the ability to adapt one's reactions swiftly and adequately to a changing situation, may be viewed as a preference for change and unexpected events. If so, then the positive correlation with extraversion and sensation seeking is consistent with the theoretical rationale.

Strelau, Angleitner, and Ruch (1990) applied the same questionnaire (STI) in four independent studies of German samples. These studies were not included in their meta-analysis. In all, 863 persons (369 females and 494 males) aged 15–80 were studied. Item analysis, reliability assessment, and correlations between SE, SI, and MNP scales yielded results similar to those obtained in the meta-analysis. The mean number of items that did not meet the difficulty criterion in the four studies ranged from 12 (MNP) to 18 (SI) and the proportion of items that correlated less than 0.20 with their own scale ranged from 23 percent (SI) to 42 percent (MNP). Cronbach alpha reliability coefficients approached 0.80, whereas the

---

[1] The Polish adaptation of the Maudsley Personality Inventory was developed by Mieczysław Choynowski (1977) and is known as the Eysenck Personality Inventory. Brzozowski and Drwal (1995) were responsible for the Polish adaptation of the Eysenck Personality Questionnaire–Revised. These two researchers wrote a comprehensive manual of the test that they called the Eysenck Personality Questionnaire. Ewa Oleszkiewicz-Zsurz (1986) is the author of the Polish adaptation of the Sensation Seeking Scale IV and Dorota Żychowska (unpublished) developed the Polish adaptation of the Sensation Seeking Scale V. Kazimierz Wrześniewski and Tytus Sosnowski (1987) were responsible for the Polish adaptation of the State–Trait Anxiety Inventory.

Table 2.1 STI scales related to other temperament scales: Meta-analysis

	STI Scales							
	SE			SI			MO	
Temperament scale	No.	*M*	Range	No.	*M*	Range	No.	*M*	Range
Extraversion	21	.38	.07 to .60	19	.01	-.22 to .32	18	.49	.15 to .73
Neuroticism	20	-.43	-.13 to -.56	19	-.34	-.20 to -.59	18	-.22	-.01 to .35
Psychoticism	9	-.04	-.26 to .16	9	-.29	-.03 to -.54	8	-.02	-.18 to .13
Anxiety	13	-.57	-.39 to -.72	12	-.42	-.20 to -.59	11	-.31	-.18 to -.60
SSS-Total	5	.16	-.07 to .28	4	-.16	-.29 to .11	4	.31	.12 to .63
SSS-TAS	5	.26	.12 to .36	4	.04	-.12 to .30	4	.30	.18 to .51
SSS-ES	5	.07	-.17 to .28	4	-.12	-.29 to .18	4	.19	-.03 to .32
SSS-Dis	5	.02	-.12 to .17	4	-.24	-.09 to -.33	4	.18	.04 to .48
SSS-BS	5	.12	-.03 to .31	4	-.18	-.27 to .00	4	.22	.11 to .47

Note. SE = Strength of Excitation; SI = Strength of Inhibition; MO = Mobility of the Nervous Processes; SSS = Sensation Seeking Scale; TAS = Thrill and Adventure Seeking; ES = Experience Seeking; Dis = Disinhibition; BS = Boredom Susceptibility; No. = number of samples from which the average (M) correlation was calculated; M = mean of coefficients of correlation between scales. Range includes distribution of correlations across samples. From *Pavlovian Temperament Survey (PTS): An International Handbook* by J. Strelau, A. Angleitner, and B. H. Newberry, 1999, p. 14. Copyright 1999 by Hogrefe & Huber Publishers. Reprinted with permission.

correlations between the STI scales confirm the lack of orthogonality of these scales. This is especially true of the correlations between scales SE and MNP, which range from 0.43 to 0.59.

Questionnaires measuring extraversion, neuroticism, and psychoticism (EPI or EPQ) and sensation-seeking scales (SSS-IV or SSS-V) were administered to all four samples. Anxiety was not assessed in these studies but an abbreviated version of the Personality Research Form was used in the largest sample (428 individuals including 184 males) of 15- to 18-year-olds. The Personality Research Form developed by Jackson (1967) has fifteen content scales and two control scales. Murray's (1938) need theory was the rationale for the construction of the content scales.

As far as the relationship between the basic CNS properties and extraversion, neuroticism, psychoticism, and sensation seeking (with its four components) is concerned, the results of the four studies confirmed the patterns that emerged in the meta-analysis. However, interesting relationships were found between the Pavlovian temperament constructs and the personality traits postulated by Jackson. The SE scale correlated positively with the Need for Achievement, Dominance, and Endurance scales. Since strength of excitation is understood as an activity-oriented temperament trait (see Mangan, 1982; Strelau, 1983), and Pavlov understood it as resistance to intensive stimuli, these findings are quite surprising. The SI scale, in turn, correlated negatively with the Aggression and Impulsiveness scales and this pattern corresponds to the defining characteristics of strength of inhibition. Finally, mobility of the nervous processes correlated positively with scales covering various aspects of social behavior: Affiliation, Dominance, and Inhibition. Even if it is not easy to explain these relationships directly, they are consistent with our expectations.

The two series of psychometric studies using the Temperament Questionnaire/Strelau Temperament Inventory can be summarized as follows.

- The itemmetric analysis of the questionnaire yielded unsatisfactory results; too many items of the different TQ/STI scales are either too difficult or not difficult enough and many items correlate too weakly (< 0.20) with their own scale. These findings suggest that the SE, SI, and MNP scales have unsatisfactory validity.

- The TQ/STI scales are not mutually orthogonal; this has resulted in serious critique of the questionnaire even though the established patterns appear to correspond to Pavlov's theory. Taking the factor analysis of the scales as our point of departure, it is clear that the questionnaire has poor validity. But if we consider the outcomes of studies in which the questionnaire was used, this psychometric tool appears to have good construct validity if Pavlov's theory is the criterion. I shall return to this critique in my discussion of the research on the construction of the next version of the questionnaire.

- The TQ/STI scales have satisfactory reliability that does not depart significantly from analogous parameters of other personality scales, including temperament scales.

- The TQ/STI has high external validity if the relationships between the TQ/STI scales and other personality (temperament) scales that draw on the Pavlovian constructs of higher nervous activity are the criterion (Spence, Eysenck, Zuckerman).

The Temperament Questionnaire/Strelau Temperament Inventory, which was used for more than twenty years to study the functional role of temperament and its relationships with behavior, will be the topic of the next chapter. Here I will briefly outline the next stage of the research on the construction of another questionnaire measuring basic CNS properties for which the TQ/STI was the point of departure.

2.6
The PTS Temperament Questionnaire: The final step in the construction of a psychometric instrument for the assessment of the basic Pavlovian CNS properties

Strelau and Angleitner (1994), taking into consideration the critique of the TQ/STI and also the fact that this questionnaire was popularized in more than a dozen countries, and remembering that nearly all of these foreign adaptations consisted of translating the items of the English-language version into other languages, decided to construct a new version of the questionnaire. Their goal was to eliminate the shortcomings of the Temperament Questionnaire/Strelau Temperament Inventory and develop an inventory that could be used in cross-cultural comparisons. There are many good reasons to study temperament from a cross-cultural perspective.

Most temperament researchers agree that temperament is rooted in specific physiological or biochemical mechanisms (see Cloninger, 1986; Eysenck & Eysenck, 1985; Kagan, 1994; Strelau, 1998; Zuckerman, 1994), and it is hardly surprising that these mechanisms are not genetically determined to a considerable extent. Therefore it is highly probable that as far as the defining components of temperament traits are concerned, there should not be any major differences between populations representing various ethnic or national groups. The distinguishing factors are largely environmentally (and culturally) determined behaviors in which the defining components of temperament, which are universal, are expressed. For example, need for stimulation may manifest itself in African tribes in hunting dangerous animals, and in Western culture it may find an outlet in extreme sports. Presumably this universality of temperament is to be found not only in its different traits but also in their configurations—as demonstrated in research on the three Eysenckian personality (temperament) superfactors (Eysenck, 1991; Eysenck & Eysenck, 1985) or in the research on the Big Five factor model of personality (see Digman, 1989; McCrae & Costa, 1987).

Many theories of temperament attribute specific adaptive functions to the different temperament traits. In a general sense, the interaction of those traits and environmental influences—which are specific for the various ethnic or national groups—leads to a variety of developmental and behavioral outcomes. In the context of child development studies, Super and Harkness (1986) postulated the existence of a *sui generis* "developmental niche" and suggested that the interaction between the child's temperament traits and the physical and social environment that fills this niche leads to the development of various forms of adaptation. They also claimed that the same temperament traits play various roles depending on the nature of this niche.

We can imagine a similar ethnic or national niche as the context within which temperament traits and their behavioral manifestations develop (see Wachs &

Kohnstamm, 2001). As Margaret Kerr (2001) pointed out when treating culture as a context for temperament, there are psychological and social environmental characteristics that favor certain temperamentally determined behaviors and these culturally favored behaviors increase the likelihood of goodness of fit. Thomas and Chess (1977), who introduced the goodness-of-fit concept to the study of temperament, were among the first researchers to demonstrate that the same temperament trait in children (i.e., activity) leads to various educational outcomes depending on whether the child is brought up in an upper-class white family or a lower-class Puerto Rican family. Strelau and Angleitner (1994) quote many other arguments supporting the meaningfulness of studying temperament in a cross-cultural context and the development of psychometric instruments that would allow researchers to consider cultural context when diagnosing temperament.

Whether construction of a temperament inventory that takes conceptual and metric equivalence into consideration will succeed (see Poortinga, 1989) largely depends on the degree to which the instrument is based on the universal aspects of the studied phenomenon. This is known as the etic approach in cross-cultural psychology. The opposite approach, which concentrates on culturally specific aspects, is known as the emic approach (see Berry, 1969; also Zawadzki, 2002).

In our own research, which we initially conducted on a German population (Strelau & Angleitner, 1994; this also applies to our studies of American and Polish subjects), we applied a procedure that took both universal and culturally specific aspects into account. This resulted in constructing a radically modified questionnaire—known outside Poland as the Pavlovian Temperament Survey (PTS; Strelau, Angleitner, & Newberry, 1999) and in Poland as the PTS Temperament Questionnaire (Strelau & Zawadzki, 1998). Work on this questionnaire proceeded in three stages:

- Operationalization of the theoretical constructs—that is, strength of excitation, strength of inhibition, and mobility of the nervous processes—on whose basis the three scales were constructed.

- Generation of a large pool of items for each scale to cover a heterogeneous range of behaviors and situations found in culturally heterogeneous populations.

- Selection of those items from the larger pool that were most representative for the particular language (cultural) version.

Because of this procedure, every version of the PTS questionnaire included the universal defining components of the SE, SI, and MNP scales and language-specific (culturally specific) items selected from the general pool and identical in all language versions. The following defining components are identical in all language versions of the PTS (Strelau, Angleitner, & Newberry, 1999, p. 17; see also Strelau & Zawadzki, 1998).

Strength of excitation:

- Threatening situations do not stop the individual from undertaking previously planned activities/actions.
- The individual is prone to undertake activity under highly stimulating conditions.
- The individual prefers to carry out risky and/or demanding activities.
- Performance of activity under social and/or physical load does not evoke emotional disturbances.
- Under conditions of high stimulating value, the individual's performance does not decrease significantly.
- The individual is resistant to fatigue when engaging in long-lasting and/or intensive activity.
- The individual is able to react adequately under strong emotional tension.

Strength of inhibition:

- The individual easily refrains from behavior that for social reasons is not expected or not desired.
- The individual has no difficulty delaying task performance when such delay is expected.
- Once starting to perform a task or react to a situation, the individual is able to interrupt the action when needed.
- If circumstances require, the individual is able to delay his or her reaction to acting stimuli.
- The individual is able to refrain from expressing his or her emotions when withholding that expression is desirable.

Mobility of the nervous processes:

- The individual reacts adequately to unexpected changes in the environment.
- The individual adapts quickly to new surroundings.
- The individual passes easily from one activity to another.
- The individual easily changes mood from positive to negative and vice-versa, according to the meaning of the situation.
- The individual prefers situations that require him or her to perform different activities simultanously.

The point of departure for constructing the PTS questionnaire was a pool of 377 items generated with respect to all seventeen defining components. Expert

judges reduced this pool to 252. All the language versions of the PTS questionnaire (of which there are now about twenty) were constructed on the basis of this
252-item pool. A detailed account of the procedure that led to the development of
this diagnostic instrument is provided in the Polish version of the PTS questionnaire manual (Strelau & Zawadzki, 1998) and in the international sixteen-lan-
guage manual; there are also scoring keys for each language version (Strelau,
Angleitner, & Newberry, 1999).

Below is merely a selection of the findings of the meta-analyses that were performed on the data for the sixteen language versions, which were administered to a
total of 13,393 individuals (6,351 males and 7,042 females) aged 10–85. Reliability
of the PTS questionnaire—assessed on the basis of the Cronbach alpha coefficient—
ranges from 0.79 (SI) to 0.87 (MNP); when collapsed for gender, it ranges from 0.80
(SI) to 0.86 (MNP) for men and from 0.78 (SI) to 0.87 (MNP) for women. The correlations between the different scales (SE – SI = 0.25; SE – MNP = 0.52; and SI –
MNP = 0.21) corroborate our earlier findings (see section 2.4). This pattern of correlations is consistent with Pavlov's opinion and suggests that mobility and strength
of excitation are not orthogonal traits. When the same statistical software was
applied to the data gleaned from all sixteen studies conducted within the PTS construction project, the same structure of Pavlovian temperament scales was obtained
without exception, thus strongly corroborating the universality of Pavlov's theory.
Meta-analysis of the correlation coefficients between age and the different PTS
scales revealed that these scales do not correlate with age (SE = –0.02; SI = 0.08;
MNP = 0.03). A similar pattern of lack of correlation was found between gender and
SI (–0.04) and MNP (–0.01) with one exception—that is, SE (M = –0.17; code: 1 =
males, 2 = females). The pattern of this last finding shows that men have a slightly
higher level of strength of excitation than women.

The most interesting results, however, illustrate the correlation between the
PTS scales and the scales of several psychometric instruments that measure other
dimensions of personality (temperament) and whose authors—with only a few
exceptions—refer in one way or another to the arousal construct (more on arousal in section 3.1). On the one hand, these research findings tell us that the PTS is
a valid instrument, and on the other they allow us to place Pavlovian temperament
among other theories of temperament or personality. In the following presentation
of research findings, I shall limit myself to data collected on Polish, German, and
American samples numbering from 2,304 to 5,281 individuals in all (the only
exception being the assessment made with the Impulsiveness Questionnaire I_7,
which was administered to a total of 940 men and women). The results of these
comparisons, which include the medians of the means for the different samples,
are presented in Table 2.2. The number of samples ranged from five to fourteen
(with the exception of I_7 where only three samples were tested). A more detailed
account of these comparisons, including the sample frequencies and demographic
characteristics, can be found elsewhere (Strelau, Angleitner, & Newberry, 1999).

Table 2.2 Relationships between the basic nervous system properties measured by means of the PTS questionnaire and selected temperament/personality traits: Studies based on Polish, German, and American samples

Temperament/personality trait	No.	N	SE	SI	MO
Extraversion	14	5281	0.39	-0.08	0.51
Neuroticism	14	5281	-0.45	-0.32	-0.39
Psychoticism (EPQ-R)	8	4098	0.17	-0.17	0.06
Openess to experience	6	3268	0.12	0.10	0.21
Agreeableness	6	3268	0.04	0.33	0.16
Conscientiousness	6	3268	0.18	0.20	0.16
Sociability (EAS-TS)	6	2586	0.14	-0.15	0.27
Activity (EAS-TS)	6	2586	0.24	-0.07	0.24
Distress (EAS-TS)	6	2586	-0.42	-0.29	-0.39
Fear (EAS-TS)	6	2586	-0.45	-0.23	-0.34
Anger (EAS-TS)	6	2586	-0.20	-0.39	-0.14
Activity level-general (DOTS-R)	5	2493	0.09	-0.24	0.04
Activity level-sleep (DOTS-R)	5	2493	-0.06	-0.14	-0.02
Approach-withdrawal (DOTS-R)	5	2493	0.43	0.10	0.60
Flexibility-rigidity (DOTS-R)	5	2493	0.41	0.20	0.56
Mood quality (DOTS-R)	5	2493	0.21	0.01	0.39
Rhythmicity-sleep (DOTS-R)	5	2493	-0.08	0.02	-0.11
Rhythmicity-eating(DOTS-R)	5	2493	0.01	0.06	-0.04
Rhythmicity-daily habits (DOTS-R)	5	2493	0.00	0.00	-0.09
Distractibility (DOTS-R)	5	2493	0.26	0.22	0.15
Persistence (DOTS-R)	5	2493	0.17	0.19	0.11
Thrill and adventure seeking (SSS-V)	6	2304	0.33	0.00	0.29
Disinhibition (SSS-V)	6	2304	0.23	-0.26	0.12
Experience seeking (SSS-V)	6	2304	0.27	-0.05	0.25
Boredom susceptibility (SSS-V)	6	2304	0.20	-0.11	0.20
Sensation seeking-general	6	2304	0.37	-0.14	0.28
Impulsiveness (I_7)	3	940	0.18	-0.42	0.25
Venturesomeness (I_7)	3	940	0.51	-0.09	0.37
Empathy (I_7)	3	940	-0.25	-0.05	-0.15

Note. No. = number of samples; N = number of subjects. For the remaining abbreviations, see Table 2.1. The Eysenck Personality Questionnaire–Revised (EPQ-R), one of the three NEO inventories (NEO-FFI, NEO-PI, NEO-PI-R), and the Sensation Seeking Scale–Form V (SSS-V) were administered to Polish (P), German (G), and American (A) samples; the EAS Temperament Survey (EAS-TS) and the Revised Dimensions of Temperament Survey (DOTS-R) were applied in samples P and G, whereas measures by means of the I_7 Impulsiveness Questionnaire (I_7) were taken in samples G and A.

I shall limit my presentation of the patterns of relationships between basic CNS properties measured by the PTS and other personality traits, mainly temperament, to those data that shed light on the questionnaire's convergent and divergent validity. I shall focus only on those findings that correlate at $r \geq 0.30$ (convergent validity) or those for which no correlation or only a very weak correlation was found ($r \leq 0.10$; divergent validity). Taking these criteria into consideration, one may say that:

- Strength of excitation is positively correlated with extraversion, approach, flexibility, thrill and adventure seeking, general sensation seeking, and venturesomeness and negatively correlated with neuroticism, distress, and fear. SE does not correlate or correlates very weakly with agreeableness, general activity, activity-sleep, and rhythmicity (of sleep, eating, and habits).

- Strength of inhibition is positively correlated with agreeableness and negatively correlated with neuroticism, anger, and impulsiveness. SI does not correlate or correlates very weakly with openness, activity, approach, mood quality, and rhythmicity (of sleep, eating, and habits).

- Mobility of the nervous processes is positively correlated with extraversion, approach, flexibility, positive mood, and venturesomeness and does not correlate or correlates very weakly with neuroticism, distress, and fear. MNP also does not correlate or correlates very weakly with psychoticism, general activity, activity-sleep, and rhythmicity (of sleep and habits).

If we refer to the defining components of all three PTS scales, we come to the obvious conclusion that this psychometric instrument has good convergent validity and this conclusion holds for all three scales of the questionnaire. The negative correlation between all three PTS scales and neuroticism merits special attention. This result seems rather surprising although it is consistent with Pavlov's (1928, 1938) opinion that the weak type is low on all three properties of the nervous system and therefore its characterization has been limited to weakness of the excitation process (see Figure 1.1). We also see quite considerable convergence of relationships between strength of excitation and mobility of the nervous processes on the one hand and temperament (personality) traits on the other. This is quite understandable if we remember that the links between the two CNS properties are quite strong. As far as divergent validity is concerned, it is noteworthy that rhythmicity—in all its varieties—is not related to the Pavlovian constructs and this refers to all three CNS properties. What is really surprising, however, is the lack of any connection whatsoever between activity (general and sleep) on the one hand and SE and MNP on the other. This finding tends to refute the reliability of these two PTS scales. But if we remember that the Revised Dimensions of Temperament Survey (Windle & Lerner, 1986) and the Emotionality–

Activity–Sociability Temperament Survey (Buss & Plomin, 1984) measure activity that is manifested in motor reactions only (expansiveness and number of movements), then the fact that no correlation was found is easier to understand.

Diagnosis of temperament traits on the basis of the TQ/STI and PTS questionnaires and verification of the psychometric value of these diagnostic instruments were not ends in themselves. The questionnaires were used in research whose main purpose was to test the broadly conceived, hypothetical functional significance of temperament as defined in the first stage of research within the framework of the Regulative Theory of Temperament. This will be the topic of chapter 3.

Chapter 3

An outline of the Regulative Theory of Temperament and the first stage of research on the functional role of temperament

Pavlov's theory of the basic properties of the central nervous system (CNS)—whose adaptive functions he emphasized in his accounts—and my own psychological interpretation of these properties served as the point of departure for the Regulative Theory of Temperament (RTT). Many other researchers also contributed to the development of this theory, as I will demonstrate in this chapter that presents the theoretical rationale and our own early studies of the first version of the RTT.

3.1
Origins of the Regulative Theory of Temperament

Pavlov (1928, 1938) defined the basic CNS properties—strength of excitation, strength of inhibition, and mobility of the nervous properties—in terms of their role in the individual's adaptation to environmental demands (see section 1.1). In a way this compelled me, as a close follower of his ideas, to adopt the functional approach to temperament and its empirical investigation. This functional paradigm, which was also present in the approach of the Russian neo-Pavlovians— Boris Teplov (1956), Vladimir Nebylitsyn (1972), and Wulf Merlin (1973) are among the most distinguished—contrasted with the traditional, static approach of the adherents of constitutional typologies of temperament (see Conrad, 1941; Kretschmer, 1944; Sheldon & Stevens, 1942) who concentrated on describing individual physical and psychological characteristics.

One factor that had a major impact on the development of the theory of temperament, which has provided the foundation for the research that my close collaborators and I have conducted for about fifty years, was the Action Theory of my mentor Tadeusz Tomaszewski (1963; see also 1978). This theory says that the most important factors in the regulation of the individual's relationship with the environment are actions (i.e., individual activity) and that the proper philosophy of psychological research is to study human beings in the environment in which they live. The concept of regulation encouraged Tomaszewski (1984) to develop a more comprehensive "regulative theory." This theory inspired many more detailed conceptualizations—including my own theory of temperament, in which the concept of regulation played a central role (see Kurcz & Reykowski, 1975; Kurcz & Kądzielawa, 2002; Łukaszewski, 1974).

According to Tomaszewski (1984), regulation takes place at two different levels that he called traces and templates. He focused mainly on the latter, an approach that emphasizes the role of internal representations of reality in the regulation of the individual's relationship with the physical and social environment. These representations (templates) are the mechanism whereby actions are given proper direction and controlled. To ensure direction and control of one's actions, one must continually compare the actual state of affairs with the template. Tomaszewski (1984) introduced the following simple formula to describe the directed dynamics of human activity:

$$T \rightarrow R$$

in which T is the task that defines the individual's direction of activity and R is the result or outcome to which the individual aspires.

As far as traces are concerned, Tomaszewski reserved this term for the organism's internal structures. These structures have the status of intervening variables and their function is to moderate[1] task-outcome relationships. The shaping of this basic "T → R" relationship is controlled not only by external factors or environmental demands, but also by internal factors that regulate behavior (understood as more or less static structures for which the symbol "O" was used in traditional psychology). These structures include, for example, temperament—present from early childhood—and the rich repertoire of personality traits that is woven onto this basic canvas. Elsewhere I discussed the origins of my theory of temperament and its similarities to Tomaszewski's regulative theory at length (Strelau, 2002).

At the Eighteenth International Congress of Psychology in Moscow in 1966, I met Hans Eysenck and his most outstanding disciple, Jeffrey Gray. This encounter, my first with Western psychologists, had a major impact on my thinking about temperament (see the Introduction). Eysenck's (1970) theory of extra-

---

[1] In this and the subsequent chapters, the term "moderate" is used in the sense that Folkman and Lazarus (1988) applied it to those psychological variables (largely personality traits and intellectual qualities, including intelligence) which exist prior to the situation (stimulus, task, demand) that evokes a particular response or behavior. The moderating role of these variables consists of constituting antecedent conditions that influence other conditions.

version-introversion was greatly influenced by Pavlov's theory of excitation-inhibition (see Strelau, 1998, 2001a), whereas Gray (1964) was the first researcher to place the concept of strength of nervous system in the wider context of arousal theory. Gray gave individual differences in level of arousal the status of a stable property that he called arousability.

Arousability, understood as a permanent tendency to be more or less aroused, resembles strength of excitation understood as a trait, in accordance with Pavlov's suggestions. The stronger the nervous system (i.e., the more resistant the individual is to intensive stimulation), the lower that individual's chronic level of arousal and hence the lower his or her arousability and vice-versa. A weak nervous system—that is, one characterized by low endurance—is related to a chronically elevated level of arousal and hence higher arousability (for a detailed account of these patterns, see Strelau, 2001b).

Influenced by these two researchers with whose ideas I became thoroughly acquainted, I decided to pay more attention to the arousal construct. Arousal, also called activation or energy mobilization (Duffy, 1957), is defined by the authors of this "energetic" concept as a basic trait of behavior that is expressed in the intensity of all reactions; hence it is sometimes referred to as behavioral intensity. This construct has been discussed by Freeman (1948), Duffy (1951), and Malmo (1959). Elisabeth Duffy particularly emphasizes individual differences in level of arousal.

In similar stimulus situations, different individuals will have different levels of arousal and will revert to their previous level of functioning at different speeds. Moreover, it has been proven that these individual differences are stable. In other words, if the individual responds intensively in one situation, he or she will also respond intensively—relatively to other individuals—in other situations (Duffy, 1957, p. 268). The importance of the two constructs, arousal and arousability, for the study of the physiological bases of temperament, including their role in the development of the Regulative Theory of Temperament (see below), has been discussed many times (see Strelau, 1994, 2001b).

One source of the Regulative Theory of Temperament was the deep conviction, rooted in the hundred-year-old tradition of research and theorizing on temperament (see Strelau, 1998, 2001a), that temperament traits—which are present in human beings from birth and can also be found in animals—have to do mainly with the formal characteristics of behavior. Regardless of the differences between theories of temperament, two aspects of behavior (energy level and temporal characteristics) can be found in practically every theory (see Strelau, 1983, 1998). As opposed to formal characteristics, content-related (substantive) characteristics tell us about the individual's relationship with the external world, other people, and himself or herself and are expressions of that individual's other personality traits, unrelated to temperament.

Finally, I must stress that my early collaborators and students greatly contributed to the development of the Regulative Theory of Temperament. Two of them merit special attention—Andrzej Eliasz and Tatiana Klonowicz. Eliasz, who studied temperament mostly in natural settings, also greatly contributed to the development of my own theory of temperament. On this canvas he developed his own Transactional Model of Temperament (Eliasz, 1981, 1985). Klonowicz, in turn, enriched this theory with empirical data and thus greatly contributed to the empirical verification of the Regulative Theory of Temperament.

The Regulative Theory of Temperament was first formulated in the early 1970s and its inchoate version was presented at length in *Temperament, Personality, Activity* (Strelau, 1983). The theory was slightly modified in the 1990s. Most of the changes involve the structure of temperament itself and temperament assessment and hence two phases in the evolution of the theory can be distinguished, each of which has its own specific empirical focus. Most of this book is devoted to the second phase of RTT research. Below is a very brief discussion of the first phase.

3.2
Development of the Regulative Theory of Temperament: Phase one

After more than a dozen years of research conducted in the Pavlovian and neo-Pavlovian tradition, represented mainly by Russian researchers as far as temperament is concerned, I decided to refrain from using Pavlovian terms (strength of excitation, strength of inhibition, mobility of the nervous processes, and type of nervous system) to describe temperament. There were several reasons for this and I shall now review them briefly (for a more detailed justification, see Strelau, 1983).

• CNS properties have the status of explanatory concepts; they also limit the hypothetical physiological mechanism to cortical processes and structures (see the introduction to chapter 2). However, the findings reported in the literature suggest that temperament has much more extensive physiological bases including subcortical structures, particularly the reticular activation system, the autonomic nervous system, or the endocrine system. My collaborators and I pointed this out more than thirty years ago (Strelau, Klonowicz, & Eliasz, 1972).

• Although Pavlov's theory of nervous system types does not refer directly to existing physiological mechanisms but instead to conceptual processes and CNS properties, it is essentially a physiological theory of temperament. My objective, however, was to develop a theory of this component of personality in which human behavior plays the leading role.

- In my own research on the diagnosis of temperament traits, I demonstrated that partiality prevails (see chapter 1). This finding has been corroborated in many studies conducted by Russian psychologists (see Nebylitsyn, 1976; Teplov, 1985; for a review of the research on the partiality of CNS properties, see Strelau, 1972a, 1983). I therefore decided to measure temperament by means of the questionnaire method in the hope that this would allow me to diagnose traits understood as a general tendency toward specific behaviors. Subsequently I realized that questionnaires do not allow us to identify the physiological mechanisms that underlie temperament (see chapter 2).

The definition of the theoretical construct of temperament that emerged from numerous sources was the point of departure for the Regulative Theory of Temperament. As I wrote in *Temperament, Personality, Activity*, "By *temperament* I mean relatively stable features of the organism, primarily biologically determined, as revealed in the formal traits of reactions which form the energy level and temporal characteristics of behaviour" (Strelau, 1983, p. 171).

By relatively stable I mean, above all, that temperament traits (compared with other personality traits) belong to the most stable ones. This does not mean, however, that they cannot change—mainly due to processes of organismal maturation (Strelau, 1978) but also to environmental factors, particularly extreme ones such as prolonged hyperstimulation or deprivation. I shall discuss the relative stability of temperament traits more thoroughly in the next chapter.

The above definition also stresses that temperament cannot be reduced to behavior. Temperament is a theoretical construct that is used to explain behavior. It has the status of trait, understood as a generalized tendency toward specific behaviors as manifested in behavior consistent with that tendency (Strelau, 2006).

When we say that temperament or its traits are primarily biologically determined, we mean that temperament is the result of biological evolution and that human beings—as well as animals—are born with specific temperament traits. The postulated primary biological determination of temperament does not contradict the postulate that temperament can change as a result of environmental influences.

Crucial for the Regulative Theory of Temperament is the part of the definition which says that temperament is about the formal traits of behavior and that these traits are expressed in the energy level and temporal characteristics of behavior. In the next chapter, where the basic propositions of the RTT are outlined, arguments in favor of the focus on these aspects of behavior will be presented.

In the first stage of development of the RTT, I postulated the existence of two basic temperament traits responsible for individual differences in the energy level of behavior, reactivity, and activity, and I shall argue below that these two concepts have specific meaning in the theory.

3.2.1. Reactivity as a primary temperament trait

The reactivity concept evolved at our laboratory in the 1960s and early 1970s (Eliasz, 1974; Strelau, 1969, 1970). It has its source in many observations, later experimentally confirmed, which suggest that people differ with respect to the intensity of their reactions or the intensity of their behavior in response to stimuli or situations and that these differences are relatively stable. A classic example of individual differences in the intensity of response to stimulation is the research on the sensory sensitivity threshold, which demonstrated that when this threshold is repeatedly measured in the same individual, the outcome is relatively stable (Duffy, 1972; Eysenck, 1981; Haslam, 1972; Nebylitsyn, 1976; Petrie, 1967; Teplov, 1972). In the research on the sensory sensitivity threshold, response intensity is basically constant because it is the smallest detectable reaction— although individuals do differ with respect to the intensity of the stimulus that evokes this reaction, and this is the measure of the individual differences that interests us here.

Many studies illustrating individual differences in reaction intensity (amplitude) can be found in the literature. Researchers have focused on conditioned reflex activity, orienting responses measured on the basis of electrodermal activity and the bioelectrical activity of the brain, or the amplitude of evoked potentials. Individual differences in the intensity (amplitude) of these reactions are assumed to be the psychophysiological correlates of a number of personality traits, including temperament. This is true of the research on extraversion (Eysenck, 1967), anxiety (Spence, 1956), stimulation reducing-augmenting (Petrie, 1967), sensation seeking (Zuckerman, 1979) and strength of excitation (Nebylitsyn, 1976; Strelau, 1969). These studies are reviewed at length elsewhere (Strelau, 1983).

I proposed the term "reactivity" to describe the individual-specific tendency to react with a given intensity (magnitude). Understood in this context, reactivity is a temperament trait and this trait determines the relatively stable individual differences in reaction intensity. Thus reactivity has the status of a psychological concept in the RTT, as opposed to the use of the term in physiology where reactivity is defined as the capacity of the nervous system to react to stimulation of the receptors (see Konorski, 1967; Sosnowski & Zimmer, 1993; for an extensive review of the concept of reactivity and its applications in the psychology of individual differences, see Janke and Kallus, 1995). To appreciate how my collaborators and I understood this term, it is important to remember our assumption that reactivity may be expressed in reactions to stimuli whatever their intensity and that it determines the organism's sensitivity (sensory and emotional) and efficiency (endurance). Sensitivity is measured mainly in terms of the sensitivity threshold, whereas efficiency (endurance) is expressed in reactions and behavioral responses to intensive or prolonged stimuli. We also assumed, drawing mainly on research conducted in Teplov's laboratory (Teplov & Nebylitsyn, 1963), that the sensitivity threshold-efficiency (endurance) threshold ratio is relatively constant. Hence if we view reactivity as a dimension, we can say that at one extreme we have individuals who are very sensitive and not very efficient, whereas at the other extreme we have individuals who are typically not very sensitive but highly efficient (see Figure 3.1).

I have given a more detailed account of the concept of reactivity as a temperament trait and of the hypothetical physiological mechanisms of reactivity elsewhere (Strelau, 1983). Here I shall simply point out that the RTT assumes that a whole complex of neurobiochemical mechanisms lies at the basis of reactivity, and that these mechanisms determine individual differences in the intensity of behavior and intensity of reactions to stimuli (situations). Hence drawing on a theory proposed by Williams (1956), who introduced the concept of biochemical individuality in order to underscore the fact that every individual has his or her own specific system of biochemical mechanisms, I coined the term "neurohormonal individuality." This concept emphasizes the fact that reactivity is determined by an individually specific configuration of neural mechanisms (the physiology and biochemistry of the CNS and the autonomic nervous system) and hormonal mechanisms responsible for the regulation of the energy level of reactions (behavior). Borrowing from Gray (1964) the concept of stimulation augmenting/reducing, which he used to compare strength of excitation and individual differences in level of arousal, we may say that highly reactive individuals are individuals whose physiological mechanism of temperament augments stimulation. In turn, in low-reactive individuals this mechanism reduces stimulation.

It can easily be inferred from this account that the concept of reactivity has a great deal in common with the concept of strength of excitation: individuals low in reactivity can be compared with individuals with high strength of excitation, whereas highly reactive individuals can be compared with individuals with a weak nervous system type. At the level of behavioral indicators, both concepts refer to the same behavior but we must remember that the Strength of Excitation scale measures behaviors indicative of efficiency (endurance), whereas the reactivity concept includes sensitivity. However, as we can see in Figure 3.1, the RTT assumes that the relationship between the two extremes is relatively constant. Therefore reactivity has usually been assessed by means of the Strength of Excitation scale of the Temperament Questionnaire/Strelau Temperament Inventory (TQ/STI; see, e.g., Eliasz, 1981; Strelau, 1983) and recently Eliasz and his collaborators have used the Pavlovian Temperament Survey (PTS) questionnaire to measure reactivity (see, e.g., Eliasz, 2001; Zalewska, 2003).

Although one difference between reactivity as it is used in the RTT and strength of excitation is that the former is a psychological concept whereas the latter is a physiological one, there are other differences as well (see Strelau,

1983). The most important difference is that the physiological mechanism of reactivity is not identical with the physiological mechanism of strength of excitation. The latter concept is narrower because, as far as the postulated physiological mechanism of reactivity is concerned, the CNS properties are but only one of the chains in the mechanism codetermining the level of reactivity.

3.2.2. Activity as a temperament trait

According to the RTT, the energy level of behavior includes both reactivity and activity understood as a trait. Activity is a concept found in most theories of temperament and is viewed as one element of temperament structure. Heymans and Wiersma (Heymans, 1908) were probably the first to identify this trait on the basis of empirical findings. Although these researchers also identified two other temperament traits (emotionality and perseveration), activity is one of the temperament traits most frequently mentioned. As a rule the concept is limited to the motor characteristics of behavior, such as motor expansiveness or speed and intensity of movement (see Buss & Plomin, 1984; Guilford, Zimmerman, & Guilford, 1976; Thomas & Chess, 1977; Thurstone, 1951). In the RTT activity has broader connotations than motor characteristics alone.

The concept of activity was introduced to the RTT in the early 1970s (Eliasz, 1974; Strelau, 1970, 1974a). Tomaszewski's regulative theory (see section 3.1) largely influenced how the concept is understood in the Regulative Theory of

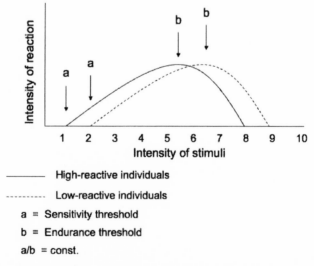

Figure 3.1. A model of reaction intensity (magnitude) in high-reactive and low-reactive individuals. From *Temperament, Personality, Activity* by J. Strelau, 1983, p. 178. Copyright 1983 by Academic Press. Reprinted with permission.

Temperament. In the RTT activity has the status of a regulator of need for stimulation and is determined by individual level of reactivity. Activity is also conceived to be a temperament trait, which determines the number and range of activities of a given stimulating value that the individual undertakes.

In order to correctly understand the relationships between reactivity and activity, we must turn to Donald Hebb's (1955) theory of optimal level of arousal. According to this theory, individuals provide themselves with stimulation to achieve an optimal level of arousal. Stimulation that is too intensive motivates the individual to undertake actions that will reduce the level of arousal evoked by that stimulation to the optimal level or vice-versa. If stimulation is too low, the individual will seek stimulation so as to achieve an optimal level of arousal. According to the RTT, activity is the individual property that regulates the process of reinstatement or maintenance of an optimal level of arousal. Many other conceptualizations of the organism's regulative functions with respect to energy level—where optimal arousal or stimulation are the regulative standard—have been presented in the literature (see Berlyne, 1960; Fiske & Maddi, 1961; Helson, 1964; Leuba, 1955). However, Hebb and Berlyne's theories of optimal level of arousal come close to our own understanding of the regulative function of activity.

Drawing upon the work of these researchers, Eliasz (1974) introduced a new concept to the RTT: the standard of stimulation regulation. According to this standard, the individual strives to maintain an optimal level of arousal that should be viewed as a band located in the middle of the level-of-arousal continuum. Eliasz explains that this level is optimal for well-being and willingness to cope with tasks of various levels of difficulty and to reduce the psychophysiological costs of coping with moderately difficult tasks (Eliasz, 1981). Low-reactive individuals have a wider range of optimal arousal than high-reactive individuals, says Eliasz. Ilin (1978) voiced a similar opinion about the strength of the nervous system and suggested that the distance between sensitivity and efficiency (endurance) is greater in strong types of CNS than in the weak type. The proposals of both Eliasz and Ilin disagree with Teplov and Nebylitsyn's (1963) hypothesis that the distance between sensitivity and efficiency (endurance) is constant, as shown in Figure 3.1. The hypothesis put forward by these two neo-Pavlovians was rejected in the second phase of development of the RTT because our empirical research failed to corroborate it (see Zawadzki & Strelau, 1995). Elsewhere I have given a detailed analysis of the constructs of reactivity and activity as they were understood in the RTT and the relationships between them (Strelau, 1983).

3.2.3. The temporal characteristics of behavior

The temporal characteristics of behavior are the second basic component of the formal characteristics of behavior. There are many temporal descriptors of behavior; a small sample includes reaction speed, mobility, stability, tempo, lability, and rhythmicity, all of which have been discussed and/or studied beginning with the ancient typology of temperaments proposed by Hippocrates-Galen (see Strelau, 1983). Our own research endeavors concentrated mainly on mobility. One of the main reasons was that the RTT originated from Pavlov's theory of basic CNS properties (1938) and Teplov's (1956) elaboration of Pavlov's ideas. Another reason was that we already had a psychometric tool with which to assess behavioral mobility – the Temperament Questionnaire/Strelau Temperament Inventory (see chapter 2) with its Mobility of the Nervous Processes scale. At the behavioral level, this scale applies to behavior that can be viewed as the defining components of mobility. When Pavlov characterized mobility of the nervous processes, he referred to the speed with which the nervous processes catch up with ongoing changes in the individual's environment. Mobility thus conceived is expressed in the capacity to react swiftly and adequately to ongoing changes and the capacity to switch from one form of activity to another, and the items of the Mobility of Nervous System scale were selected accordingly.

Mobility of behavior is the temperament trait that seems to be particularly important for activity in situations demanding adequate adjustment to rapidly changing conditions. When I say change of behavior, I mean shifting within the existing repertoire of acquired reactions and actions, not the ability to learn new behaviors. Behavioral mobility is a bit like so-called functional mobility—a concept introduced by Vvedensky and submitted to psychological interpretation by Khilchenko (1958) and Troshikhin, Moldavskaya, and Kolchenko (1978). Troshikhin noticed that functional mobility is the product of a complex physiological mechanism that includes the receptor-effector system and the central nervous system. One must surely agree that the mechanism is complex.

Ewa Goryńska (Goryńska & Strelau, 1979) factor-analyzed six temporal characteristics of behavior—persistence, recurrence, mobility, regularity, speed, and tempo—and obtained two factors. She called the first factor perseveration (after Heymans, 1908) and the second factor liveliness. The factor solution demonstrates that both factors are characterized by mobility to a similar extent, albeit with opposite signs (negatively with perseveration and positively with liveliness). Meta-analysis of the research findings, in which mobility of the nervous processes and strength of excitation were assessed using various language versions of the TQ/STI (Strelau, Angleitner, & Ruch, 1990) or PTS (Strelau, Angleitner, & Newberry, 1999), revealed that the two traits are positively correlated. The mean correlation for the TQ/STI was 0.56 (Strelau, Angleitner, & Ruch, 1990) and the mean correlation for the PTS was 0.52 (Strelau, Angleitner, & Newberry, 1999).

The RTT, though deeply rooted in Pavlov's typology, postulated the existence of temperament traits that were defined by Pavlov in behavioral rather than physiological terms. However, no theoretically consistent adequate diagnostic tool was constructed to test the temperament traits postulated by the RTT (reactivity,

activity, and mobility of behavior). Hence most research on the functional significance of temperament was conducted using the Temperament Questionnaire/ Strelau Temperament Inventory to assess reactivity and mobility of behavior. Activity, which has no equivalent in the TQ/STI scales, was measured—or to be more precise, controlled—by focusing on the stimulating value of various forms of activity and behavior in both laboratory and natural settings. The next section reviews this research very briefly.

3.3
The functional significance of the temperament traits postulated by the RTT

In the studies of the functional significance of temperament conducted at our laboratory, my colleagues and I concentrated on the regulative function of temperament traits. We devoted most of our attention to reactivity and activity and assumed that activity is a regulator of the stimulating value of actions or situations in which the individual participates (see Strelau, 1974b, 1982, 1983, 1985). Many of my graduate and postgraduate students contributed to this research and the findings reported in several works qualifying for tenure (professorship) were also conducted within the RTT paradigm (see Eliasz, 1981; Klonowicz, 1984; Terelak, 1982).

The majority of studies conducted within the RTT paradigm investigated the relationship between level of activity—as expressed in the stimulating value of various actions—and the individual's reactivity. These studies fall into three thematic groups: (a) reactivity and style of action; (b) choice of actions and situations of given stimulating value and level of reactivity; and (c) reactivity and its relationship to effectiveness and psychophysiological costs of action in situations differing in stimulating value.

3.3.1. Reactivity and style of action

Style of action, also called style of activity, has long been the object of interest of psychologists of temperament both in Europe and the United States. Russian psychologists who studied the types of nervous system (Merlin, 1973; Teplov, 1956) viewed style of action as enduring ways and forms of reactions determined by type of CNS. They defined style in terms of the relationship (equilibrium or lack of equilibrium) between operant (performance-related) and orienting actions. Style of behavior is a central concept in Thomas and Chess's (1977) theory of temperament. According to these researchers, when we characterize an individual's temperament on the basis of his or her behavior, the fundamental question is how or in what way the behavior proceeds. Buss and Plomin (1975) took a similar stance on style when they made a distinction between style and content of behavior and pointed out that style refers to how a reaction proceeds irrespective of its content.

In the research conducted within the RTT paradigm, style of action is defined as the individual's typical way of performing actions. Here style of action, which is shaped by the environment on the basis of inherent temperament, is viewed as one of the regulators of need for stimulation.

Drawing on Tomaszewski's (1967) Action Theory, I focused on the functional aspect that underscores the role played by various elements in the action structure in the attainment of any goal. From this perspective Tomaszewski distinguished two kinds of action, basic and auxiliary, which became the point of departure for the styles of action that I proposed. Basic actions are actions that lead directly to outcome attainment. Auxiliary actions, meanwhile, are actions that organize the setting so that basic actions can be performed. Auxiliary actions increase the probability that the goal of the action in question will be achieved (see Figure 3.2).

Auxiliary actions include preparation, correction, control, and protection. Auxiliary actions reduce the risk of failure when performing a task, especially when the individual is in a difficult situation or under stress. In temperament research we study the relationship between basic and auxiliary actions from the perspective of the stimulating value of the action or the situation in which that

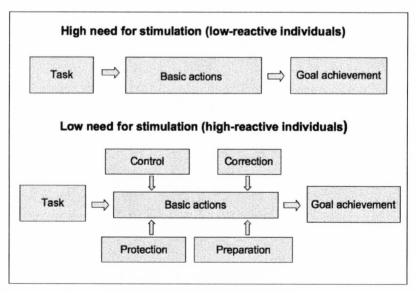

Figure 3.2. The specific activity structure during the realization of the same goal depending on reactivity-determined need for stimulation. From *Psychologia różnic indywidualnych* [Psychology of Individual Differences] by J. Strelau, 2006, p. 256. Copyright 2006 by Wydawnictwo Naukowe Scholar. Reprinted with permission.

action is performed. In general, when a person engages in auxiliary actions, he or she reduces the stimulating value of the action that leads to goal attainment. Hence we may presume that individuals whose physiological mechanism augments stimulation (i.e., high-reactive individuals) will perform more auxiliary actions to reduce the stimulating value of the action they are performing or the situation in which that action is being performed, compared with individuals low in reactivity who have a tendency to reduce stimulation. This logic led to the formulation of the following hypothesis. In high-reactive individuals there is a predominance of auxiliary actions over basic actions; thus I called this style of action the adjunctive style. In low-reactive individuals either the two types of actions are balanced or there is a predominance of basic actions over auxiliary actions; I called this style the straightforward style (Strelau, 1995b, 1996). These patterns are presented in schematic form in Figure 3.3.

The role that temperamentally determined style of action plays in the regulation of level of arousal—determined by the situation and the type of action performed—has been demonstrated in several studies where reactivity was assessed by means of the TQ, observation sheet (see section 2.1), or one of the laboratory methods (for a description see Strelau, 1983). Presented in Table 3.1, these studies consistently showed a predominance of the adjunctive style over the straightforward style in high-reactive persons. They also showed that if a person is free to choose the style of action that best suits his or her level of reactivity, there will be no difference in the level of performance.

We can also look at style of action from the perspective of the stress theory proposed by Stevan Hobfoll (1989; see also Schönpflug, 1993). Applying Hobfoll's

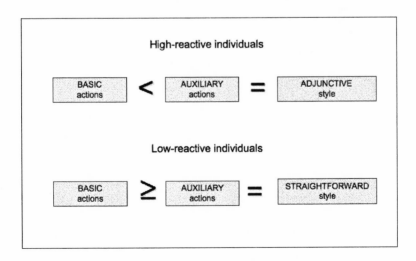

Figure 3.3. Typical action styles for individuals differing in level of reactivity.

Table 3.1 Studies demonstrating dominance of the adjunctive style (BA < AA) over the straight-forward style (BA ≥ AA) in low-reactive individuals (LR) compared with high-reactive (HR) individuals

Author	Study
Uszyńska, 1971	Twenty foundry workers aged 23–47 were studied in a natural on-the-job setting, which consisted of preparing, casting, and removing molds. HR individuals performed significantly more AA and took longer time to perform.
Strelau & Krajewski, 1974	Fifteen LR and 19 HR drivers were selected from a sample of 117 taxi drivers. It was found, for example, that the HR drivers spent significantly more time during the week checking their cars even though systematic, professional checkups were regularly conducted at the taxi base. This was a self-report, questionnaire study.
Mündelein, 1981	Examinees in a laboratory setting role-played insurance agents. During three hours of work at a computer calculating client damages, computer overload and interference were signaled. By pressing the appropriate key, examinees could allegedly avoid computer breakdown. HR individuals pressed the safety key significantly more often and spent significantly more time pressing the key.
Cymes, 1974	Thirty-eight HR and 39 LR individuals were selected from a pool of 169 secondary school pupils. They were requested to memorize $1\frac{1}{2}$ pages of a text describing the anatomy of the liver using their most preferred aids and methods. The HR pupils resorted to significantly more auxiliary actions (e.g., underlining, copying difficult fragments of the text, dividing the text into smaller portions, taking notes, etc.).
Czyżkowska, 1974 Materska, 1978 Klonowicz, 1974	In a series of studies, subjects were forced to adopt the auxiliary action style while performing construction tasks (e.g., Mechano) by alternating an algorythmic instruction—which forced them to perform auxiliary actions—and a heuristic instruction. The latter instruction allowed the subjects to adopt their preferred performance style. HR subjects (a) preferred AA (Czyżkowska), (b) had a higher AA to BA ratio (Materska), and (c) made more effort to solve the task with the heuristic instruction (Klonowicz).
Friedensberg, 1985	Five groups of subjects aged 6, 8, 10, 13, and 16 were studied. The subjects were requested to solve the Link Cube (10–16-year-olds) or its simpler version, the Red Block Test (6–8-year-olds). In all cohorts HR subjects adopted a more adjunctive style, although the cohorts differed as to the actual type of auxiliary actions performed.

terminology, we may say that auxiliary actions help to preserve (protect) resources. High-reactive individuals, compared with individuals low in reactivity, have a smaller pool of resources and therefore are mainly concerned with their preservation. By applying the adjunctive style of action, they perform more auxiliary actions. Due to these actions, they are able to avoid stressful situations or reduce the stress involved and thereby preserve their resources. This style of action enables them to avoid failure and maintain an appropriate level of efficiency when performing in highly stimulating conditions. In other words, the temperamentally determined style of action—viewed from the perspective of resource management—can be characterized in terms of gains and losses: gains flowing from auxiliary actions that predominate in highly reactive individuals are greater than the costs of coping with stress (Strelau, 1995b, 1996).

3.3.2. Performance of activities of a particular stimulating value, or preference thereof, and level of reactivity

No diagnostic tool had been developed prior to the early 1990s to measure activity understood as a temperament trait that regulates the number and range of actions undertaken and the choice of environments in terms of their stimulating value. The Temperament Questionnaire/Strelau Temperament Inventory—which had been used since the early 1970s—measured only strength of excitation (reactivity according to the interpretation adopted in this chapter), mobility of the nervous processes (mobility of behavior), and strength of inhibition (behavior control). In our research we assumed that activity could be measured in terms of professional or recreational activities that an individual undertakes and which expert judges have rated as differing in stimulating value, or situations (contexts) that the individual either chooses or avoids because of their stimulating value. We also studied declared preferences for particular occupations differing in stimulating value and managerial styles differing in the amount of stimulation they provided. In nearly all these studies, we wanted to identify the relationship between level of reactivity (usually measured by means of the TQ but assessed in a few cases by means of laboratory methods) and the stimulating value of an activity or the situation (context) in which that activity was performed. The results have been presented extensively in many publications (see Strelau, 1974b, 1983, 1985), and therefore here I shall only give a general outline of a small selection of these studies.

One of the first of these investigations (Danielak, 1972) tried to establish the relationship between reactivity and activity by comparing two groups, lawyers and librarians, with respect to level of reactivity. Because these two professions differ in the stimulating value of the activities they involve, office workers with a legal education represented an intermediate group. All three groups had similar educational status.

The point of departure for this study was the assumption that if people enjoy a certain level of freedom of choice of occupation, they will choose an occupation that corresponds to their typical trait activity. According to the RTT, activity has the status of a regulator of need for stimulation that is determined by the individual's level of reactivity, and therefore the studied groups should differ in level of reactivity. We also assumed that other variables responsible for choice of occupation (e.g., interests, abilities) are randomly distributed in all three groups, and therefore the groups should not differ with respect to these variables. Expert judges rated the stimulating values of the three occupations, largely on the basis of the social threat involved. The legal profession rated highest and the job of librarian rated lowest in stimulating value. The office workers were given an intermediate rating on this criterion. Level of reactivity was measured by means of the TQ inventory (Strength of Excitation scale). Two extreme groups with respect to this trait were selected using the quartile distribution—high-reactive individuals below the cutoff point for the first quartile and low-reactive individuals above the cutoff point between the third and fourth quartiles. The results of the normative sample (Stawowska, 1973) were the criterion. As we predicted, the vast majority of lawyers had low levels of reactivity whereas the relationships were reversed in the librarian group: here the majority had high levels of reactivity. The office workers had intermediate levels of reactivity. The differences in the frequency distributions of high-reactive and low-reactive individuals in the three professional groups were significant ($\chi^2 = 5.991$; $p < 0.05$).

Maria Popielarska (1972) conducted a similar study, based on a similar rationale, on groups differing in degree of physical threat relating to sports activities. The group engaged in the most physically hazardous activities included mountain climbers and glider pilots, whereas the group representing the least threatening activities did not engage in sports of any sort. Basketball and volleyball players from factory clubs represented the intermediate group. The results of this study corroborated Maria Danielak's (1972) findings despite the fact that two different criteria of activity-related threat were applied—social threat and physical threat. The majority of the mountain climbers and glider pilots (high physical threat group) was low reactive, whereas the majority of the people in the group that did not engage in any kind of sport was high reactive. The basketball and volleyball players had an intermediate level of reactivity. The difference in the frequency distributions of high-reactive and low-reactive persons was significant ($\chi^2 = 12.086$; $p < 0.01$).

If the hypothesis that people differing in level of reactivity will also vary in their preference for activities differing in stimulating value is legitimate, this pattern should show up most fully when we compare activities that are extremely stimulating. In order to cope successfully with highly stimulating activities for a long time, the individual must have an appropriate level of efficiency (endurance) and resistance to stress—both of which are typical for low-reactive people. High-reactive people will avoid such activities because, if performed for a long time, they will lead to overstimulation and psychological dysfunction. In low-reactive individuals the relationship between level of reactivity and the stimulating value of occupational activities that are low in stimulating value may not show up because the shortage of stimulation during performance of job-related activities can easily be offset by the pursuit of highly stimulating activities (e.g., sports, gambling) after work. Also, these individuals may have a number of self-stimulating mechanisms to compensate for lack of occupational stimulation.

No studies have been conducted to test this hypothesis directly. However, at the time we used the Temperament Questionnaire in our research, a number of scattered studies were conducted that might shed light on the relationship between level of reactivity and highly stimulating professional activity. All these studies were performed on men only. The relationship between level of reactivity and occupational activity, analyzed in terms of the stimulating value of the activity, may follow a different pattern in women because men and women have different levels of reactivity. Research conducted by Strelau (1983) and Stawowska (1973) on a normative group of 2,520 men and women (including 1,255 women) revealed that women have significantly higher levels of reactivity than men, as measured by means of the TQ inventory.

Table 3.2 presents the results of studies of six independent groups (male) performing highly stimulating activities or choosing highly stimulating situations (contexts) according to the ratings of expert judges.

Without exception, the data in Table 3.2 support the hypothesized relationship between level of reactivity and the stimulating value of occupational activities or situations (contexts). They do not tell us anything about the direction of the causal relationship, however. Do people choose occupations and job-related activities that correspond to their level of reactivity, or does their level of reactivity change as a result of prolonged performance of highly stimulating occupational activities, leading to greater organismal resistance to intensive stimulation (i.e., to reduction of the level of reactivity)?

The study conducted by Eliasz (1981) partly answers this question. This author assumed that the physiological mechanisms that underlie reactivity may be modified in the process of stimulation regulation in such a way that their functioning adjusts to the level of satisfaction of the individual need for stimulation, leading eventually to changes in level of reactivity. This change in level of reactivity may occur in response to the stimulating value of the physical or social environment or the individual's own activity.

In one of his studies of 15- and 16-year-olds, Eliasz (1981) formulated the following hypothesis. Youngsters who live in the inner city (a highly stimulating environment) for a long time gradually become less reactive; the environment hardens them and makes them more resilient to intensive stimulation. The study was run on 225 schoolboys. Part of this group (n = 102) had lived in the suburbs

Table 3.2 Reactivity level in men performing activity in highly stimulating professions compared with standardization sample

Study	Sample	Reactivity level M	Standard scores (C scale)
Stawowska, 1973	Standardization sample (N = 1265)	56.0	5
Ciosek & Oszmiańczuk, 1974	Fishermen on long-term voyages (N = 70)	70.1	8
Terelak, 1974	Pilots (N = 115)	64.4	7
	Pilots (N = 95)	62.2	6
Zarzycka, 1980	Railroad engineers (N = 59)	66.1	7
Eliasz, 1981	Steelworkers (N = 192)	61.8	6
Terelak, 1982	Participants in an Antarctic expedition (N = 21)	65.7	7
Karwowska-Szulkin, 1989	Top managers (> 1000 employees) with more than 10 years of professional experience (N = 168)	65.3	7

Note. Scale C = centile scale. Reactivity level was measured by means of the Strength of Excitation scale; higher scores mean lower level of reactivity. Adapted from *Temperament, Personality, Activity* by J. Strelau, 1983, p. 230. Copyright 1983 by Academic Press. Reprinted with permission.

(an environment low in stimulation) for at least five years, whereas the remainder (n = 123) had lived for an equally long time in the inner city. Without going into the details of this study, suffice it to say that the physical properties of the environment were the only controlled variable on which the two groups differed. Level of reactivity was measured by means of the Temperament Questionnaire. Eliasz found that level of reactivity in the boys living downtown was significantly lower (p < 0.01) than that of the boys living in the suburbs. None of the boys had any control over the choice of environment and therefore this result cannot be explained in terms of preference for the dwelling place because of its stimulating value. The author suggests that his findings support the hypothesis that the physiological mechanism underlying reactivity was modified by the environment, although he is aware that longitudinal studies would need to be done to test this hypothesis.

In another study conducted on 192 steelworkers aged 25–50, Eliasz (1981) controlled two independent variables—the stimulating value of the residential macro-environment and working conditions. One group consisted of men who lived in houses on busy roads where the level of stimulation was high; another group was composed of men who lived in suburban areas where the level of stimulation was low. Stimulation at work (an old steel mill in Silesia) was measured against three criteria: noise, physical hazards (number and nature of accidents at work), and high temperature. Two groups were selected—a group of men working in highly stimulating departments and men working in much less stimulating departments. Eliasz assumed that reactivity has no effect on place of residence in Poland, whereas it may have an effect on place of work due to such factors as selection or preference in accordance with one's individual level of reactivity. Level of reactivity was measured by means of the Temperament Questionnaire. The men were divided into four groups according to two criteria: highly versus poorly stimulating dwelling environment and relatively light versus hard working conditions. Both environments (residential and occupational) were assumed to be constant.

Analysis of the findings suggested several interesting conclusions. When light working conditions were analyzed, the author found that men living in macro-environments differing in their stimulating value also differed in their level of reactivity. This result is consistent with the findings of the schoolboy study. However, in the present study conducted on adult males, a highly stimulating residential macro-environment correlated with a higher level of reactivity. Eliasz predicted this on the assumption that when adults are submitted to prolonged and intensive macro-environmental stimulation, they switch from active regulation of stimulation (negative feedback loop) to passive regulation of stimulation (positive feedback loop). The exact moment when this switch takes place, says Eliasz (1981), is a function of "the product of the discrepancy between the optimal and actual stimulation and the duration of this discrepancy" (p. 191).

Regardless of how we interpret this outcome, it certainly shows that the residential macro-environment—which was beyond the control of the studied men, perhaps with only a few exceptions—was related to their level of reactivity. It is possible that level of reactivity changed in response to environmental influence, but we cannot say for certain because this would need a longitudinal research design. However, Eliasz's findings also revealed that when the residential macro-environment is constant, difficult working conditions are related to level of reactivity. Individuals who work in highly stimulating environments have a lower level of reactivity compared with individuals who work in less stimulating conditions. Since choice of workplace is largely at the worker's discretion, this result suggests the effect of preference or negative selection determined by individual level of reactivity. This finding is similar to the findings of Danielak (1972) and Popielarska (1972).

In the context of the research in which the relationship between level of reactivity and the stimulating value of undertaken activities was studied in actual job settings, we wanted to know whether occupational preferences for jobs differing in the stimulating value of the activities involved would also show up in youngsters who were yet to choose their career, and whether these preferences would be related to level of reactivity. To answer this question, Ewa Oleszkiewicz-Zsurzs (1986) conducted a study on a group of 171 secondary school students (males only) aged 16–20 as part of the research for her doctoral dissertation. She presented the students with a list of 44 occupations and asked them to choose three jobs they would like to do in the future (positive choices) and three jobs they would like to avoid (negative choices). Fifty expert judges rated the stimulating value of the 44 occupations, taking four criteria into account: social stimulation, physical threat, novel experiences and sensations, and cognitive stimulation.

The Temperament Questionnaire was used to measure reactivity. The results did not confirm the predicted relationship between level of reactivity and the stimulating value of the preferred occupations. The correlations between level of reactivity and the criteria of stimulating value were nil. Perhaps this negative outcome is not surprising if we consider that choice of career depends on a plethora of social factors (mainly familial) and also on the attractiveness of the profession. When the negative choices were analyzed, however (i.e., the occupations that the boys would not like to pursue in the future), a pattern of significant relationships emerged between the stimulating value of the rejected occupations and level of reactivity. With the exception of cognitive stimulation ($0.16, ns$), all the other correlations were significant ($p < 0.01$) and ranged from 0.26 to 0.34. These results imply that high-reactive individuals dismiss highly stimulating occupations. Oleszkiewicz-Zsurzs's study suggests that the individual's psychological make-up, including level of reactivity, may have a greater effect on rejection of undesirable occupations than on his or her choice of desirable occupations.

To conclude this presentation of research on the relationship between reactivity and the stimulating value of preferred or actually performed occupational activities, I would like to mention an interesting study that Renata Karwowska-Szulkin (1989) conducted as part of the research for her doctoral dissertation (see Karwowska-Szulkin & Strelau, 1990). Karwowska-Szulkin asked the following question: is the stimulating value of one's declared managerial style related to one's level of reactivity and can stress lead to a change of preferred managerial style depending on the level of this temperament trait? Managing a large enterprise employing hundreds or even thousands of people is an extremely stimulating activity; it involves making decisions that often have far-reaching consequences, not only for the firm itself but also for its employees. Adequate functioning in the managerial role is very demanding and stressful and involves considerable psychophysiological costs (Mintzberg, 1980; Shinn et al., 1984). Managers often function at or even beyond the limits of their capacity (Cooper & Payne, 1979). Hence "their preferred action style is the result of coping mechanisms or stress avoidance" (Karwowska-Szulkin, 1989, p. 5). If so, then managerial style should be related to reactivity.

I shall now concentrate on this part of Karwowska-Szulkin's study, which also had a number of other objectives. The study was run on 168 male directors or deputy directors of large enterprises (more than one thousand employees) aged 39–62 ($M = 51$) who had been in a managerial position for no less than eleven years ($M = 14.9$). Managerial style was assessed by means of an unauthorized scale called the Managerial Grid (Blake & Mouton, 1964). This scale covered ten categories of managerial functioning and enabled individual assessment in terms of preference of five different managerial styles. These styles reflect the level of activity and involvement with which managers concentrate on tasks (production) or people (employees).

- Strong focus on tasks and people (9,9).
- Strong focus on tasks and weak focus on people (9,1).
- Weak focus on tasks and strong focus on people (1,9).
- Average focus on tasks and people (5,5).
- Weak focus on tasks and people (1,1).

Fourteen expert judges, former directors of enterprises, rated the styles in terms of their difficulty and stressfulness. They based their ratings on four criteria: scope of responsibility with respect to superiors and employees; involvement with the enterprise; conflicts with superiors and employees; and level of control of the enterprise. The level of difficulty and stressfulness of the managerial style was the measure of the stimulating value of that style. The expert judges rated style 9,9 as the most stimulating and style 1,1 as the least stimulating. Styles 9,1 and 1,9 were midway and style 5,5 received ambiguous ratings. Reactivity was assessed by means of the Temperament Questionnaire. Professional competence and length of employment were both controlled and a stressful situation in which the directors' competency was questioned was specially arranged. Here I shall limit my account to the relationship between reactivity and managerial style, controlling for length of employment.

First, as predicted, the examined directors had lower levels of reactivity than the normative group (see Table 3.2). The data suggested that preferred managerial style is a function of the interaction between level of reactivity and length of employment. Preference for style 1,1 (the least stimulating style) was higher in high-reactive directors than low-reactive directors, independently of length of employment but also increasing with length of employment. In the low-reactive men, the low preference for this managerial style became even lower the longer the men had been working with the enterprise (see Figure 3.4). The statistical analysis revealed that reactivity and length of employment account for 34 percent of the variance of style 1,1. Quite the opposite pattern emerged for style 9,9 although high-reactive and low-reactive directors who had not been employed for very long did not differ significantly in their preference for this style (the most stimulating of all). As predicted, the majority of directors who preferred this style were low reactive.

A second interesting result emerged from this study. There was no significant relationship between level of reactivity and quality of managerial style (people versus tasks), which means that there is no relationship between reactivity and preference with respect to people-focus versus task-focus. On the other hand, a significant relationship was found between the formal characteristics of the various styles (read "their stimulating value") and reactivity. This finding is consistent with the RTT assumption that temperament traits are mainly about the formal characteristics of behavior (Strelau, 1983, 2001a).

The data presented in this section unequivocally demonstrate that reactivity is related to the type of activity performed or preference for activity of a particular stimulating value. The more stimulating the task or the setting in which activity is performed, or the greater the preference for such stimulation, the lower the reactivity. This is consistent with the assumption that trait reactivity is negatively correlated with stimulation-seeking activity where activity is understood as a temperament trait (Strelau, 1983). We still do not know whether the relationship between the stimulating value of individual activity or the individual's environmental setting is determined by the physiological mechanism that underlies reactivity, or whether this mechanism can be modified by the activities that individual performs or by the individual's environmental setting. The studies presented here, especially those conducted by Eliasz (1981), suggest that the biologically determined stimulation-regulating mechanism that is at the root of reactivity can

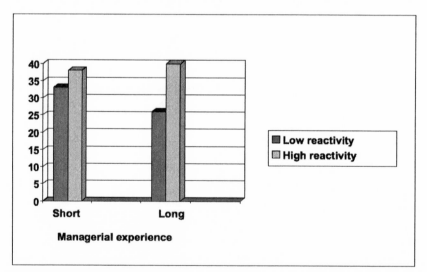

Figure 3.4. Preferred managerial style as the effect of the interaction between level of reactivity and duration of employment. From "Reactivity and the Stimulative Value of Managerial Styles" by R. Karwowska-Szulkin and J. Strelau, 1990, *Polish Psychological Bulletin, 21*, p. 55. Copyright 1990 by Committee for Psychological Sciences, Polish Academy of Sciences. Reprinted with permission.

change in response to the environment. However, only longitudinal research will give us more insight into the role of the environment—including one's own activity—in the development of level of reactivity and other temperament traits. Indirectly the answer to this question can be gleaned from research conducted within the behavior genetic paradigm, which will be discussed in chapter 8.

3.3.3. Reactivity as related to effectiveness and its psychophysiological costs in situations differing in stimulating value

Both in our laboratory and elsewhere, many investigations have been conducted to determine the relationship between neo-Pavlovian temperament traits and effectiveness. Much of this research has concentrated on reactivity or its equivalent, strength of excitation (high strength of excitation = low reactivity and vice-versa; see section 3.2.1). In these studies, most of which were conducted in the laboratory, the manipulated variable was either task difficulty or the stimulating value of the setting in which people differing in level of reactivity performed these tasks. Some researchers also controlled level of arousal "online" by registering such indices as electrodermal activity, heart rate, or psychometric measure of arousal (see Strelau, 1983). Depending on the specific nature of the study, various indicators (criteria) of reactivity were adopted—for example, alpha rhythm amplitude (see Maciejczyk, 1974; Terelak, 1974) or psychophysiological indicators of strength of excitation typically used in Russian laboratories, such as the motor reaction time curve, a measure of CNS strength often used in our laboratory by Tatiana Klonowicz (1974; for a description of this method, see Strelau, 1983). Here I shall present only two studies in which reactivity was assessed by means of the Temperament Questionnaire. Many studies of this problem, in which reactivity was measured either by the questionnaire method or various laboratory methods, have been discussed elsewhere (see, e.g., Strelau, 1974b, 1983, 1985).

One study that provided a remarkable illustration of the role played by reactivity in the effectiveness of behavior, conducted in a natural setting, was Żmudzki's (1986) study of a group of highly qualified sportsmen (weightlifters). I often mention this study, in which reactivity was measured by means of the TQ, because it shows quite dramatically how reactivity can act as a moderator in performance under extreme stress.

Żmudzki studied a national sample of 75 weightlifters. Their mean age was 23.3 and they had been competing for an average of 5.3 years. Reactivity was measured with the Strength of Excitation scale of the Temperament Questionnaire. Three groups were selected on the basis of the quartile distribution: low reactive ($n = 19$), moderately reactive ($n = 38$), and high reactive ($n = 18$). Only the extreme groups will be the subject of this presentation. Reactivity (and also neuroticism, which will not be discussed here) was measured once at a training session. Four indicators of level of arousal were also applied: state anxiety, assessed by the State-Trait Anxiety Inventory (Spielberger, Gorsuch, & Lushene, 1970); two measures of arterial blood pressure (systolic and diastolic); and heart rate. Level of arousal was measured numerous times, both in normal conditions and during competitions. The mean score was the indicator of level of arousal in a nonstressful setting—that is, during daily training sessions. In the competitive setting, level of arousal was measured after the contestants had been weighed and before they began to warm up. The dependent variable in this study was level of performance of the sports task in two contests, snatch and clean-and-jerk, in a stressful setting (the Polish national championship). Level of arousal and level of performance were assessed during ten different contests and every weightlifter was assessed on at least three occasions. Level of performance (a relative score, computed separately for each contestant) was measured by means of a seven-point scale with "unsuccessful trial" at one extreme (this applies to either snatch or clean-and-jerk) and a record-breaking score at the other. The competitive setting was more stressful than the training setting for all the competitors, as attested to by the fact that the arousal scores in both groups (high reactive and low reactive) were significantly higher ($p > 0.01$) in the former than the latter setting. The most important finding of this study for our purposes, as predicted, was that low-reactive contestants were more effective than high-reactive contestants in the stressful setting (see Figure 3.5).

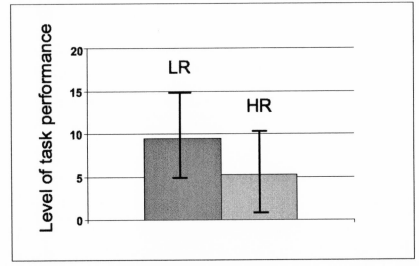

Figure 3.5. Level of task performance in a highly stressful competitive setting in high-reactive and low-reactive weightlifters. LR = low-reactive men; HR = high-reactive men. Adapted from *Poziom reaktywności a powodzenie w trakcie startu u zawodników w podnoszeniu ciężarów* [Level of Reactivity and Success During Competition in Weightlifters] by A. Żmudzki, 1986, p. 84. Copyright 1986 by Wydawnictwa Instytut Sportu. Reprinted with permission.

Żmudzki's (1986) finding that level of performance of a sports task (weightlifting) under stress is related to reactivity is very important for at least three reasons. First, the study in which it was obtained was run in a natural setting. Second, obviously competition in so prestigious an event as the Polish national championship is very stressful and the psychophysiological measures confirmed this. Third, the score that Żmudzki used was based on at least three independent measures because all the contestants took part in at least three competitions, and some even took part in ten.

Most studies on the relationship between level of performance (effectiveness) or task difficulty and level of reactivity were conducted by Tatiana Klonowicz (see 1974, 1984, 1985, 1987a, 1987b). I often quote this research in my own publications (e.g., Strelau, 1983, 1988). Klonowicz included psychophysiological variables—for example, electrodermal activity, cardiovascular activity, or state anxiety—in her research. Depending on the specific nature of the study in question, she controlled these variables at different stages (before, during, or after the experiment) and used them as indicators of the effort needed to perform the activities or level of arousal.

Following is a synopsis of one of Klonowicz's (1992) complex studies that illustrates the relationship between level of reactivity as measured by the Temperament Questionnaire and functioning under stress. This study involved a series of trials conducted on the same individuals. Let me focus here only on those trials in which Klonowicz used the TQ to measure reactivity and mobility of behavior.

The study was run on a group of 23 professional simultaneous interpreters aged 30–42 (about one-third of the subjects were men and two-thirds were women) and 40 students of applied linguistics aged 22–26 who were training to be simultaneous interpreters. One of the main objectives of this study was to determine whether the effort required to translate simultaneously, a highly stimulating task (stressful setting), depends on level of reactivity.

The professional simultaneous interpreters were studied in a natural setting (a conference lasting several days) in two different conditions—translating from Polish into a foreign language (French, German, Russian, or Spanish) and translating from one of these languages into Polish. The effort invested in the task was measured on the basis of cardiovascular activity (systolic and diastolic blood pressure, heart rate) and intensity of emotional states measured by means of the State-Trait Personality Inventory (Spielberger, 1979) in the Polish adaptation by Wrześniewski (1984). This inventory has three scales (Anxiety, Anger, and Curiosity), all of which can be administered in their state format or trait format. Only emotional states were assessed in this study. Effort was measured twice, prior to the onset of interpretation (anticipatory phase) and directly after completion of the task. In order to eliminate the novelty factor, all measures were taken on the second day of the conference.

Reactivity correlated significantly (from 0.38 to 0.61) with heart rate, systolic blood pressure, and state anxiety. These correlations emerged regardless of the direction of the translation (from Polish to a foreign language or vice-versa). No direct correlation was found between mobility of behavior and effort, but when partial correlations were analyzed, mobility accounted for about 15 percent of the variance. Klonowicz conducted a similar study in a quasi-natural setting on students of applied linguistics and received similar results (correlations from 0.22 to 0.56) to those she obtained for professional interpreters.

Klonowicz (1992) also studied the same professional interpreters in the laboratory in an experimental setting and found that the relationship between effort and reactivity only emerged when the task was very difficult (i.e., stressful). The subjects performed three activities differing in their level of difficulty: (a) they listened to a short text in Polish through headphones (listening); (b) they listened to and repeated a text in Polish (echoing); and (c) they listened to a message and translated it, aloud and simultaneously, into a foreign language (simultaneous interpretation). The effort involved in performing these different activities was measured by monitoring changes in heart rate. Klonowicz found a positive correlation between heart rate and reactivity but only in the simultaneous translation setting. No correlation emerged in the listening and echoing settings. This outcome corroborates my own finding that temperament traits show up mainly in difficult, stressful situations (Strelau, 1983, 1995b).

3.4
Concluding remarks

In the almost forty years since the development of the Temperament Questionnaire (Strelau, 1969), its English-language equivalent the Strelau Temperament Inventory (Strelau, 1972b), and their more recent modification the Pavlovian Temperament Survey, hundreds of works have been published in which these questionnaires are one of the diagnostic instruments. In addition to my many students and coworkers who typically use one of the versions of this inventory, many students of my former students and collaborators have also used the TQ or PTS to assess reactivity. One example is the book edited by Andrzej Eliasz and Magdalena Marszał-Wiśniewska (1992), which summarizes the research conducted by Eliasz's team during that period. Empirical research is presented in twelve chapters of the book and the Temperament Questionnaire was used in ten of these chapters. The PTS, which was constructed just six years ago, has also been used in many studies (see, e.g., Brandstätter and Eliasz, 2001; Dudek, 2003; Klonowicz, 2001a; Strelau, Angleitner, & Newberry, 1999; Strelau and Zawadzki, 1998; Strzałecki, 2003; Zalewska, 2003). In my reprint files, I have found more than thirty works by non-Polish authors who have used the STI—not to mention many studies conducted in Eastern Europe, mainly in Russia, where these inventories are particularly popular (see Bodunov, 1993).

The intent of this chapter was not to present the results of the many studies in which the aforementioned questionnaires were used to measure temperament in a variety of settings depending on the purpose of the study and the interest of the researcher. The main focus of this book is the Regulative Theory of Temperament and investigations corroborating its theoretical assumptions. Both versions of the questionnaire, the TQ/STI and the PTS, have close affinity with Pavlov's theory of basic CNS properties. This theory, as indicated in section 3.1, was but one of the points of departure for the development of the RTT—whose most recent version will be discussed in the next chapter.

Chapter 4

The Regulative Theory of Temperament: A theoretical framework for temperament research at the turn of the twenty-first century

As we know from the theoretical discussion in chapter 3, the basic outline of the Regulative Theory of Temperament (RTT) was developed in the 1980s. For the sake of greater clarity, the theory was presented in the form of five postulates (Strelau, 1993), most of which were concerned with the formal characteristics of behavior. As a result of research conducted by my collaborators, graduate and postgraduate students, and me, the number of postulates increased to nine (Strelau, 1996) and then subsequently to ten (Strelau, 2001a). During this last phase of research, two of my closest collaborators—Bogdan Zawadzki and Włodzimierz Oniszczenko—greatly contributed to the present version of the theory and the accumulation of empirical findings testing the theory's validity.

4.1.
Basic propositions of the Regulative Theory of Temperament

The term "postulate" is often used in science (mathematics and logic) to mean an axiom, a statement that is accepted without having to be demonstrated. In everyday life the term is used to underscore the wishful or imperative nature of our endeavors. For these reasons I am going to present the RTT in the form of propositions to indicate that what I intend to put forward are assumptions or statements that provide the rationale for empirical testing, although some of these propositions—particularly those that refer to the formal characteristics of behavior—are more like postulates. This chapter is structured around these ten propositions.

- Proposition 1. Temperament manifests itself in the formal characteristics of behavior.

- Proposition 2. The formal characteristics of behavior may be described in terms of energetic and temporal categories.

- Proposition 3. There exist relatively stable individual differences in formal characteristics of behavior and these differences have the status of traits.

- Proposition 4. Every behavior, independent of the kind and content, may be described in terms of energy and time; thus individual differences in temperament are common (universal).

- Proposition 5. Individual differences in the intensity and temporal characteristics of behavior and reactions may be observed from the very beginning of neonatal life; thus temperament traits are present from early infancy.

- Proposition 6. Irrespective of the specific nature of typical human and animal behavior, the behavior of all mammals (and probably all vertebrates) may be characterized by means of properties that refer to the categories of intensity and time.

- Proposition 7. Considering Propositions 5 and 6, it is reasonable to assume that temperament is the outcome of biological evolution; therefore some genetic bases, as well as physiological mechanisms codetermining individual differences in temperament, must exist.

- Proposition 8. Although temperament traits are relatively stable, they undergo gradual, biologically and environmentally determined, ontogenetic changes.

- Proposition 9. Temperament has a regulative function that modifies (moderates) the stimulating (energetic) and temporal values of behavior and reactions and the situations in which individuals find themselves.

- Proposition 10. The role of temperament in the regulation of human beings' relationships with the world shows up mainly in difficult situations or extreme behaviors.

4.2.
Temperament manifests itself in the formal characteristics of behavior that can be described in energetic and temporal terms (Propositions 1 and 2)

The proposition concerning the formal characteristics of behavior is based on the conviction that for hundreds of years, the formal characteristics of behavior have been the most frequently mentioned property defining the essence of temperament. In the eighteenth century, Immanuel Kant ([1798] 1912) distinguished four types of temperament on the basis of two criteria—vital energy (*Lebenskraft*), which ranges from excitability to drowsiness; and the dominant characteristic of behavior (emotion versus action). "Each temperament may be characterized by means of vital energy [*intension*] or by release [*remissio*]" (Kant, [1798] 1912, p.

228). These were a reinterpretation of the four classical temperaments described in the ancient Greek typologies of Hippocrates and Galen (see Figure 4.1).

Kant's ideas concerning vital energy that is expressed in temperament had considerable impact on later theories of temperament. Influenced by Kant, Gerhard Ewald (1924) introduced the concept of biotonus to psychology. This concept refers to individual differences in resistance to intensive stimulation and fatigue and stated that its physiological basis should be traced to the quality and speed of metabolism. Earlier Wilhelm Wundt (1887), who understood temperament as a disposition that applies to drives and emotions, had added the concept of time to the typology of temperaments in addition to the existing concept of energy. He distinguished four temperaments that also drew on the Hippocrates-Galen typology but were based on two dimensions, strength-weakness and speed-slowness. Wundt applied these dimensions to the emotional sphere to distinguish the four temperaments shown in Figure 4.1.

William Stern (1921) summarized the existing ideas on temperament by quoting sixteen typologies whose authors refer in their descriptions of temperament to formal traits, which in general boil down to the energetic or temporal characteristics of behaviors and reactions.

Many researchers have emphasized the formal characteristics of behavior and reactions in which temperament is manifested and have subjected this sphere of personality to empirical research. For example, the pioneers of psychometric and

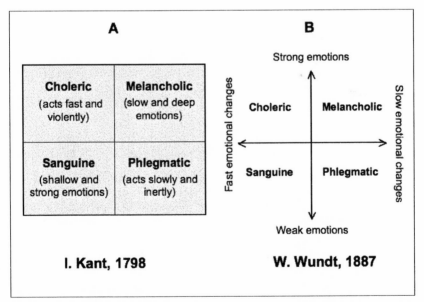

Figure 4.1. The Hippocrates-Galen typology according to Immanuel Kant (A) and Wilhelm Wundt (B). From *Psychologia różnic indywidualnych* [Psychology of Individual Differences] by J. Strelau, 2006, p. 20. Copyright 2006 by Wydawnictwo Naukowe Scholar. Reprinted with permission.

experimental personality studies, Heymans and Wiersma (Heymans, 1908), distinguished three facets of temperament—primary-secondary function, emotionality, and activity—which actually have to do with formal characteristics. The first of these three facets, also called perseveration, relates to the duration of mental processes and behavior and the speed with which these processes move from one state to another. Emotionality stems from the energetic perspective because it pertains to excitability and emotional sensitivity, regardless of sign. In turn, activity can be measured by the amount of time a given action or behavior has been performed. The very names of the properties of the nervous system, which were discussed at length in chapters 1 and 2 and formed the basis of Pavlov's typology (Pavlov, 1938), underscore the fact that temperament is about the formal characteristics of behavior. Russian psychologists, influenced by Pavlov, defined temperament as a dynamic characteristic of behavior that is expressed in individual differences in the speed and intensity of reactions (behaviors) determined by the type of nervous system (e.g., Merlin, 1973; Rusalov, 1979; Teplov, 1956).

Hans Eysenck (1970), whose ideas and empirical investigations on extraversion and neuroticism had substantial impact on the development of many conceptions of temperament that were formulated in the second half of the twentieth century, also belongs to those ranks of temperament researchers who refer to formal characteristics. This is most evident in one of the two postulates that underlie his experimental research on extraversion. Eysenck argued that individuals differ in the speed and strength with which they enter a state of excitation or inhibition, and also in the speed with which inhibition subsides (Eysenck, 1970). In Eysenck's laboratory such formal characteristics as speed of classical conditioning, sensory sensitivity threshold, or speed of reaction or activity served to locate people on the extraversion-introversion continuum. Animal studies of extraversion (Garau & Garcia-Sevilla, 1985; Simonov, 1987), emotionality (Broadhurst, 1975), neuroticism (Gray, 1982), and many other temperament traits in animals are also based on these formal characteristics.

Many American temperament researchers, most of whom concentrate on child studies, also claim that temperament is largely about formal characteristics. Gordon Allport and Solomon Diamond, who defined temperament in terms of the formal characteristics of behavior, contributed greatly to this research, which began to develop dynamically in the mid-twentieth century. Allport (1937), the pioneer of personality psychology understood in terms of traits, reduced temperament to the emotional sphere, which he described by means of such categories as strength, sensitivity, speed, and changeability. Diamond (1957), on the other hand, who also greatly contributed to the ideas of American temperament researchers, defined temperament "in terms of the ease of arousal of *unlearned* patterns of adaptive behavior" (p. 95, emphasis added).

The pioneers of temperament research in children, Alexander Thomas and Stella Chess (1977), subordinated their categories of temperament to the main idea that the child's temperament has to do with how the child behaves (i.e., its style of behavior, not the contents of that behavior). Many theories of temperament referring to the stylistic properties of behavior were inspired by Thomas and Chess (see, e.g., Carey, 1986; Maziade, 1988; Windle & Lerner, 1986). Of the three temperament traits distinguished by Buss and Plomin (1975, 1984)—emotionality, activity, and sociability—the first two also refer to the formal characteristics of reactions and behavior. Emotionality is the ease with which the individual reacts with intense arousal, whereas level of activity refers to total energy output. According to these writers, activity has two components—vigor and tempo—and is therefore a combination of energetic and temporal characteristics. Goldsmith and Campos (1986) voiced the opinion that infant temperament is expressed in primary emotions and suggested that the manifestations of these emotions should be measured on the basis of relatively stable temporal and energetic parameters of the general level of arousal.

These ideas, which provide a random illustration of how temperament is understood, led me to conclude that temperament is about the formal characteristics of behavior and that this (among other things) is what distinguishes it from those spheres of personality that emphasize the contents of behavior and reactions. These contents are largely expressed in the individual's attitude toward himself or herself, other people, and the world in general (Strelau, 1984, 1987a). If we consider the formal characteristics of behavior, we must say that its description in terms of energy and time—concepts that originated in physics—basically exhaust the abundance of temperament traits described in formal terms.

4.3.
There are relatively stable individual differences in the formal characteristics of behavior and these differences have the status of traits (Proposition 3)

If we were to treat the concept of stability literally, we would have to say that it does not apply to human beings or any other living organisms. Both mental phenomena and all the biological functions change with time, as do their underlying structures. Hence when we refer to relatively stable temperamental characteristics, this can mean at least three different things (Strelau, 1986).

- Temperament does not change from hour to hour, overnight, or from week to week. The difficulty lies in the lack of unambiguous criteria on whose basis we can assess relative stability. Obviously stability of temperamental characteristics is more a matter of time measured in months or even years (see Guerin & Gottfried, 1994; Roberts & DelVecchio, 2000; Thomas & Chess, 1986). It is highly probable, however, that temperament will change in response to drastic events or prolonged environmental influence that chronically exceeds the band of optimal stimulation regulation (see section 3.2.2; Eliasz, 1981).

- Compared with other personality characteristics, the specific behaviors or characteristics in which temperament is manifested are less prone to change. Temperamental stability can probably be compared to the stability of the intelligence quotient (Carroll, 1993; Deary, 2000).

- Temperamental characteristics do not change or change only slightly if we compare an individual's temperament with his or her age group at various stages of life. This underscores the fact that changes are related to human biological development. For example, if a 6-year-old girl is diagnosed as an introvert compared with her peer reference group, then at the age of 20 or 60 she will still be an introvert compared with her peers. However, the behaviors and reactions on whose basis we infer introversion will change throughout the life-cycle. Thomas and Chess (1977) observed that the way temperament expresses itself changes with age, but what "remains consistent over time is the definitional identity of the characteristic" (p. 159).

Regardless of their theoretical rationale, temperament researchers assume that there are relatively stable individual differences in temperament. In order to emphasize this relative stability, they describe temperament and its structure with the help of such concepts as trait, type, property, disposition, style, dimension,

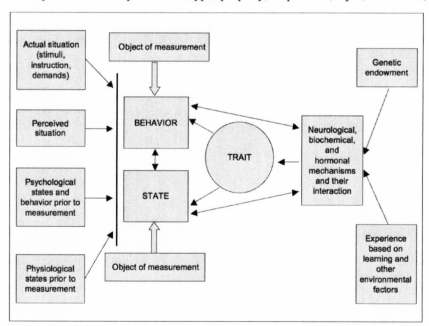

Figure 4.2. The hypothetical status of traits. From "The Concept and Status of Trait in Research on Temperament" by J. Strelau, 2001c, *European Journal of Personality, 15,* p. 319. Copyright 2001 by John Wiley & Sons. Reprinted with permission.

factor, or category (for a detailed account of the similarities and differences between these concepts, see Strelau, 1998, 2006). Here let me focus only on the concept of trait from which all the remaining concepts derive.

The ontological status of the trait, as it is understood in the Regulative Theory of Temperament, cannot be reduced to behaviors or processes and states that take place in the individual organism (human or animal). Trait—understood as a generalized tendency toward specific behaviors manifested in various tendency-consistent situations or settings—is determined by internal mechanisms, inborn or acquired, but cannot be reduced to these mechanisms alone (see section 1.5). The trait is the outcome of specific connections between many internal mechanisms and has a discrete status, expressed in the tendency to behave (react) in a specific way. This tendency, which has a genetic background, can be modified by ontogenetically developing physiological mechanisms and external contingencies (such as learning and other environmental factors) that affect the individual from the moment of conception. Since we still do not fully understand the biological bases of traits, we must assign them the status of a hypothetical construct (see Strelau, 2001c, 2006). As illustrated in Figure 4.2, what we measure is not the trait per se but the behaviors and processes (states) in which it is expressed. Traits are difficult to measure, however, because all our behaviors and reactions result from the trait and many other physical, physiological, and psychological factors that make it very difficult to draw inferences about traits.

By aggregating behaviors and states over many different situations and periods of time, it is possible to grasp the expression of a trait (see section 1.5). Questionnaire measures of temperament, for example, are based on this assumption.

4.4
Individual differences in temperament are universal, present from the onset of neonatal life, and found in both humans and animals (Propositions 4–6)

When we say that individual differences in temperament traits are universal, we mean that every behavior—whether manifested in the emotional, cognitive, or motor sphere, and whatever its content and goal—can be described in energetic (e.g., intensity, strength, amplitude, energy, effort, etc.) and temporal (e.g., speed, rhythmicity, mobility, duration, etc.) terms. The proposition that individual differences in temperament are universal distinguishes the Regulative Theory of Temperament from many other conceptions of temperament. Many temperament researchers limit this sphere of personality to emotional characteristics, just as Allport did long ago (Allport, 1937). This is how Gray (1991), Goldsmith and Campos (1990), Kagan (1994), and Mehrabian (1991)—to name but a few—view temperament. Until the late 1980s, temperament research within the RTT paradigm tended to ignore the emotional side of behavior. One reason for this was that existing diagnostic instruments (the Strelau Temperament Inventory and Pavlovian Temperament Survey) did not have scales directly measuring this sphere of human functioning.

Temperament, as opposed to other areas of personality, is present from the beginning of neonatal life (see Kagan, 1994; Rothbarth, 1989). Several question-naires have been constructed that can be used to diagnose temperament from the first months of life (see Bates, Freeland, & Lounsbury, 1979; Medoff-Cooper, Carrey, & McDevitt, 1993; Sanson et al., 1987). Moreover, several instruments also assess temperament in neonates (Koženi & Šulcová, 1994) and there have even been attempts to diagnose this sphere of personality in the prenatal phase (Eaton & Saudino, 1992), on the assumption that temperament traits are already manifested in the mother's womb in the movements of the unborn baby.

Studies of temperament in children are the domain of American psychologists. Alexander Thomas and Stella Chess (1957, 1977) initiated them in the early 1950s and were followed by a galaxy of American researchers, several of whom enjoyed great popularity—for example, Mary Rothbart (1989; Garstein & Rothbart, 2003; Rothbart, Ahadi, & Evans, 2000), Hill Goldsmith (1989; Goldsmith & Campos, 1990; Lemery et al., 1999), Arnold Buss and Robert Plomin (1975, 1984), and Jerome Kagan (1994).

In the first phase of research conducted within the RTT paradigm, children—especially preschool children—were not the subject of research apart from a few exceptions (see Friedensberg, 1985). This is largely because our diagnostic tools (the Strelau Temperament Inventory and Pavlovian Temperament Survey) were not adapted to parental or teacher assessment of children's temperament. The only instrument that measured reactivity in children was the Reactivity Rating Scale con-structed by Ewa Friedensberg (1982) and presented at length by Strelau (1983). This scale enabled researchers to assess reactivity by means of observation, beginning at the preschool stage.

It is indisputable that temperament traits found in human beings can also be found in animals. Calvin Hall (1941) reviewed the research on temperament in animals more than eighty years ago. Diamond (1957), one of the pioneers of personality research and author of *Personality and Temperament*, was emphatic that the concept of personality includes both temperament traits—which are present in humans and animals—and traits that are specific to human beings only. In his laboratory studies, Ivan Pavlov (1938) clearly demonstrated that animals have temperament and believed that the types of nervous system were the physiological basis of the four classical temperaments. He even identified these types with temperaments, which is unequivocally expressed in the title of one of his lectures: "Physiological Study of the Types of Nervous Systems, *i.e.*, of Temperaments" (Pavlov, 1928, p. 370).[1]

---

[1] This school of research, which involved the study of the basic properties of the nerv-ous system in various species (dogs, rats, mice, monkeys, horses, sheep, and guinea pigs), became very popular among Russian researchers (see Strelau, 1983).

On the basis of many years of research conducted on rats, Jeffrey Gray (1967, 1981, 1982) developed a neuropsychological theory of anxiety and proposed a modification of Eysenck's theory. Laboratory studies of rats led Gray to conclude that the two basic dimensions proposed by Eysenck—extraversion and neuroticism—are derived from two more basic dimensions, impulsivity and anxiety. On this basis Gray (1991) constructed his neuropsychological model of temperament, which he applied to human beings.

Within the last quarter-century, dozens or even hundreds of studies of animal temperament have been conducted (see, e.g., Gershenfeld & Paul, 1998; Gosling & John, 1999; Steimer, la Fleur, & Schulz, 1997). The temperament of rats has also been studied in our laboratory, focusing mainly on stimulation seeking, emotionality, and open field behavior (see Matysiak, 1993; Pisula, 1994; Pisula, Ostaszewski, & Matysiak, 1992).

4.5
Temperament, which is the result of biological evolution, undergoes gradual changes (Propositions 7 and 8)

The fact that temperament traits are manifested as early as the neonatal stage and can even be found in the animal world entails the proposition that temperament traits are rooted in innate physiological and biochemical mechanisms. Genetic determination is one of the defining elements of Buss and Plomin's (1984) conceptualization of temperament according to which "temperaments are *inherited personality traits, present in early childhood*" (p. 84). Nearly every investigator of temperament views the significant contribution of the genetic factor to the variance of the studied traits as supporting the claim that temperament is what he or she is studying. Without going into the details of heritability of temperament (this problem will be discussed in chapter 8, devoted largely to our own research), most investigators of this aspect of personality have found that the heritability of temperament traits falls in the 0.30–0.60 range (see Gjone & Stevenson, 1997; Goldsmith, 1986; Loehlin, 1986; Oniszczenko, 2005; Saudino et al., 1995; Strelau, 1998), and if the error of measurement typical for self-rating is eliminated, it can even exceed 0.80 (see Wolf et al., 2004).

It should also be pointed out that research conducted within the behavior genetic paradigm has demonstrated that individual differences in characteristics that are far removed from temperament are also genetically determined to a certain extent. This has been found, for example, in studies of individual differences in social or religious attitudes (see Bouchard et al., 2003, 2004; Tesser, 1993; Waller et al., 1990). This research—as well as research indicating that personality traits not normally classified as temperamental, such as agreeableness or conscientiousness (see Bergeman et al., 1993; Bouchard, 1994; Jang, Livesley, & Vernon, 1996)—also show considerable heritability scores. This means that heritability is not unique for temperament vis-à-vis other mental phenomena. Contribution of heritability to the variance of temperament traits is necessary but not sufficient.

Temperament traits, strongly rooted in biological mechanisms and primarily genetically determined, may be significantly modified under the influence of environmental factors, as powerfully attested to by research conducted within the behavior genetic paradigm (Bouchard & McGue, 1990; Goldsmith, 1994; Oniszczenko, 2005). If the genetic factor accounts for 30–60 percent of the variance of temperament traits, then of course the remaining part of the total variance can only be accounted for by the contribution of environmental factors, beginning with the conditions of fetal development and ending with the influence of the social and physical environments. Even if we assume that about 20 percent of the contribution to demonstrated individual differences is absorbed by measurement error (the reliability of psychometric measures of temperament is about 0.80; see Strelau, 1998), other environmental factors still account for a considerable portion of the variance. The research cited earlier, as well as many other studies including our own (see chapter 8), has demonstrated unequivocally that the environment that makes us differ from one another with respect to temperament traits is the nonshared environment—that is, the one that leads to differences between members of the same family (see Oniszczenko, 2005; Strelau, 1998).

Many temperament researchers link the behaviors in which temperament traits are expressed to physiological or biochemical correlates that they see as the biological mechanisms underlying temperament (see Cloninger, Svrakic, & Przybeck, 1993; Eysenck & Eysenck, 1985; Kagan, 1994; Zuckerman, 1994). For example, Gray (1981, 1991) traces the physiological foundations of his anxiety dimension to the hippocampus, septum, and Papez ring, structures that form the so-called behavioral inhibition system. Gray relates the second of his temperament traits, impulsiveness, to the functioning of neural structures in the thalamic nuclei and neocortex, structures that form the two motor systems—the caudate and accumbens systems. These structures form the behavioral activation system. Reactivity of both these systems determines individual differences in temperament traits. Jerome Kagan (1994), in turn, who distinguished two categories of temperament on the basis of his child studies—inhibited temperament and uninhibited temperament—attributed individual differences in these temperaments to the reactivity threshold of specific neural structures. These structures are the limbic system, especially the amygdala and the hypothalamus, and other related systems—the pituitary-adrenal axis, the reticular activating system, and the sympathetic chain of the autonomic nervous system. As I said before, temperament traits do not differ from other personality traits as far as heritability is concerned. They probably do differ, however, in that researchers usually suggest hypothetical underlying physiological or biochemical mechanisms for the basic temperament traits, as illustrated in Table 4.1.

Table 4.1 Arousability and selected temperament traits

Author	Arousability		Biological mechanisms
H. J. Eysenck	Extraversion	Introversion	Cortico-reticular loop
H. J. Eysenck	Emotional stability	Neuroticism	Visceral brain (limbic system)
A. H. Buss & R. Plomin	Low emotionality	High emotionality	Autonomic nervous system
J. Strelau	Low emotional reactivity	High emotional reactivity	Limbic system and autonomic nervous system
J. Strelau	High activity	Low activity	Cortical structures and brainstem reticular formation
M. Zuckerman	Sensation seeking	Sensation avoidance	Catecholamine system
I. P. Pavlov	High strength of excitation	Low strength of excitation	Cortical and subcortical centers
J. A. Gray	Low anxiety	High anxiety	Behavioral inhibition system
J. A. Gray	High impulsivity	Low impulsivity	Behavioral activation system
J. Kagan	Uninhibited temperament	Inhibited temperament	Limbic system (amygdala and hypothalamus)
C. R. Cloninger	Harm avoidance	No harm avoidance	Serotonin activity in the limbic system
C. R. Cloninger	Novelty seeking	Novelty avoidance	Activity of dopaminergic paths in the *locus cinereus*
C. R. Cloninger	Reward dependence	Reward independence	Basal noradrenegic activity

Note. From *Psychologia różnic indywidualnych* [Psychology of Individual Differences] by J. Strelau, 2006, p. 265. Copyright 2006 by Wydawnictwo Naukowe Scholar. Reprinted with permission.

Irrespective of the specific nature of temperament traits and the biological mechanism that allegedly explains individual differences in these traits, most temperament researchers attach critical significance to the arousal (activation) construct and its trait equivalent, arousability (both constructs were discussed in section 3.1). Although different temperament scholars may understand the concept of arousal and its derivative (arousability) differently, the two concepts are a bridge linking various theories of temperament (Strelau, 2001b). The differences in how these concepts are understood are partly determined by the fact that, depending on the hypothetical physiological or biochemical mechanism of temperament traits, researchers measure arousal at different levels—from neurotransmitters to behavior. Hence we speak of biochemical, hormonal, neurotransmitter, autonomic, cortical, behavioral, or general arousal. Measurement at these different levels, based on different level-appropriate indicators, naturally yields different outcomes—a fact that Fahrenberg pointed out very clearly (1992; see also Strelau, 1991). We know from the research that current level of arousal (also interpreted in terms of activation) depends on the stimuli or situation (setting), as well as on the state of the organism prior to stimulation onset (e.g., fatigue, mood, etc.). But regardless of the type of activation being measured, its level also depends on individual differences in the reactivity of the underlying biological mechanisms. These individual differences in the reactivity of the biological mechanisms that determine level of activation (arousal) are at the root of arousability, as illustrated in Figure 4.3.

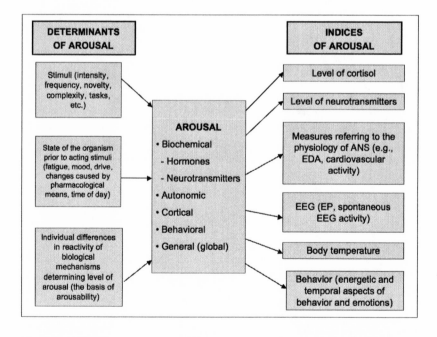

Figure 4.3. Arousal: Its indicators and determinants. ANS = autonomic nervous system; EDA = electrodermal activity; EP = evoked potential. From "The Place of the Construct of Arousal in Temperament Research" by J. Strelau, 2001b. In R. Riemann, F. M. Spinath, and F. Ostendorf (Eds.), *Personality and Temperament: Genetics, Evolution, and Structure*, p. 118. Copyright 2001 by Pabst Science Publishers. Reprinted with permission.

Although the biological mechanisms to which temperament researchers refer explain its physiological foundations, however, they cannot explain individual differences in temperament. They can only explain behavior or states assumed to be manifestations of these traits. For example, if we refer to the physiological mechanism underlying Zuckerman's (1994) sensation seeking or Cloninger's (1986) novelty seeking—activity of catecholamine amines in both cases—this is not sufficient to account for individual differences within these traits. The reason is that individual differences in temperament depend on individual differences in the sensitivity or reactivity of these mechanisms.

> The biological properties that underlie individual differences in behavior apply to the more or less formal characteristics of these physiological and biochemical mechanisms. . . . They can only be explained when we refer to such properties as individual differences in the sensitivity of the postsynaptic receptor neurones, differences in synaptic transmission, differences in the amount of excreted neurotransmitters, and differences in the reactivity of the neural structures involved in catecholaminergic activity. (Strelau, 2006, p. 263)

4.6
Temperament has a regulative function that shows up mainly in difficult situations or extreme behaviors (Propositions 9 and 10)

Proposition 9 says that the regulative function of temperament is to moderate the energetic (stimulating) and temporal values of both behaviors and situations in which individuals have found themselves, in accordance with their temperament traits. This proposition gives temperament traits the status of an intervening variable—that is, one that moderates (see chapter 3, note 1, for a definition of this term) the relationship between the stimulus, or more widely the situation, and the response (behavior) evoked by that stimulus (situation). Stagner (1984) comments that the intervening variable is anchored in the input variables (stimulus) and output variables (response). But the regulative function of temperament also recognizes that individuals organize their behavior or seek situations that correspond to their temperament traits. In this sense these traits also have a motivational component and this component is most salient in activity that, according to the RTT, is a temperament trait. The regulative function of temperament seemed so obvious that it was not mentioned in the original list of RTT postulates; it was only after twenty years of research that this proposition was included among the ten RTT postulates (Strelau, 2001a). The regulative function of temperament is discussed in detail in section 3.2, where reference is made primarily to the concepts of reactivity and activity that were introduced in the early phase of development of the RTT. Eliasz (1981), who introduced the concept of standard of stimulation regulation that is so important for the theory (see section 3.2.2), made this standard the point of departure for his Transactional Model of Temperament (Eliasz, 1985).

The temperament traits belonging to the energetic characteristics and temporal characteristics have different adaptive functions, although both are based on similar biological mechanisms responsible for regulating the level of arousal. Individual differences in the reactivity of these mechanisms determine the tendency toward chronically elevated or suppressed level of arousal. This tendency has the status of trait and therefore the concept of arousability was introduced (after Gray, 1964) to the RTT (see section 3.1).

Temperament traits, determined by level of arousal and their underlying neurobiochemical mechanism, are the principal moderator of the stimulating and temporal value of behaviors, reactions, and stimuli. This moderating or modifying role of temperament traits (the traits will be discussed in the next chapter) is illustrated in Figure 4.4.

As already noted in section 3.2.1 in the discussion of the physiological bases of reactivity—and this also applies to other temperament traits based on the physiological and biochemical mechanisms responsible for regulating the level of

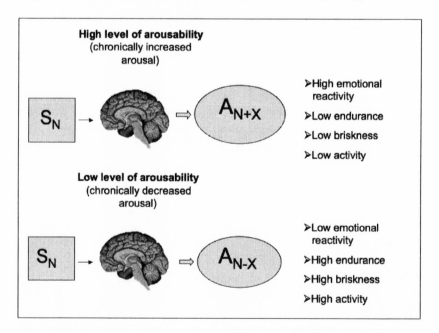

Figure 4.4. Temperament traits and the underlying arousability level: The regulators of the relationship between the stimulus (situation) and the response (behavior). From *Psychologia różnic indywidualnych* [Psychology of Individual Differences] by J. Strelau, 2006, p. 264. Copyright 2006 by Wydawnictwo Naukowe Scholar. Reprinted with permission.

arousal—there are individual differences in level of arousability. Drawing on the concepts of augmentation/reduction of stimulation, we may say that individuals who have temperament traits typically associated with a high level of arousability have a stimulation-augmenting mechanism. Stimulation (sensory, motor, emotional, cognitive) of a given intensity (S_n) leads to a higher level of arousal than that intensity of stimulation would imply (A_{n+x}). Individuals who have temperament traits typically associated with a low level of arousability have a stimulation-reducing mechanism; stimulation of the same intensity leads to a lower level of arousal than that intensity of stimulation would imply (A_{n-x}).

Our research spanning more than thirty years has shown that the regulative function of temperament may assume many different forms. It is expressed in the preferred style of activity (preference for activity of a particular stimulating value), the choice of situations and actions corresponding to one's temperament traits, or the drop in performance level (effectiveness) or psychophysiological costs in situations whose stimulating value is inconsistent with the individual's temperament traits. The research illustrating the regulative functions of temperament was reviewed in detail in section 3.3 (see also Strelau, 1983).

Mary Rothbart and her collaborators (Rothbart, 1989, 1991; Rothbart, Derryberry, & Posner, 1994; Rothbart & Posner, 1985) proposed a developmental model of temperament that strongly emphasized the regulative functions of temperament traits in children. In this model temperament is defined as constitutionally determined individual differences in reactivity and self-regulation (Rothbart & Derryberry, 1981). According to these authors, reactivity means physiological and behavioral excitability, whereas self-regulation means processes (such as attention, approach, withdrawal, attack, or withholding reactions) that modify reactivity. This concept of self-regulation has great affinity with the RTT concept of activity, which regulates the individual's typical level of reactivity (see section 3.2.2). Rothbart (1989) says that "our constructs of reactivity and self-regulation are very similar to Strelau's" (p. 59).

Many studies (see, e.g., Kagan, 1994; Nebylitsyn, 1972; Pavlov, 1938), including our own studies conducted since the 1960s (Strelau, 1974b, 1982, 1983, 1985; see also Eliasz, 1981; Klonowicz, 1984), suggest that the role of temperament is most prominent in extreme conditions when the individual is under great stress. If we agree with Proposition 5, which says that temperament traits are present from the neonatal period, then obviously human beings experience stressors and stressful states vis-à-vis their particular temperament traits from a very early age. It is these traits that moderate the state of stress. I have devoted several publications to the relationship between temperament and various aspects of stress (Strelau, 1988, 1995b, 1996, 2001d). Here suffice it to say that beginning in the early 1990s, our investigations into the relationship between temperament and stress have been rooted in the temperament-stress model. This model, which will be discussed in chapter 6, illustrates the role of temperament in the functioning of the individual in difficult or even extreme situations. The relationship between temperament and stress is manifested not only with respect to stressors, but also with respect to coping with stress and the psychological and psychophysiological consequences of the state of stress. We have not studied the direct relationship between temperament and the state of stress because this state is hard to investigate. We make inferences about this state on the basis of the operating stressors and above all on the basis of the consequences to which this state leads.

4.7
The definition of temperament as proposed by the RTT

Throughout my research (see Strelau, 1965b, 1969, 1983), I have tried to define temperament and, depending on the level of advancement of these studies, these definitions have been modified. On the basis of the above propositions, I proposed a rather classical definition of temperament that includes the *genus proximum* and *differentia specifica*. It describes what temperament is and to which category it belongs; it also tells us about the populations to which temperament applies and about its origins.

> Temperament is what we call the basic, relatively stable personality traits that apply mainly to the formal characteristics (energetic and temporal) of reactions and behaviors. These characteristics manifest themselves from early childhood and have their counterpart in the animal world. Although temperament is originally determined by innate neurobiochemical mechanisms, it undergoes gradual changes due to maturation and individual-specific interplay between the genotype and the environment. (Strelau, 2001a, p. 184)

The remaining chapters present a selection of the research that my collaborators, students, and I have conducted during the last fifteen years. The presentation begins with our studies of the structure of temperament and an account of a psychometric instrument that measures traits distinguished within this structure.

Chapter 5

The structure of temperament and a psychometric instrument with which to measure it

L ong-standing attachment to the Pavlovian (1938) temperament constructs in general, and the practice of assessing the traits postulated by the Regulative Theory of Temperament (RTT) in its first phase of development— that is, reactivity, activity, and mobility of behavior—by means of a psychometric instrument diagnosing basic central nervous system (CNS) properties in particular, made it virtually impossible to test many of the propositions of the RTT. Below is a list of some of the major shortcomings of this stage of research in our laboratory through the late 1980s.

- According to the RTT, temperament is a psychological construct whereas Pavlovian temperament originated in the conceptual theory of the nervous system, as attested to by the very names of the temperament traits postulated by this theory—strength of excitation, strength of inhibition, and mobility of the nervous processes.

- Foreign researchers identified the RTT with Pavlov's nervous system typology because RTT research was typically conducted using the Strelau Temperament Inventory (STI) and Pavlovian Temperament Survey (PTS) questionnaire scales, which corresponded to the Pavlovian traits (see Angleitner et al., 2001; Kagan, 1994; Plomin, 2001).

- The inverse relationship between the sensitivity threshold and the efficiency (endurance) threshold (see Figure 3.1), postulated by Teplov and Nebylitsyn (1963) and adopted as one of the assumptions of our understanding of reactivity, was not empirically corroborated in our research. Reactivity viewed as the equivalent of strength of excitation refers to efficiency (endurance) only (Strelau & Zawadzki, 1993).

- Although activity understood as a temperament trait is crucial for the RTT, our diagnostic instruments did not allow us to measure it. Activity was controlled by taking into consideration the different stimulating values of various types of behavioral activity and activity in laboratory or natural settings (see section 3.3).

- Although the Mobility of Nervous Processes scale of the Temperament Questionnaire (TQ) and STI and PTS questionnaires is psychologically interpreted as the ability to modify one's behavior (reaction) rapidly, adequately to the changing environment (Strelau & Zawadzki, 1998), this scale does not cover the entire sphere of temporal characteristics of behavior. Ewa Goryńska (1982; see section 3.2.3) distinguished six dimensions of the temporal characteristics of behavior that, when factor-analyzed, yielded two factors: perseveration and liveliness. Both factors were similarly loaded with mobility of behavior, albeit with opposite signs.

- Nearly all theories of temperament (see Strelau, 1998) limit it to the emotional sphere (e.g., Kagan, 1994) or include characteristics of emotional functioning in the postulated temperament structure (e.g., Thomas & Chess, 1977). As conveyed by the title of one of my publications, "Emotion as a Key Concept in Temperament Research," emotions are a core concept in temperament studies (Strelau, 1987b). The RTT also assumes (see Proposition 4) that the energetic and temporal features of temperament are expressed in all behaviors, regardless of their type and content, and therefore also in the emotions. The TQ, STI, and PTS, however, measured this sphere of human functioning only indirectly, as manifested in those items that refer to emotional endurance in difficult or stressful situations (see Strelau, Angleitner, & Newberry, 1999).

These shortcomings of the Regulative Theory of Temperament, particularly in how the traits composing the structure of temperament were operationalized, led us to conduct an in-depth investigation into the structure of temperament. The first four RTT propositions formulated in chapter 4 provided the starting point for these studies, which were soon followed by research on the development of a diagnostic instrument to measure the traits identified in this structure. The basic outline of this project was pursued by Bogdan Zawadzki (1992) in his doctoral dissertation. The details of the research conducted during the last decade on the structure of temperament and its psychometric assessment have been discussed in numerous publications (see Strelau & Zawadzki, 1993, 1995; Zawadzki & Strelau, 1995) and particularly in the *Formal Characteristics of Behavior–Temperament Inventory Manual* (FCB-TI; Zawadzki & Strelau, 1997).

5.1
The procedure leading to identification of temperament structure according to the RTT

The research on temperament structure was inseparable from the work on the development of the psychometric instrument for the assessment of the traits identified within this structure. The rationale behind this approach is based on two premises. First, to construct a psychological theory that cannot be empirically verified is to sentence the theory to oblivion. Second, once we have determined the object of our research—in our case the structure of temperament—then it is only natural that we should want to determine the procedure that will lead to the desired effect.

The point of departure for our investigation into the structure of temperament as it is defined in the RTT was the belief that the formal characteristics of behavior are manifested in two basic spheres—that is, the energetic and temporal characteristics of behavior and reactions. More than thirty years ago, I wrote (Strelau, 1974a) that by the energetic characteristics of behavior (ECB) we mean "all those characteristics which are determined by individual differences in the physiological mechanisms responsible for the energy level of the organism, i.e., for the accumulation and release of stored-up energy" (p. 11), and by the temporal characteristics of behavior (TCB) we mean "a group of characteristics of the dynamics of reaction over time" (p. 20). I presumed that the physiological bases of temporal characteristics could be traced to the lability and mobility of the nervous processes. In this case lability is understood as a conceptual CNS construct referring to the speed of origination and extinction of nervous processes, whereas mobility refers to the speed of change of CNS processes.

From the very beginning of our investigation into the structure of temperament, we acted on the assumption—which also underlay the studies of temperament presented in this chapter—that the characteristics identified within both the ECB and TCB participate in the regulation of stimulation. Both these characteristics are based on mechanisms that are responsible for individual differences in level of arousal. Ever since the experimental studies of reaction times conducted in Wilhelm Wundt's laboratory, we have known that the energetic characteristics of behavior (reaction time, like reaction amplitude) depend on the strength of the stimulus. In physiological terms we would say that they depend on the level of arousal (activation) evoked by the stimulus. Hence we would predict—and our research to date has confirmed (Strelau, 1969, 1983; Strelau & Zawadzki, 1998)—that the components of the energetic characteristics of behavior and the temporal characteristics of behavior should correlate, just as body weight and height correlate. If so, then we should basically strive to identify—by means of factor analysis—the psychological constructs for which ECB and TCB have shared variance.

We abandoned this seemingly methodologically sound approach, however, on the assumption that although energetic and temporal characteristics correlate strongly, they serve different functions in the regulation of level of arousal—or, to put it another way, in the regulation of level of stimulation (see Eliasz, 1981; Klonowicz, 1992; Strelau, 1983, 1993). For many years the functional significance of temperament, to which RTT Propositions 9 and 10 mainly refer, has been the main line of research in our laboratory. To return once again to our correlation between weight and height, it is hardly conceivable that one factor extricated on the basis of these two components (i.e., body mass) has the same practical significance as each of the components (i.e., weight and height). Although dieticians use the so-called Body Mass Index (see, e.g., Frankenfield et al., 2001; Malina & Katzmarzyk, 1999), this index provides for changes in the contribution of the variance of the two component variables, height and weight, in the population. The index takes into consideration the fact that height and weight are or are not in mutual harmony with respect to age and gender because domination of one of the components is a source of pathology (e.g., overweight or underweight), which in turn leads to other health-related consequences.

The suggestion that each of the characteristics, ECB and TCB, be treated separately, primarily on functional grounds, affected later studies of the structure of temperament and its assessment. Both structure and assessment—which are closely related—are based on the psychometric approach.

5.1.1. Temperament traits that compose the energetic characteristics of behavior

The two basic traits postulated by the RTT, reactivity and activity (as defined in sections 3.2.1 and 3.2.2), were subjected to in-depth analysis in order to identify the components of the energetic characteristics of behavior, within these constructs, that could be operationalized. As far as reactivity is concerned, two thresholds were distinguished—the sensory sensitivity threshold and the emotional sensitivity threshold. The other extreme of the reactivity-resistance (also called endurance) dimension was collapsed into three components: resistance to fatigue, resistance to distraction, and emotional resistance. Hence five components were distinguished within the reactivity construct (Strelau & Zawadzki, 1993, pp. 317, 319):

- Sensory sensitivity: the ease with which the individual reacts to stimuli whose stimulating value is very low, expressed in all modalities of sensory stimulation.
- Emotional sensitivity: the ease with which emotions are generated in response to weak emotogenic stimuli.
- Resistance to fatigue: the adequacy of response in situations (settings) requiring prolonged or highly stimulating activity.

- Resistance to distraction: the adequacy of response to situations in which there is strong adventitious stimulation (e.g., physical discomfort, noise, pain, temperature, or other intensive stimuli).

- Emotional resistance: the ability to control emotional reactions in response to intensive emotogenic stimuli.

Activity, a temperament trait that—according to the RTT—serves as a regulator of need for stimulation, is both a direct and indirect source of stimulation (for a detailed explanation of this point, see Strelau, 1983). Activity as a direct source of stimulation is expressed in at least two different ways. In physical (motor) activity, all sorts of movements cause arousal in the receptors, which in turn is conveyed to the higher nervous centers. This type of stimulation is produced on the basis of the well-known mechanism of reciprocal afferentation. Thus one may say that it is not motor activity by itself but changes in the receptor that influence the level of arousal. But activity is a direct source of stimulation mainly because actions themselves are stimulating. This is expressed in the level of difficulty, complexity, uncertainty, or riskiness of performed actions and activities.

Thanks to activity, the individual may pursue (seek) or avoid situations or environments that have a particular stimulating value. "This means that activity as the 'organizer' of the type and amount of stimulation should be treated here as an indirect source of stimulation" (Strelau, 1983, p. 188). The role of activity as a regulator of the stimulating value of the environment was recognized quite early (Helson, 1964). It is worth noting that activity understood as a temperament trait has nothing to do with the content of the activity in question, only with its stimulating value.

Taking into consideration these two different mechanisms underlying the regulation of activity-related stimulation, we (Strelau & Zawadzki, 1993, p. 319) distinguished two components of activity:

- Activity as a direct source of stimulation: the quantity and range of behaviors (reactions) characterized from the point of view of their stimulating value.

- Activity as an indirect source of stimulation: behaviors whose purpose it is to provide the organism with stimulation or avoid stimulation from without.

5.1.2. Temperament traits that compose the temporal characteristics of behavior

Until recently the temporal characteristics of behavior had been limited to mobility of behavior as measured by the Mobility of Nervous Processes scale of the TQ, STI, and PTS. This understanding of the temporal characteristics of behavior needed a major revision. Previously Ewa Goryńska (1982; Goryńska & Strelau, 1979) had demonstrated that the temporal characteristics of behavior were much more complex and could not possibly be reduced to only one trait, mobility (see section 3.2.3). Drawing on Goryńska's work, we distinguished five TCB components (persistence, recurrence, mobility, speed, and tempo) and defined them as follows (Strelau & Zawadzki, 1993, pp. 319–320):

• Mobility: the ease with which behavior is altered in response to changes in the environment.

• Speed: the minimal reaction time to stimuli or other external environmental demands.

• Tempo: the frequency of occurrence of homogeneous reactions (actions) within a specified unit of time (e.g., the number of movements performed in natural conditions or the number of uttered words).

• Persistence: continuation of reactions (behavior) or states after the stimulus (situation) has ceased despite the presence of other stimuli.

• Recurrence: the number of repetitions of the same reactions (behaviors) or states after the stimulus that evoked these reactions (behaviors) has abated.

We discarded the sixth component, regularity. This trait was included in the Revised Dimensions of Temperament Survey (DOTS-R; Windle & Lerner, 1986; see Śliwińska, Zawadzki, & Strelau, 1995) where it was represented in as many as three scales: Rhythmicity-Sleep, Rhythmicity-Eating, and Rhythmicity-Daily Habits. We concluded, however, that rhythmicity is largely determined by environmental factors (home, nursery school, secondary school, workplace) and can therefore hardly be viewed as a typical temperament trait.

5.1.3. The structure of temperament according to the RTT

The formal characteristics of behavior were the defining components of the ECB and TCB. Hence the energetic characteristics had seven components (sensory sensitivity, emotional sensitivity, emotional resistance, resistance to distraction, resistance to fatigue, activity as a direct source of stimulation, and activity as an indirect source of stimulation). The temporal characteristics had five components (speed, tempo, persistence, recurrence, and mobility). At this point our research began to focus not only on the structure of temperament, but also on the development of a psychometric measure of the traits identified within this structure (see section 5.2). However, I will limit my discussion to those procedural stages that led directly to identifying the structural characteristics of temperament.

The defining components of the ECB and TCB were the point of departure for the generation of behaviors and reactions in which these characteristics are expressed. We distinguished about six hundred statements describing the manifestations of temperament within the twelve defining components. On the basis of the data from successive stages of the psychometric studies (see section 5.2), Zawadzki (1992; see also Strelau & Zawadzki, 1993; Zawadzki & Strelau, 1997) performed two factor analyses (Principal Components, Varimax)—one for the ECB and one for the TCB—to determine the structure of temperament. These analyses were performed independently on two samples, a construction sample and a verification sample. Each sample consisted of more than one thousand individuals matched for age, gender, and education. When the defining components of temperament were factor-analyzed, six factors were extracted—including four factors for the ECB (sensory sensitivity, emotional reactivity, endurance, and activity) and two factors for the TCB (briskness and perseveration), as shown in Table 5.1.

It is noteworthy that with respect to both the ECB and TCB, the factor analysis yielded the same factors in both groups (construction and verification samples). On the basis of this research—which was further corroborated in later replication trials—we concluded that the RTT structure is composed of six traits whose definitions, presented in many publications (Strelau, 2001a; Strelau & Zawadzki, 1993, 1995; Zawadzki & Strelau, 1997), are given below.

• Briskness (BR): the tendency to react quickly, keep a high tempo in performing activities, and shift easily in response to changes in the surroundings from one behavior (reaction) to another.

• Perseveration (PE): the tendency to continue and repeat behavior and experience emotional states after cessation of stimuli (situations) evoking this behavior or states.

• Sensory sensitivity (SS): the ability to react to sensory stimuli whose stimulating value is low.

• Emotional reactivity (ER): the tendency to react intensively to emotion-generating stimuli, expressed in high emotional sensitivity and low emotional endurance.

• Endurance (EN): the ability to react adequately in situations requiring prolonged or highly stimulating activity or under conditions of intensive external stimulation.

• Activity (AC): the tendency to undertake highly stimulating behaviors or behaviors providing intensive external (environmental) stimulation.

Taking into consideration the effectiveness of the individual's regulation of stimulation—one of the central RTT constructs justifying the relationships and interactions between the traits identified in the structure of temperament—we must say that the links between these traits have adaptive significance, as discussed extensively by

Table 5.1 Factor matrices (after rotation: Principal Components, Varimax) of the temporal and energetic characteristics of behavior

Energetic characteristics (ECB)	Samples									
	Construction sample Factor					Verification sample Factor				
	I	II	III	IV	h^2	I	II	III	IV	h^2
Sensory sensitivity	0.04	-0.01	0.10	0.99	0.99	0.07	-0.01	0.09	0.99	0.99
Emotional sensitivity	-0.23	-0.87	-0.23	0.10	0.88	-0.22	-0.89	-0.19	0.10	0.89
Emotional endurance	0.38	0.79	0.21	0.11	0.83	0.42	0.75	0.22	0.13	0.87
Endurance-distractors	0.83	0.31	0.11	0.01	0.80	0.79	0.38	0.14	0.03	0.78
Endurance-fatigue	0.87	0.21	0.20	0.05	0.84	0.88	0.20	0.20	0.08	0.86
Activity-direct	0.05	0.16	0.89	0.06	0.83	0.08	0.15	0.90	0.06	0.84
Activity-indirect	0.28	0.23	0.78	0.08	0.74	0.25	0.19	0.84	0.07	0.80
Eigenvalue	1.72	1.61	1.56	1.02	5.91	1.70	1.60	1.66	1.02	5.98

Temporal characteristics (TCB)	Samples				
	Construction sample Factor			Verification sample Factor	
	I	h^2		I	II	h^2
Speed	0.70	-0.33	0.60	0.74	-0.29	0.63
Tempo	0.82	0.17	0.70	0.80	0.19	0.68
Persistence	-0.26	0.77	0.67	-0.29	0.77	0.68
Recurrence	0.02	0.87	0.75	0.03	0.86	0.75
Mobility	0.68	-0.44	0.66	0.74	-0.31	0.64
Eigenvalue	1.71	1.67	3.38	1.81	1.56	3.37

Note. In respect to ECB, factor II in the construction sample appeared as factor III in the verification sample. For clarity, factor II in the verification sample has the status of factor III. Adapted from "The Formal Characteristics of Behaviour–Temperament Inventory (FCB-TI): Theoretical Assumptions and Scale Construction" by J. Strelau and B. Zawadzki, 1993, *European Journal of Personality, 7*, p. 326. Copyright 1993 by John Wiley & Sons. Reprinted with permission.

Zawadzki and Strelau (1997) and illustrated in the empirical studies that will be discussed in subsequent chapters. Suffice it to say here that depending on the configuration of traits in the ECB, stimulation regulation may have different levels of effectiveness. For example, if high stimulus processing potential (high endurance and low emotional reactivity) is accompanied by high activity, we have effective stimulation regulation. If, however, stimulus processing potential is low (low endurance and high emotional reactivity) but activity is high, stimulation regulation will not be effective. As noted by Zawadzki and Strelau (1997), TCB component traits contribute to the process of stimulation processing: they can either increase or reduce stimulation input (the main function of briskness) or discharge level of arousal to a greater or lesser extent (the main function of perseveration).

5.2
The Formal Characteristics of Behavior–Temperament Inventory

It would be impossible to give an account here of all the stages of the research that led to the construction of the inventory known as the Formal Characteristics of Behavior–Temperament Inventory. Work on the development of this inventory is presented in detail in the test manual (Zawadzki & Strelau, 1997; see also Strelau & Zawadzki, 1993, 1995). The very name of the questionnaire emphasizes the important RTT distinction—that is, concentration on the formal aspects of behavior rather than the content.

5.2.1. The FCB-TI: Construction and basic psychometric parameters

From the very beginning of our work on the FCB-TI, we followed the research strategy already applied by Strelau and Angleitner (1994) during the construction of the PTS. We wanted to root the inventory firmly in a cross-cultural paradigm to ensure that it could be adapted to various cultures and languages without compromising its validity. Toward this end we followed a two-step strategy.

First, the points of departure are the operationalized defining components of the scales—reflecting the structure of temperament—and these components are universal; that is, they are understood identically in all cultures and languages (the etic approach[1]). The defining components are the points of departure for the generation of the items. Temperament traits are expressed in behaviors that may be culturally specific; therefore it is necessary to generate an item pool for each component that taps behaviors found in various cultures. This item pool is the same for all language versions and refers to as many behaviors and situations as possible in which temperament traits may be manifested.

---

[1] For an explanation of the terms "etic" and "emic," see Berry (1989).

Second, the emic approach takes the cultural specificity of the population into consideration. Applying an appropriate psychometric procedure, those items selected from the item pool are most representative for the defining component in question. This explains why more than six hundred items were generated with respect to the twelve defining components (see section 5.1.3). Following the final itemmetric analysis, the item pool was reduced to 381. This pool was the point of departure for the further stages of the construction of the FCB-TI.

There is no space here to document all the stages of the development of this inventory and therefore I shall outline them schematically in Figure 5.1.

The psychometric characteristics illustrating the goodness of the FCB-TI have been presented on numerous occasions and it would be difficult to cite them here. I shall therefore limit myself to a psychometric presentation of the FCB-TI scales based on the median from six independent samples numbering from $N = 392$ to $N = 1,012$ (4,245 respondents in all). These data are presented in Table 5.2. Special attention should be paid to the reliability of the FCB-TI scales measured with the Cronbach alpha coefficient. Reliability is satisfactory for scales SS, PE, and BR (from 0.72 to 0.78) and very satisfactory for scales ER, EN, and AC (from 0.83 to 0.86).

Temporal stability of the scales measured twice within a two-week interval on two independent samples ($N = 96$, aged 15–22; $N = 90$, aged 16–69) ranges from 0.76 (BR) to 0.85 (ER). Only scale SS has a lower stability coefficient ($r = 0.68$). When stability was measured within a six-month interval, also on two independent samples ($N = 90$, aged 15–20; $N = 65$, aged 18–69), the results (except SS – $r = 0.55$) were in the 0.69 (BR) to 0.83 (ER) range. In other words, reliability is satisfactory and meets one of the defining criteria of the RTT (i.e., temporal stability). Also, the values of the correlation coefficients do not depart from the parameters of other renowned instruments diagnosing personality, including tem-

Table 5.2 Psychometric characteristics of FCB-TI scales: Median scores based on six independent samples ($N = 4,245$)

FCB-TI scale	*Me*	*SD*	Kurtosis	Skewness	Cronbach alpha
Briskness	14.55	3.70	-0.14	-0.62	0.77
Perseveration	12.72	4.17	-0.21	-0.45	0.78
Sensory Sensitivity	15.34	3.16	0.42	-0.86	0.72
Emotional Reactivity	11.85	4.63	-0.58	-0.38	0.83
Endurance	8.75	4.98	-0.76	0.24	0.86
Activity	10.08	4.68	-0.65	-0.13	0.83

Note. Me = median; *SD* = standard deviation.

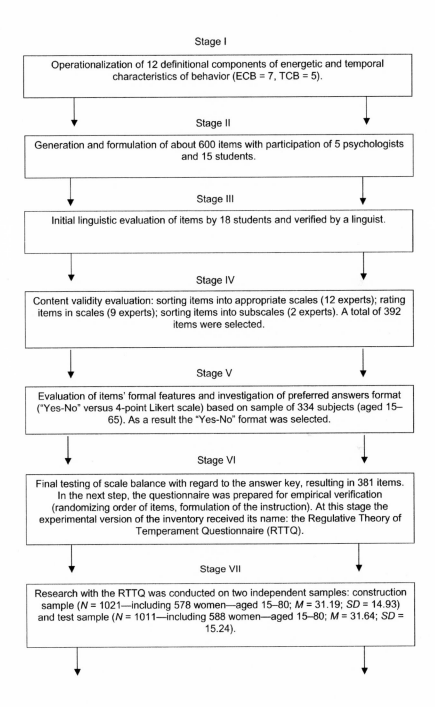

Figure 5.1. Continued on page 100.

Figure 5.1. Continued from page 99.

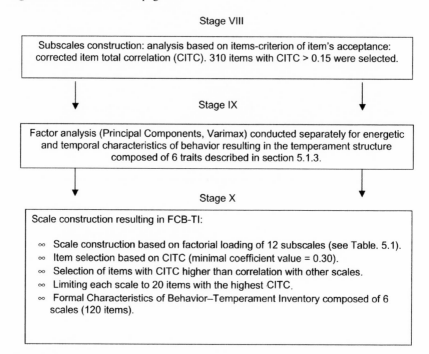

Stage VIII

Subscales construction: analysis based on items-criterion of item's acceptance: corrected item total correlation (CITC). 310 items with CITC > 0.15 were selected.

Stage IX

Factor analysis (Principal Components, Varimax) conducted separately for energetic and temporal characteristics of behavior resulting in the temperament structure composed of 6 traits described in section 5.1.3.

Stage X

Scale construction resulting in FCB-TI:

∞ Scale construction based on factorial loading of 12 subscales (see Table. 5.1).
∞ Item selection based on CITC (minimal coefficient value = 0.30).
∞ Selection of items with CITC higher than correlation with other scales.
∞ Limiting each scale to 20 items with the highest CITC.
∞ Formal Characteristics of Behavior–Temperament Inventory composed of 6 scales (120 items).

Figure 5.1. Outline of the construction of the Formal Characteristics of Behavior–Temperament Inventory (FCB-TI). ECB = energetic characteristics of behavior; TCB = temporal characteristics of behavior. Adapted from *Formalna Charakterystyka Zachowania–Kwestionariusz Temperamentu (FCZ-KT). Podręcznik* [Formal Characteristics of Behavior–Temperament Inventory (FCB-TI): Manual] by B. Zawadzki and J. Strelau, 1997, pp. 46–47. Copyright 1997 by Pracownia Testów Psychologicznych PTP. Reprinted with permission.

perament (see Angleitner & Riemann, 1991; Eysenck, Eysenck, & Barrett, 1985; Slabach, Morrow, & Wachs, 1991).

When trying to determine the psychometric goodness of any assessment instrument, it is essential to answer one of the most important questions regarding validity—that is, to what extent the scales of a given inventory measure the constructs (traits, factors) they are supposed to measure. In fact most research conducted with the FCB-TI during the last fifteen years answers this question, although the criteria or types of validity varies depending on the nature of the study. Here I shall limit myself to assessing the criterion validity of the FCB-TI where the results of self-report studies were compared with descriptions of the same temperament traits obtained by means of rating scales.

As far as self-report—the most typical approach in questionnaire studies—is concerned, respondents refer to their own memory resources and, depending on how the questionnaire is constructed, use these resources to share information about the frequency or intensity of behavior or reactions that are presumably manifestations of particular traits (in our case temperament traits) or about their preferences for such behaviors and reactions. Rating involves assessment of the behaviors and reactions by an external observer—usually a friend, relative, or acquaintance who has frequent contact with the subject of assessment. In this case ratings are usually based on observations made in a variety of situations over a longer period of time. When rating is performed by means of questionnaires, the questionnaire items are generally formulated in the third-person singular.

Comparing self-reports and ratings by third parties is a favorite way of estimating the validity of a psychometric instrument among adherents of the Big Five personality traits (see Hofstee, 1994; McCrae & Costa, 1987; Ostendorf & Angleitner, 1994). This method of estimating the validity of psychometric instruments is based on one of the major psychometric canons proposed many years ago by Campbell and Fiske (1959), who made a distinction between convergent and discriminant validity. When a similar assessment of the same traits on the basis of different methods (self-report vs. rating) is reached, this is a sign of convergent validity—as is convergence between the ratings of different raters if more than one observer rated the same individual.

Studies of the validity of the FCB-TI on the basis of comparisons of self-report and rating by others, and between rating by two independent peers, were conducted within the framework of the Polish-German Twin Project. This project was conducted by a group of German researchers headed by Alois Angleitner and a group of Polish researchers working under my direction. The studies were run on monozygotic (identical) and dizygotic (fraternal) twins using five psychometric instruments including the FCB-TI. The German sample numbered 2,087 males and females (aged 14–80) and the Polish sample numbered 1,092 males and females (aged 16–63). Each twin was rated by two peers who were different for twin and co-twin. Most peers were recruited among spouses, good friends, and relatives and their age was similar to that of the twins. A comprehensive report of this program is given elsewhere (Strelau, 1998). The findings relating to the validity of the FCB-TI are shown in Table 5.3.

The correlation coefficients for both the German and Polish samples oscillate around 0.50 or more, both for convergence between self-reports and ratings by peers and convergence between two independent ratings by peers of the same individuals. As far as the ratings are concerned, the mean correlation coefficient was as high as 0.60 (Polish sample).[2] It is worth noting that the lowest values for both validity

---

[2] In other studies conducted at our laboratory on three independent samples, much smaller ($N = 67$–97 rated individuals) and more heterogeneous with respect to the study objective, convergence between two ratings was smaller than convergence between self-rating and rating by others—although both measures oscillated around 0.50–0.60 (Zawadzki & Strelau, 1997).

Table 5.3 Reliability scores and rater agreement on temperament scales: Self-report and peer rating data from German (G) and Polish (P) samples

FCB-TI scale	Self-report[1]		Peer rating[2]	
	G	P	G	P
Briskness	0.50	0.48	0.55	0.62
Perseveration	0.42	0.46	0.48	0.58
Sensory Sensitivity	0.40	0.40	0.42	0.47
Emotional Reactivity	0.54	0.56	0.66	0.63
Endurance	0.46	0.53	0.53	0.58
Activity	0.57	0.65	0.66	0.71
Mean	0.49	0.51	0.56	0.60

Note. [1]Correlations between self-report and average peer report; [2]intraclass correlations (ICC including Spearman–Brown correction for 2 raters). Adapted from *Temperament: A Psychological Perspective* by J. Strelau, 1998, p. 304. Copyright 1998 by Plenum Press. Reprinted with permission.

measures (from 0.40 to 0.47) were obtained for sensory sensitivity, perhaps because it is the most difficult to observe (in oneself and another), whereas the highest values were obtained for those traits that are most clearly expressed in behavior such as activity (correlations between 0.57 and 0.71). Our correlation coefficients, both between self-rating and peer rating and between independent peer ratings, are similar or higher than the correlations for the Big Five (e.g., McCrae et al., 1998) and other personality traits including temperament (see Gervai, Turner, & Hinde, 1993; Hayes & Dunning, 1997; Osterman et al., 1994; Schmitz et al., 1996). These results attest to the validity of the FCB-TI scales.

The following basic question must now be asked: what is the relationship between the presented psychometric instrument for the assessment of RTT traits and other questionnaires also aimed to assess temperament, but temperament that is understood differently and whose structure is also different? Efforts to test hypotheses about the similarity or dissimilarity of these traits are tests of the theoretical validity of the FCB-TI and will be discussed in the next section.

5.2.2. Relationships between the FCB-TI scales and scales representing similar personality constructs

I mentioned in chapter 4 that many temperament researchers trace the biological foundations of temperament to the physiological or biochemical mechanisms that are responsible for regulation of level of arousal, although the concept is variously understood depending on the CNS structures and functions involved (see Figure

4.3). The purported mechanisms include Pavlov's (1938) typology of the nervous system; Eysenck's (1970; Eysenck & Eysenck, 1985) biological theory of psychoticism-extraversion-neuroticism (PEN); the behavior genetic theory of temperament by Buss and Plomin (1975, 1984); Zuckerman's (1979, 1994) biological theory of sensation seeking; or Cloninger's psychobiological model of temperament (Cloninger, 1986; Cloninger, Svrakic, & Przybeck, 1993). In our own research, we focused mainly on searching for the relationship between these concepts of temperament—all of which offer a psychometric instrument measuring the postulated traits—and the RTT. In the so-called psychometric Big Five theory (see Costa & McCrae, 1988, 1992), at least two postulated factors (extraversion and neuroticism) are also temperament constructs. They are understood much as Eysenck understood them and therefore this five-factor model of personality also became a focus of our research. Representatives of these conceptualizations of temperament—except the Big Five researchers—make reference to the arousal or arousability construct, also present in the RTT, or suggest that specific physiological or biochemical mechanisms underlie selected temperament traits (see Table 4.1).

Since the RTT strongly emphasizes the fact that temperament traits refer to the formal characteristics of behavior—as, to a certain extent, do the theories proposed by Pavlov, Eysenck, or Buss and Plomin (see section 4.1)—we also studied the relationships between RTT traits and the theory of temperament formulated by Thomas and Chess (1977, 1986). The latter stress the "stylistic" nature of temperament, the "how" of the individual's behavior as opposed to the content.[3]

The temperament traits postulated by the above scholars—except Cloninger—were frequently subjected to our investigation within the RTT framework (see Strelau, 1993, 1998; Strelau & Zawadzki, 1997; Zawadzki & Strelau, 1997). Here let me cite some of the findings of a factor analysis of 33 temperament traits included in the aforementioned theories of temperament that refer to the concepts of arousal or the formal characteristics of behavior. This analysis helped us to outline the structure of temperament (personality) and also show where RTT traits fit into this structure and how they relate to the remaining constructs. The study presented below (Zawadzki and Strelau, 1997) was run on 919 respondents (including 443 females) between the ages of 17 and 77.

Temperament traits were measured by means of the two questionnaires developed in our laboratory, the FCB-TI (the temperament traits postulated by the

---

[3] In addition to the theories of temperament mentioned here, many other theories focus on the study of children beginning from infancy—e.g., Rothbart's developmental model of temperament (Rothbart, 1989; Rothbart, Ahadi, & Evans, 2000); the emotional theory of temperament by Goldsmith and Campos (1982, 1990); or Kagan's (1994) theory of inhibited/disinhibited temperament. Because the RTT and diagnostic instruments proposed within the framework of this theory concentrate mainly on adults and adolescents, the constructs proposed by these theories were not subjected to our RTT studies.

RTT; Zawadzki & Strelau, 1997) and PTS (Pavlovian temperament traits; Strelau & Zawadzki, 1998), and the Polish adaptations of the following inventories:

- Eysenck Personality Questionnaire–Revised (EPQ-R): Eysenckian temperament dimensions (Brzozowski & Drwal, 1995).
- DOTS-R: temperament traits postulated by Thomas and Chess (Śliwińska, Zawadzki, & Strelau, 1995).
- Emotionality–Activity–Sociability Temperament Survey (EAS-TS): temperament traits postulated by Buss and Plomin (Oniszczenko, 1997).
- NEO Five Factor Inventory (NEO-FFI): the factors incorporated in the Big Five (Zawadzki et al., 1988).

The factor analysis was conducted by means of the reduced Principal Components method with orthogonal Varimax rotation. The criterion for factor identification was 5 percent of explained variance (the Cattell scree-test).

As far as the relationships between temperament traits postulated by the RTT and the traits postulated by the aforementioned theories are concerned, we formulated several hypotheses (see Zawadzki & Strelau, 1997) based largely on the findings of our earlier correlation studies. We predicted that briskness and endurance (FCB-TI), and strength of excitation and mobility (PTS), would emerge in the temperament structure as positive factor loadings and that perseveration and emotional reactivity (FCB-TI), neuroticism (EPQ-R and NEO-FFI), and emotionality components (EAS-TS) would emerge in the same structure as negative factor loadings. We also predicted that activity (FCB-TI) would combine in one factor with activity (EAS-TS and DOTS-R) and mobility and extraversion (EPQ-R and NEO-FFI). We further hypothesized that rhythmicity measured with three DOTS-R scales would not correlate with RTT traits because this trait is largely determined by environmental demands and contingencies. We did not formulate any hypotheses concerning the location of sensory sensitivity in the temperament structure. The results of the factor analysis are presented in Table 5.4.

As we can see from the table, the scales in factor I—which has been identified as emotionality/endurance—fulfilled our expectations. This also applies to factor II, which has been identified as extraversion/activity. None of the FCB-TI scales emerged in factor III (social conformity). The configuration of traits in this factor is more akin to character than temperament. We formulated this hypothesis based on a number of correlation analyses—including factor analyses—presented elsewhere (Strelau & Zawadzki, 1996, 1997), which indicated that together psychoticism, conscientiousness, and agreeableness create a factor that is very poorly or not at all characterized by temperament traits. As far as factor IV (openness/rhythmicity) is concerned, it is worth noting that the three rhythmicity scales are completely unrelated to any FCB-TI scales except sensory sensitivity (where

Table 5.4 Temperament structure based on measurement of 33 temperament traits, representing conceptualizations referring to biological mechanisms or formal characteristics of behavior

Inventory/Scale	I	II	III	IV	V
FCB-TI					
Briskness	0.57				0.44
Perseveration	-0.80				
Sensory Sensitivity				-0.43	0.38
Emotional Reactivity	-0.92				-0.32
Endurance	0.89				
Activity			0.67		
PTS					
Strength of Excitation	0.80				
Strength of Inhibition	0.60		0.53		
Mobility of Nervous Processes	0.61	0.45			
EAS-TS					
Emotionality-Fear	-0.69				
Emotionality-Distress	-0.74	-0.44			
Emotionality-Anger	-0.55		-0.50		
Activity		0.48			0.50
Sociability		0.68			
DOTS-R					
Activity Level-General		0.56			0.33
Activity Level-Sleep					
Approach-Withdrawal	0.33	0.62			
Flexibility-Rigidity	0.58			-0.33	
Mood Quality		0.64			
Rhythmicity-Sleep				0.66	
Rhythmicity-Eating				0.69	
Rhythmicity-Daily Habits				0.66	
Distractibility					0.51
Persistence					0.64
EPQ-R					
Extraversion		0.78			
Neuroticism	-0.78				
Psychoticism			-0.87		-0.30
Lie Scale			-0.62	0.31	
NEO-FFI					
Neuroticism	-0.72	-0.47			
Extraversion		0.84			
Openness to Experience				-0.60	
Agreeableness			0.86		
Conscientiousness			0.44		0.60

Note. Adapted from *Formalna Charakterystyka Zachowania–Kwestionariusz Temperamentu* (FCZ-KT). *Podręcznik* [Formal Characteristics of Behavior–Temperament Inventory (FCB-TI): Manual] by B. Zawadzki and J. Strelau, 1997, p. 94. Copyright 1997 by Pracownia Testów Psychologicznych PTP. Reprinted with permission.

the relationship is negative). As predicted, this configuration of traits confirms the divergent validity of the FCB-TI. FCB-TI scales emerged—albeit with less factor loading—in factor V, defined as attention concentration and characterized most strongly by persistence, distractibility (DOTS-R), conscientiousness (NEO-FFI), and activity (EAS-TS). This applies to briskness and sensory sensitivity and also to emotional reactivity (negative sign). We did not predict this configuration of temperament traits. I would like to conclude this part of the discussion of the validity of the FCB-TI scales by noting that the structure of factors I and II confirms the questionnaire's convergent validity, whereas the structure of factor III and—to a certain extent—factor IV confirms the questionnaire's divergent validity.

The foregoing analysis does not include Zuckerman's (1979) sensation seeking. In another study (Strelau & Zawadzki, 1997) conducted on a sample of 317 respondents (including 155 females) aged 15–23 ($M = 19.1$; $SD = 2.4$), the Sensation Seeking Scale (SSS-V)[4] was administered jointly with the EPQ-R, PTS, and FCB-TI. We predicted that sensation seeking would produce one factor with activity, briskness, and endurance and would also be chracterized (with a negative sign) by emotional reactivity. Factor analysis with an enforced three-factor solution (subordinated to the three Eysenckian superfactors, PEN) indicated that the four scales of the SSS-V (Thrill and Adventure Seeking, Experience Seeking, Disinhibition, and Boredom Susceptibility) combine into one factor with four FCB-TI scales: Briskness, Endurance (positive sign), Emotional Reactivity, and Perseveration (negative sign). This factor was loaded with Activity to a negligible extent (0.12). The analysis did not include the SSS-V–General Scale, however. The correlation coefficients between the total score of the SSS-V and the FCB-TI scales are highest for the Activity scale. In two samples, the first of which was described above and the second of which consisted of 217 respondents (including 169 females) aged 15–69 ($M = 22.9$; $SD = 9.83$), the correlations are 0.50 and 0.56, respectively (see Strelau & Zawadzki, 1995; Strelau & Kaczmarek, 2004). Hence we can conclude that the predicted relationships between the FCB-TI scales and the SSS-V scales have been empirically supported, providing yet another argument in favor of the validity of the FCB-TI.

Our research to date has not taken Robert Cloninger's (1986, 1997) psychobiological model of temperament into consideration. This model has gained considerable popularity within the last decade. The traits identified by Cloninger's model—novelty seeking, harm avoidance, and reward dependence, all of which have alleged biochemical mechanisms (see Table 5.4), and persistence, a trait introduced more recently (Cloninger et al., 1994)—virtually prompt the urge to compare them with the tem-

---

4 Dorota Żychowska developed the Polish adaptation of the SSS-V as part of the research for her master's thesis, but the questionnaire's psychometric properties have not been published.

perament traits postulated by the RTT. Novelty seeking, a trait that finds expression in exploratory behavior and the search for novel and rewarding stimuli, ought to correlate with such RTT traits as activity and briskness. Harm avoidance (on the other hand), which is manifested in shyness, proneness to fatigue, and fear of uncertainty, should correlate with such RTT traits as emotional reactivity, perseveration, and low endurance. Reward dependence, a trait whose defining characteristics are communicativeness and easy conditioning of stimuli (especially social ones), ought to correlate with activity. And finally, persistence should correlate with endurance.

Elżbieta Hornowska (2003) investigated the relationships between the traits postulated by the RTT and those postulated by Cloninger on a Polish sample, and Angleitner and Spinath (2003) conducted an analogous study on a German sample. The Polish sample numbered 382 respondents (including 245 women) aged 18–83 ($M = 32.6$; $SD = 13.40$) and the German sample numbered 213 respondents (including 149 women) aged 16–62 ($M = 23.7$; $SD = 7.10$). In both these studies, a number of personality inventories were administered including the FCB-TI and the Temperament and Character Inventory (TCI; Cloninger et al., 1994). Hornowska (2003) developed the Polish adaptation of the TCI and Richter and his collaborators (Richter et al., 1999) were responsible for the German adaptation of the inventory. The results of these studies are presented in Table 5.5.

As we see in the table, with the exception of reward dependence, the results of the Polish and German samples are consistent in the direction and strength of the relationships between the compared traits. As predicted, both studies demonstrated that novelty seeking correlates most strongly with activity and briskness. The largest number of significant relationships was found for harm avoidance, which

Table 5.5 Relationship between RTT traits and temperament traits postulated by Cloninger's theory based on FCB-TI and TCI measures

RTT trait	Novelty seeking		Harm avoidance		Reward dependence		Persistence	
	P	G	P	G	P	G	P	G
Briskness	0.15	0.21	-0.51	-0.38	-0.07	0.15	0.16	0.27
Perseveration	-0.01	-0.06	0.48	0.59	0.37	0.02	0.00	-0.04
Sensory sensitivity	0.11	0.10	-0.10	0.07	0.03	0.19	0.06	-0.07
Emotional reactivity	-0.11	-0.13	0.72	0.71	0.28	-0.22	-0.17	-0.21
Endurance	0.06	0.10	-0.57	-0.38	-0.24	0.11	0.15	0.33
Activity	0.45	0.33	-0.54	-0.36	0.09	0.43	0.17	0.24

Note. P = Polish sample; G = German sample. For Polish data see Hornowska (2003); for German data see Angleitner and Spinath (2003).

correlated with emotional reactivity and perseveration and also (negatively) with endurance, activity, and briskness. The predicted relationship between reward dependence and activity was only found in the German sample. As far as this temperament trait—which was assessed by means of the TCI—is concerned, the results for the two samples are divergent and do not lend themselves to any far-reaching conclusions. Persistence correlates most strongly with endurance, as predicted, although this correlation is weak in the Polish sample. In general, with a few exceptions the relationships between the RTT traits and the temperament traits postulated by Cloninger follow the patterns that can be predicted on the basis of the defining components of the scales used to assess these traits, providing yet another piece of evidence in favor of the validity of the FCB-TI scales.

The rationale behind the construction of the FCB-TI was to develop an inventory that could easily be adapted to various cultures and languages without detracting from validity and equivalence (see section 5.2). Bogdan Zawadzki and a group of psychologists accepted the challenge and developed seven different cultural adaptations of the questionnaire according to a set of standard rules (Zawadzki et al., 2001). The results of these studies, which also confirmed the universal structure of temperament, are presented very briefly in the next section, drawing on Zawadzki's (2002) text.

5.3
Cross-cultural studies of the assessment and structure of temperament using the FCB-TI

When working on the PTS, we had already adopted a procedure permitting the cross-cultural investigation of the assessment and structure of Pavlovian temperament (Strelau & Angleitner, 1994; Strelau, Angleitner, & Newberry, 1999; Strelau & Zawadzki, 1998). The defining components of temperament—sixteen in our case—were assumed to be etic and common to all the studied cultures (see section 5.2.1). Those items, on the other hand, that were generated within each defining component—selected from a pool of 381 items—and were specific for each language version had the status of emic items (see section 2.6).

In his cross-cultural studies on the assessment and structure of temperament within the RTT paradigm, Zawadzki adopted very refined and methodologically sophisticated research procedures. Taking the research strategies proposed by Berry (1989; see also van de Vijver & Hambleton, 1996) as his point of departure, he applied two strategies in order to construct a universal version of the FCB-TI: an etic-emic strategy and an etic strategy. The point of departure for both these strategies was the 381-item pool generated for the Polish version (see section 5.2.1). The essential elements of the two strategies are presented most concisely in Figure 5.2.

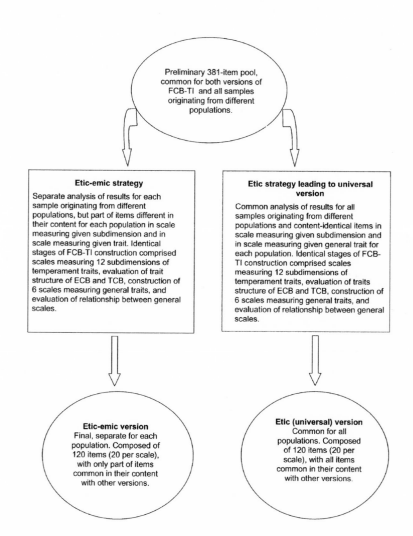

Preliminary 381-item pool, common for both versions of FCB-TI and all samples originating from different populations.

Etic-emic strategy

Separate analysis of results for each sample originating from different populations, but part of items different in their content for each population in scale measuring given subdimension and in scale measuring given trait. Identical stages of FCB-TI construction comprised scales measuring 12 subdimensions of temperament traits, evaluation of trait structure of ECB and TCB, construction of 6 scales measuring general traits, and evaluation of relationship between general scales.

Etic strategy leading to universal version

Common analysis of results for all samples originating from different populations and content-identical items in scale measuring given subdimension and in scale measuring given general trait for each population. Identical stages of FCB-TI construction comprised scales measuring 12 subdimensions of temperament traits, evaluation of traits structure of ECB and TCB, construction of 6 scales measuring general traits, and evaluation of relationship between general scales.

Etic-emic version
Final, separate for each population. Composed of 120 items (20 per scale), with only part of items common in their content with other versions.

Etic (universal) version
Common for all populations. Composed of 120 items (20 per scale), with all items common in their content with other versions.

Figure 5.2. Outline of the construction of the etic-emic version and the etic (universal) version of the FCB-TI. ECB = energetic characteristics of behavior; TCB = temporal characteristics of behavior. Adapted from *Temperament—geny i środowisko. Porównania wewnątrz- i międzypopulacyjne* [Temperament—Genes and Environment: Intrapopulation and Interpopulation Comparisons] by B. Zawadzki, 2002, p. 83. Copyright 2002 by Gdańskie Wydawnictwo Psychologiczne. Reprinted with permission.

The studies were run on eight samples representing eight populations from eight different countries: the Netherlands, South Korea, Germany, Poland, Russia, the United States, Ukraine, and Italy. The samples ranged from 204 (including 139 females) to 1,012 (including 578 females) in the Netherlands and

Poland,[5] respectively. A total of 3,723 individuals (including 2,296 females) aged 14–85 ($M = 30.89$; $SD = 13.89$) were studied.

5.3.1. Construction of the etic-emic version of the FCB-TI

First, the entire 381-item pool was translated into seven languages. Then construction of the etic-emic versions of the questionnaire, separately for each sample, began. Initially all the defining components of temperament (seven for the temporal characteristics of behavior and five for the energetic characteristics of behavior) and then the six scales measuring the six RTT traits were subjected to psychometric analysis. The procedure was identical for all the FCB-TI language versions. As in the Polish version, 120 items were selected (20 items per scale). The Polish and Russian versions had the largest number of shared items (81 items, 68 percent) and the Italian and Korean versions had the fewest (56 items, 47 percent). On average the various language versions had 60 percent shared items (72 out of 120; Zawadzki et al., 2001). The items were selected on the basis of the corrected item-scale correlation.

The Cronbach alpha reliabilities for the eight etic-emic versions of the questionnaire are presented in Table 5.6. It is not hard to see that the coefficients are satisfactory for all the scales ($M = 0.80$) although they vary from country to country (from 0.64 to 0.87).

The scales' validity was also measured by comparing the interscale correlations for each sample in order to determine whether the pattern of correlations resembled the one that emerged for the Polish sample. Eight covariance matrices were developed and compared by means of the LISREL technique. The goodness-of-fit indicators suggested that there was considerable cross-cultural equivalence of the relationships between the FCB-TI scales (Zawadzki et al., 2001).

In the etic-emic version, the factors and their structure as well as the questionnaire items—which are the same for all the populations—are the etic elements. However, there are also items that take into consideration the culturally determined specificity of the behavioral manifestations of temperament traits; these are the emic elements. As Zawadzki's research suggests, this approach to the construction of the FCB-TI enables us to identify universal traits of temperament and its structure and hence also allows for cross-population studies. Because the culturally specific (emic) items may affect the scales' validity (Strelau & Angleitner, 1994), however, it is difficult to demonstrate their universality unequivocally. Zawadzki's studies of the etic-emic version of the FCB-TI were simply a point of departure for a more ambitious project: construction of an etic version of the questionnaire for the cross-population comparison of temperament traits.

---

[5] The Polish data are based on the construction sample, which provided the basis for construction of the FCB-TI.

Table 5.6 Mean reliability scores (Cronbach alpha) for eight culturally different FCB-TI scales: Etic-emic version

FCB-TI scale	M	Range
Briskness	0.77	0.73-0.81
Perseveration	0.78	0.76-0.86
Sensory Sensitivity	0.76	0.64-0.80
Emotional Reactivity	0.81	0.74-0.87
Endurance	0.84	0.78-0.87
Activity	0.82	0.77-0.84
M	0.80	0.77-0.82

Note. Adapted from "The Comparison of Two Basic Approaches of Cross-Cultural Assessment of Strelau's Temperament Dimensions in Eight Countries" by B. Zawadzki, F. J. R. van de Vijver, A. Angleitner, A., V. de Pascalis, B. Newberry, W. Clark et al., 2001, *Polish Psychological Bulletin, 32*, p. 138. Copyright Committee for Psychological Sciences, PAN. Reprinted with permission.

5.3.2. Construction of the etic version of the FCB-TI

It has been demonstrated that environment has a significant effect on individual differences in temperament (see, e.g., Loehlin, 1992; Lynn & Martin, 1995). Studies of RTT traits have also corroborated this finding (Oniszczenko, 2005; Zawadzki, Strelau, Oniszczenko et al., 2002; see chapter 8). If so, then we should also expect populations representing various cultures or countries—that is, living in various environments (social, political, economic, climatic, etc.)—to differ in their temperament traits. Genetic factors also affect these differences, as has been demonstrated by Lynn and Martin (1995) in their cross-cultural studies of Eysenckian personality dimensions.

In order to determine the extent to which the environment affects cross-population differences in temperament traits and structure, Zawadzki controlled six socioeconomic indices: per capita gross national product (GNP) in U.S. dollars, GNP according to purchasing power parity (PPP), GNP dynamics, population density (PD), per capita energy usage (EU), and the personal development index (PDI) including longevity and scholarization (an index composed of the degree of illiteracy and number of years of education). The studied samples represented a variety of countries and differed greatly in geographical longitude but hardly at all in geographical latitude. Hence they also did not differ very much as far as climate, a significant determinant of differences in temperament, is concerned (Lynn & Martin, 1995).

In order to develop a questionnaire that would not only detect individual differences in temperament traits in each of the eight samples but also identify between-sample differences, an etic version of the FCB-TI had to be constructed. The procedure for constructing this universal version of the FCB-TI (i.e., one where all the items were identical with respect to content for all populations despite their cultural differences) was similar to the procedure adopted for constructing the etic-emic version of the questionnaire. Exploratory factor analysis was used to extract subscales, separately for the temporal characteristics of behavior and the energetic characteristics of behavior, and also to actually construct the scales. The main difference was that to develop the etic version, all the samples were combined into one supersample ($N = 3,723$). Before this was done, however, the results for all 381 items were standardized separately for each national version.

The standardized data for all the respondents (data accumulated for eight countries) were factor-analyzed, after which each cultural version of the FCB-TI was factor-analyzed separately. In order to determine the degree of convergence between the "general" temperament traits and the factors obtained for the different cultures, the factor solutions were compared—separately for each country—with factors obtained for the aggregated sample. The Tucker *phi* coefficient was applied. The coefficient was high for all the comparisons and ranged from 0.954 to 0.999,[6] which shows that the factor structure is very similar regardless of which cultural version is used.

Not only standardized data but also raw scores were subjected to statistical analysis. As in the case of the etic-emic version, the etic version involved constructing a 120-item questionnaire with 20 items per scale; the only difference was that in the etic version, all the items had identical content. In order to find out whether the etic scales differed between samples, one-way analysis of variance was performed. The *eta*^{2} (η^2) coefficient was used to calculate the proportion of variance accounted for by differences between the samples (see Brzeziński & Stachowski, 1981). Next, in order to identify the relationships between the FCB-TI scales and socioeconomic variables, the FCB-TI scale scores were correlated with the socioeconomic data. In this case the former were the dependent variables and the latter were the independent variables. According to Zawadzki (2002), this approach—rooted in the cross-cultural research paradigm—is based on the assumption that factors on which the studied populations differ relate to psychological variables in predictable ways.

Zawadzki found statistically significant differences between the samples for all the scales but the differences are not large; η^2 values for the different scales range from 2 percent to 6 percent ($M = 4$ percent). This result suggests that although there are differences between the populations regarding temperament

---

[6] A Tucker *phi* coefficient lower than 0.90 indicates that the compared factors do not have the same meaning as far as psychological interpretation is concerned.

traits, these differences are negligible compared with the differences within the samples. As Zawadzki (2002, p. 152) points out in referring to one of the experts in cross-cultural differences (Leung, 1989):

> [T]he between-sample differences with respect to the scores on the FCB-TI scales are smaller than the within-sample differences. This pattern is viewed...as one of the basic indicators of the diagnostic validity of a research instrument...and in this sense the universal version of the FCB-TI complies with this demand.

Analyzing the relationships between differences in FCB-TI scale scores for all samples and the sociocultural variables for the population from which these samples are recruited suggests that these variables are related. The correlation coefficients are moderate to high but because there were so few samples (just eight!), only some of them are statistically significant. Table 5.7 shows these relationships for normalized scores.

The data presented suggest, among other things, that temperament traits are related to such socioeconomic factors as per capita gross national product (BR, PE, SS–positive, ER–negative); per capita energy usage (ER–negative, EN–positive); population density (EN, AC–negative); and the personal development index (PE–positive, AC–negative). Not all these relationships can be easily inter-

Table 5.7 Coefficients of Pearson correlation between normalized scores of the etic version of FCB-TI scales and sociocultural variables: Data from eight countries

FCB-TI scale	GNP	PPP	EU	PD	PDI	GNP dynamics
BR	0.53*	0.48	0.37	-0.48	0.44	-0.61
PE	0.51*	0.47	-0.16	0.50	0.55*	-0.58
SS	0.54*	0.41	0.34	-0.21	0.44	-0.59
ER	-0.52*	-0.50	-0.66**	-0.07	-0.47	0.32
EN	0.11	0.12	0.65**	-0.67**	-0.04	0.07
AC	-0.38	-0.45	0.15	-0.74**	-0.56*	0.48

Note. FCB-TI = Formal Characteristics of Behavior–Temperament Inventory: BR = Briskness; PE = Perseveration; SS = Sensory Sensitivity; ER = Emotional Reactivity; EN = Endurance; AC = Activity; GNP = Gross national product in US dollars; PPP = GNP according to purchasing power parity; EU = per capita energy usage; PD = population density; PDI = personal development index (including longevity and scholarization). $*p > 0.10$; $**p > 0.05$. Adapted from *Temperament—geny i środowisko. Porównania wewnątrz- i międzypopulacyjne* [Temperament—Genes and Environment: Intrapopulation and Interpopulation Comparisons] by B. Zawadzki, 2002, p. 153. Copyright 2002 Gdańskie Wydawnictwo Psychologiczne. Reprinted with permission.

preted. If we consider the contents of the RTT traits (see section 5.1.3), the negative relationship between emotional reactivity and such socioeconomic factors as GNP and EU is understandable because it is highly probable that when these latter values are low, this means considerable individual stress. As Lynn (1981, after Zawadzki, 2002) pointed out, socioeconomic factors should be viewed as indicators of the stressfulness of conditions of life. Of course we may ask why the remaining socioeconomic factors are unrelated to ER. In an analogous analysis in which Zawadzki excluded the data for Russia and Ukraine, the negative relationship with ER was found for all the socioeconomic factors.

As far as emotional reactivity and endurance are concerned—that is, temperament traits that are most strongly related to socioeconomic factors—Zawadzki conducted a regression analysis in which he entered GNP, PPP, and EU as explanatory variables and an additional explanatory variable (PD) for endurance. All three socioeconomic factors emerged as predictors of emotional reactivity. Partial correlations accounted for 45 percent of the variance between the samples for ER and the direction of the relationships was as predicted: more stimulating conditions of life and lower affluence are related to high emotional reactivity. As far as endurance is concerned, the results were also in the predicted direction. Endurance was higher for less dense and more affluent populations (i.e., populations living in less stimulating conditions). The explanatory variables accounted for 50–70 percent of the between-sample variance of endurance.

Other analyses in which Zawadzki compared the structure of the TCB and ECB subdimensions and the relationships between temperament traits employed the following procedure. The scores for all 3,723 respondents were combined into one supersample (within-population data) and the structure of the subdimensions and temperament traits identified for this supersample were compared with analogous between-population data. In this case the data for the eight samples were processed as if they were data for eight respondents. The within-population analysis was based on standardized scores obtained separately for each version of the FCB-TI. The between-population data were analyzed on the basis of normalized scores. Both approaches yielded the same factor solution. Two factors were identified for TCB: perseveration, with highest factor loadings on continuation and repetition; and briskness, with the highest factor loadings on speed and tempo. The Tucker coefficients corroborate the similarity of the TCB factor structure (0.902 for the within-population data and 0.954 for the between-population data).

As far as ECB is concerned, the factor solutions for the two versions (within and between population) are less convergent. In both these versions, emotional sensitivity and emotional resistance produce one factor—emotional reactivity. The same holds for resistance to fatigue and resistance to distractors, both of which contribute to the same factor—endurance. The Tucker coefficients of factor similarity were high for both these factors (ER = 0.927; EN = 0.923). Factor III, identified as activity, has the least factorial similarity (Tucker *phi* = 0.850).

This is because at the within-population level this factor is characterized by indirect and direct activity (as predicted), whereas at the between-population level it is only characterized by indirect activity and resistance to distractors. Factor IV, sensory sensitivity, confirms the opinion that this factor—already extracted on the basis of studies of the original (Polish) version of the FCB-TI—is no artifact. This factor has a rather low Tucker index (0.890), probably because it is also characterized by other subdimensions (mainly emotional sensitivity and resistance) at the between-population level and is therefore not orthogonal—as opposed to the within-population level.

The vast majority of Zawadzki's (2002) findings, presented here very briefly and selectively, support the conclusion that temperament traits and the structure of temperament are universal. The traits postulated by the RTT can be identified at both the within-population and between-population levels. The cross-cultural research paradigm that Zawadzki applied, a paradigm that is unique as far as temperament studies are concerned, is an important contribution to the empirical testing of the first four of the ten propositions postulated by the Regulative Theory of Temperament.

The FCB-TI is meant for respondents upward of 13–14 years old and cannot be used to assess temperament in younger children. In this latter case, psychometric methods based on ratings—usually by the parents but also by caregivers and teachers—are employed. Włodzimierz Oniszczenko and Anna Radomska initiated a successful attempt to develop a questionnaire rooted in the Regulative Theory of Temperament. The results of their studies on this questionnaire will be briefly presented in the next section.

5.4
The Children's Temperament Questionnaire based on the Regulative Theory of Temperament

Taking as their point of departure the structure of temperament postulated by the RTT and Oniszczenko's (1997) previous experience with the Polish adaptation of Buss and Plomin's (1984) EAS Temperament Questionnaire, which assesses temperament in children aged 3–11, Oniszczenko and Radomska (2002) developed an inventory called the Children's Temperament Questionnaire (CTQ). Construction of this questionnaire proceeded in three stages.

In stage one items for the six postulated temperament traits were generated. Expert judges helped to select 111 items with satisfactory content validity. It must be stressed that, following the example of Buss and Plomin, the authors made sure that the wording of the items was concise but that a wide range of child behavior was covered.

As in the FCB-TI, respondents were to respond in a "Yes-No" format. The selected list of items was submitted to empirical verification in stage two.

Mothers (their demographic characteristics are not provided) were asked to use the list to rate their children's temperament. A total of 312 children (including 157 girls) aged 7–12 ($M = 9.0$; $SD = 1.54$) were rated. The item pool was then reduced to thirty with five items per temperament trait, to produce six CTQ scales.

In stage three this questionnaire was subjected to psychometric evaluation. Reliability and validity were tested on a sample of 577 children (including 289 girls) aged 7–13 ($M = 10.2$; $SD = 0.50$). Again, only the mothers were asked to make the ratings. The reliability coefficients (Cronbach alpha and test-retest) for the CTQ scales are presented in Table 5.8.

As we can see from this table, all the scales except sensory sensitivity have satisfactory reliability within the 0.63–0.74 range. These values are comparable with the reliability of the EAS Temperament Inventory for Children where there were also five items per scale. Repeated measurement of temperament after an interval of two weeks and then nine months yielded surprisingly high correlation coefficients, which attest to the satisfactory stability of the measured traits. The average test-retest reliability for the six CTQ scales was $M = 0.71$ (two weeks) and $M = 0.65$ (nine months).

The authors of this study limited their evaluation of the validity of the CTQ to the relationships between the various scales and their relationship with the scales of the Buss and Plomin inventory. Based on the outcomes of validity studies of the FCB-TI (Zawadzki & Strelau, 1997), the authors predicted that the scales would not be orthogonal. Oniszczenko and Radomska's (2002) results only partly confirmed this hypothesis. As expected, briskness correlates positively with

Table 5.8 Reliability coefficients (Cronbach alpha) and temporal stability of the Children's Temperament Questionnaire

FCB-TI scale	Cronbach alpha	Test-retest 2 weeks	Test-retest 9 months
Briskness	0.63	0.64	0.56
Perseveration	0.68	0.79	0.74
Sensory Sensitivity	0.50	0.64	0.64
Emotional Reactivity	0.74	0.71	0.60
Endurance	0.69	0.73	0.72
Activity	0.66	0.73	0.72

Note. All coefficients of correlation are statistically significant (p = 0.05). From "Kwestionariusz Temperamentu dla Dzieci (KTD) oparty na Regulacyjnej Teorii Temperamentu—wersja eksperymentalna" [Temperament Inventory for Children (TIC) Based on the Regulative Theory of Temperament: Experimental Version] by W. Oniszczenko and A. Radomska 2002, *Psychologia–Etologia–Genetyka, 5,* p. 91. Copyright 2002 by Wydawnictwo Naukowe Scholar. Reprinted with permission.

endurance (0.25) and activity (0.43), and emotional reactivity correlates positively with perseveration (0.20) and negatively with endurance (–0.37). Contrary to the authors' expectations, and to the findings for studies using the FCB-TI, they found no correlation whatsoever between activity on the one hand and any of the traits on the other, and they also found positive correlations between sensory sensitivity on the one hand and endurance (0.22) and briskness (0.30) on the other. It should be pointed out that these correlation coefficients are statistically significant. Perhaps the presence or absence of relationships between the temperament traits postulated by the RTT found by Oniszczenko and Radomska are age specific. The authors' findings concerning interstructural relationships should be treated as a moderately strong argument supporting the validity of their questionnaire.

Oniszczenko and Radomska obtained more convincing evidence of the validity of the CTQ when they correlated the inventory's scales with the scales of the children's version of the EAS Temperament Inventory, which has four scales: Emotionality, Activity, Sociability, and Shyness. As predicted, the following CTQ traits correlated significantly and positively with the traits measured by Buss and Plomin's questionnaire: briskness correlated with activity (0.44) and sociability (0.29); emotional reactivity and perseveration correlated with emotionality (0.42 and 0.14, respectively); and activity correlated with activity (0.61). Several negative correlations were also found: between briskness and shyness (–0.35), endurance and emotionality (–0.21), and activity and shyness (–0.55). These results are highly reminiscent of the relationships that Zawadzki and Strelau (1997) identified between RTT traits and the traits postulated by these American researchers when they correlated the scores on the FCB-TI and the adult version of the EAS.

Although the CTQ still lacks sufficient empirical support confirming its validity, it holds great promise as a psychometric tool of RTT traits and has been applied in several studies (see, e.g., section 7.2.2.4 and chapter 8). The FCB-TI, on the other hand, is an instrument of proven psychometric value and my coworkers, students, and I have used it to conduct many studies of the functional role of RTT traits. These studies, based on the last two RTT propositions (see section 4.1), will be discussed in chapters 6 and 7.

Chapter 6

Temperament as a moderator of stressful phenomena

Ever since the days of Hippocrates and Galen, temperament researchers have noted the relationship between temperament and various aspects of stress, viewing the former either as an immediate determinant of behavior under stress—as aptly illustrated in the difficult temperament concept developed by Thomas and Chess (1977)—or as a factor linking directly or indirectly to stress-related behavior disorders. A classic example of the latter case is Pavlov's (1938) account of the responses of dogs differing in type of nervous system to a flood in his laboratory. Dogs with a weak nervous system, the equivalent of the human melancholic type, developed an intense and persistent neurosis in response to this traumatic event.

The constitutionalists (see Kretschmer, 1944; Sheldon & Stevens, 1942), who denied that the environment plays any role in temperament, viewed temperament as a determinant of the emergence or aggravation of various mental disorders. Both Kagan (1994)—who studied temperament in the inhibited and disinhibited child—and Nebylitsyn (1972)—who conducted neurophysiological studies of Pavlov's temperament constructs—found that temperament shows up most vividly when the individual is in an extreme situation and under intense stress (see section 4.6). This finding is also one of the propositions of the Regulative Theory of Temperament (RTT). Elsewhere I have discussed the role of temperament as a variable remaining in specific relationships with phenomena generally referred to as stress or the consequences of the state of stress (see Strelau, 1995b, 1998, 2001d) and have paid attention to the specific nature of this problem depending on the subject of study—be it the child or the adult.

Why, we may ask, is temperament an important moderator of stress? If we accept the definition of temperament proposed in this book (see section 4.7), which underscores the fact that temperament traits are about the energetic and temporal characteristics of behavior, then obviously they will participate in moderating (for a definition of the term "to moderate," see chapter 3, note 1) all aspects of stress, which can be characterized in terms of energy or time. Lazarus

(1991, 1993) points out that the emotions are one of the most fundamental constructs in our understanding of stress, a tenet that has been reflected in my own definition of psychological stress. Nearly all theories of temperament relate the phenomenon to the emotions and two RTT temperament properties do so directly—the energetic characteristics of temperament (emotional reactivity) and the temporal characteristics of temperament (perseveration).

In the following presentation of the research on the relationships between temperament and stress conducted within the RTT paradigm, I shall focus first on the explication of various stress-related phenomena because the concept of stress and its components has not been clearly defined in psychology.

6.1
The stress concept underlying the research conducted within the RTT paradigm

Within the last decade, once we had an adequate instrument with which to assess RTT temperament, we conducted many studies of the relationships between temperament and stress. In most cases my temperament-stress model was the point of departure (Strelau, 1995b, 1998; see section 4.6). This model illustrates the relationships between temperament on the one hand and various stress-related phenomena on the other (i.e., stressors, the state of stress, and the consequences of stress; see Figure 6.1). It follows from this model that the state of stress (induced by various stressors and modified by temperament traits[1]) as well as ways of coping with stress are the crucial link in this causal chain because it leads directly to the consequences of stress—be they health, psychological, or other. The problem is that the state of stress (here psychological stress) has only very rarely been subjected to empirical investigation. State of stress is usually inferred on the basis of the magnitude, intensity, or duration of the factors that evoke it (stressors) or on the basis of psychological, health, or biochemical changes induced by the state of stress. Hence when studying the role of temperament in relation to stress, we focused on stressors and the consequences of the state of stress. One of the factors that directly affects state of stress is coping with stress, defined as a regulative function and consisting either of maintaining an adequate balance between demands placed on the individual and that individual's capacity to deal with these demands or reducing the discrepancy between demands and capacity. In our research we also wanted to know whether the temperament traits postulated by the RTT relate in any way to coping, as illustrated in Figure 6.1.

---

[1] The state of stress can also be moderated by personality variables that do not belong to the temperament category and that developed prior to the stressor evoking this state—for example, self-esteem (Ormel & Schaufeli), locus of control (e.g., Parkes, 1984), or self-confidence (e.g., Holohan & Moos, 1986).

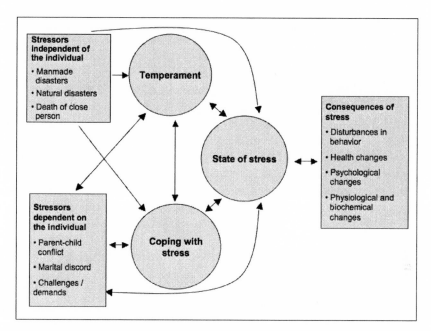

Figure 6.1. Hypothetical relationships between temperament and various aspects of stress. Adapted from "Temperament" [Temperament] by J. Strelau, 2000. In J. Strelau (Ed.), *Psychologia. Podręcznik akademicki. Vol. 2. Psychologia ogólna*, p. 715. Copyright 2000 by Gdańskie Wydawnictwo Psychologiczne. Reprinted with permission.

Stress and its definition have been the topic of thousands of publications ever since Selye (1956) introduced the term a half-century ago. Various disciplines (e.g., biology, medical studies, or even technology) have given different meanings to the term, however. Even psychologists have failed to reach consensus regarding the meaning of the term "psychological stress" (e.g., Hobfoll, 1989; Lazarus, 1966, 1993; Lazarus & Folkman, 1984; see also Heszen, 2000; Strelau, 1995b). Most of the research presented in this chapter is based on the following definition of stress:

> Psychological stress is understood here as a state characterized by strong negative emotions, such as fear, anxiety, anger, hostility, or other emotional states evoking distress, accompanied by physiological and biochemical changes that exceed the baseline level of arousal. (Strelau, 1998, p. 362)

In those works where I discussed the relationships between temperament and stress-related phenomena more comprehensively (see Strelau, 1995b, 1998), I largely focused on the theoretical discussion legitimizing the relationships we have been seeking. I cannot ignore them here completely and therefore the next two sections will refer to this discussion, beginning with the moderating effect of temperament on the situations (stressors) that lead to the state of stress.

Except for the general statement that stress is caused by stressors, researchers disagree about what factors produce the state of stress. The opinion presented in this book, and shared by many writers (see, e.g., Krohne & Laux, 1982; McGrath, 1970; Schultz & Schönpflug, 1982; Tomaszewski, 1975), is that the state of stress is brought about by the lack of equilibrium between demands placed on the individual and that individual's capacity to meet these demands. The intensity of this state is a function of the level of discrepancy between demands and capacity, as illustrated in Figure 6.2.

Broadly speaking, demands are situations that evoke the state of stress—that is, stressors. Whereas Lazarus (1966, 1991) claims that appraisal (either conscious or unconscious) of threat is what causes stress, I distinguish between objective and subjective demands (see Figure 6.2). Objective demands exist regardless of whether the individual perceives them; they include disasters, catastrophes, and all sorts of extreme changes (e.g., the death of a significant other). Many authors share the opinion that objective stressors (demands) do indeed exist (see, e.g., Freedy, Kilpatrick, & Resnick, 1993; Hobfoll, 1989, 1998; Pellegrini, 1990). Nearly thirty years ago, Holmes and Rahe (1967) demonstrated considerable agreement on the significance of various life-events among both individuals and groups. The correlation between the intensity of a life-event and the time needed to adjust to that event is very high (about 0.90) regardless of gender, age, or level of education. Subjective demands are demands that result from an individual's specific appraisal. It is not hard to conceive that subjective demands may only be investigated in human beings, whereas states of stress evoked in animals can only be studied in terms of objective stressors (demands).

Capacities of the individual are determined by psychological and physical fac-

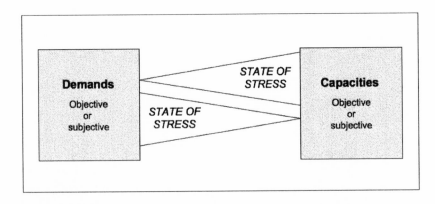

Figure 6.2. The state of stress caused by lack of balance between demands and the capacity to meet these demands.

tors, both inherited and acquired during the life-span. These factors include intelligence, all sorts of abilities and skills, knowledge, acquired experience with respect to a given stressful situation or similar situations, coping strategies, personality traits including temperament, physical attributes, or current physical and psychological conditions (i.e., at the time when stressors are operating). Capacities may also be objective and subjective. Objective capacities actually exist and can usually be measured. Subjective capacities are a function of individual appraisal. For example, a highly intellectually capable individual whose intelligence has been tested and confirmed (an objective capacity) may feel that his or her intellect is mediocre and inferior (a subjective capacity).

This consensus on the state of stress exemplifies the interactive approach because the state of stress results from the interaction between demands (actual or perceived) and capacities appropriate to these demands, whether these capacities actually exist or are simply appraised as such by the individual. Many conceptualizations of stress have adopted an interactive approach. Let me limit myself to the two most popular ones. Lazarus (1991; Lazarus & Folkman, 1984) points out that the relationship between the individual and the environment must be appraised as taxing or beyond the individual's coping capacity. This is a subjective (perceived) relationship. Hobfoll (1989, 1991; see also Schönpflug, 1993), meanwhile, defines stress in terms of resources and argues that we can only understand potential or actual loss of valued resources (i.e., the reason for stress) if we look at the relationship between resource input and resource retrieval. Hobfoll points out that not only perceived loss but also real loss is viewed as a source of stress. I must emphasize that the approach wherein the causes of the state of stress are conceived not only in terms of threat appraisal but also in terms of objective factors is not inconsistent with the interactive approach. Often both objective and subjective stressors coincide to evoke the state of stress. The effect of these stressors is moderated by individually specific temperament traits and hence they affect the relationships between stressors and the state of stress.

6.2
Temperament as a moderator of situations that evoke the state of stress

I do not intend to defend the claim that temperament viewed as a moderator of the stressor-state of stress relationship always plays an important role in the development of that relationship in every difficult or stressful situation. I do think, however, that there are at least three significant reasons why it is worth concentrating on temperament if we want to gain a better understanding of the relationship between stressors and the state of stress.

- Temperament affects the stimulating value of demands.
- Temperament has a regulative function: it helps to maintain an optimal level of arousal (stimulation regulation standard; see section 3.2.2) that is disrupted in stressful situations.
- The state of stress involves experiencing negative emotions and temperament traits are expressed, among other things, in the tendency to experience emotions—including negative ones.

Ever since Selye (1975) postulated that "deprivation of stimuli and excessive stimulation are both accompanied by an increase in stress, sometimes to the point of distress" (p. 21), researchers have viewed the intensity of demands as a stressor. Some researchers have noted that temperament traits or the individual's typical level of arousal (arousability; see section 3.1) significantly affect tolerance of intense life-events. For example, Rahe (1987)—who discussed life-events in terms of stimulation intensity leading to a specific level of arousal—believed that the latter may be moderated by temperament traits. Depending on the nature of the specific life-event, various temperament traits may moderate (enhance or reduce) the stimulating value of these events. Ursin (1980) in turn argued that intense life-events lead to heightened arousal that reduces the individual's tolerance of these events due to stimulus augmentation. Tolerance of life-events may also be reduced when stimulation is extremely low (e.g., in situations of deprivation, isolation), in which case the process of stimulation reduction is responsible. Ursin failed to notice, however, that in both cases—stimulation excess and stimulation deficit—individual differences in temperament play a moderating role in the development of stressor (life-event) intensity.

As we can see in Table 4.1, there are a number of temperament traits for which low arousability is typical (e.g., extraversion, sensation seeking, low emotional reactivity, or a strong type of nervous system). Individuals who have these traits are more tolerant of highly stimulating life-events because their typical stimulation-reducing mechanism lowers the stimulating value of the events (stressors) themselves. However, if the same temperament traits interact with demands whose stimulating value is low, they act as moderators that lead to reduced tolerance of situations whose stimulating value is weak. An opposite pattern can be observed for temperament traits that are rooted in high arousability (e.g., introversion, sensation avoidance, high emotional reactivity, or a weak type of nervous system), all of which typically have a stimulation-augmenting mechanism. This pattern is illustrated in Figure 6.3. It is worth quoting Eysenck (1983) who, drawing upon the research on neuroticism, said that "ceteris paribus high N individuals live a more stressful life, not in the sense that they necessarily encounter more stressful stimuli (although that may be so) but because identical stressful stimuli produce a greater amount of strain in them" (p. 126). According to Eysenck, tension and state of stress are synonymous.

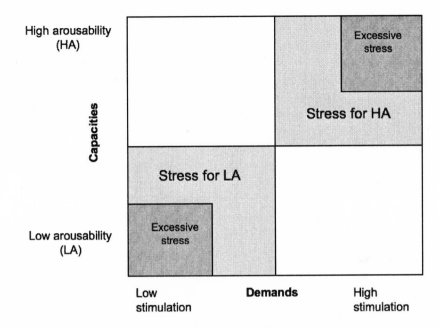

Figure 6.3. The level of arousability (here capacity) that underlies temperament traits co-determines the extent to which that stimulation (here demands) evokes a state of stress. Adapted from "Temperament and Stress: Temperament as a Moderator of Stressors, Emotional States, Coping, and Costs" by J. Strelau, 1995b. In C. D. Spielberger and I. G. Sarason (Eds.), *Stress and Emotion: Anxiety, Anger, and Curiosity* (Vol. 15), p. 225. Copyright 1995 by Hemisphere Publishing. Reprinted with permission.

Insufficient arousal (caused by weak stimuli whose stimulating value is low) and excessive arousal (caused by stimuli whose stimulating value is high) generate negative emotions, a fact recognized by Wilhelm Wundt (1887; see also Berlyne, 1960; Hebb, 1955) more than a hundred years ago. If these negative emotions are intense, a state of stress ensues. Stimuli of moderate intensity, meanwhile, which cause a level of arousal within the middle range of the arousal continuum and ensure optimal arousal (see the stimulation regulation standard in section 3.2), generate positive emotions and hence a sense of well-being. Level of arousal is moderated by temperament traits that are rooted in the mechanism responsible for level of arousability. Hence temperament traits act as a moderator of level of arousal because, by augmenting or reducing the level of stimulation, they have an effect on whether a particular life-event will evoke arousal that remains in the optimal range (see Eliasz, 1981) or arousal that either exceeds or does not reach this range—in which case negative emotions and the state of stress will ensue.

It follows from this discussion that temperament traits indirectly affect the tinge of the emotions that an individual experiences because they moderate the level of arousal evoked by a given stressor. In and of themselves, however, these traits may generate specific emotions irrespective of any life-events (Strelau, 1987b). Many writers, beginning with Gordon Allport (1937), have viewed temperament as a purely emotional construct. For example, according to Gray (1991), "[T]emperament reflects individual differences in predispositions towards particular kinds of emotion" (p.106). In turn, Goldsmith and Campos (1990) stated that "temperament can be defined fruitfully as individual differences in tendencies to express the primary emotions" (p. 1945). Temperament traits that refer to negative emotions, such as neuroticism or emotionality, act as moderators of the state of stress whatever their specific nature because they either enhance or reduce the emotional response to stressors. The extent of this emotional impact depends on individual differences in the strength of the tendency to experience such emotions. Buss and Plomin (1984) pointed this out emphatically when they said that "emotionality equals distress, the tendency to become upset easily and intensely" (p. 54).

Research conducted within the RTT paradigm has shed some light on the moderating role of one temperament trait—emotional reactivity—on the relationship between experienced stressors (life-events) and the state of stress, measured in terms of the state's consequences for mental health or mental disorder. The study in question, conducted by Małgorzata Trzcińska (1996), was conceived with the following hypothesis in mind: the tendency toward disordered behavior is a function of temperament and life-events (stressors) with temperament acting as a moderator of the individual's sensitivity to these events. The Formal Characteristics of Behavior–Temperament Inventory (FCB-TI) was used to measure temperament. The stressors experienced by the individual were assessed by means of Rahe's Recent Life Changes Questionnaire (RLCQ 1987; Sobolewski, Strelau, & Zawadzki, 1999). This inventory measures two indicators—an individual one and a normative one—of life-changes (stressors) rated for significance and the difficulty involved in adjusting to them. The individual index represents the subjective (individual) appraisal of stressor intensity, whereas the normative index is a standardized measure of the intensity of life-changes based on normative ratings by a sample that is representative for the population.

Three psychometric instruments were used to measure mental health:

- The Mental Health Inventory (Veit & Ware, 1983), adapted to Polish conditions by Cupas (1997). This questionnaire has five scales whose specific composition gives insight into two dimensions of mental health: psychological distress (anxiety, depression, and loss of behavioral and emotional control) and psychological well-being (general positive affect and emotional ties).

- Goldberg's General Health Questionnaire in its thirty-item version in its preliminary, unauthorized Polish adaptation by Trzcińska (1996). The Polish adaptation of the questionnaire measures one factor, general mental health.

- The Neurotic Symptoms Inventory by Aleksandrowicz and his collaborators (Aleksandrowicz et al., 1981) measures neurotic disorders.

The study using the RLCQ and FCB-TI was conducted on two groups. The first group was composed of two hundred men and women aged 22–75 ($M = 32.4$; $SD = 11.90$) who also took the Mental Health Inventory and General Health Questionnaire (Trzcińska, 1996). The second group (ninety students aged 21–24; unpublished data) was also administered the Neurotic Symptoms Inventory. As it happened, the temperament trait that moderated the stressor value in all three assessments of mental health was emotional reactivity (see Table 6.1).

As we can see, the correlations between the individual and normative life-change indicators (on the one hand) and the three measures of mental health (on the other) are very low or nil. However, when emotional reactivity as a moderator of this relationship is included in the equation, the correlations increase significantly—suggesting that emotional reactivity, treated as a moderator of the stressor/state-of-stress relationship (measured in terms of the consequences of this state), significantly affects the strength of the relationship between stressors and mental health. This pattern showed up in all three measures of mental health and in both the individual and normative indicators of the magnitude of life-changes.

This study was a point of departure for a second study measuring the effects of both emotional reactivity and activity. The latter variable was introduced because Sobolewski (Sobolewski, Strelau, & Zawadzki, 2001) demonstrated that although temperament traits are unrelated to stressors over which the individual has no control (see Figure 6.1), activity as measured by the FCB-TI is the only temperament trait that is related to stressors over which the individual has control. Another novel-

Table 6.1 Correlation between psychological health and life-changes moderated by emotional reactivity

Life-change index (RLCQ)	Psychological health indices					
	GHQ-30		S-II		MHI	
	r	R	r	R	r	R
Individual index	0.27	0.41	0.21	0.58	-0.23	0.44
Normative index	0.22	0.39	0.13	0.57	-0.03	0.48

Note. RLCQ = Recent Life Changes Questionnaire; GHQ = General Health Questionnaire; S-II = Neurotic Symptoms Inventory; MHI = Mental Health Inventory. All correlations are multiple (R) and significant on level $p < 0.001$. Adapted from *Psychologia temperamentu* [Psychology of Temperament] (2nd ed.) by J. Strelau, 2001a, p. 417. Copyright 2001 by Wydawnictwo Naukowe PWN. Reprinted with permission.

ty in this study was that rather than focusing on a general measure of health, we measured the relationships between stressors (life-events) and temperament traits on the one hand and the two extremes of the mental health continuum—the negative extreme expressed in anxiety and depression and the positive extreme, which in general terms may be called psychological well-being—on the other. In order to get closer to the causal relationships between the studied variables, the data were subjected to hierarchical regression analysis (Strelau & Zawadzki, 2005a).

The study was run on 1,327 men and women (including 525 men) aged 19–81 ($M = 36.3$; $SD = 11.09$). Mental health was assessed by means of the Mental Health Inventory with its two basic dimensions, psychological distress and psychological well-being. Life-events were assessed by means of Rahe's Recent Life Changes Questionnaire. Since the individual and normative scores were highly correlated ($r = 0.81$), only the normative score, the objective measure of life-changes, was analyzed. Both temperament traits, emotional reactivity and activity, were measured by means of the FCB-TI.

This study drew on the hypothesis that life-events affect life-changes (which are manifested in discomfort or well-being) and that emotional reactivity and activity moderate this relationship. It was predicted that emotional reactivity would increase the level of psychological distress, whereas activity would enhance psychological well-being.

Because the distribution of the RLCQ scores was far from normal, the scores were square-rooted before they were subjected to regression analysis. The contribution of age and gender was removed from all the variables by means of linear regression and the data were presented in the form of standardized residuals. Hierarchical regression analysis was conducted in a top-down fashion (beginning with the highest level of interaction). Below is a presentation of the outcomes of the hierarchical regression based on the final model of analysis only, separately for psychological distress, psychological well-being, and life-events—all of which were treated as dependent variables. Three predictors of psychological distress and psychological well-being were analyzed: life-events, emotional reactivity, and activity. In turn, for life-events the only predictors were emotional reactivity and activity. The outcomes of these analyses are presented in Table 6.2.

The most striking outcome of the analyses is that for all three variables, only additive effects emerged—no interactions. As predicted, emotional reactivity emerged with life-events as a predictor of psychological distress and both factors account for 22 percent of the variance of this dependent variable. Emotional reactivity accounts for more of the variance than life-events. No effect of activity emerged from this analysis, due perhaps to the specific status of activity. On the one hand, activity is a regulator of level of arousal; on the other, it has an indirect effect on the individual's adjustment to the environment (see Zawadzki, 2001). It may well be that activity plays a more complex role than emotional reactivity. Depending on the individual's typical level of arousability, the stimulating value

Table 6.2 Outcomes of hierarchical regression based on the final model of analysis separately for psychological distress, psychological well-being, and life-events

Psychological distress				
Final model	F	R	R^2	Predictor	Partial correlation
LE and ER	189.76[a]	0.47	0.22	LE	0.24*
				ER	0.42

Psychological well-being				
Final model	F	R	R^2	Predictor	Partial correlation
LE, ER, and AC	87.75[b]	0.41	0.17	LE	-0.11*
				ER	-0.30*
				AC	0.20*

Life-events				
Final model	F	R	R^2	Predictor	Partial correlation
ER and AC	15.69[a]	0.15	0.02	ER	0.07*
				AC	0.15

Note. LE = life-events; ER = emotional reactivity; AC = activity; F = test for coefficient of regression; R = correlation between dependent variable and linear combinations of predictors; R^2 = variance explained by the model. [a]$df = 2/1324$; [b]$df = 3/1323$; *$p < 0.05$. Adapted from "The Functional Significance of Temperament Empirically Tested: Data Based on Hypotheses Derived from the Regulative Theory of Temperament" by J. Strelau and B. Zawadzki, 2005a. In A. Eliasz, S. Hampson, and B. de Raad, (Eds.), *Advances in Personality Psychology*, Vol. 2, p. 27. Copyright 2005 by Psychology Press. Reprinted with permission.

of activity adequate for that level may have a positive effect on mental health, whereas stimulating values of activity departing from that level may lead to behavior disorder. This is one of the reasons why activity does not contribute significantly to the variance of psychological distress.

Low emotional reactivity, high activity, and a low level of life-events are predictors of psychological well-being. If we remember that in almost all the studies conducted to date, extraversion correlates with positive emotions (see Eysenck & Eysenck, 1985) and psychological well-being (e.g., Cooper, Okamura, & McNeil, 1995; Pavot, Fujita, & Diener, 1997; Ryan & Frederick, 1997) and that activity correlates strongly with extraversion (correlations between these variables ranged from 0.65 to 0.76 in four independent trials; Zawadzki & Strelau, 1997), then this finding is not surprising.

The role of temperament traits as predictors of life-events departs from our expectations, however. As we can see in Table 6.1, emotional reactivity emerged as a quite evident moderator of the relationship between life-events and mental disorder measured by means of three questionnaires. In this study the role of emotional reactivity—like the role of activity—was minimal; both these variables account for just 2 percent of the variance of life-events. We found in another study (Sobolewski, Strelau, & Zawadzki, 2001) that activity correlated positively with stressors defined as challenges, whereas the same temperament trait did not correlate with stressors over which the individual had no control. Life-events as assessed by the RLCQ include stressors that depend on the individual as well as stressors that are beyond the individual's control, and this perhaps explains why activity contributes so negligibly to the variance of life-events. As far as emotional reactivity and its relationship with stressors are concerned, our analyses based on the hierarchical regression model (Strelau & Zawadzki, 2005a) suggest that Trzcińska's (1996) findings should be treated with caution.

This study shows how hard it is to evaluate stressors on their own without also looking carefully at the state of stress. The state of stress, in turn (i.e., the central link in stress-related phenomena; see Figure 6.1), shows up mainly in its consequences. Most of our attention, however, was devoted to the role of temperament as a moderator of the relationship between the state of stress and its consequences—the topic of the next section.

6.3
Temperament as a moderator of the consequences of the state of stress

Stella Chess and Alexander Thomas conducted a longitudinal study of temperament for more than thirty years. The study began when their subjects were infants. These researchers found that lack of stress may lead to poor adjustment. "New demands and stresses, when consonant with developmental potentials, are constructive in their consequences" (Chess & Thomas, 1986, p. 158). In other words, a slight discrepancy between demands and capacities—as long as it is not chronic—may actually encourage optimal adaptation to the environment and environmental expectations. These same writers also point out that excessive demand-related stress with which the individual is unable to cope will lead to behavior disorder or even pathology, as demonstrated in their own research (Thomas & Chess, 1977) and that of their successors (e.g., Kyrios & Prior, 1990; Maziade, 1988; Windle, 1989).

State of stress leads to organismal changes that may affect the individual's psychological functioning, leading (for example) to depression, elevated anxiety, or reduced adaptive capacity. It may also lead to changes in the individual's physiology and biochemistry that manifest themselves in the form of various psycho-somatic conditions and other health problems. Thanks to research confirming these patterns, stress has become one of the main focuses of interest of health psychology (see Heszen-Niejodek & Sęk, 1997; Sheridan & Radmacher, 1998). Taking the concept of arousal as his point of departure, Richard Rahe (1987) formulated a hypothesis that greatly contributed to the understanding of the connections between state of stress and health.

> The brain, with its rich interconnections and multiple influences on all organ systems of the body, appears to respond to psychosocial stresses primarily through neurotransmitters and hormonal pathways. . . . These brain effects are thereby transmitted to most of the organ systems of the body; which of these many alterations are singled out for study depends on the physiological interests of the investigators. (p. 229)

State of stress should be viewed as one of the many risk factors for behavior disorders or even pathology. Many studies conducted by temperament psychologists—or personality psychologists more generally—have demonstrated that temperament traits may increase or reduce the psychophysiological costs of one and the same stressor (for examples of research referring to temperament traits measured by means of the Temperament Questionnaire/Strelau Temperament Inventory [TQ/STI], see section 3.3). They may also enhance or reduce the risk of psychological disorder and pathology. This research has been discussed elsewhere (see Strelau, 1995b, 1998, 2001d).

This review—as well as the research conducted by my collaborators—encouraged me to introduce the term "temperament risk factor" (TRF) after Carey (1986 p. 40), albeit with a different meaning. Carey limited the scope of the concept to the excessive stress that children with difficult temperament experience in their interactions with the environment. In order to give this concept more universal meaning, spreading over all populations regardless of their age and the theory of temperament adopted (Carey restricted the term to the concept of difficult temperament proposed by Thomas and Chess), I expanded the definition of temperament risk factor.

> By temperament risk factor (TRF) I mean any temperament trait or configuration of traits that in interaction with other factors acting excessively, persistently, or recurrently (e.g., physical and social environment, educational treatment, situation, the individual's characteristics) increases the risk of developing behavior disorders or pathology or that favors the shaping of a maladjusted personality. (Strelau, 1998, p. 376)

This definition unequivocally implies that it only makes sense to treat temperament traits as risk factors if we view them in the context of other variables with which they interact. In other words, the same temperament traits or configurations that are a temperament risk factor in one situation need not be a risk factor in a different situation. If we distinguish between absolutely risky and relatively risky behavior, as Jeffery (1989) did, then we will have to conclude that TRF belongs to the group of relative risk factors. Other stressors (life-events) being equal, this risk is measured in terms of the probability of dysfunction in individuals with TRF compared with the probability that similar dysfunction will emerge in individuals who do not have this TRF.

Within the last decade, research conducted by my collaborators, postgraduate and graduate students, and me has focused largely on the moderating role of temperament as it is manifested in the consequences of the state of stress. This role is probably most pronounced when the individual has experienced trauma caused by stressors over which he or she had no control (catastrophes, disasters, etc.). Our studies of this problem area have been sufficiently comprehensive to merit a separate chapter (see chapter 7). In all these studies, temperament was assessed by means of the FCB-TI, an offshoot of the Regulative Theory of Temperament. I emphasize this fact because many studies of the role of temperament as a moderator of stress-related phenomena have been conducted with the help of earlier measures of temperament, the TQ/STI or Pavlovian Temperament Survey, presented very selectively in chapter 3.

The work of Tatiana Klonowicz and Andrzej Eliasz deserves special attention. Klonowicz demonstrated that simultaneous interpreters differing in level of reactivity incur different psychophysiological costs on the job (see section 3.3.3). Klonowicz (2001b) also found that reactivity and mobility, treated as individual resources, affect the goodness of "person-environment" fit measured in terms of psychological well-being. Eliasz, in turn, conducted a series of studies in which he demonstrated the moderating role of reactivity in the development of Type A Behavior (Eliasz, 2001; Eliasz & Wrześniewski, 1988; Strelau & Eliasz, 1994).

The next section briefly presents two areas of research that illustrate the role played by temperament in the individual's experience of the consequences of the state of stress — that is, somatic disease and professional burnout.

6.3.1. Temperament as a risk factor for somatic disease

The idea that temperament traits are related to disease has been present in the scientific literature ever since the philosophers of antiquity, Hippocrates and Galen, first suggested it. From the very beginning, it was believed that the "physiological mechanisms" of temperament (rather than temperament as such) are the factors responsible for these maladies. In his *De temperamentis*, Galen (2nd century B.C.) wrote that the four humors distinguished by Hippocrates (4th century B.C.) — blood (*sanguis*), bile (*chole*), black bile (*melas*), and phlegm (*phlegma*) — to which Galen ascribed the four temperaments (the sanguine, the choleric, the melancholic, and the phlegmatic) are the direct sources of these conditions. This idea has been a recurrent theme throughout the centuries and researchers, most of whom have referred to the temperaments distinguished by Hippocrates-Galen, have attributed the origins of various diseases (primarily mental ones) to the postulated physiological mechanisms that presumably underlie these temperaments—most frequently, the composition of the blood, hormonal dynamics, and so on (see Strelau, 1998).

6.3.1.1. The relationships between psychosomatic disease and personality

Empirical research on the relationships between the four temperaments and mental disease has been conducted since the beginning of the twentieth century. Initially constitutional approaches predominated, leaving no room for any discussion of the role of environmental factors in the etiology of these diseases (see Conrad, 1941; Kretschmer, 1944; Sheldon & Stevens, 1942). As Hans Eysenck's theory of personality became popular in Europe in the second half of the twentieth century, however, researchers also began to study the relationships between somatic illness and the personality dimensions that Eysenck proposed (i.e., neuroticism, extraversion, and psychoticism). Kissen and Eysenck (1962; Kissen, 1964) found a significant relationship between the Eysenckian personality traits and lung cancer in human males. Bendien and Groen (1963) found connections between neuroticism and coronary heart disease in the patients whom they studied. At about the same time, Coppen and Metcalfe (1963) focused on the link between cancer and extraversion. Based on these and similar studies—whose findings are far from unequivocal—Eysenck (1983) formulated the so-called inoculation hypothesis, which says that highly neurotic introverts who are exposed to prolonged stress are less sensitive to the negative effects of permanent tension and hence run less risk of getting cancer (the so-called inoculation effect).

Some of the most groundbreaking investigations ever conducted in this field are those by Grossarth-Maticek (1980) and his collaborators (Grossarth-Maticek, Bastiaans, & Kanazir, 1985; Grossarth-Maticek & Eysenck, 1991) of the relationship between lung cancer and coronary heart disease on the one hand and personality traits on the other. This ten-year project consisted of three independent prospective studies, one run in the former Yugoslavia and two run in Heidelberg, Germany. The Heidelberg subjects were divided into two groups—one composed of men and women who, according to the opinions of close relatives, lived under constant stress and one that did not experience constant stress. Between 800 and 1,300 randomly selected healthy men and women participated in the project. The mean age of the subjects was 60 in Yugoslavia and 50 in Germany. All three groups were administered the same questionnaire that taps four personality types:

- Type I (the cancer-prone type) is excessively cooperative and unassertive, suppresses negative emotions, avoids conflicts, is overpatient, and responds defensively to stress. This type is referred to as Type C in the literature.

- Type II (known as Type A) is susceptible to coronary heart disease and is incessantly irritated and angry, emotionally unstable in his or her relationships with other people, aggressive, and hostile.

- Type III, which has no counterpart in the literature, has been referred to as the hysterical type, one that oscillates between maladjustment and anger.

- Type IV (or Type B) is psychologically healthy.

The mortality statistics computed for these men and women ten years after they were psychometrically assessed revealed that in all three groups the number of deaths from cancer was highest in Type I (Type C) persons, whereas mortality due to heart disease was highest in Type II (Type A) persons. The Heidelberg studies also revealed that mortality due to either cancer or heart disease was higher in men and women whom observers had rated as permanently stressed than in those who were not subject to continual stress. On the basis of these and earlier findings, Eysenck (1988) formulated the following causal hypothesis concerning the relationship between personality and cancer:

> Both personality and the immune system can be affected by features of the endocrine system, so that the apparent correlation between personality and cancer, say, is in fact mediated by ACTH [adrenocorticotropic hormone], cortisol, the endogenous opiates, etc., which have been shown to affect both personality and the immune system. (p. 137)

In Eysenck's opinion, high neuroticism, high psychoticism, and introversion are conducive to cancer. More than a decade after the Grossarth-Maticek, Bastiaans, and Kanazir (1985) study, however, Smedslund (1995) conducted a study that failed to find any significant relationship between his personality types and cancer. Smedslund did not include Type III in his study but Grossarth-Maticek before him had found no relationship between this type and somatic diseases either. Smedslund's study, conducted on five thousand younger men and women ($M = 42.2$) than those investigated by Grossarth-Maticek, revealed that persons representing Type IV (the healthy type) had heart disease significantly less frequently than persons representing Types I and II. However, several variables (such as age, exercise, smoking, and diet) confounded the relationships between these types and coronary heart disease. The studies cited therefore suggest that not only biological factors but also environmental factors and one's own activity play an important role in the etiology of somatic disease.

Returning to the research initiated by Eysenck's personality theory, Schmitz (1992, 1993) — who studied men and women suffering from somatic conditions —

demonstrated that the personality types distinguished by Grossarth-Maticek may be described in terms of the Eysenckian concepts of neuroticism, extraversion, and psychoticism. In addition, many studies of the relationships between personality and somatic disease have been conducted within the last decade, including studies of cancer and heart disease (see, e.g., Amelang, 1997; Chen et al., 2000; Denollet, 1997; Watten et al., 1997). The results are far from clear. Whiteman, Deary, and Fowkes (2000) reviewed more than forty years of research on personality and coronary heart disease and concluded that there is a connection between Type A and hostility-related personality traits, albeit not a very powerful one because Type A personality accounts for only about 2 percent of the variance of this heart condition.

Taking this work as their point of departure, my graduate students and collaborators set out to determine the relationship between RTT traits and the most frequently researched somatic diseases—that is, cancer and heart disease.

6.3.1.2. Our own research

My graduate students conducted a preliminary study of temperament and somatic disease[2] on small samples of patients with coronary heart disease (men) and breast cancer (women). Each patient group was matched with a group of healthy controls. Because RTT temperament traits had not yet been studied in the context of somatic disease, no specific hypotheses were formulated except for the prediction that emotional reactivity—the trait with the greatest affinity with neuroticism—should be higher in patients with coronary heart disease than in healthy controls. As far as the five remaining temperament traits are concerned, the study was more exploratory in kind. The outcomes of the studies in which only age and gender (in addition to type of disease) were controlled revealed that patients and healthy controls differed with respect to only two temperament traits, emotional reactivity and activity, and that these differences were only present in men (see Table 6.3). As for the women with breast cancer, represented by four samples of patients, only in one sample was a significant relationship found between the tumor and temperament; this was a relationship between cancer and emotional reactivity. Other than in the men with coronary heart disease, emotional reactivity was higher in healthy women.

The graduate students' studies of somatic disease and temperament no doubt have many shortcomings, including the small samples and lack of control of

---

[2] Somatic diseases were not the only ones whose relationship with RTT traits has been investigated. For example, in her doctoral dissertation written under Andrzej Eliasz's supervision, Ewa Habrat (1997; see Strelau, 2001a) found that patients with bipolar affective disorder in depression or remission differed significantly from the control group. Compared with normal controls, the patients had lower briskness, endurance, and activity and higher emotional reactivity and perseveration.

Table 6.3 Differences in emotional reactivity and activity between patients with coronary heart disease (men), patients with breast cancer (women), and healthy controls

Author	Patients	Samples of healthy controls	Illness	Difference in ER	Difference in AC
Wenglorz, 1996	$N = 80, M = 49.6;$ $SD = 7.79$	$N = 37, M = 48.5;$ $SD = 8.49$	CHD	*ns*	P > H
Szczerbicka, 1996	$N = 29, M = 49.9;$ $SD = 8.68$	$N = 21, M = 51.28;$ $SD = 7.0$	CHD	P > H	P > H
Duda, 1996	$N = 49, M = 52;$ 38-70[1]	$N = 38, M = 49;$ 35-75[1]	BC	*ns*	*ns*
Szlachta, 1996	$N = 95$, 38-70[2]	Equivalent sample[3]	BC	*ns*	*ns*
Siwak, 1999	$N = 43, M = 51.5;$ $SD = 7.95$	$N = 42, M = 53.5;$ $SD = 7.21$	BC	*ns*	*ns*
Bobrowska, 1997	$N = 50, M = 54;$ $SD = 11$	$N = 50, M = 51;$ $SD = 11$	BC	*ns*	*ns*
Zianowicz, 1998	$N = 35, M = 47$	Equivalent sample[3]	BC	P < H	*ns*

Note. ER = emotional reactivity; AC = activity; CHD = coronary heart disease; BC = breast cancer; P = patients; H = healthy controls. [1]No *SD* data; [2]no *M* and *SD* data; [3]data about healthy controls lacking.

many biological and social variables known to interact with variables that contribute to the etiology of these diseases (such as diet, smoking, or recreational habits; see Whiteman, Deary, & Fowkes, 2000). This preliminary work encouraged Zawadzki (2001; Strelau & Zawadzki, 2005a) to undertake more in-depth studies of the relationships between somatic conditions and temperament. These new studies focused exclusively on emotional reactivity, the trait closely related to neuroticism, and activity. The latter temperament trait is related to extraversion and has been studied by researchers of somatic disease who have investigated the contribution of personality to the etiology of these conditions since the 1960s.

The studies presented here are rooted in hypotheses that draw indirectly on the data reported in the literature. Meta-analysis of the findings concerning the relationship between personality traits on the one hand and cardiovascular disease and cancer on the other suggests that certain personality traits (e.g., depressiveness) are a common risk factor for both these maladies, whereas other personality traits (e.g., extraversion) are specific risk factors for these diseases (see Friedman & Booth-Kewley, 1987; McGee, Williams, & Elwood, 1994; Miller, Smith,

& Turner, 1996). Emotional reactivity, a factor closely related to neuroticism but also to depression, was assumed to be a common risk factor for men with myocardial infarction and women with breast cancer. Activity, a temperament trait closely related to extraversion but also to psychoticism (see Strelau & Zawadzki, 1997), is a specific risk factor. High activity seems to be related to hostility (one of the components of psychoticism) and susceptibility to myocardial infarction, whereas low activity is related to submissiveness and lung cancer. It was also predicted that temperament traits are an indirect risk factor for both these pathologies, via the aforementioned personality syndromes. Finally, it was assumed that smoking, a direct risk factor for lung cancer, is related to temperament.

The study was run on patients—men and women who had lung cancer or who had experienced myocardial infarction. The lung cancer sample numbered 135 patients (96 men and 39 women) aged 27–72 ($M = 54.6$; $SD = 8.57$), including 119 smokers. The myocardial infarction sample numbered 74 patients (50 men and 24 women) aged 31–75 ($M = 54.9$; $SD = 10.01$), including 44 smokers. An additional group of 120 healthy individuals (79 men and 41 women) aged 30–77 ($M = 52.6$; $SD = 10.19$) was also recruited; there were 63 smokers in this group. All three groups were of similar age ($F = 1.97$; $df = 2, p = 0.65$). The diagnoses of lung cancer were submitted, with the patients' permission, by the supervising physicians. The cardiac patients were tested within one to three months of their first infarction.

Personality was assessed by means of Zawadzki's (2001) Personality Pattern Inventory, a fifty-item questionnaire with three scales corresponding to three factors obtained by means of factor analysis (Principal Components, Varimax): Depressiveness, Hostility, and Submissiveness. It has satisfactory reliability and validity. Both Zawadzki's own work, which has been presented in detail elsewhere (see Zawadzki, 2001; see also Strelau & Zawadzki, 2005a), and work reported in the literature (see Eysenck, 1994; McGee, Williams, & Elwood, 1994; Temoshok & Dreher, 1992; Williams & Barefoot, 1988) suggest that the depressiveness syndrome correlates with both Type A and Type C and may be a nonspecific risk factor for both myocardial infarction and lung cancer. Submissiveness, in turn, may be viewed as an axial component of Type C and hence a risk factor for lung cancer, whereas hostility may be an analogous component of Type A personality and a risk factor for coronary heart disease and myocardial infarction.

The FCB-TI was used to measure the two temperament traits investigated in the Zawadzki study, emotional reactivity and activity. Information on smoking behavior was gleaned from the medical interview. Patients were divided into two groups, smokers and nonsmokers. Individuals who had not smoked for at least two years (both patients and healthy controls) were classified as nonsmokers.

Path analysis was used to analyze the data separately for two groups—healthy controls and patients with lung cancer ($N = 255$) and healthy controls and patients with myocardial infarction ($N = 194$). The application of regression analysis and transformation of the scores on each scale into standardized residuals made it possible to eliminate the effect of gender and age. Path analysis was performed using LISREL 8 software (Jöreskog & Sörbom, 1993). Temperament traits were given the status of explanatory variables; health status was the explained variable; and the personality syndromes and smoking were treated as moderators (intervening variables). By applying chi^2 statistics in the path analysis (see Pedhazur & Pedhazur-Schmelkin, 1991), it was possible to eliminate all nonsignificant relationships or relationships that would only worsen the overall goodness of fit for the full model.

The full path model for lung cancer (temperament traits, personality syndromes, and smoking included) is presented in Figure 6.4. As predicted, depressiveness and submissiveness—but above all smoking—are directly related to lung cancer and should be viewed as predictors of this type of cancer. Both the temperament traits directly relating to the personality syndromes (i.e., emotional

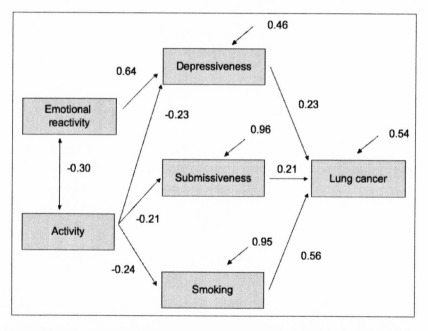

Figure 6.4. Path model illustrating the relationships between temperament traits (emotional reactivity and activity), personality syndromes (depressiveness and submissiveness), and smoking on the one hand and lung cancer on the other. Adapted from "Temperamentalny czynnik ryzyka chorób somatycznych—raka płuca i zawału serca" [Temperament as a Risk Factor of Somatic Diseases: Lung Cancer and Myocardial Infarction] by B. Zawadzki, 2001. In W. Ciarkowska and A. Matczak (Eds.), *Różnice indywidualne. Wybrane badania inspirowane Regulacyjną Teorią Temperamentu Profesora Jana Strelaua*, p. 43. Copyright 2001 by Interdisciplinary Center for Behavior Genetic Research, Warsaw University. Reprinted with permission.

reactivity with depressiveness and activity with depressiveness and submissiveness) affect lung cancer indirectly. This indirect effect also emerged for temperament and smoking.

The full path model for myocardial infarction is shown in Figure 6.5. As we can see from this figure, depressiveness and hostility are directly related to myocardial infarction, whereas smoking—contrary to expectations—is not. In this model, emotional reactivity has an indirect effect on myocardial infarction by way of depressiveness and hostility, whereas activity has an indirect effect via hostility. Like emotional reactivity, activity is related to smoking.

As we see from Table 6.4, which summarizes the two path analyses presented above, most of the findings are as predicted (see Zawadzki, 2001; Strelau & Zawadzki, 2005a). In order to test the model's goodness of fit, chi^2 statistics were applied. The data in Table 6.4 point to several conclusions.

First, depressiveness is a common risk factor for both somatic diseases—lung

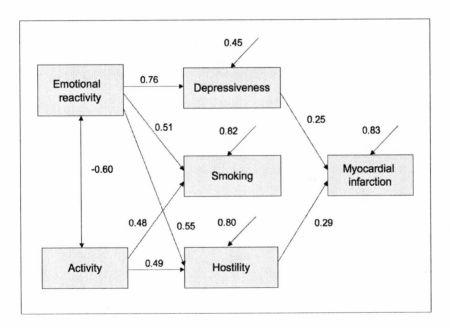

Figure 6.5. Path model illustrating the relationships between temperament traits (emotional reactivity and activity), personality syndromes (depressiveness and hostility) and tobacco smoking on the one hand and myocardial infarction on the other. Adapted from "Temperamentalny czynnik ryzyka chorób somatycznych—raka płuca i zawału serca" [Temperament as a Risk Factor of Somatic Diseases: Lung Cancer and Myocardial Infarction] by B. Zawadzki, 2001. In W. Ciarkowska and A. Matczak (Eds.), *Różnice indywidualne. Wybrane badania inspirowane Regulacyjną Teorią Temperamentu Profesora Jana Strelaua,* p. 45. Copyright 2001 by Interdisciplinary Center for Behavior Genetic Research, Warsaw University. Reprinted with permission.

Table 6.4 Results of path analysis for relationships between temperament traits (emotional reactivity and activity), personality syndromes (depressiveness, submissiveness, and hostility), smoking, and myocardial infarction and lung cancer

Variable	Emotional reactivity	Activity	Illness
Lung cancer (chi^2 = 7.15; df = 7, p = 0.41)			
Illness	0.15* (0.18*)	-0.23* (-0.13*)	
Smoking		-0.24*	0.56*
Depressiveness	0.64*	-0.23*	0.23*
Submissiveness		-0.21*	0.21*
Myocardial infarction (chi^2 = 4.70; df = 7, p = 0.70)			
Illness	0.35* (0.32*)	0.15 (0.13)	
Smoking	0.51*	0.48*	
Depressiveness	0.76*		0.25*
Hostility (corr.)	0.55*	0.49*	0.29*

Note. *p < 0.05 (two-tailed test); corr. = data corrected for hostility after extracting the influence of depressiveness (based on analysis of linear regression). In parentheses are the scores for the relationship between temperament traits and illness for models with smoking extracted. Adapted from "Temperamentalny czynnik ryzyka chorób somatycznych—raka płuca i zawału serca" [Temperament as a Risk Factor of Somatic Diseases: Lung Cancer and Myocardial Infarction] by B. Zawadzki, 2001. In W. Ciarkowska and A. Matczak (Eds.), *Różnice indywidualne. Wybrane badania inspirowane Regulacyjną Teorią Temperamentu Profesora Jana Strelau*, p. 44. Copyright 2001 by Interdisciplinary Center for Behavior Genetic Research, Warsaw University. Reprinted with permission.

cancer and myocardal infarction—because it directly facilitates the emergence of these conditions. Second, hostility and submissiveness are specific risk factors: hostility predicts myocardial infarction, whereas submissiveness predicts lung cancer. Third and finally, temperament traits (emotional reactivity and activity) are not direct risk factors for either of these somatic conditions; rather, they are temperament risk factors that are conducive to the development of maladaptive personality. High emotional reactivity is a predictor of both depressiveness and hostility and hence is related to both myocardial infarction and lung cancer. Depending on its intensity, activity can be a specific predictor of personality syndromes. High activity goes hand in hand with hostility and thus is related to myocardial infarction, whereas low activity has affinity with depressiveness and hence to lung cancer. This pattern of findings corroborates the findings of Eliasz (2001) and Klonowicz and Eliasz (2004), who demonstrated that misfit between temperament traits and other personality traits that help to control stimulation may lead to maladaptive behavior when stressors are present.

Zawadzki's work (2001; Strelau & Zawadzki, 2005a), conducted within the RTT paradigm, is a convincing demonstration of the temperament risk factor concept. The next section will present the results of a study conducted by one of my collaborators, Joanna Korczyńska, in the context of a short review of the research on staff burnout.

6.3.2. Temperament and staff burnout

It must be stressed that staff burnout has rarely been studied within the individual differences paradigm despite Burisch's (2002) warning that if we neglect the role of personality dispositions in burnout research, we shall merely accumulate more data within the next few decades but no new knowledge. Several personality traits—for example, hardiness (McCranie, Lambert, & Lambert, 1987; Topf, 1989), locus of control (Perlman & Hartman, 1982; Lunenburg & Cadavid, 1992), coping style (Nowack, 1991)—or selected temperament traits such as approach-avoidance or adaptability (Rowe, 1997) have been studied as possible intervening variables in the development of burnout.

6.3.2.1. Staff burnout: Definition and assessment

The concept of staff burnout was originally introduced into the research literature by Freudenberger (1974), who then proceeded to study the phenomenon at length. According to Freudenberger, burnout is an extreme state of exhaustion of the resources at the individual's disposal—mainly the need for energy. Burnout is closely related to high arousal leading to organismal overload due to functioning in occupational situations that may be termed "very demanding." Thus defined, Freudenberger views burnout as a homogeneous, structurally undifferentiated phenomenon closely related to stress. According to the model presented in Figure 6.1, burnout may be viewed as a psychological consequence of the state of stress, and its specific nature lies in the fact that it refers to human occupational functioning that is both highly exhausting and long term. Freudenberger and Richelson (1980) observe that a number of individuals who operate in such conditions are prone to burnout, an approach that highlights the role of individual differences.

Two years after Freudenberger first introduced the concept, Christina Maslach (1976, 1982) also began to study burnout. She gave a detailed account of the phenomenon based on numerous interviews, case studies, experiments, and questionnaires conducted in a variety of professional settings (Maslach & Jackson, 1981). According to Maslach, burnout occurs in the helping professions[3] (see Maslach,

---

[3] This opinion, which is shared by most burnout researchers, explains why teachers and nurses are the two professions in which the phenomenon has been studied most frequently.

1993). Like most burnout researchers who adopt a social psychological approach, Maslach attributes the phenomenon to extrinsic rather than intrinsic factors (Maslach & Leiter, 1997). Pines, Aronson, and Kafry (1981; after Burisch, 2002) are particularly ardent advocates of this point of view. In their work on the origins of burnout, for example, they argue that there are "bad situations, not bad people" (p. 60). Christina Maslach and Susan Jackson (Maslach & Jackson, 1986) defined burnout in an exploratory study. Their definition fully corresponds to a diagnostic instrument that these writers constructed to measure burnout. Maslach (1993) writes, "We define burnout as a psychological syndrome of emotional exhaustion, depersonalization, and reduced personal accomplishment that can occur among individuals who work with other people in some capacity" (p. 20).

Maslach points out that emotional exhaustion, closely related to intensive arousal of the organism, is most similar to stress and the energetic approach to exhaustion introduced by Freudenberger. However, she limits exhaustion to feelings of being emotionally overextended. Depersonalization is expressed in reacting to other people in a heartless, negative, and dehumanized fashion. Reduced personal accomplishment manifests itself in the feeling that one lacks competence and success at work. The term "feeling" as it is applied in the context of emotional exhaustion and personal accomplishment reflects Maslach's (1993) cognitive approach to staff burnout. According to Leiter and Maslach (1988), the first syndrome of burnout is emotional exhaustion, which leads to depersonalization and a reduced sense of personal accomplishment. Leiter (1993) modified this "phasal" conceptualization somewhat; he thinks that reduced sense of personal accomplishment develops independently of the two remaining phases of staff burnout.

Maslach and Jackson (1986) not only defined burnout—a concept firmly rooted in psychometric research—but also developed a questionnaire, the Maslach Burnout Inventory (MBI), which fully corresponds to the above definition that emphasizes the three-dimensional structure of burnout. The MBI has three scales whose names correspond to the three dimensions of burnout.

Despite its short history of just over thirty years, staff burnout has accumulated a large body of research literature. A review of this canon reveals that burnout is variously understood. More than twenty years ago, Perlman and Hartman (1982) identified over fifty definitions of burnout. Nearly all burnout researchers quote the pioneers of this area, Freudenberger and Maslach. The great popularity of Maslach's approach in particular should probably be attributed to the fact that she not only described the phenomenon, but also developed a psychometric tool with which to measure it—a tool that is both reliable and valid.

Polish burnout researchers also refer mainly to Maslach's conceptualization, but they draw attention to the importance of individual differences as well. Helena Sęk and her collaborators (see Beisert, 2000; Pasikowski, 2000; Sęk, 1996, 2000) have conducted the largest number of studies of this phenomenon in

Poland.[4] Their model of staff burnout includes personal attributes as variables that interact with both the stressful situation at work and staff burnout. The problem of individual differences is not conspicuous in this team's research, however. Like Sęk and her collaborators, Noworol and Marek (1993) took Maslach's conceptualization as a point of departure to introduce their typological model of staff burnout. This model assumes that various professions have their own paths of burnout, which represent the dynamics of the process over time, and they distinguish various clusters depending on the intensity of the process. According to Noworol and Marek, there are also individuals who burn out differently, not according to their path; this suggests that individual differences are at work.

If we look at the problem of staff burnout from the perspective of the regulative functions of temperament, it is worth mentioning two studies, one conducted by Lucyna Golińska and Waldemar Świętochowski (1998) and the other by Maria Kliś and Joanna Kossewska (1998). The first pair of researchers, who used the STI to measure temperament, discovered that increased depersonalization and reduced personal accomplishment in teachers correlate negatively with strength of excitation (high reactivity). Kliś and Kossewska, who administered the STI and the Eysenck Personality Inventory, found that (a) emotional exhaustion correlates positively with neuroticism and negatively with extraversion; (b) reduced personal accomplishment correlates positively with extraversion, strength of excitation, and mobility of the nervous processes; and (c) both these nervous system properties also correlate positively with depersonalization. In other words, the two pairs of researchers obtained contradictory findings concerning the relationships between temperament as measured by the STI and the three dimensions of staff burnout. This dilemma calls for further discussion. It should also be mentioned that both studies (and to the best of my knowledge, the same is true for all studies of burnout in Poland) used the MBI, albeit in different adaptations, to measure burnout.

Within the context of these studies, Joanna Korczyńska—one of my postgraduate students—conducted a large study of burnout in prison staff within the individual differences paradigm.

6.3.2.2. Burnout studies within the RTT paradigm

Because burnout should be seen as a consequence of an intense and prolonged state of stress, research on RTT traits and staff burnout fits into the temperament-stress model. Assuming that the probability of burnout increases with the increase in risk factors for this syndrome, Korczyńska (2004) introduced several variables that could

---

[4] Parallel to Helena Sęk's work on staff burnout in Poznań, a group of researchers in Kraków also began to study this phenomenon (see Noworol & Marek, 1993; Schaufeli, Maslach, & Marek, 1993).

contribute to the development of burnout in prison staff. She based her predictions on an analysis of the existing literature and our own previous research. In addition to RTT traits, her key variables, Korczyńska also studied coping style and locus of control (personality variables) and measured the stressful situation itself, paying particular attention to those aspects of the situation that were specific to the work of prison staff. Korczyńska wanted to know whether temperament traits are a risk factor for burnout in prison staff and whether these traits are specific for different positions in the job hierarchy. Furthermore, she wanted to determine the degree to which other variables controlled in this study and related to temperament would predict the different syndromes of staff burnout. Drawing on Noworol and Marek's (1993) model of staff burnout, Korczyńska conducted a number of correlational analyses and several cluster analyses of her data. For example, she performed separate analyses for selected work departments and positions.

In my discussion of Korczyńska's study, I shall concentrate on the temperament risk factor for staff burnout. One of the author's original contributions was to study burnout within the context of the structural diagnosis of temperament proposed by Zawadzki and Strelau (1997), a tenet of which is that a specific configuration of temperament traits has functional significance for the individual's adaptation to the stimulating demands of the environment. In this context we say that temperament structure may be harmonious or disharmonious, largely with respect to its energetic characteristics as manifested in emotional reactivity, endurance, and activity. This structure also applies, albeit secondarily, to temporal characteristics that are "energetic 'channels': they increase stimulation input, a basic function of briskness, or discharge arousal, a basic function of perseveration" (Zawadzki & Strelau, 1997, p. 36).

In the following presentation of Korczyńska's findings, I shall focus on four basic trait configurations—two of which are structurally harmonized and two of which can be said to be in structural disharmony (Zawadzki & Strelau, 1997). The temperaments distinguished within the harmonious structure are:

- A temperament with a high stimulation-processing capacity typical of individuals who are enduring and very active and have a low level of emotional reactivity. This temperament structure resembles the sanguine temperament of the ancient Greeks.

- A temperament with a low stimulation-processing capacity typical of individuals who are highly reactive emotionally, inactive, and lacking in endurance. This configuration resembles the classic melancholic temperament.

The temperaments distinguished within the disharmonious temperament structure are:

- A temperament with ineffective stimulus-processing regulation due to high stimulation-processing capacity, expressed in high endurance and low emotional reactivity on the one hand and lack of stimulation seeking and hence low activity on the other. This configuration reminds us of the phlegmatic temperament.

• A temperament with ineffective stimulus-processing regulation due to low stimulation-processing capacity typical of individuals who are highly reactive emotionally, lack endurance, yet tend to be very active—which is inadequate to their poor stimulation-processing capacity. This configuration resembles the choleric temperament.

The different combinations of the characteristics of energetic stimulation processing—endurance, activity, and emotional reactivity—yield eight different temperament structures that have more or less affinity with either the harmonious or disharmonious structures.

Korczyńska tested 672 prison workers (including 97 women). The sample was heterogeneous with respect to position and department. The respondents' age ranged from 22 to 53 ($M = 37.3$; $SD = 6.61$) and they had employment histories ranging from six months to 29 years. This group was recruited from prison staffs throughout Poland and is very similar to the representative sample for the population of prison workers, making Korczyńska's study particularly interesting.

The author used the FCB-TI to measure temperament and Noworol's (1998) adaptation of the MBI (Maslach, Jackson, & Leiter, 1996) to measure burnout.[5] In accordance with Maslach's structure of staff burnout, the MBI has three scales: Emotional Exhaustion, Depersonalization, and Reduced Personal Accomplishment. In the Polish adaptation, the latter scale was constructed in reverse form as a Personal Accomplishment scale; this means that high scores on the Personal Accomplishment scale indicate feelings of personal accomplishment. The author also included the Coping Inventory for Stressful Situations, a questionnaire developed by Endler and Parker (1990) in the Polish adaptation by Szczepaniak, Strelau, and Wrześniewski (1996); the I-E at Work, a measure of locus of control adapted by Gliszczyńska (1990); and two tests of her own construction, the Social Support at Work Scale and the Stressful Situations at Work Scale.

Korczyńska's findings have been discussed comprehensively in her doctoral dissertation (2001; see also Korczyńska, 2004). Here I shall focus only on those themes that interest us most from the point of view of the regulative function of temperament and its relationships with staff burnout.

The preliminary findings concerning the relationships between the different temperament traits and the three syndromes of burnout are presented in Table 6.5. As we can see in this table, all the studied temperament traits except sensory sen-

---

[5] When she began her study, Korczyńska did not have access to Pasikowski's (2000) authorized adaptation of the MBI, but it must be pointed out that Noworol's and Pasikowski's adaptations do not differ significantly.

Table 6.5 Coefficients of Pearson correlation between burnout syndromes and temperament traits for prison workers ($N = 672$)

Temperament trait	Emotional exhaustion	Personal accomplishment	Depersonalization
Briskness	-0.17*	0.23*	-0.14*
Perseveration	0.26*	-0.11*	0.19*
Sensory sensitivity	-0.07	0.11*	-0.06
Emotional reactivity	0.37*	-0.25*	0.25*
Endurance	-0.36*	0.25*	-0.24*
Activity	-0.21*	0.23*	-0.16*

Note. *p < 0.01. From "Temperamentalny czynnik ryzyka wypalenia zawodowego na przykładzie pracowników służby więziennej" [Temperament Risk Factor of Professional Burnout in Prison Service Personnel] by J. Korczyńska, 2004. In J. Strelau (Ed.), *Osobowość a ekstremalny stres*, p. 327. Copyright 2004 by Gdańskie Wydawnictwo Psychologiczne. Reprinted with permission.

sitivity correlate significantly—albeit weakly or moderately—with the three syndromes of staff burnout. In contrast to the Emotional Exhaustion and Depersonalization scales, high scores on the Personal Accomplishment scale imply lack of burnout and hence low scores on this scale mean that the burnout syndrome is present.

As we expected, emotional reactivity and perseveration correlate positively with emotional exhaustion and depersonalization, whereas endurance, activity, and briskness correlate negatively with these burnout syndromes. The link between temperament and reduced personal accomplishment is not so consistent because, as we can see from the data, high scores on the Briskness, Endurance, and Activity scales correlate with lack of reduced personal accomplishment and this is quite logical. But the positive correlation between emotional reactivity and high lack of reduced personal accomplishment is hard to explain theoretically. In general, the pattern of relationships between temperament traits and the syndromes of staff burnout is consistent with the postulates of the Regulative Theory of Temperament because it has emerged in those situations where the individual incurs psychological costs of functioning in highly stimulating conditions.

In order to find out how the temperament structures outlined above—encompassing three traits relating to energetic stimulation processing—are linked to burnout syndromes, Korczyńska divided her respondents into two groups, taking the median as her criterion. She did so separately for each of the three temperament traits and obtained eight structural configurations of temperament. She then investigated their relationships with the respective burnout syndromes by means of analyses of variance. The results of these analyses are presented in Table 6.6.

Table 6.6 Eight structural configurations of temperament related to three syndromes of burnout

No.	Group	Emotional exhaustion	Personal accomplishment	Depersonalization
I	Low AC Low ER Low EN (N = 66)	30.08	34.52	16.47
II	Low AC Low ER High EN (N = 72)	26.52	37.31	14.19
III	High AC Low ER Low EN (N = 64)	28.83	37.03	15.53
IV	*High AC* *Low ER* *High EN* *(N = 162)*	*24.96*	*39.45*	*13.67*
V	**Low AC** **High ER** **Low EN** (N = 171)	**36.90**	**33.65**	**18.56**
VI	Low AC High ER High EN (N = 30)	30.35	33.37	17.20
VII	High AC High ER Low EN (N = 84)	33.73	35.62	17.18
VIII	High AC High ER High EN (N = 23)	32.91	28.56	14.00
F		15.50*	6.75*	8.50*

Note. ER = emotional reactivity; EN = endurance; AC = activity. *$p < 0.01$. Division of groups is based on median scores: high scores = $\geq Me$; low scores = $< Me$; AK – Me = 9.5; RE – Me = 9.0; WT – Me = 10.0. Configuration of temperament traits illustrating low energetic stimulation processing (melancholic) is indicated by boldface type and the one illustrating high energetic stimulation processing (sanguine) is indicated by italics. From "Temperamentalny czynnik ryzyka wypalenia zawodowego na przykładzie pracowników służby więziennej" [Temperament Risk Factor of Professional Burnout in Prison Service Personnel] by J. Korczyńska, 2004. In J. Strelau (Ed.), *Osobowość a ekstremalny stres*, p. 329. Copyright 2004 by Gdańskie Wydawnictwo Psychologiczne. Reprinted with permission.

Assuming that Korczyńska's respondents work in conditions that require considerable resistance to highly stimulating stressors, it was predicted that the temperament structure with poor stimulation-processing capacity would (under these circumstances) be a risk factor for burnout. This is the "melancholic" temperament, which has poor endurance, is very reactive emotionally, and is inactive. On the other hand, the temperament structure that has high stimulation-processing capacity, represented by men and women who are enduring, emotionally nonreactive, and very active (the "sanguine" temperament), should act as a protective "buffer" against burnout. Of the eight temperament structures presented in Table 6.6, the group representing the temperament with the poorest stimulation-processing capacity (group V) scored highest on emotional exhaustion and depersonalization (and had intermediate scores—neither very low nor very high—on personal accomplishment), thus confirming the hypothesis that this temperament structure is a TRF for staff burnout. The "sanguine" temperament, in turn (high activity, high endurance, and low emotional reactivity; group IV) obtained scores indicating the lowest level of all three burnout syndromes compared with the seven other temperament structures. In other words, this temperament structure can be viewed as a buffer protecting against burnout.

One more conspicuous pattern of results is worth mentioning. If we look at all four structural configurations of temperament that include high emotional reactivity (the structures represented by groups V–VIII), a sign of poor emotional resistance, we find that the burnout syndrome is most pronounced in these groups. This result suggests that emotional reactivity may be a particularly potent risk factor for people working in the prison setting.

Korczyńska subjected her data to cluster analysis to discover whether the specific configuration of studied variables was conducive to burnout or immunity against burnout. By applying the k-means method, she obtained nine clusters (see Table 6.7) containing six variables: burnout, temperament traits, coping with stress, locus of control, social support, and stressor intensity.

Two of the nine clusters are typical for intense burnout, which is expressed in emotional exhaustion and depersonalization; reduced personal accomplishment has a developmental dynamic that is independent of the two remaining syndromes of burnout (see Leiter, 1993; section 6.3.2.1). In Table 6.7 the configuration of burnout syndromes illustrating the highest level of this variable is indicated by boldface type, whereas the configuration for the lowest level of burnout is indicated by italics. As we can see, compared with the remaining clusters, high burnout (clusters M_1 and M_9) goes with high emotional reactivity, low endurance, and low activity. It also goes with emotion-oriented coping style with a high ratio of expected support to received support, external locus of control, and high stressor ratings. To a certain extent, an opposite configuration of variables is found for syndromes that are indicative of low burnout (clusters M_2 and M_5). Compared with the remaining clusters, these clusters represent low emotional reactivity

Table 6.7 Cluster analysis illustrating specific configurations of studied variables conducive to burnout or immunity against burnout in prison service personnel

Variable	M_1 (113)	M_2 (88)	M_3 (4)	M_4 (31)	M_5 (91)	M_6 (107)	M_7 (76)	M_8 (88)	M_9 (74)	F^*
Burnout										
Emotional burnout	**38.59**	*21.04*	22.75	29.90	*23.92*	32.78	24.76	33.48	**38.54**	31.57
Personal accomplishment	34.58	*38.05*	41.00	35.52	*40.93*	34.60	40.93	32.30	**33.23**	11.94
Depersonalization	**20.35**	*12.02*	13.50	15.94	*11.66*	16.83	12.86	17.50	**20.12**	27.17
Temperament										
Emotional reactivity	**11.15**	*6.37*	3.00	9.10	*7.24*	9.93	7.71	10.13	**10.69**	13.54
Endurance	**8.29**	*12.21*	15.50	10.39	*11.69*	9.16	11.54	9.34	**8.18**	9.94
Activity	**8.23**	*9.74*	15.25	10.50	*11.39*	8.77	11.07	8.84	**7.99**	7.69
Locus of control	13.16	*17.72*	18.75	14.29	*17.42*	12.85	16.12	12.25	**12.20**	19.45
Emotion-oriented coping	**46.77**	*36.12*	28.25	41.45	*38.63*	43.68	38.88	43.81	**44.70**	16.73
Task-oriented coping	**58.34**	*60.25*	60.50	57.32	*58.57*	57.92	61.46	52.22	**58.46**	10.74
Avoidance	**43.46**	*36.75*	36.25	42.26	*42.30*	40.19	39.17	42.37	**40.65**	6.05
Social support										
Expected support	**40.22**	*38.67*	18.50	30.32	*46.29*	42.38	53.39	29.47	**50.58**	119.85
Received support	**31.21**	*32.91*	26.00	39.71	*46.08*	26.56	35.82	29.08	**21.46**	87.50
Stressors-general score	**36.73**	*22.01*	25.75	33.71	*24.55*	34.51	27.44	33.58	**41.12**	41.47

Note. *All F scores are significant ($p < 0.01$). Number of subjects representing the separate clusters is in parenthesis. Social support relates to family members and friends. Locus of control = general score of the I-E at Work scale. The configuration of burnout symptoms illustrating the highest level is indicated by boldface type and the lowest level of these symptoms is indicated by italics. Because of the small number of subjects representing cluster M_3 this configuration of burnout symptoms was not taken into account. Adapted from "Temperamentalny czynnik ryzyka wypalenia zawodowego na przykładzie pracowników służby więziennej" [Temperament Risk Factor of Professional Burnout in Prison Service Personnel] by J. Korczyńska, 2004. In J. Strelau (Ed.), *Osobowość a ekstremalny stres*, pp. 332–333. Copyright 2004 by Gdańskie Wydawnictwo Psychologiczne. Reprinted with permission.

combined with high endurance and high activity (activity is average in cluster M_2), internal locus of control, task-oriented coping (only cluster M_2), and low stressor ratings.

The results of the cluster analysis confirm the hypothesis that burnout measured in terms of emotional exhaustion and depersonalization is related to temperament. Also, the configurations of the remaining traits controlled in Korczyńska's study in the clusters indicating both high and low burnout are consistent with expectations and other findings reported in the literature. This approach to burnout research, based on the individual differences paradigm, has yielded outcomes that shed new light on the origins of this phenomenon; they strongly suggest that personality traits, mainly temperamental ones, play an important role in the development of staff burnout alongside such factors as stressful aspects of the situation and work organization.

Korczyńska's findings show very clearly that the configuration of temperament traits indicating poor stimulation-processing capacity is a temperament risk factor for staff burnout in the prison setting, which is surely very stressing. Prison functionaries rank among the top ten most stressful professions, largely because of the specific nature of relationships between the staff and convicts. This applies particularly strongly to those employees who have direct contact with the prisoners—that is, those who work in the security and detention departments (73.3 percent of the studied sample). Korczyńska (2001, 2004) discusses these occupational hazards at length. Her study demonstrates once again that temperament traits show up most conspicuously when people are functioning in difficult and highly stimulating situations.

The regulative function of temperament is clearest when the individual is in an extremely stressful situation such as a catastrophe or disaster (see section 6.3). These independent stressors will be discussed in the next chapter.

Chapter 7

Temperament and extreme stress

D isasters and catastrophes, both extreme stressors, have afflicted humanity since the beginning of time. Until recently their consequences—such as loss of life and property or threatened survival—were known only to the local community because there were no mass media by which to publicize them. For some time, however, we have been aware of the range and consequences of disasters throughout the world. Veisaeth (1995) compiled statistics of these life-events. According to his estimates, one billion men, women, and children experienced disasters or catastrophes of one kind or another between 1967 and 1991 alone, resulting in the death of over seven million people. According to the most recent data collected by Fran Norris and her collaborators (Somasundaram et al., 2003), every year 197 catastrophes occur throughout the world. These include earthquakes, floods, hurricanes, fires, and technological disasters. One particular type of catastrophe that has not been included in these statistics is the proliferation of world terrorism (see Ursano, Fullerton, & Norwood, 2003)—although we know that nearly three thousand lives were lost in the tragedy in New York on 11 September 2001.

In Poland awareness of the consequences of disasters and the need to counteract them did not mature until this phenomenon occurred on an unprecedented scale. In 1997 an enormous flood, known as the Flood of the Century, devastated our country. Massive areas in southern Poland were affected. More than 150,000 people suffered, mainly from loss of property and threats to physical survival; 48 people lost their lives. Heitzman (1998) reported that about 20,000 people required psychiatric and psychological assistance. In the aftermath of these events, the Scientific Research Committee—encouraged by the psychological community—announced a competition for a project called Men and Women in the Face of Disaster. This was the first competition ever to be commissioned by the committee. A team under my supervision participated in this project. Bogdan Zawadzki, Włodzimierz Oniszczenko, Beata Kozak, and Adam Sobolewski made major contributions and my graduate students at Warsaw University and the Silesian University also did their part.[1]

---

[1] Studies of victims of the Flood of the Century within the project Men and Women in the Face of Disaster were also conducted by psychologists from the Institute of Psychology, Opole University, under the supervision of Krzysztof Kaniasty. The results of these studies are reported extensively in two monographs (see Bokszczanin, 2003; Kaniasty, 2003).

This chapter gives a concise presentation of the results of these studies and their sequels.

If we look at Propositions 9 and 10 (see chapter 4) of the Regulative Theory of Temperament (RTT) and the temperament-stress model presented in Figure 6.1, we shall see that it is quite justified to join the school of research on the psychological aspects of the consequences of disasters. Our studies were based on the belief, also well documented in the literature (see, e.g., Lauterbach, 2006; Lauterbach & Vrana, 2001; McFarlane, 1989, 2006; McFarlane, Clayer, & Bookless, 1997), that if we want to understand the psychological consequences of trauma, we cannot limit ourselves to analysis of the extent, intensity, or duration of the disaster itself or the social context within which the victim of trauma functions afterward (e.g., the role of social support). We must also consider the role of the individual's psychological makeup including individual differences. Therefore our research focused largely—though not exclusively—on the role of temperament as a codeterminant of the psychological consequences of trauma.

When we began to work on this problem, we had no instrument with which to measure these consequences, which have been defined since the early 1980s as post-traumatic stress disorder (PTSD; APA, 1980, 1994). At the time we did not have access to the only PTSD assessment inventory that had been adapted in Poland by Krzysztof Kaniasty (2003), the Revised Civilian Mississippi Scale (RCMS) originally developed by Norris and Perilla (1996). Hence drawing on our rich experience in the construction of original psychometric instruments assessing individual differences and the adaptation of existing ones (see, e.g., Strelau, 1995c), we decided to construct our own inventory. The first section of this chapter presents this work.

7.1
Construction of the PTSD Inventory as a point of departure for the study of the relationships between temperament and the psychological consequences of disasters

Experts who have developed instruments assessing PTSD have taken the description of this disorder first provided in the *Diagnostic and Statistical Manual of Mental Disorders* (DSM-III), published by the American Psychiatric Association, as their point of departure. In this manual threatening life-events (such as the threat of loss of life, health, or property or the death of another) are viewed as etiological factors for PTSD and labeled criterion A (see APA, 1980). Twelve symptoms of the disorder have been distinguished and divided into three groups, based on three criteria: obsessive recall of the trauma (criterion B); obsessive avoidance and numbness (criterion C); and persistent hyperarousal (criterion D). The revised edition of DSM-III (APA, 1987) includes the subjective experiences of fear, terror, and helplessness in addition to objective life-events as etiological determinants of PTSD. This addition was probably made under the influence of Lazarus's phenomenological-cognitive theory of stress (Lazarus & Folkman, 1984), which is popular among psychiatrists and clinical psychologists. The number of symptoms in this version has also been increased to seventeen but the number and quality of the three criteria remain unchanged. The next edition of the manual, DSM-IV, introduced only minimal modifications in the description of PTSD. This disorder and its assessment have been widely discussed (see, e.g., APA, 2000; Foa, Keane, & Friedman, 2000; Hobfoll & de Vries, 1994; Roussis & Wells, 2006).

Most instruments used to assess PTSD have been constructed by psychiatrists and have a structured interview format. Another common element is that they faithfully adhere to the three DSM criteria, assess them on the basis of seventeen (previously twelve) symptoms, and measure either frequency or intensity of these criteria and symptoms. This pattern began to weaken, however, when researchers began constructing questionnaires based on psychometric criteria to assess PTSD (see Strelau et al., 2002). Although these questionnaires also assumed the criteria and symptoms provided in successive editions of the DSM as their point of departure, the number of factors (which should be viewed as equivalent to the criteria provided in the manuals) varies from two to more than three. This is because the empirical data were factor-analyzed. For example, the RCMS by Norris and Perrilla (1996) has four subscales that correspond to the four factors extracted in the process of factor analysis: Intrusion, Avoidance, Numbing, and Arousal. Research based initially on seventeen (twelve) PTSD symptoms often led the constructors of questionnaires to measure this disorder to a two-factor solution. For instance, the Impact Event Scale (Horowitz, Wilner, & Alvarez, 1979) measures intrusion and avoidance. A group of Canadian researchers (Taylor et al., 1998) also obtained a two-factor solution when they administered three universally recognized tests of PTSD. The factors they obtained are intrusion-avoidance and hyperarousal-numbing. When these factors are correlated, they give a general factor suggesting that the structure of PTSD is hierarchical.

Taking a more comprehensive review of the assessment tools used to measure PTSD as our point of departure, our team set out to construct two questionnaires—a factorial one and a clinical one—with which to assess the post-traumatic symptoms. A detailed account of this work is given elsewhere (see Strelau et al., 2002; Zawadzki, Strelau, Bieniek et al., 2002; Zawadzki et al., 2004). The research was based on the following rationale:

• Both questionnaires—the factorial one and the clinical one—should refer to the defining criteria and symptoms of PTSD provided in DSM-IV.

- PTSD is a multidimensional construct; therefore if we want to determine its structure, we must take as our starting point the questionnaire items on whose basis the factors have been identified in the exploratory factor analysis—hence the factorial version of the questionnaire.

- According to the definition of PTSD in DSM-IV, the instrument that will assess this disorder must take all the criteria and symptoms into consideration—thus forming the basis for the clinical version of the questionnaire.

- The factorial version of the questionnaire should be used for quantitative assessment only—that is, assessment of PTSD with lack of the phenomenon at one end of a continuum and high intensity of the phenomenon at the other.

- In addition to quantitative diagnosis, the clinical version of the questionnaire should also enable qualitative diagnosis of PTSD.

- Assessment of trauma-induced psychological disorders should focus on two time spans—within a few weeks of the trauma and not less than three months after the trauma. The first assessment should diagnose the acute form of PTSD and the second assessment should diagnose various stages of chronic PTSD.

The list of PTSD symptoms that may be viewed as defining components of the three basic criteria (B, C, and D) of PTSD has been widely published, including by our team (see, e.g., Strelau et al., 2002; Zawadzki, Strelau, Bieniek et al., 2002; Zawadzki et al., 2004). To facilitate better understanding of the nature of PTSD and the relationships between this syndrome—as described in DSM-IV (APA, 2000, pp. 467–468)—and various dimensions of personality in general and temperament in particular, the symptoms are listed below.

Criterion B: The traumatic event is persistently reexperienced.

- Reccurent and intrusive distressing recollections of the event.
- Recurrent distressing dreams of the event.
- Acting or feeling as if the traumatic event were recurring.
- Intense psychological distress at exposure to internal or external cues that symbolize or resemble the traumatic event.
- Physiological reactivity on exposure to internal or external cues that resemble the traumatic event.

Criterion C: Persistent avoidance of stimuli associated with the trauma and numbing of general responsiveness.

- Efforts to avoid thoughts, feelings, or conversations associated with the trauma.
- Efforts to avoid activities, places, or people that arouse recollections of the trauma.

- Inability to recall an important aspect of the trauma.
- Markedly diminished interest or participation in significant activities.
- Feeling of detachment or estrangement from others.
- Restricted range of affect.
- Sense of a foreshortened future.

Criterion D: Persistent symptoms of increased arousal.

- Difficulty falling or staying asleep.
- Irritability or outbursts of anger.
- Difficulty concentrating.
- Hypervigilance.
- Exaggerated startle response.

When we constructed our PTSD inventory, we included one additional criterion—consequences of symptoms in the form of clinically meaningful stress or disruption of social, occupational, or other functions.

- Psychosomatic disturbances.
- Specific ways of coping with stress.
- Changes in personality.

The initial pool consisted of 444 items generated by our research team (including graduate students). All items were rated by expert judges who were requested to assign them unequivocally to the DSM-IV criteria, reject repetitious items, and correct any linguistic deficiencies. This procedure resulted in a reduced list of 138 items. Next this item list was used in a pilot study of 76 individuals (including 45 females) aged 15–76 ($M = 41.4$; $SD = 13.93$) who had experienced the flood. A four-point scale of symptom frequency was adopted (from 1 = never experienced the symptom to 4 = always experienced the symptom). This stage resulted in rejection of an additional 23 substantively or psychometrically flawed items and 10 items constituting a separate Social Support scale, thus leaving a final pool of 105 items. All the symptoms except criterion C, "loss of memory of the events," were represented by two to eight items: 34 items in criterion B; 32 items in criterion C; 23 items in criterion D; and 16 items for the additional criterion. This pool was the point of departure for construction of the two versions of the PTSD questionnaire. From this point on, however, a different procedure was adopted for each questionnaire.

In accordance with our assumptions, the clinical version of the PTSD questionnaire (PTSD-C) was to serve largely practical purposes. Hence the studies of the clinical version and their outcomes will be omitted here. Suffice it to say that construction of this version was based on the Item Response Theory (see Hullin, Drasgow, & Parson, 1983) and a detailed account of the construction procedure can be found elsewhere (Zawadzki, Strelau, Bieniek et al., 2002).

7.1.1. The factorial version of the PTSD questionnaire

The studies on which construction of the factorial version of the PTSD questionnaire (PTSD-F) was based were conducted on a group of flood victims living in the Racibórz, Kłodzko, and Kędzierzyn-Koźle regions, which had suffered seriously in the Flood of the Century. This group, henceforth called the "construction" sample, consisted of 396 individuals aged 13–85 (M = 35.8; SD = 15.78), including 207 females aged 13–78 (M = 36.8; SD = 15.33) and 185 males aged 14–85 (M = 34.7; SD = 16.23). Information on gender is missing for four respondents.

The sample was tested two years after the flood. All respondents filled in various questionnaires including the experimental version of the PTSD questionnaire. This questionnaire had 105 randomly arranged items and a four-point response scale. All respondents who completed this questionnaire were requested to rate each item for the frequency of reactions or behaviors indicative of a particular symptom "just after the flood" and "two years after the flood"—that is, within the last few weeks of the testing. It must be stressed that the first of the two ratings (just after the flood) is retrospective and may be inaccurate due to imperfect memory of the experiences at that time and later experiences relating directly or indirectly to the trauma.

Work on the construction of the questionnaire was based on the assumption that all symptoms are strongly correlated (the clinical diagnosis of PTSD rests on this assumption), but on the other hand—despite their covariance—the symptoms belonging to the separate categories should also have their own specific content characteristics. In other words, in addition to the general (global) assessment of PTSD intensity, the questionnaire should also enable assessment of specific dimensions (factors) within the structure of the PTSD syndrome. Authors of psychometric instruments measuring PTSD who have based their work on factor analysis have provided the rationale for this procedure (see Brett & Ostroff, 1985; Cordova et al., 1995; Horowitz, Wilner, & Alvarez, 1979; Taylor et al., 1998).

The data were analyzed using the Principal Components method, Cattell's scree test, and the Oblimin oblique rotation on the assumption that the factors that emerged would not be orthogonal. The analysis, whose details are discussed elsewhere (see Strelau et al., 2002), led to the identification of two factors: intrusion-hyperarousal (I-H; factor I) and avoidance-numbing (A-N; factor II). These factors emerged for both testing situations, "just after the flood" and "two years after the flood." Intrusion-arousal consists of items from criteria B and D and typical items illustrating its content are:

- I feel sick when I hear about similar tragic events.
- I find it hard to stop recalling past events.
- Everything associated with the experienced event terrifies me.

Avoidance-numbing consists of items from criterion C and typical items illustrating its diagnostic characteristics are:

- I feel that most things have become unimportant to me.
- I avoid any mention of what happened.
- I feel that I have nothing to look forward to in life.

Many items had high factor loadings in both factors. In order to eliminate these items, another criterion (in addition to factor loading) was adopted—that is, the size of criterion difference between factors (see Zakrzewska, 1994). When this procedure was applied, the number of items meeting both psychometric criteria was reduced to fifteen per factor. Corrected "item-total" correlations (CITC) ranged from 0.65 to 0.90 for factor I (I-H) and from 0.45 to 0.82 for factor II (A-N). Analogous coefficients for a selection of thirty items relating to the general (global) diagnosis of PTSD range from 0.43 to 0.77.

This procedure resulted in the construction of the factorial version of the PTSD questionnaire. This questionnaire has thirty items with fifteen per scale (Intrusion-Hyperarousal and Avoidance-Numbing). As we assumed, the two scales are significantly correlated—0.60 (just after the flood) and 0.57 (two years after the flood). Depending on the specific nature of the study concerned, the PTSD-F has been used either to assess the two dimensions or general PTSD, in which case the thirty-item pool is treated as a General Scale. It must be emphasized very strongly that the psychometric instrument constructed according to the adopted procedure does not diagnose PTSD unequivocally, although that is what clinicians would like it to do. This is because the questionnaire rests on the assumption that the intensity of PTSD symptoms may be viewed as a dimension with lack of PTSD symptoms (resistant to this disorder) at one extreme and intense symptoms at the other (see Figure 7.1). This instrument corresponds to the idea emphatically voiced by Bonanno (2004) that trauma may lead to a variety of consequences. In some individuals the traumatic experience may lead to post-traumatic symptoms consequences, whereas in other individuals resistance to trauma may develop. Ruscio, Ruscio, and Keane (2002) argue in favor of the existence of latent PTSD structures whose symptoms are not intense enough to diagnose PTSD. Other researchers (Anthony, Lonigan, & Hecht, 1999; Brewin, Dalgleish, & Joseph, 1996) in turn suggest that there is a subtle line between ordinary reactions to stressful situations and the disorder identified as PTSD.

The questionnaire was subjected to a number of psychometric procedures in order to assess its psychometric goodness. A selection of the results of these procedures will be discussed in the following section.

7.1.2. Studies of the psychometric goodness of the PTSD-F

The basic (construction) sample (N = 396) was used to estimate the reliability of the two PTSD-F scales, I-H and A-N, as well as the General Scale. The Cronbach alpha coefficient was computed for the whole sample, separately for men and women, and also for three cohorts selected from the whole sample (under 20, 20–49, and over 49 years of age), separately for the testing directly after the flood and two years later. This procedure was introduced in order to prove whether reliability of the PTSD scales is consistent across age, gender, and time of assessment. A total of 36 Cronbach alpha coefficients were obtained; their values ranged from 0.89 to 0.96. When the coefficients were corrected for age, gender, and both these demographic variables together, the original results were practically replicated and varied from 0.88 to 0.96.

The two-factor structure of PTSD, determined on the basis of studies of the construction sample, was subjected to further testing. Three years after the flood, PTSD was assessed in 179 flood victims—91 females and 88 males aged 12–75 (M = 37.1; SD = 14.45)—from the Racibórz area. These individuals had not been tested before.

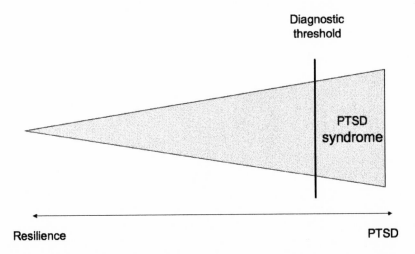

Figure 7.1. The dimensional approach to assessment of PTSD intensity. From "Temperament as Predictor of Maladaptive Behavior Under Extreme Stress: The Polish Studies of Natural Disasters" by J. Strelau, M. Kaczmarek, and B. Zawadzki, 2006. In Q. Jing, M. R. Rosenzweig, G. d'Ydewalle, H. Zhang, H.-C. Chen, and K. Zhang (Eds.), *Progress in Psychological Science around the World: Vol. 2. Social and Applied Issues*, p. 142. Copyright 2006 by Psychology Press. Reprinted with permission.

This sample, which we will call the "verification" sample, was used to test the factor structure of PTSD. The same procedure was used to identify the factors as in the construction sample. The results are almost perfect replicas of the original factor findings. Additionally, in both samples the factors tap identical psychological contents—as illustrated by the high Tucker coefficients of factor similarity, which range from 0.978 to 0.994 for I-H and from 0.961 to 0.992 for A-N.

A subgroup of 102 flood victims (including 55 women) was isolated from the construction sample and subjected once again to an assessment of PTSD. This step shed more light on the dynamic of PTSD at three points of time—just after the flood, two years after the flood, and three years after the flood. Figure 7.2 shows that this dynamic corroborates the pattern reported in the literature (see Kaniasty, 2003; Klonowicz, 2000) and hence supports the validity of the PTSD-F. PTSD is most pronounced directly after the trauma and its symptoms are least evident three years after the flood. This pattern emerged for both subscales (I-H and A-N) and also for the General Scale. The differences between the means for all three diagnostic moments are significant.

Four years after the Flood of the Century, Poland was once again devastated by a serious flood in the northern part of the country. We tested the victims in sever-

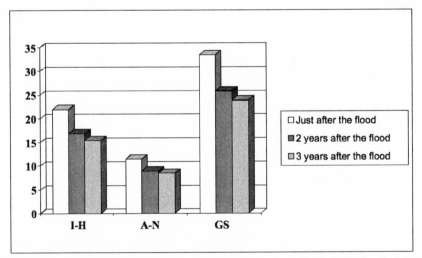

Figure 7.2. The temporal dynamics of PTSD symptom intensity in 1997 flood victims assessed just after the flood, two years, and three years after the flood. I-H = Intrusion-Hyperarousal; A-N = Avoidance-Numbing; GS = General Scale. From "Kwestionariusz PTSD—wersja czynnikowa (PTSD-C). Konstrukcja narzędzia do diagnozy głównych wymiarów zespołu stresu pourazowego" [The Factorial Version of the PTSD Inventory (PTSD-F): The Development of a Questionnaire Aimed at Assessing Basic Dimensions of Post-Traumatic Stress Disorder] by J. Strelau, B. Zawadzki, W. Oniszczenko, and A. Sobolewski. 2002, *Przegląd Psychologiczny, 45*, p. 167. Copyright 2002 by Polish Psychological Association. Reprinted with permission.

al districts of the City of Gdańsk (Strelau et al., 2004). The sample, which was tested three months after the flood, numbered 422 individuals (including 237 females)
aged 9–84 ($M = 35.3$; $SD = 14.96$). Combined with the studies reported above, this
study provided much new information on the validity of the PTSD-F.

We also studied the psychological consequences of trauma experienced by
coalminers in a mining catastrophe. This study was run by Agnieszka Kowalczyk
(2000) on 52 men aged 23–54 ($M = 37.4$; $SD = 7.41$) within from several months
to two years of the accident. The reliability parameters for both PTSD-F subscales and the General Scale were almost identical with those obtained for the
flood victims. The correlations between scales I-H and A-N are also comparable.

In order to determine whether the factor structure of PTSD symptoms that we
had repeatedly obtained was specific for flood victims, we combined the scores
of the miners and the verification sample of flood victims ($N = 179$), having first
standardized the scores separately for each group. We then factor-analyzed these
data once again, employing the same procedure that we applied to the construction sample. The results fully corroborated the previous structure of PTSD symptoms.

Once we had gathered empirical material from several samples of trauma victims, we were able to conduct several collective analyses, all of which yielded
convincing evidence of the validity of the PTSD-F. This work is discussed at
length elsewhere (Zawadzki et al., 2004). A meta-analysis of the data on the
effects of demographic variables on the intensity of PTSD symptoms collected
from 60,000 victims of various kinds of disasters and catastrophes demonstrated
beyond doubt that these symptoms are more intense in women and in individuals
with lower socioeconomic status (SES). They are also reportedly more pronounced in children than adults (Norris et al., 2002b).

Table 7.1 shows the relationships between PTSD symptoms and such demographic variables as gender, age, and education (treated here as an SES indicator).
The figures in the table are cumulated scores for four samples: the construction
sample ($N = 396$), the verification sample ($N = 179$), the Gdańsk flood victims ($N
= 422$), and the miners ($N = 52$). In order to submit the data to global analysis, the
correlation coefficients were first transformed into Fisher z values and then their
means were calculated.

As we predicted, the intensity of PTSD symptoms is higher in women, older
respondents (as already demonstrated in the study of the construction sample),
and the less educated. The intensification of PTSD symptoms in the elderly found
in our studies contradicts our expectation and is inconsistent with American findings (see Kaniasty, 2003; Norris, Friedman, & Watson, 2002a), probably
because—at least in Poland—older people have fewer resources with which to
cope with stress effectively (Hobfoll, 1989). Education proved to be the weakest
predictor of PTSD, probably because our samples were rather homogeneous
(most respondents had primary education). Also, education is only one element

Table 7.1 Correlations between PTSD and demographic characteristics (gender, age, and education): Aggregated/cumulated results from four samples ($N = 1,049$)

| | Time of PTSD diagnosis | | | | | |
| | Few weeks after trauma | | | Present state (1–3 years after trauma) | | |
Variable	I–H	A–N	General	I–H	A–N	General
Gender	-0.36	-0.17	-0.30	-0.33	-0.15	-0.28
Age	0.25	0.19	0.24	0.29	0.19	0.27
Education	-0.10	-0.08	-0.08	-0.16	-0.08	-0.13

Note. I-H = Intrusion-Hyperarousal; A-N = Avoidance-Numbing; General = General PTSD-F Scale. Education was divided into higher (high school and college) and lower (primary education); in the case of gender and education, the coefficient *Eta* was applied. Adapted from "Diagnoza zespołu stresu pourazowego. Charakterystyka psychometryczna wersji czynnikowej i wersji klinicznej kwestionariusza PTSD" [The Diagnosis of PTSD: Psychometric Characteristics of the Factorial and Clinical Version of the PTSD Inventory] by B. Zawadzki, J. Strelau, W. Oniszczenko, A. Sobolewski, and A. Bieniek, 2004. In J. Strelau (Ed.), *Osobowość a ekstremalny stres*, p. 220. Copyright 2004 by Gdańskie Wydawnictwo Psychologiczne. Reprinted with permission.

of socioeconomic status (the other one is income) and we know from the American research that SES is strongly related to PTSD.

In two samples of flood victims in which PTSD was assessed three years after the trauma (the verification sample [$N = 179$] and a second sample that was tested twice [$N = 102$]), which we shall analyze conjointly here and call the "Silesian" sample, and also in the sample of flood victims from Gdańsk, trauma intensity (TI) was measured at two different points in time—three months after the trauma, then again three years after the trauma. The following measures of trauma were used: threat to life, material losses, financial problems, housing problems, status, and material situation. In accordance with DSM-IV and other extensive empirical findings (for a review see Kaniasty, 2003; Klonowicz, 2000; Norris, Friedman, & Watson 2002a; Norris et al., 2002b), a positive relationship was predicted between trauma intensity and psychological consequences of the trauma. This pattern also emerged consistently in our studies (see Table 7.2): without exception, all 33 correlation coefficients showing the relationship between the trauma and the intensity of post-traumatic symptoms are positive. This finding is another argument supporting the validity of the PTSD-F.

Our publications (see Strelau et al., 2002; Zawadzki et al., 2004) also provide many other arguments supporting the validity of this questionnaire. I shall not critique them here because it seems that the data presented in this section sufficiently attest to the validity of our diagnostic instrument. The next section will focus on the role of individual differences, mainly temperament, in the modera-

Table 7.2 Relationship between trauma and intensity of post-traumatic symptoms

	Time of PTSD diagnosis					
	Just/directly after trauma[1] and 3 months later[2]			3 years after trauma[1]		
Trauma characteristic	I–H	A–N	General	I–H	A–N	General
Threat to life	0.29*	0.22*	0.28*	0.29*	0.20*	0.28*
	0.21*	0.18*	0.21*	—	—	—
Material losses	0.28*	0.25*	0.28*	0.27*	0.23	0.28*
	0.21*	0.18*	0.22*	—	—	—
Financial problems	—	—	—	0.43*	0.46*	0.48*
Housing problems	—	—	—	0.37*	0.39	0.41*
Material status	0.28*	0.32*	0.32*	0.33*	0.37*	0.38*
and situation	0.18*	0.09*	0.15*	—	—	—

Note. For abbreviations see Table 7.1. [1]Data from Silesian sample ($N = 179 + N = 102$); [2]data from Gdańsk sample ($N = 422$). Upper row: coefficients of correlation for the Silesian sample; lower row: coefficients of correlation for the Gdańsk sample. In both samples in which PTSD symptoms were measured directly or three months after trauma, housing problems were not taken into account. In the Silesian sample three years after trauma, the measure of material status and situation was lacking. Adapted from "Diagnoza zespołu stresu pourazowego. Charakterystyka psychometryczna wersji czynnikowej i wersji klinicznej kwestionariusza PTSD" [The Diagnosis of PTSD: Psychometric Characteristics of the Factorial and Clinical Version of the PTSD Inventory] by B. Zawadzki, J. Strelau, W. Oniszczenko, A. Sobolewski, and A. Bieniek, 2004. In J. Strelau (Ed.), *Osobowość a ekstremalny stres*, p. 231. Copyright 2004 by Gdańskie Wydawnictwo Psychologiczne. Reprinted with permission.

tion of the relationship between the trauma experience and its psychological consequences measured in terms of PTSD symptoms.

7.2
Temperament as a moderator of the relationship between experienced trauma and its psychological consequences

As I wrote in the introduction to this chapter, our research on the role of temperament and other variables as moderators of the relationship between the trauma experience and its psychological consequences was conducted within the framework of a project called Men and Women in the Face of Disaster. This project, on which we worked between 1999 and 2002, was the point of departure for the research conducted by Bogdan Zawadzki and his collaborators and also under my supervision—in both cases with the major contribution of Magdalena Kaczmarek. This later work also focused on other populations (e.g., fire victims), new problems that emerged during subsequent studies, and the cross-cultural perspective, and involved researchers who study extreme stress and its consequences in other European countries.

Research on trauma and its psychological consequences, and the contribution of individual differences as a moderator of this relationship, is a relatively new area of investigation. For many years researchers were strongly convinced that trauma intensity is the principal—if not the only—determinant of PTSD (see Lauterbach & Vrana, 2001; Ozer et al., 2003). What follows is a brief review of research highlighting the role of individual differences.

7.2.1. The role of individual differences in the moderation of the trauma-psychological consequences relationship: A research review

As Bogdan Zawadzki and I pointed out in an article in the *Polish Psychological Bulletin* (Strelau & Zawadzki, 2004), in recent years there has been an increasing number of publications on the determinants of PTSD in which the same tendency has emerged whatever the specific nature of the trauma. Specifically, more attention is being paid to the role of individual differences in susceptibility to exposure to traumatic events and the consequences of such events as expressed in the intensity, duration, and frequency of PTSD (see Lauterbach, 2006). The reason why researchers are showing increasing interest in individual differences as determinants of the psychological consequences of trauma due to extreme stressors (disasters, all sorts of catastrophes, terror, rape, physical violence, etc.) is that trauma intensity accounts for only part of the variance of PTSD or its symptoms, usually no more than 50 percent (see Lauterbach, 2006; Norris, Friedman, & Watson, 2002a; Ozer et al., 2003).

A pioneer of the use of the individual differences paradigm in PTSD research was Alexander McFarlane (1986, 1989). In one of his studies, conducted on firemen exposed to Australian bush fire (an extreme stressor), he found that neuroticism is one of the determinants of PTSD incidence irrespective of when PTSD is measured—directly after the disaster or later. The firemen were tested within four, eleven, and 29 months of the bush fire. Both variables directly relating to the disaster and pre- and post-traumatic variables were measured in this study. When pre-traumatic variables such as extraversion and neuroticism, the history of pre-traumatic mental disorder, or earlier traumatic experiences were analyzed, it was found that neuroticism was the most powerful predictor of PTSD symptoms. It was also found that the significance of neuroticism increased with time, whereas the contribution of the trauma itself to PTSD diminished with time.

Studies of PTSD in Vietnam War veterans also suggested that in addition to traumatic events relating to the war itself, biologically, psychologically, and socially determined individual vulnerability also affects the intensity of PTSD (Kulka et al., 1990).

Studies of vulnerability to PTSD and other determinants of this syndrome based on the individual differences paradigm have focused on many different phenomena and it would be difficult to mention all of them here (see Strelau & Klonowicz, 2006). For example, the role of gender (King et al., 1998), individual experiences (McFarlane, 1992), style of upbringing (Kulka et al., 1990), parental mental disease history (McFarlane, 1986), coping style (Spurrell & McFarlane, 1993), or personality traits (see Fauerbach et al., 2000) have all been investigated. In studies of the role of individual differences treated as moderators of the trauma-psychological consequences relationship, personality traits in general and temperament traits in particular have had a prominent place. The list of traits includes neuroticism, extraversion, sensation seeking, and hardiness (Davidson, Kudler, & Smith, 1987; Dekel et al., 2004; Lee et al., 1995; McFarlane, 1989, 1992; Pengilly & Dowd, 2000). Their moderating role in the trauma-psychological consequences relationship varies and depends largely on the underlying neurophysiological mechanisms. In general, those personality traits that typically accompany chronically reduced level of arousal (i.e., low arousability) act as buffers and reduce the impact of trauma caused by extreme stressors. Those personality traits, on the other hand, that accompany enhanced arousability (particularly neuroticism and anxiety) act as augmenters and amplify the effect of the traumatic experience. In their review of the literature, Schnurr and Vielhauer (2000) found that neuroticism in particular is a risk factor for PTSD.

The most remarkable study of personality predictors of PTSD is probably the one conducted by Lauterbach (2006; Lauterbach & Vrana, 2001). This researcher studied a sample of students who claimed to have experienced trauma. He controlled such personality variables as borderline personality disorder, antisocial personality disorder, sensation seeking, psychoticism, extraversion, and neuroticism (Eysenck's three superfactors) and treated all these variables as predictors of trauma intensity and retraumatization. His results suggest that personality variables explain just as much variance as trauma intensity—that is, over 40 percent of the variance of PTSD (Lauterbach & Vrana, 2001).

Although research to date has shown that the neuroticism-PTSD relationship is the most evident one, it has also been reported in the literature that PTSD is related to extraversion and conscientiousness (see Fauerbach et al., 2000; Talbot et al., 2000). Therefore in his next study, also conducted on students ($N = 566$), Lauterbach (2006) included the personality variables that are assessed by the NEO Personality Inventory–Revised. This personality questionnaire not only measures the Big Five personality factors (neuroticism, extraversion, openness to experience, conscientiousness, and agreeableness) but also the components of these factors. By conducting several regression analyses, Lauterbach was able to demonstrate that neuroticism, conscientiousness, and extraversion are predictors of PTSD intensity. When he further analyzed only the six components of neuroticism (hyperarousal, anxiety, depression, aggression/hostility, impulsiveness, and shyness), he found that they all predict PTSD symptoms.

Taking as our point of departure the abundant literature illustrating the role of individual differences in the relationship between experienced trauma and its psychological consequences, we designed a study to address (among other things) the moderating role of RTT traits in this relationship. This work will be discussed in the next section.

7.2.2. Our own studies of the role of temperament as a moderator of PTSD symptoms

Our research was based on the model of the relationships between temperament and various stress-related phenomena presented in chapter 6 (see Figure 6.1). However, as can be seen in Figure 7.3, this model was refined for the purpose of the present study.

Although our main concern in this study was the relationship between stressors and the consequences of the state of stress as modified by temperament traits, we

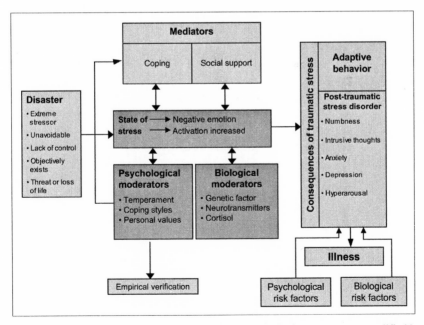

Figure 7.3. Disaster, an extreme stressor, and its psychological consequences modified by biological, psychological, and environmental variables.

also included several other personal and situational variables. As far as the former variables are concerned, we focused on coping styles (see Strelau & Zawadzki, 2006; Strelau et al., 2004). This variable will be discussed in the next chapter in the context of behavior genetics. We also studied the value system (Kaczmarek et al., 2003); biological factors, mainly the genetic determinants of vulnerability to PTSD (see chapter 8); and biochemical variables. In our first study, conducted on a group of victims of the Flood of the Century, we controlled the levels of neurotransmitters and cortisol. We did so on the assumption, based on the literature (see the review by Strelau, 1998), that cortisol is directly related to the state of stress and hence may be considered a measure of stress intensity. Dopamine (a neurotransmitter that regulates level of arousal) and serotonin (which regulates emotional processes) are also related to this state. Our results were negative (see Oniszczenko et al., 2002). The lack of any relationship between PTSD and the biochemical correlates of the state of stress that emerged from our study can probably be attributed to the fact that we did not measure these variables until two years after the trauma.

As far as situational variables are concerned, we studied social support (Miazga, 2001; Michałowska, 2001; Wróbel, 2001). However, our measure of social support based on a provisional five-item scale was psychometrically unsatisfactory and therefore I shall not present it here. Preliminary PTSD research convinced us that in order to account for the variance of trauma-related disorders, it is also necessary to measure the intensity of the experienced trauma and the consequences of prolonged trauma that do not show up until long after the disaster. From the very beginning, we concentrated not on individuals but on two-generation family members who experienced the flood, mainly because we wanted to measure the contribution of the additive genetic factor to the experienced consequences of trauma. This was possible due to the family study method used as one of the behavior genetic paradigms. Incidentally, we found that this research model also captures such family effects as the parental induction of PTSD intensity in children or the reciprocal induction of PTSD intensity by spouses.

This chapter will deal with four issues that are central to our studies of the psychological consequences of disasters: the relationships between PTSD and temperament traits (discussed in the next section); temperament and trauma as predictors of PTSD; the specific nature of this contribution depending on the age of the flood victims and isolated PTSD components; and the role of family induction in determining the relationships among trauma, temperament, and PTSD.

7.2.2.1. PTSD and temperament traits

The existing research on the relationships between stress and temperament, extensively reviewed in chapter 6, allowed us to formulate several hypotheses concerning the relationships between RTT traits and PTSD. We predicted that emotional reactivity (ER)—which augments the stimulating value of the trauma experience, particularly with respect to negative emotions—and the related perseveration (PE) should correlate positively with PTSD. Endurance, briskness, and activity, all of which are signs of high stimulation processing capacity and stimulation seeking, should act as PTSD buffers and therefore should correlate negatively with this psychological disorder.

We have presented the results of these studies in many publications (see Strelau, Kaczmarek, & Zawadzki, 2006; Strelau & Zawadzki, 2004, 2005a, 2005b, 2006; Strelau et al., 2002). This section will therefore present only those findings that we obtained in stage one of the study, which was conducted on the flood victims (the construction sample; see section 7.1.1). This sample numbered 378 individuals (including 199 females) aged 13–85 years.[2]

We also conducted an analogous study on a group of 52 miners who had survived a mining catastrophe, likewise discussed in this chapter (see section 7.1.2). PTSD-F was used to measure PTSD but only the general score was analyzed. Temperament was assessed by means of the Formal Characteristics of Behavior–Temperament Inventory (FCB-TI). The relationships that were the focus of this study were measured twice in both groups, immediately after the trauma (retrospective data) and two years later. The results are presented in Table 7.3.

As we can see from the table, the pattern of correlation coefficients is just as predicted. Emotional reactivity and perseveration are positively correlated with PTSD in the two groups, both immediately after the trauma and two years later. Briskness,

Table 7.3 Correlations between temperament traits and PTSD

| | Flood survivors | | Coalminers | |
FCB-TI scale	PTSD-FWA	PTSD-2YA	PTSD-FWA	PTSD-2YA
Briskness	-0.20*	-0.26*	-0.29*	-0.33*
Perseveration	0.27*	0.19*	0.39*	0.25*
Sensory Sensitivity	-0.06	-0.17*	-0.16	-0.29*
Endurance	-0.27*	-0.25*	-0.53*	-0.51*
Emotional Reactivity	0.38*	0.40*	0.57*	0.57*
Activity	-0.12*	-0.11*	-0.29*	-0.48*

Note. PTSD = intensity of PTSD total; FWA = few weeks after trauma; 2YA = 2 years after trauma. $*p < 0.05$ (two-tailed test). Adapted from "Trauma and Temperament as Predictors of Intensity of Posttraumatic Stress Disorder Symptoms After Disaster" by J. Strelau and B. Zawadzki, 2005b, *European Psychologist, 10,* p. 129. Copyright 2005 by Hogrefe & Huber Publishers. Reprinted with permission.

---

[2] This number is smaller than the number of respondents whose results were used to construct the PTSD questionnaire ($N = 396$). This is because the data on temperament were not available for all respondents.

endurance, and activity are negatively correlated with PTSD. It is worth pointing out that regardless of who was studied (flood victims or miners) and when they were tested (directly after the trauma or two years later), the correlation between PTSD and temperament is strongest for emotional reactivity. This lends indirect support to the striking regularity with which neuroticism, which is closely related to emotional reactivity (see Strelau & Zawadzki, 1997), is one of the best personality predictors of PTSD (see Lauterbach & Vrana, 2001; McFarlane, 1989; Schnurr & Vielhauer, 2000). Endurance, a temperament trait indicative of high stimulation processing capacity, is a particularly potent buffer protecting against PTSD—especially in miners.

However, in order to determine the extent to which the temperament traits measured in this study can be viewed as predictors of PTSD or buffers protecting against this disorder, we conducted a step-by-step regression analysis for the two groups for the two different points in time, directly after the trauma and two years later. The results of this analysis are presented in Table 7.4.

As far as the flood victims are concerned, the multiple correlations for the two points of time range from 0.38 to 0.43 and account for 0.14–0.19 percent of the variance. These values are higher among the miners because here the multiple correlations range from 0.57 to 0.62 and account for 33–39 percent of the variance. It is noteworthy that in both groups and at both points in time, emotional reactivity is the temperament trait that accounts for the largest portion of the variance of PTSD. In the flood victim group, sensory sensitivity is an additional predictor (but only two years after the flood), whereas significant predictors in the miner group are also endurance (immediately after the flood) and activity (two years after the flood). In our later studies, we tested not only the effect of temperament but also the effect of the intensity of the trauma and its temporal consequences, both of which were treated as variables relating to PTSD intensity.

7.2.2.2. Temperament traits and trauma as predictors of PTSD

That the extent of experienced trauma affects the intensity and duration of PTSD has been known ever since the disorder was first studied (see, e.g., Green et al., 2003; Kaniasty, 2003; Norris et al., 2002b; Ozer et al., 2003). Therefore it was legitimate to measure the intensity of the trauma experience in addition to the individual differences variables. It has been demonstrated that the intensity of PTSD—or to be more precise its temporal dynamics, at least as far as catastrophes are concerned—largely depends on secondary stressors that are the consequence of the trauma (Kaniasty, 2003). These stressors are caused by the fact that victims are often left without means of subsistence that would allow them to maintain a standard of living similar to the one they had prior to the disaster (see Norris, Friedman, & Watson, 2002a). We therefore decided to include this rarely investigated aspect of trauma in our studies.

Table 7.4 Results of hierarchical regression analysis with temperament traits as predictors of PTSD in flood survivors and coalminers

Flood survivors						
Few weeks after trauma						
Model	F	F_{change}	R	R^2	Predictor	Partial correlation
ER	62.95 $(a)^*$		0.38	0.14	ER	0.38*
2 years after trauma						
Model	F	F_{change}	R	R^2	Predictor	Partial correlation
ER	72.55 $(a)^*$	—	0.40	0.16	ER	0.40*
+ SS	42.60 $(b)^*$	10.76*	0.43	0.19	ER	0.40*
					SS	0.17*
Coalminers						
Few weeks after trauma						
Model	F	F_{change}	R	R^2	Predictor	Partial correlation
ER	24.46 $(c)^*$		0.57	0.33	ER	0.57*
+ EN	15.66 $(d)^*$	4.94*	0.62	0.39	ER	0.38*
					EN	-0.30*
2 years after trauma						
Model	F	F_{change}	R	R^2	Predictor	Partial correlation
ER	23.41 $(c)^*$	—	0.57	0.33	ER	0.57*
+ AC	15.39 $(d)^*$	5.34*	0.62	0.39	ER	0.45*
					AC	-0.31*

Note. ER = emotional reactivity; SS = sensory sensitivity; EN = endurance; AC = activity. a – df = 1/376; b – df = 2/375; c – df = 1/50; d – df = 2/49; *p < 0.05. Adapted from "Trauma and Temperament as Predictors of Intensity of Posttraumatic Stress Disorder Symptoms After Disaster" by J. Strelau and B. Zawadzki, 2005b, *European Psychologist, 10*, p. 130. Copyright 2005 by Hogrefe & Huber Publishers. Reprinted with permission.

A series of investigations checking the effect of trauma intensity and the consequences of prolonged trauma, in addition to several other variables, was conducted on a sample of flood victims from Gdańsk (the 2001 flood) and a sample of victims from Silesia who had experienced the Flood of the Century and in whom PTSD was assessed three years after the event. Sample A, the Gdańsk sample, originally numbered 384 individuals[3] (including 217 females) aged 14–84 (M = 35.5; SD = 14.39) and was tested twice—three months after the trauma and fifteen months after the trauma. When the sample was tested the second time (sample B), it numbered 321 individuals (including 181 females) and the respondents' age ranged from 15 to 76 (M = 37.2; SD = 14.41). The Silesian sample (sample C) numbered 279 individuals (including 146 females) aged 13–75 (M = 36.2; SD = 14.55).

Trauma was measured with a six-item questionnaire covering three issues: life threat during the flood, injuries, and material losses. The data concerning these aspects of the trauma were dichotomized according to a "Yes-No" format (trauma present or absent). This way we were able to calculate a trauma intensity index ranging from 0 (all three aspects of the trauma absent) to 3 (all three aspects of the trauma present). In sample A only TI was assessed; in samples B and C, the consequences of prolonged trauma (CPT) were also evaluated. These consequences were again measured against three criteria: financial problems, housing problems, and status and material situation. CPT was calculated in the same way as TI and could also range from 0 to 3. As far as sample C is concerned, only two aspects of TI were assessed: threat to life during the flood and material losses. As always, temperament was assessed with the FCB-TI. A detailed account of the methods of measuring trauma intensity and the consequences of prolonged trauma has been given elsewhere (see Strelau & Zawadzki, 2005b, 2006).

I shall not present the data on the relationships between temperament and the general PTSD score for the three samples (A, B, or C). All I want to say is that the configuration of these relationships is identical to the one in Table 7.3, the only difference being that the values of the correlation coefficients are slightly different. However, the differences between the present correlations and the ones presented in Table 7.3 are negligible: the various temperament traits and trauma intensity do not correlate significantly. Out of eighteen correlation coefficients (TI was measured in all three samples for all six temperament traits), only three are statistically significant and range from 0.12 to 0.13.

A different pattern emerged for the relationships between temperament traits and the consequences of prolonged trauma. When the consequences of trauma were assessed fifteen months after the disaster (sample B), a statistically signifi-

---

[3] This number is lower than the original sample (N = 422; see section 7.1.2) because the analyzed variables were not measured in all respondents.

cant correlation was found with all temperament traits except activity. CPT correlated positively with emotional reactivity (0.19) and perseveration (0.18) and negatively with briskness (–0.22), sensory sensitivity (–0.13), and endurance (–0.17). This correlation pattern suggests that ER and PE may increase the likelihood that secondary stressors will emerge or affect stressor appraisal. The highest negative correlation coefficient was found for briskness. This makes sense if we consider that the definition of briskness includes the tendency to switch easily from one behavior (reaction) to another appropriate to the changing environment (see section 5.1.3). It is noteworthy that an analogous assessment conducted much later—that is, three years after the flood (sample C)—did not reveal this pattern. Only emotional reactivity correlates significantly and positively (0.24) with the consequences of prolonged trauma. These findings have been presented comprehensively elsewhere (see Strelau & Zawadzki, 2005b).

The research that has been conducted on the relationship between PTSD and temperament traits has unequivocally demonstrated that emotional reactivity is the best temperamental predictor of PTSD. Therefore in our effort to identify the role of trauma (its intensity and long-term consequences) and individual differences as predictors of PTSD, we subjected this temperament trait to our next regression analysis. General PTSD was the dependent variable and trauma intensity, consequences of prolonged trauma, and emotional reactivity were treated as predictors of PTSD intensity. These variables were entered into a hierarchical regression analysis, separately for PTSD diagnosed three months (sample A), fifteen months (sample B), and three years (sample C) after the trauma. The results of this analysis are displayed in Table 7.5.

As we can see from this table, regardless of when the PTSD symptoms were assessed, trauma intensity and emotional reactivity are significant predictors of PTSD. When emotional reactivity was entered into the model, the proportion of explained variance increased by 9 percent (sample B) to 13 percent (sample A). The TI x ER interaction, on the other hand, did not increase the proportion of explained variance. It is noteworthy that inclusion of CPT in the model in samples B and C significantly increased the proportion of explained variance from 19 percent (sample A) to 33 percent (sample C) and 40 percent (sample B), respectively. Also, when PTSD was assessed again three years after the flood, the best predictors of PTSD symptoms were CPT and ER. This confirms the findings reported by other researchers (Kaniasty, 2003; Norris et al., 2002b) indicating that secondary stressors are important determinants of PTSD and that emotional reactivity has a chronic effect on the symptoms of this disorder. The significant interaction between these variables (CPT x ER) also suggests that if secondary stressors are experienced, their effect on PTSD will be greater in individuals whose level of emotional reactivity is high than in individuals whose level of emotional reactivity is low.

Our studies have demonstrated that in addition to trauma, temperament traits—especially emotional reactivity—are important predictors of PTSD and

Table 7.5 Results of hierarchical regression analysis with trauma and emotional reactivity as predictors of PTSD: Three months, fifteen months, and three years after flood

3 months after flood						
Model	F	F_{change}	R	R^2	Predictor	Partial correlation
TI	26.31 (a)*	—	0.25	0.06	TI	0.25*
+ ER	45.29 (b)*	60.20*	0.44	0.19	TI	0.29*
					ER	0.37*
+ TI x ER	30.25 (c)*	0.32	0.44	0.19	—	—

15 months after flood						
Model	F	F_{change}	R	R^2	Predictor	Partial correlation
TI	68.73 (d)*	-	0.42	0.18	TI	0.42*
+ PTC	70.03 (e)*	58.70*	0.56	0.31	TI	0.44*
					PTC	0.40*
+ ER	68.08 (f)*	44.65*	0.63	0.40	TI	0.43*
					PTC	0.36*
					ER	0.35*
+ Both interactions	41.50 (g)*	1.38	0.63	0.40	—	—

3 years after flood						
Model	F	F_{change}	R	R^2	Predictor	Partial correlation
TI	25.28 (h)*	—	0.29*	0.08	TI	0.29*
+ PTC	33.43 (i)*	38.16*	0.45	0.20	TI	0.17*
					PTC	0.35*
+ ER	40.20 (j)*	43.36*	0.55	0.31	TI	0.17*
					PTC	0.29*
					RE	0.37*
+ PTC x ER	32.90 (k)*	7.91	0.57	0.33	Trauma	0.16*
					PTC	0.31*
					ER	0.37*
					Interaction	0.17*

Note. TI = Trauma Intensity Index; PTC = prolonged trauma consequences; ER = emotional reactivity. a – df = 1/382; b – df = 2/381; c – df = 3/380; d – df = 1/319; e – df = 2/318; f – df = 3/317; g – df = 5/315; h – df= 1/276; i – df = 2/275; j – df = 3/274; k – df = 4/273. *p < 0.05. Adapted from "Trauma and Temperament as Predictors of Intensity of Posttraumatic Stress Disorder Symptoms After Disaster" by J. Strelau and B. Zawadzki, 2005b, *European Psychologist, 10*, p. 131. Copyright 2005 by Hogrefe & Huber Publishers. Reprinted with permission.

correspond well to McFarlane's (1992) observation that "genetic and personality-based vulnerability to the development of pathological pattern of arousal is an important predisposing factor in the development of the disordered arousal in PTSD" (p. 443).

In the next stage of our investigations into the role of temperament in the development of PTSD symptoms, we concentrated on the specific nature of temperament-PTSD relationships depending on structural PTSD factors (components), including the age of the flood victims.

7.2.2.3. Temperament and trauma as predictors of PTSD components depending on the age of the flood victims

Meta-analysis of the data from sixty independent studies revealed that demographic variables, including the age of the victims of trauma, are a significant predictor of PTSD intensity and duration (see Kaniasty, 2003; Norris, Friedman, & Watson, 2002a; Norris et al., 2002b). Such consequences of trauma as secondary stressors also depend on the age of the victims. For example, financial strife secondary to loss of property will predictably be more intensely experienced by adults than children who are not directly involved in coping with this type of problem. Hence secondary stressors will have a greater effect on PTSD intensity in adults than children.

The PTSD-F has two scales corresponding to its two factors: Intrusion-Hyperarousal and Avoidance-Numbing (see section 7.1.1). In addition to emotional reactivity, the temporal characteristics of temperament can be expected to predict both these PTSD components. Briskness, a temporal trait that is expressed in the capacity to adapt to novel conditions, may act as a buffer against avoidance symptoms. Perseveration, the tendency to continue and repeat reactions, may be viewed as a predictor of intrusive symptoms. This concisely presented rationale was the point of departure for another series of studies whose details have been presented elsewhere (Strelau, Kaczmarek, & Zawadzki, 2006).

As part of this project, three samples of flood victims were studied. The first, from southern Poland (Maków Podhalański and Budzów), consisted of 124 children (including 59 boys) aged 8–13 ($M = 10.3$; $SD = 1.50$). The remaining samples were recruited from the Gdańsk flood victims (the 2001 flood). The latter were divided into two samples of different ages—youths and adults. The second sample consisted of 71 flood victims (including 22 boys [youths]) aged 14–21 ($M = 17.0$; $SD = 2.27$). The third sample consisted of 196 flood victims (including 87 men) aged 22–75 ($M = 44.9$; $SD = 9.73$). This particular division into three cohorts was based on theoretical assumptions concerning stages of life (see Levinson, 1990). Youths are more mature than children and resemble adults more than children as far as psychological functioning is concerned. On the other hand, youngsters of this age usually go to school and live with their parents, on whom they are economically dependent—making them more akin to children than adults (Strelau, Kaczmarek, & Zawadzki, 2006).

Unlike the youths and adults, all measures for the child sample are based on parental ratings (in 90 cases both parents provided the ratings and in 34 cases only one parent provided the ratings). All three samples have one factor in common, however: PTSD was always assessed two years after the trauma.

PTSD symptoms were diagnosed by means of the PTSD-F. Three scores were obtained: General, I-H, and A-N. Children were diagnosed with the help of the children's version of the PTSD-F(C) developed by Kaczmarek (2004; Kaczmarek & Zawadzki, 2006). This instrument, which is administered to parents, has two scales corresponding to the two factors that this researcher identified: Intrusion-Avoidance and Passive Avoidance-Hyperarousal. It also measures general PTSD, as reflected in the general score. All in all, the scale has twenty items (eleven for Intrusion-Avoidance and nine for Passive Avoidance-Hyperarousal). The reliability and validity of this diagnostic instrument are discussed elsewhere (Kaczmarek, 2004; see also Strelau, Kaczmarek, & Zawadzki, 2006). Trauma intensity and the consequences of prolonged trauma were assessed by means of the questionnaire discussed in section 7.2.2.2. Adult temperament was assessed by means of the FCB-TI, whereas children's temperament was assessed by means of the Children's Temperament Questionnaire developed by Oniszczenko and Radomska (2002; see section 5.4 for a brief description). This is the children's equivalent of the FCB-TI and has analogous scales. The scores of both parents were averaged for the PTSD-F(C) and Children's Temperament Questionnaire unless only one parent provided the ratings.

It also needs to be added that PTSD-F Intrusion-Hyperarousal and PTSD-F(C) Intrusion-Avoidance are labeled "Intrusion" and PTSD-F Avoidance-Numbing and PTSD-F(C) Passive Avoidance-Hyperarousal are labeled "Avoidance." This was possible because of the content overlap of the two factors used to construct the two PTSD questionnaires (see Strelau, Kaczmarek, & Zawadzki, 2006).

The results of this study are presented at length elsewhere (Strelau, Kaczmarek, & Zawadzki, 2006). I shall limit myself here to the relationships between general PTSD and its components on the one hand and trauma indices (TI and CPT) on the other, and to the three temperament traits selected for this study (emotional reactivity, briskness, and perseveration). I shall present the results separately for children, youths, and adults. Also, in order to facilitate inferences concerning the predictive values of trauma and temperament traits, I shall present the outcomes of the regression analysis in which these variables were treated as predictors of PTSD symptoms. The correlations between these variables are given in Table 7.6.

One striking finding is that the sign of the correlation coefficients is the same for all three groups. This applies to all the variables whose relationships with PTSD and its components were tested. Of the 45 coefficients of correlation, 35 are significant. The correlations were weakest in the youth group, in which trauma intensity failed

Table 7.6 Correlation between temperament traits and trauma (intensity and prolonged consequences) and PTSD (general and symptoms)

Variable	General PTSD		
	Children	Adolescents	Adults
Trauma intensity	0.43*	0.11	0.38*
Prolonged trauma consequences	0.22*	0.18	0.32*
Emotional reactivity	0.45*	0.26*	0.49*
Briskness	-0.42*	-0.23*	-0.48*
Perseveration	0.40*	0.12	0.38*
	Intrusion symptoms		
Variable	Children	Adolescents	Adults
Trauma intensity	0.41*	0.10	0.32*
Prolonged trauma consequences	0.25*	0.24*	0.26*
Emotional reactivity	0.27*	0.23*	0.46*
Briskness	-0.25*	-0.06	-0.36*
Perseveration	0.33*	0.12	0.44*
	Avoidance symptoms		
Variable	Children	Adolescents	Adults
Trauma intensity	0.28*	0.10	0.38*
Prolonged trauma consequences	0.10	0.08	0.32*
Emotional reactivity	0.47*	0.25*	0.43*
Briskness	-0.45*	-0.38*	-0.51*
Perseveration	0.31*	0.10	0.24*

Note. *$p < 0.05$ (two-tailed test). Adapted from "Temperament as Predictor of Maladaptive Behavior Under Extreme Stress: The Polish Studies of Natural Disasters" by J. Strelau, M. Kaczmarek, and B. Zawadzki, 2006. In Q. Jing, M. R. Rosenzweig, G. d'Ydewalle, H. Zhang, H.-C. Chen, and K. Zhang (Eds.), *Progress in Psychological Science Around the World: Vol. 2. Social and Applied Issues,* p. 149. Copyright 2006 by Psychology Press. Reprinted with permission.

to correlate significantly with any PTSD symptoms. This also applies to CPT (with the exception of intrusion: –0.27). The correlations with temperament were also weaker in this group compared with children and adults and no correlation whatsoever was found for perseveration and the different PTSD symptoms. The correlations between all three temperament traits and all three PTSD measures were strongest in children and adults and the sign of these correlations was as predicted. Also, in all three groups emotional reactivity correlated positively with all PTSD symptoms. The correlation between the consequences of prolonged trauma and all PTSD symptoms was most pronounced in adults. This is understandable if we consider that responsibility for mitigating the consequences of flooding lies with the adults and that this process may take many years. If we look at the magnitude of the correlation coefficients and their between-group consistency, we will come to the unequivocal conclusion that temperament traits are the best predictors of PTSD symptoms. The correlation coefficients (regardless of sign) fall in the 0.25–0.47 range for children, 0.06–0.38 range for youths (only in this group are four of the nine correlations between temperament and PTSD statistically insignificant), and 0.24–0.51 range for adults.

If we look separately at the different PTSD symptoms and their relationships with temperament traits, the following patterns emerge. As far as briskness is concerned, in all three groups the correlations are most powerful for avoidance, lending support to our expectation that briskness acts as a buffer against this category of PTSD symptoms. If we look at perseveration, we shall see that it correlates more strongly with intrusion (this is most pronounced in adults; in the adolescent group, the correlation coefficients are insignificant but the pattern is as predicted). This result is consistent with our hypothesis that perseveration is a predictor of this PTSD category (i.e., avoidance).

Regression analysis based on the "introduction" of all the independent variables included in the model (step-by-step regression analysis) is discussed elsewhere (Strelau, Kaczmarek, & Zawadzki, 2006). Suffice it to say that it confirmed the dominant role of emotional reactivity as a predictor of the intensity of PTSD and its components (intrusion and avoidance). Briskness predicts avoidance and perseveration predicts intrusion. Trauma intensity and the consequences of prolonged trauma are also significant predictors of PTSD and its components. The patterns reported here emerged in all three groups of flood victims, albeit with different strength. Building on the step-by-step regression analysis, we conducted a hierarchical regression analysis. The results of this analysis are presented in Table 7.7.

As we see in this table, the contribution of the variables that were treated as predictors of the intensity of PTSD and its components was most significant (as predicted) in the adult group. When only the two aspects of trauma and emotional reactivity were included in the model, the latter variable accounted for the largest portion of the variance. As far as intrusion is concerned, all four variables (TI, CPT, ER, and PE) account for the variance in more or less equal proportions. The same applies to avoidance with one exception, briskness, which stands out in the configuration of variables as a predictor of this group of PTSD symptoms.

In children a similar pattern emerged to that in the correlation analyses. Consequences of prolonged trauma do not predict PTSD. This applies to all three

Table 7.7 The results of regression analysis with trauma characteristics, their consequences, and selected temperament traits as predictors of PTSD intensity (total and symptoms): Stepwise method

Statistics/Variables	General PTSD		
	Children	Adolescents	Adults
R	0.54*	0.26*	0.62*
R^2	0.29	0.07	0.39
Trauma intensity	0.35*	—	0.31*
Prolonged trauma consequences	—	—	0.28*
Emotional reactivity	0.38*	0.26*	0.47*

Statistics/Variables	Intrusion symptoms		
	Children	Adolescents	Adults
R	0.45*	0.24*	0.59*
R^2	0.20	0.06	0.35
Trauma intensity	0.32*	—	0.24*
Prolonged trauma consequences	—	0.24*	0.23*
Emotional reactivity	—	—	0.25*
Perseveration	0.19*	—	0.25*

Statistics/Variables	Avoidance symptoms		
	Children	Adolescents	Adults
R	0.57*	0.38*	0.63*
R^2	0.33	0.14	0.40
Trauma intensity	—	—	0.30*
Prolonged trauma consequences	—	—	0.24*
Emotional reactivity	0.39*	—	0.19*
Briskness	-0.36*	-0.38*	-0.33*

Note. R = multiple correlation; R^2 = explained variance; * $p < 0.05$ (two-tailed test). For each independent variable, partial correlation. Adapted from "Temperament as Predictor of Maladaptive Behavior Under Extreme Stress: The Polish Studies of Natural Disasters" by J. Strelau, M. Kaczmarek, and B. Zawadzki, 2006. In Q. Jing, M. R. Rosenzweig, G. d'Ydewalle, H. Zhang, H.-C. Chen, and K. Zhang (Eds.), *Progress in Psychological Science Around the World: Vol. 2. Social and Applied Issues*, p. 152. Copyright 2006 by Psychology Press. Reprinted with permission.

assessments. Trauma intensity, on the other hand, is a predictor of PTSD and as far as general PTSD is concerned, TI and ER predict the disorder to the same extent. Perseveration is the only temperament trait that predicts intrusion (as predicted), whereas briskness predicts avoidance on par with emotional reactivity (also as predicted).

A different pattern from those found for children and adults emerged for youths. The proportion of explained variance in the child and adult groups ranged from 0.20 (intrusion in children) to 0.40 (avoidance in adults), whereas in the youth group the proportion of explained variance was very small and ranged from 0.06 (intrusion) to 0.14 (avoidance). Emotional reactivity is the only significant predictor of general PTSD. This temperament trait did not emerge as a predictor of either intrusion (for which CPT is the only predictor) or avoidance. The only predictor of avoidance in this group is briskness. In all three groups, high briskness acts as a buffer against the symptoms of avoidance. The results of the regression analysis for youths do not contradict our expectations, although they confirm them only partially, hence making them difficult to interpret—all the more so since PTSD was assessed at the same point in time in all three groups (two years after the trauma) and youths experienced the same trauma as children and adults and were interviewed by the same interviewers as the adults.

It is clear that of all the temperament traits that we measured, emotional reactivity played the most central role as a predictor of PTSD and its components. This pattern emerged in all our studies and analyses. As we predicted, briskness and perseveration emerged as predictors of specific PTSD symptoms: briskness predicts avoidance and perseveration predicts intrusion. Our findings also lend support to Lauterbach's opinion, based on his own research (Lauterbach, 2006; Lauterbach & Vrana, 2001), concerning the multivariate model of determinants of the intensity of PTSD symptoms. In addition to personality traits, trauma — both its intensity and its prolonged action—is an equally valid predictor of the psychological consequences of disaster, although this relationship tends to vary depending on the age of the flood victims. The fact that the consequences of prolonged trauma do not show up in children and show up only minimally in youths (with respect to intrusion symptoms) suggests that parents open a "protective umbrella" over their children to shield them from secondary stressors, whereas their protective devices during the actual trauma resulting directly from the flood are negligible or totally absent.

This argument leads us to the next section on the relationships between temperament and extreme stress. In this section we will discuss how the consequences of disaster expressed in PTSD symptoms show up in the family because in the contingency we studied (i.e., flooding), family members who relate to one another in various ways all experience the same trauma.

7.2.2.4. Trauma, temperament, and family induction of PTSD

All disasters (including floods) affect the social communities or groups that live within their range of impact. Hence the consequences of trauma should be analyzed not only from the perspective of the individual but also—as Hobfoll and de Vries (1994; see also Kaniasty, 2003) have pointed out—from the perspective of the entire community, including families. On a smaller scale, the one on which we focused, this applies to the family as well. This work has been presented in detail elsewhere (see Kaczmarek, 2004; Kaczmarek & Zawadzki, 2006; Zawadzki, Strelau, Kobyłka et al., 2002).

When studying PTSD in firemen, McFarlane (1989) focused on the coexistence of PTSD symptoms within the family due to familial induction. Another study has shown that the likelihood of PTSD is much higher in mothers whose offspring demonstrate PTSD symptoms (Foy & Goguen, 1998; Green et al., 1991). But on the other hand, it has been argued (Green et al., 2000) that PTSD in children depends on the intensity of maternal PTSD. All these family studies are flawed in that researchers attribute PTSD to family members without heeding other factors that may be responsible for intrafamilial similarities—for example, shared trauma-related experiences or genetically determined personality traits. Only when we have eliminated the effect of these variables can we say that we are dealing with induction of PTSD within the family that is unrelated to shared experience or similar personality traits.

When we set out to study familial induction of PTSD, we assumed that covariance of PTSD within the family is determined by common experience of the same disaster and by the fact that family members (parent-child relations) share similar, genetically determined temperament traits. Because these factors determine the individual intensity of PTSD, one should not view them as variables that induce the disorder within the family. Induction means the mutual effects of PTSD symptoms on family members, leading to the increasing similarity of PTSD symptom intensity among family members. In other words, increased similarity of symptoms in different family members may lead to a situation where one of the predictors of PTSD—in addition to trauma and individual characteristics—is PTSD in other family members.

It still remains to be determined which family member will become the source of induction. If induction depends on the intensity of PTSD symptoms, then the mother should be the source of induction because we know from the existing research that PTSD is more intense in women than men (and this has been confirmed regardless of the disaster and the country being investigated; see Klonowicz, 2000; Norris et al., 2002b). Other researchers have pointed out that PTSD symptoms are more intense in people who have family responsibilities than single people (Foa, Keane, & Friedman, 2000). This in turn suggests that both the father and the mother can induce PTSD; depending on the specific culture or community, one or the other parent may be more responsible.

Our main hypothesis was that coexistence of PTSD in family members is caused by similarity of the traumatic experience, similarity of temperament in parents and offspring (limited here to emotional reactivity), and induction of PTSD. Not knowing which parent is responsible for inducing PTSD, we assumed that this need not be the member with the most intense PTSD symptoms.

We ran the study on familial induction of PTSD in families that had shared the consequences of flooding. These families consisted of two parents and one dependent child. The study was conducted on two samples—a sample of Silesian flood victims (the Flood of the Century in 1997) and a sample of Gdańsk flood victims (the 2001 flood). In the Silesian sample, which consisted of 72 families, PTSD was assessed three years after the flood; in the Gdańsk sample, which numbered 116 families, PTSD was assessed three months after the flood. Since the results for the two samples are similar, the only major difference being that family induction was measured either three months or three years after the flood (see Zawadzki, Strelau, Kobyłka et al., 2002), the following presentation will be limited to the more numerous sample—that is, the Gdańsk families. The mean father age was 46 ($SD = 8.28$), the mean mother age was 43 ($SD = 6.86$), and the mean age of the children (including 73 girls) was 17.4 ($SD = 4.38$).

Emotional reactivity was measured with the FCB-TI, PTSD was measured with the PTSD-F (general score only), and trauma intensity was assessed with the help of a questionnaire that was used to calculate the trauma intensity index (see section 7.2.2.2). Additionally, PTSD was diagnosed with the help of the Revised Civilian Mississippi Scale adapted by Kaniasty (2003). This inventory contributed no new information, however, and therefore the data obtained by means of this measure will be omitted.

As predicted, preliminary analysis of the data showed that PTSD symptoms were most pronounced in the mothers ($M = 38.0$; $SD = 17.15$) and least pronounced in the children ($M = 24.4$; $SD = 17.07$). This highlights the intrafamilial differences in the intensity of PTSD symptoms. It does not, however, imply that symptoms do not covary; it only suggests that further analysis should be performed separately for each family member. As far as emotional reactivity is concerned, it is highest in the mothers ($M = 12.2$; $SD = 4.32$) and lowest in the fathers ($M = 9.8$; $SD = 4.53$). The correlations between paternal, maternal, and offspring PTSD on the one hand and the two analyzed predictors of this disorder—trauma intensity and emotional reactivity—on the other do not differ from previous findings. The values of six coefficients, which range from 0.25 to 0.38, are all statistically significant and consistently suggest that trauma intensity and emotional reactivity account for similar portions of the variance of PTSD.

In order to identify the determinants of the intensity of PTSD symptoms, we applied hierarchical regression analysis and introduced the predictors into the model (separately for fathers, mothers, and children) in the following order: trauma intensity index, emotional reactivity of the family member, emotional reactivity of remaining family members, and intensity of PTSD (including intensity in remaining family members). This last variable was included to check the effect of PTSD covariance. The results of this analysis are presented in Table 7.8.

As in all our previous studies, this analysis revealed that trauma and emotional reactivity are significant predictors of PTSD symptoms. This applies to each family member—the father, mother, and child. Introducing the emotional reactivity of remaining family members into the model did not significantly increase the portion of explained variance of PTSD, but when PTSD in remaining family members was entered into the model, this significantly increased the portion of explained variance. Partial correlations between the PTSD questionnaire scores calculated separately for each family member (on the one hand) and trauma intensity, emotional reactivity, and PTSD intensity in remaining family members (on the other) revealed that (a) ER predicts PTSD in every family member; (b) maternal and offspring PTSD are predictors of paternal PTSD; and (c) both trauma intensity and paternal PTSD are predictors of PTSD in the mother and the child.

We conducted an additional analysis in which we used the raw scores to calculate the correlation coefficients between PTSD in each family member. Regardless of the configuration, these coefficients were statistically significant. They were highest for father-child PTSD (0.45) and lowest for mother-child PTSD (0.24). When trauma intensity and emotional reactivity were removed from the equation (by presenting the scores in the form of standardized residuals), the strength of the relationships decreased only slightly and was still statistically significant. This finding, obtained after the removal of trauma intensity and emotional reactivity, suggests heightened intrafamilial PTSD similarity that cannot be accounted for by these variables. The values of the correlation coefficients suggest that different family members contribute to PTSD induction to various extents.

Finally, we conducted an exploratory path analysis based on the variance/covariance outcome matrix for trauma intensity, emotional reactivity, and PTSD intensity in all family members. The model that had the best fit assumed that the father was the source of induction. The full model, which includes maternal, paternal, and child emotional reactivity and PTSD intensity separately for each family member, is displayed in Figure 7.4.

As we can see, emotional reactivity has a direct effect on PTSD in all three family members. Trauma intensity has a similar effect on PTSD intensity in the father, the mother, and the child. This means that emotional reactivity and trauma intensity, treated as independent variables (as they were in earlier one-way and two-way analyses), affected the similarity of the intensity of the trauma experience and hence the similarity between different family members. But the model also shows that familial similarity depends on the intensity of paternal PTSD because paternal induction showed up in both the mother and the child.

We also conducted a similar study on 72 Silesian families, the only difference being that PTSD was assessed three years after the trauma. Path analysis based

Table 7.8 Intensity of PTSD and its predictors—trauma intensity, emotional reactivity of the family member, emotional reactivity of remaining family members, and intensity of PTSD (including intensity in remaining family members) in flood victims three months after disaster: Hierarchical regression analysis

Mother's PTSD	R	R^2	F	df	P	F_{change}	P
Trauma	0.38	0.15	19.83	1/114	0.01		
Trauma + ER	0.46	0.21	14.91	2/113	0.01	8.66	0.01
Trauma and ER + ER of family	0.48	0.23	8.36	4/111	0.01	1.65	0.20
Trauma and ER + PTSD of family	0.52	0.27	10.37	4/111	0.01	4.82	0.01
Final model	0.52	0.26	13.89	3/112	0.01		
Father's PTSD	R	R^2	F	df	P	F_{change}	P
Trauma	0.27	0.07	9.25	1/114	0.01		
Trauma + ER	0.43	0.18	12.68	2/113	0.01	14.98	0.01
Trauma and ER + ER of family	0.43	0.19	6.39	4/111	0.01	0.25	0.78
Trauma and ER + PTSD of family	0.59	0.35	14.91	4/111	0.01	14.18	0.01
Final model	0.59	0.35	19.83	3/112	0.01		
Child's PTSD	R	R^2	F	df	P	F_{change}	P
Trauma	0.33	0.11	13.77	1/114	0.01		
Trauma + ER	0.44	0.20	13.73	2/113	0.01	12.32	0.01
Trauma and ER + RE of family	0.45	0.20	7.13	4/111	0.01	0.63	0.54
Trauma and ER + PTSD of family	0.57	0.33	13.46	4/111	0.01	10.82	0.01
Final model	0.57	0.32	18.89	3/112	0.01		

Note. R = multiple correlation; R^2 = explained variance; F = test for coefficient of regression; df = degree of freedom; p = significance of test F; F_{change} = F test indicating significant increase of explained variance; ER = emotional reactivity. Adapted from "Współwystępowanie objawów zespołu stresu pourazowego (PTSD) w rodzinach powodzian. Trauma, temperament i indukowanie rodzinne" [The Coexistence of Post-Traumatic Stress Disorder (PTSD) Symptoms in Flood Victims' Families: Trauma, Temperament, and Within-Family Contamination] by B. Zawadzki, J. Strelau, E. Kobyłka, W. Oniszczenko, P. Pawłowski, and A. Sobolewski, 2002, *Psychologia–Etologia–Genetyka, 6*, p. 19. Copyright 2002 by Wydawnictwo Naukowe Scholar. Reprinted with permission.

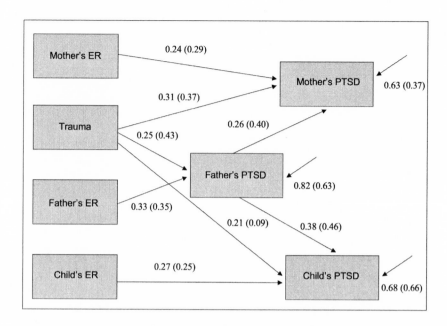

Figure 7.4. A path model of covariance of familial PTSD symptoms (trauma, emotional reactivity, and family induction) in flood victims assessed three months after the flood. Chi^2 = test value; df = degrees of freedom; $p = chi^2$ significance. Paternal PTSD (chi^2 = 1.05; $df = 1$; $p = 0.31$); maternal PTSD ($chi^2 = 20.69$; $df = 1$; $p = 0.01$); child PTSD ($chi^2 = 9.47$; $df = 1$; $p = 0.01$); full model ($chi^2 = 5.94$; $df = 7$; $p = 0.55$); without induction ($chi^2 = 35.38$; $df = 9$; $p = 0.01$). ER = emotional reactivity. Adapted from "Współwystępowanie objawów zespołu stresu pourazowego (PTSD) w rodzinach powodzian. Trauma, temperament i indukowanie rodzinne" [The Coexistence of Post-Traumatic Stress Disorder (PTSD) Symptoms in the Flood Victims' Families: Trauma, Temperament, and Within-Family Contamination] by B. Zawadzki, J. Strelau, E. Kobyłka, W. Oniszczenko, P. Pawłowski, and A. Sobolewski, 2002, *Psychologia–Etologia–Genetyka, 6*, p. 25. Copyright Wydawnictwo Naukowe Scholar. Reprinted with permission.

on the data from this study also suggests paternal induction of PTSD intensity in the mother and the child, as in the Gdańsk sample. However, prolonged stress—probably caused not only by intensity of the original trauma but also by the consequences of prolonged trauma—has a significant effect on both PTSD intensity and the intensity of emotional reactivity (although this effect was only found in the fathers and mothers, not in the children). The only factors that significantly affect offspring PTSD are emotional reactivity and paternal PTSD. These findings suggest that prolonged impact of intense stressors may modify temperament itself (emotional reactivity in this case). This is what Eliasz (1981) postulated on the basis of his work on metallurgists, but only longitudinal research can confirm this definitively.

Kaczmarek (2004; Kaczmarek & Zawadzki, 2006) conducted a similar study of schoolchildren as part of the research for her doctoral dissertation written under Bogdan Zawadzki's supervision. The purpose of this study was to determine the role of RTT traits and the social environment—represented in this case by various facets of the family environment by manifestations of parental PTSD—in the development of PTSD in children in whom the disorder was assessed two years after the flood. One of Kaczmarek's hypotheses was that the intensity of PTSD in children is affected not only by the nature and duration of the trauma and temperament traits, but also by the family climate, level of organization within the family (good climate and good organization reduce the intensity of PTSD), and level of conflict and control in the family (in this case an inverse relationship was predicted). Kaczmarek also predicted that the level of maternal and paternal PTSD would correlate positively with the level of offspring PTSD. These predictions were based on a review of the substantial literature and also on our own earlier research findings.

The study was run on 124 children (including 65 girls) and their parents from areas that had suffered from the floods in the Podhale region in southern Poland and also in the northern part of the country. The children were 8–13 years old ($M = 10.3$; $SD = 1.50$). The parents (120 mothers and 101 fathers) were 21–65 years old.

Offspring PTSD was assessed by means of the PTSD-C(C) (clinical version). This inventory was constructed by Kaczmarek and Zawadzki (2006) and administered to parents. Its construction is based on the classification criteria provided in DSM-IV. It has three scales covering seventeen PTSD symptoms: criterion B (Intrusion), criterion C (Avoidance and Numbing), and criterion D (Hyperarousal). A fourth scale, General PTSD, is the sum of the three criterion scales. The PTSD-C(C) has a total of 34 items because each symptom is represented by two items. The questionnaire has satisfactory reliability and validity (Kaczmarek & Zawadzki, 2006). Parental PTSD was assessed by means of the PTSD-F and trauma intensity and the consequences of prolonged trauma were measured with the self-report instrument described in section 7.2.2.2. Parents were also asked whether their children manifested powerful negative emotions in response to the trauma (e.g., panic, fear, or helplessness). Children's temperament was measured by means of the Children's Temperament Questionnaire developed by Oniszczenko and Radomska (2002; see section 5.4) and family climate was assessed by means of the Family Environment Scale (FES; Moos & Moos, 1994) in Oniszczenko and Ziółkowska's (2004) authorized adaptation. This scale is completed by the parents. The FES has ten subscales, five of which were analyzed in this study: Cohesion, Expressiveness, Conflict Proneness, Organization, and Control. The first three subscales assess within-family relations; the last two subscales assess maintenance of the family system.

Without going into the details of the Kaczmarek and Zawadzki (2006) study, I shall present the results of analysis based on the structural equation model that identifies the contribution of the different variables to the intensity of PTSD symptoms in children. The final model with the criteria for goodness of fit proposed by Pedhazur and Pedhazur-Schmelkin (1991) is shown in Figure 7.5

As we can see from this figure, intense negative emotions that children experienced during the flood are directly related to PTSD. Trauma intensity has a significant indirect effect on the intensity of PTSD symptoms in children (via paternal and maternal PTSD), whereas the consequences of prolonged trauma also have an indirect affect (but only via paternal PTSD). The intensity of paternal PTSD is also related to family climate (organization and conflict) and this in turn affects children's emotional reactivity. Maternal PTSD has a direct effect on children's emotional reactivity and briskness, both of which affect children's PTSD intensity; emotional reactivity augments it and briskness acts as a buffer against it.

The relationships in this model corroborate earlier findings concerning parental induction of PTSD (here both paternal and maternal) in children. The model also shows the effect of children's emotional reactivity and briskness on the intensity of PTSD symptoms. Emotional reactivity predicts PTSD and briskness acts as a buffer against PTSD. Both effects are in the predicted direction. The

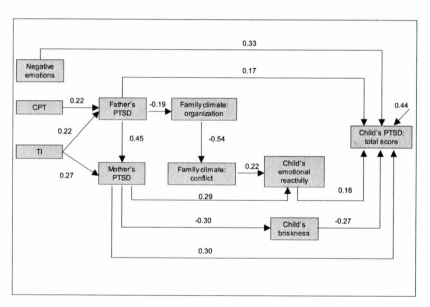

Figure 7.5. A model illustrating the relationships between the determinants of PTSD symptoms intensity in children: Path analysis. $Chi^2 = 34.28$; $df = 28$; $p = 0.19$; $GFI = 0.96$. CPT = consequences of prolonged trauma; TI = trauma intensity. From "Temperamental and Environmental Determinants of the Intensity of PTSD Symptoms in Children Two Years After a Flood" by M. Kaczmarek and B. Zawadzki, 2006. In J. Strelau and T. Klonowicz (Eds.), *People Under Extreme Stress*, p. 60. Copyright 2006 by Nova Science Publishers. Reprinted with permission.

effect of these two temperament traits is indirect, however, because it depends on the intensity of maternal PTSD and also (in the case of emotional reactivity) on conflict within the family. The findings presented within the model confirm the importance of emotional reactivity and briskness for PTSD intensity in children, but they also suggest that these temperament traits may be modified by extreme environmental impact—in line with Eliasz's (1981) findings as well as our own longitudinal study of 72 Silesian families. This study also demonstrates the importance of family organization and (above all) family conflict on the intensity of PTSD in children, but this is only an indirect effect: family organization determined by paternal PTSD affects family conflict and this in turn affects children's emotional reactivity, which is related to PTSD. Perhaps, as Kaczmarek and Zawadzki have pointed out, the reason why the effect of the family environment was so weak is that the FES is mainly used to assess family climate in dysfunctional families. It is not easy to obtain large variance of the studied facets in functional families representing the general population. In addition, the Polish adaptation of the FES is not very reliable (Kaczmarek & Zawadzki, 2006).

The studies of the relationships between temperament and PTSD intensity presented in this chapter lend support to the empirically well-founded conclusion that RTT traits, and especially emotional reactivity, play a similar role to trauma (intensity and prolonged consequences) as significant predictors of the intensity of PTSD. They also demonstrate that the intensity of post-traumatic symptoms depends on other factors, including family induction of PTSD and family climate, although the actual role of family climate is poorly documented and merits further investigation. Our findings unequivocally support my long-time claim that the importance of temperament shows up most prominently in extreme situations, and clearly disasters are one of them.

The findings concerning the family induction of PTSD presented in this chapter (see Kaczmarek & Zawadzki, 2006; Zawadzki, Strelau, Kobyłka et al., 2002), as well as Eliasz's (1981) work on temperament and functioning in situations differing in the amount of stimulation, provide strong support for the hypothesis that temperament traits may change in response to environmental pressure—although longitudinal research designs are needed to test this hypothesis. However paradoxical it may sound, the findings of behavior genetic research have provided powerful arguments supporting the role of the environment in the development of individual differences, including temperament traits. The last chapter of this book will be devoted to the work we have done within the behavior genetic paradigm.

Chapter 8

Research based on the behavior genetic paradigm conducted within the framework of the Regulative Theory of Temperament

Propositions 7 and 8 of the Regulative Theory of Temperament (RTT; see section 4.1) maintain that temperament is the result of biological evolution but also undergoes changes in ontogenesis that are determined by both biological and environmental factors. In addition, the definition of temperament given in section 4.6 underscores the fact that humans (and animals) have a specific temperament from birth. Statements such as these prompt researchers to determine the extent to which these two factors, heredity and environment, are responsible for individual differences in temperament traits. Most temperament researchers (e.g., Buss & Plomin, 1984; Diamond, 1957; Eysenck & Eysenck, 1985; Kagan, 1994), particularly those who attribute temperament to specific neurophysiological mechanisms (see Table 4.1), view the genetic contribution to temperament formation as one of the defining elements of this psychological phenomenon.

This chapter will present the findings from studies of the heritability of temperament traits that Alois Angleitner (from the University of Bielefeld) and I initiated more than ten years ago within the framework of the Polish-German Twin Study Program (PGTSP), which we codirected. This was the first work in Poland (and also in Germany to my knowledge) to be conducted within the behavior genetic paradigm. In subsequent years it stimulated a series of further studies that transcended the confines of the twin study method to include stress and its relationship to temperament (a relationship that we repeatedly confirmed; see chapters 6 and 7). A number of my colleagues and postgraduate students also joined us in this work—in particular, Włodzimierz Oniszczenko (who, together with a group of his own collaborators, widened the scope of genetic studies to include molecular genetics), Bogdan Zawadzki, Adam Sobolewski, Beata Kozak, and Anna Siwy.

It is not my intention to introduce readers to behavior genetics, a broad area of scientific investigation discussed in numerous monographs and textbooks (see, e.g., Loehlin, 1992; Oniszczenko, 2005; Plomin et al., 2001). However, to lay the groundwork for this chapter, I shall first present the theoretical and methodological foundations of our behavior genetic research.

8.1
Selected behavior genetic paradigms underlying current research

People who are unfamiliar with behavior genetics usually think that research conducted within this paradigm enables us to determine the respective contributions of genes and the environment to the studied behavior or psychological phenomena. In fact, the only legitimate conclusions that can be drawn from this research involve the degree to which the genetic factor and the environment account for individual differences (expressed in terms of amount of variance) in the measured behavior or attributes (physical and psychological). One of the assumptions of behavior genetics is that the variability of phenotypic characteristics whose distribution in the population is normal (as opposed to some pathological phenomena) is determined by the effects of many genes whose chromosomal location may vary. Inferences about the proportions to which genes and environment determine individual differences in behavior (traits) can only be made indirectly by comparing the behavior or traits of individuals who are genetically related. In other words, behavior genetics—a research approach introduced more than a century ago to the field of intelligence by Francis Galton (1883)—is based on statistics, as opposed to the genetic approach introduced by Mendel that examines specific genes.

The most popular measure of individual differences are phenotypic traits (characteristics), the variance of which can be divided into a series of partial variances relating to various genetic and environmental factors. The simplest form of phenotypic variance is the sum of two partial variances, genetic variance and environmental variance. This is reflected in the following equation:

$$V_P = V_G + V_E$$

in which V_P stands for phenotypic variance, V_G stands for genotypic variance, and V_E stands for environmental variance.

This additive form of phenotypic variance is based on the simplified assumption that genotype and environment do not correlate. Genetic variance has two components, additive genetic variance and nonadditive genetic variance. The additive genetic factor applies to that part of the genetic program which is responsible for the offspring's similarity to its parents, whereas the nonadditive genetic factor includes dominance and epistasis. Dominance is the interaction among various alleles belonging to the same gene, all of which have the same chromosomal locus, whereas epistasis is the interaction among alleles that have different chromosomal loci. Parents do not transmit the nonadditive genetic factor to their offspring and every individual except monozygotic (MZ) twins has his or her own nonadditive genetic factor (Oniszczenko, 2005; Plomin et al., 2001). If partners mate according to traits whose variance is genetically determined to some extent, their offspring will resemble them more strongly than one would expect on the basis of the contribution of the additive genetic factor alone. Assortative mating is responsible for this increased offspring-parent similarity. Most research, particularly research on personality traits, ignores this genetic factor because it assumes that these traits are randomly distributed in parents.

Paradoxical as it may sound, behavior genetics has produced some of the most convincing evidence of the role of the environment in the development of individual differences because the part of the phenotypic variance that cannot be accounted for by the contribution of genetic variance must be attributed to the contribution of environmental variance. Behavior geneticists distinguish two components of environmental variance, shared environment and nonshared environment. Shared environment refers to those elements of the environment that are responsible for the similarity of individual family members (e.g., socioeconomic status, household facilities, family atmosphere, etc.). Nonshared environment refers to those elements of the environment that are responsible for individual differences between members of the same family (e.g., having different friends and acquaintances, birth order within the family, different sensitivity to environmental stimuli, etc.). It is important to remember that the environment—in the broad sense of the term—also includes error in the measurement of behavior or traits and therefore we sometimes speak of nongenetic variance (see Oniszczenko, 2005). The different sources of phenotypic variance of behavior or traits are shown in Figure 8.1.

In order to identify the contribution of the genetic factor to the variance of behavior, behavior geneticists coined the term "heritability" (h^2). Heritability is defined as that part of the total (i.e., phenotypic) variance that must be attributed to genotypic variance (see Oniszczenko, 2005; Plomin et al., 2001). In its most rudimentary form, this can be expressed in the following formula:

$$h^2 = V_G \div (V_G + V_E)$$

Although this formula assumes that genotype and environment are unrelated, research has shown that they may correlate (GE) or interact (GxE). Genotype and environment may correlate when individuals tend to seek out environments that match their genetic endowment (we call this active correlation as opposed to passive or reactive correlation). For example, individuals whose genetic makeup facilitates the development of low emotional reactivity tend to seek highly stim-

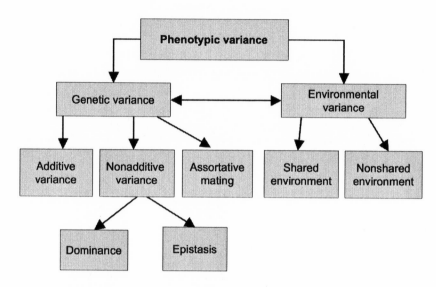

Figure 8.1. The sources of phenotypic variance of behavior or traits.

ulating environments, whereas individuals whose genetic endowment makes them prone to high emotional reactivity tend to avoid such environments. Genotype-environment interaction, in turn, can be observed when the same environment has different effects on individuals with particular genotypes. For instance, the same environment may be good for individuals with a particular genotype and bad for individuals with a different genotype. This is especially evident in education: the same educational methods will lead to different effects depending on the individual genotype. GE correlation, and particularly GxE interaction, have seldom been studied because various environmental determinants of a given trait need to be investigated. Detailed accounts of these determinants can be found in the literature (see Oniszczenko, 2005; Plomin et al., 2001; Wachs & Plomin, 1991).

In our work within the behavior genetic paradigm, we employed two methods: comparison of monozygotic and dizygotic (DZ) twins reared together and family studies. In the latter method, family members (usually parents and their offspring), genetically related in various degrees, are examined. In both cases the data were analyzed by means of the structural equation modeling method. These became the basic methods of data analysis in behavior genetics in the 1980s (see Benjamin, Ebstein, & Belmaker, 2002; Loehlin, 1992; Neale & Cardon, 1992; Plomin et al., 2001). By using these methods, it is possible to identify the specific nature of the genetic (additive and nonadditive) and environmental (shared and nonshared) components; accumulate data gleaned from many methods (e.g., comparison of MZ and DZ twins reared together, adoption studies); and perform multivariate analyses (which will be discussed in subsequent sections). These analyses enable us to answer an important question: to what degree do genetic and environmental factors contribute to the variance of the correlation between variables (e.g., emotional reactivity and PTSD)?

The point of departure for data analysis based on goodness-of-fit models are path models (Neale & Cardon, 1992). These represent latent variables—in this case genetic and environmental factors—and phenotypic variables that are observable (e.g., behavior and personality traits inferred from that behavior). Path models enable the researcher to make pseudocausal inferences (Loehlin, 1992) because latent variables are connected by means of so-called paths of influence, which run from latent to observable variables.

When MZ and DZ twins reared together are the subjects of study, the goodness of fit of the following one-way models can be tested:

- Two additive genetic models ACE and AE, where A is the additive genetic factor, C is the shared environment, and E is the nonshared environment.

- The nonadditive genetic model DE, where D is the nonadditive genetic factor (dominance and epistasis).

- The full genetic model ADE, which combines the additive and nonadditive models.

- The two environmental models CE and E.

Factor E is present in all these models because the nonshared environment also includes measurement error whose magnitude depends on the reliability of the measuring instrument. As far as personality (including temperament) self-report instruments—that is, questionnaires—are concerned, it is about 0.80. Thus on average measurement error accounts for about 20 percent of the nonshared environment. The path model for MZ and DZ twin pairs reared together is shown in Figure 8.2.

This model is based on the assumption that MZ twins share all their genes whereas DZ twins share one-half of their genes, just like ordinary siblings. It is also assumed that the shared environment is identical for each twin in the pair, whereas the nonshared environment is quite distinct (not at all shared). The only point that should be noted is the correlation between DZ twins with respect to the D factor, which is 0.25. This is because in the case of nonadditive factors, the chance that identical dominance will be present in both twins is one in four.

As far as family studies are concerned, the one-way models include the following variable configurations:

- The full genetic-environmental model including the parental mating (am) path (ACEam).

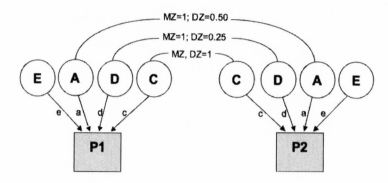

Figure 8.2. The path model for MZ and DZ twins reared together.

- The full genetic-environmental model excluding the parental mating path (ACE)
- The genetic model including the parental mating path (AEam).
- The genetic model excluding the parental mating path (AE).
- The environmental model including the parental mating path (CEam).
- The environmental model excluding the parental mating path (CE).

It is important to remember that factor D is absent in these goodness-of-fit configurations because offspring do not inherit the genetic nonadditive factor from their parents. The path model for biological families consisting of parents and their child is presented in Figure 8.3. The path model for biological families includes not only the paths for genetic and environmental influences on the father and the mother, but also the paths for parental influence on the child (separately for the father and the mother) and the paths for parental phenotypic similarity.

Structural equation modeling allows the researcher to fit the empirical data to the theoretically feasible components of phenotypic variance, represented in the path analysis, that explain the phenotypic variance most adequately. Structural equation modeling is used to analyze the data statistically and the data are also corrected for age and gender (Heath et al., 1989). The theoretical model that best fits the empirical data should not differ significantly from the empirical model. *Chi*² statistics are used to determine this: the higher the value of the *chi*² statistics, the poorer the fit of the tested model. Of all the available models, the simplest one is selected—that is, the one containing the fewest latent components. Several other criteria of goodness of fit between theoretical and empirical models are also used (see Heath et al., 1989; Neale et al., 1999; Plomin, 2001) such as the Goodness-of-Fit Index (GFI), Akaike Information Criterion (AIC), or Root

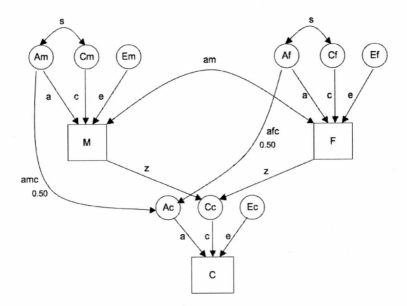

Figure 8.3. The path model for biological families consisting of parents and their child.

Mean Squared Error Approximation (RMSEA). It is assumed that of all the analyzed models, the model is best that does not differ significantly from the empirical model (a necessary condition!), has the highest GFI, the lowest possible AIC (not higher than zero; AIC equals *chi*[2] minus double the degree of freedom), and in which RMSEA is in the range from 0 to ≤ 0.05 (see Neale et al., 1999).

The RTT traits were the main focus of our behavior genetic studies. This will be discussed in the next section.

8.2
Behavior genetic studies of temperament traits

One of the most convincing pieces of evidence supporting the role of biological factors in the development of temperament are the data showing that the genetic factor is largely responsible for the development of individual differences in temperament. Genes do not affect behavior directly, however. They do so via underlying physiological and biochemical mechanisms (see Kagan, 1994; Zuckerman, 1991) and the genetically determined level of reactivity and activity of these mechanisms codetermines individual differences in temperament traits (Strelau, 1998). It is important to remember that temperament traits, like other psychological phenomena, are not located in the genes.

Temperament research based on the behavior genetic paradigm has a history of more than a half-century and I shall review it briefly in the next section.

8.2.1. Temperament studies conducted within the behavior genetic paradigm: An overview

Probably the first temperament study ever conducted within the behavior genetic paradigm was an experiment by Edward Rundquist (1933). By adopting selective breeding, this researcher was able to demonstrate that rats' motor activity in the activity wheel enabled the clear-cut selection of two strains of rats—"active" rats and "passive" rats—beginning with the fifth generation. At almost the same time, Frank Davis (1933) showed that it was possible to use selective breeding to breed aggressive and nonaggressive strains of rats. The most comprehensive research in this area, also begun in the first half of the twentieth century, was the work of Calvin Hall (1941), continued for many decades by other researchers, on the emotionality of rats and mice (see, e.g., Broadhurst & Levine, 1963; Gabbay, 1992; van der Staay, Kerbusch, & Raaijmakers, 1990). These investigators demonstrated that regardless of the indicators of emotionality, it was possible to breed strains of animals in the laboratory that differed dramatically in temperament.

From the point of view of inferences concerning the contribution of genetic factors to the variance of the studied traits, however, all these studies had two major flaws. Selective breeding can only be adopted in animals and it only allows us to infer the contribution of the additive genetic factor (i.e., that part of the genetic program which is handed down from one generation to another). The heritability identified in studies such as these is known as narrow-sense heritability. By the second half of the twentieth century, behavior genetics—which had been developing rapidly—began to study temperament and other personality traits in human beings.

Hans Eysenck and his collaborators conducted a series of pioneering studies of the heritability of human temperament. Eysenck and Prell (1951, 1956) demonstrated that the genetic factor is largely responsible for the variance of extraversion and neuroticism. In later work on more than eight hundred pairs of adult MZ and DZ twins reared together, Eaves and Eysenck (1975, 1976) showed that individual differences in extraversion and neuroticism can largely be accounted for by additive genetic variance and specific environment. Work conducted within the behavior genetic paradigm, mostly in Eysenck's laboratory, has been summarized by Eaves, Eysenck, and Martin (1989). These researchers conducted a meta-analysis of previous findings from Eysenck's superfactor psychoticism-extraversion-neuroticism (PEN) studies and found the following heritability indices (h^2) for these factors: 0.46 for psychoticism, 0.58 for extraversion, and 0.46 for neuroticism.

As early as the 1990s, John Loehlin (1992) conducted yet another meta-analysis of the data from numerous studies of the heritability of Eysenck's PEN and other traits that have been interpreted in terms of the Big Five personality traits.

Loehlin also included the results of twin studies conducted on MZ and DZ twins, adoption studies (for a full account, see Plomin et al., 2001), and family studies. This analysis led him to the following conclusion:

> Additive genetic effects under either model fell generally in the moderate range, 22% to 46%; shared family environmental effects were small, 0% to 11%; and the ambiguous third factor—nonadditive genetic . . . was intermediate at 11% to 19%. . . . The remaining variation, 44% to 55%, presumably represents some combination of environmental effects unique to the individual, genotype-environment interaction, and measurement error. (Loehlin, 1992, p. 68)

In their later studies, Loehlin and Martin (2001) also investigated the role of age and worked with three cohorts per gender. Using the goodness-of-fit method, they partly replicated their earlier findings. Heritability for extraversion and neuroticism was 0.47 and 0.40, respectively, but heritability for psychoticism (0.28) was lower than before.

A great deal of work has been done within the behavior genetic paradigm using different versions of the NEO questionnaire (the Personality Inventory, Personality Inventory–Revised, and Five Factor Inventory [FFI]; Costa & McCrae, 1989, 1992). Two scales of this questionnaire measure almost the same constructs as those proposed by Eysenck (i.e., extraversion and neuroticism). The remaining scales—Agreeableness, Conscientiousness, and to a certain extent Openness to Experience—belong to the sphere of character in the traditional sense of the word rather than temperament or personality (see Strelau & Zawadzki, 1997). Much of the work conducted with the help of these questionnaires (see Beer & Rose, 1995; Bergeman et al., 1993; Jang, Livesley, & Vernon, 1996; Riemann, Angleitner, & Strelau, 1997) has shown that the genetic factor contributes considerably (between 40 and 50 percent) to the variance of all the Big Five factors, although it must be noted that the Swedish (Bergeman et al., 1993) figures for conscientiousness and agreeableness were much lower (29 percent and 12 percent, respectively).

As far as temperament research is concerned, Marvin Zuckerman's (1979, 1994) biologically oriented sensation-seeking concept merits our attention. Work on the determinants of individual differences in sensation seeking also leads to the conclusion that the variance of this temperament trait is largely genetically determined. For example, Fulker, Eysenck, and Zuckerman (1980)—using the twin method—found that 58 percent of the variance of sensation seeking is accounted for by heritability (A + D). Nancy Pedersen and her collaborators (Pedersen et al., 1988) obtained similar results with the Swedish version of the Sensation Seeking Scale (SSS). Hur and Bouchard (1997), who used Zuckerman's SSS-V to measure sensation seeking in MZ twins reared together and separately, found that heritability for all four subscales ranged from 0.43 (Boredom Susceptibility) to 0.54 (Experience Seeking) in twins reared separately. Zuckerman

(2005) compared the findings on the heritability of sensation seeking from three independent studies in which the four basic dimensions of this temperament trait, assessed on the basis of the SSS-IV or SSS-V, were measured. Two of these studies (Hur & Bouchard, 1997; Pedersen et al., 1988) are cited above; the third study was conducted in the Netherlands (Koopmans et al., 1995). All three studies, in which the AE model obtained the best fit, adopted the method of MZ and DZ twins reared together. The mean contribution of the additive genetic variance to the variance of the different SSS subscales was 0.50 for Disinhibition, 0.54 for Threat and Adventure Seeking, 0.57 for Experience Seeking, and 0.43 for Boredom Susceptibility. In all three studies, the specific environment accounted for the remaining variance.

Much of the work on the contribution of heredity and the environment to the variance of temperament traits has been done on children, beginning with infancy. The studies conducted within the last quarter-century by researchers representing various theories of temperament development and focusing on various age groups (e.g., Goldsmith, 1989; Hwang & Rothbart, 2003; Plomin et al., 1993; Robinson et al., 1992) have not substantially altered the picture as far as the contribution of these two factors (heredity and environment) to the variance of the studied temperament traits is concerned. They have demonstrated, however, that the factors' relative contribution to individual differences in temperament may vary depending on the child's age.

Our group has not studied children—particularly children in the early developmental stage—in our own behavior genetic research, and hence I am unable to cite any data for this population. However, since the 1990s we have done considerable work on the origins of individual differences in RTT traits, the results of which will be presented in the next section.

8.2.2. RTT traits as measured by self-report and rating: Our own behavior genetic work

The need to put Proposition 7—which says, among other things, that the genetic factor plays an important role as a codeterminant of individual differences in temperament—of the Regulative Theory of Temperament (see section 4.1) to the empirical test induced me to conduct several studies within the behavior genetic paradigm. Our initial investigations within this paradigm were done in the early and mid-1990s when Alois Angleitner (Angleitner et al., 1995) and I (Strelau, Oniszczenko, & Zawadzki, 1994)—together with our collaborators—launched the Polish-German Twin Study Program. As I wrote in the introduction to this chapter, these were pioneering behavior genetic studies in both countries.

The results of the first studies adopting the method of MZ and DZ twins reared together confirmed our expectations about the significant role of the genetic factor as a determinant of individual differences in all six temperament traits. Structural equation analyses for 398 pairs of twins aged 21–66 (M = 36.1; SD = 10.73), including 205 pairs of MZ twins and 193 pairs of same-sex DZ twins, demonstrated that the best fit for temperament traits measured by means of the Formal Characteristics of Behavior–Temperament Inventory (FCB-TI) is achieved by the AE model (Strelau et al., 1995). Only in one case, briskness, did model DE give a better fit. For all traits except endurance, the genetic factor accounted for 42 percent (perseveration) to 55 percent (emotional reactivity) of the variance. As far as endurance is concerned, however, the additive genetic factor accounted for only 28 percent of the variance.

The objectives of the PGTSP were such that this program remains unique to this day. Heritability of temperament traits was studied in two culturally distinct countries, Poland and Germany, using two independent research approaches (self-report and rating). The focus was on 27 temperament traits postulated by five different theories (including the RTT). The same methods were used to assess temperament in both countries and the same method was used to identify zygoticity.

This work, discussed in detail elsewhere (see Oniszczenko et al., 2003; Zawadzki, Strelau, Oniszczenko, et al., 2002), was based on the following hypotheses: (a) heritability of temperament traits will follow similar patterns in the two culturally distinct samples; (b) the contribution of the genetic variance to the phenotypic variance of the measured traits will be evident irrespective of the method used to measure them; and (c) heritability of temperament will be particularly evident when we apply a multimethod approach (self-report and rating) that enables us to separate measurement error from specific environment. Finally, we predicted that the heritability of RTT traits would be similar to the heritability of traits postulated by other theories of temperament.

The Polish study was run on 546 pairs of twins reared together aged 17–64 (M = 34.6; SD = 10.76), including 317 pairs of MZ twins and 229 pairs of same-sex DZ twins. Of all twin pairs, 322 were female. Respondents were recruited by mail and then interviewed individually by trained interviewers (my graduate students). Spouses, friends, cousins, colleagues, other family members, or neighbors were asked to rate the twins' behavior. Each twin in a pair was rated by two people but no twin was rated by the same two people as the other twin. We obtained ratings from a total of 2,014 men and women (including 1,282 women) aged 20–71 (M = 36.4; SD = 13.56). Each pair of ratings was averaged to give one indicator.

The German study was run on 1,009 pairs of twins reared together aged 14–80 (M = 31.8; SD = 12.94), including 732 pairs of MZ twins and 277 pairs of same-sex DZ twins. There were 785 pairs of female twins. Respondents were recruited by mail. Each twin in a pair was rated by two people who, as in the Polish study, had different relationships with the twins. All in all, there were 4,036 raters (including 2,511 females) aged 13–84 (M = 33.8; SD = 13.67). Each pair of ratings was averaged to give one indicator.

In both samples zygoticity was assessed on the basis of a special questionnaire constructed at our laboratory, the Twin Physical Similarity Questionnaire (TPSQ). This questionnaire had two versions, the original Polish one (Oniszczenko & Rogucka, 1996) and its German adaptation (Angleitner et al., 1995). The TPSQ is a self-report instrument. It has 31 items pertaining to various morphological characteristics and statements concerning the extent to which parents, relatives, friends, and strangers confused twins within the pair. This questionnaire was validated by comparing its scores with morphological assessments of zygoticity performed at the Department of Anthropology, Polish Academy of Sciences. Ninety-four percent of the diagnoses obtained by means of the questionnaire were accurate.

In both the Polish and German samples, the twins' temperament was assessed by means of the same psychometric self-report and rating instruments. In the latter case (i.e., rating), the questionnaire items were worded in the third-person singular. Respondents filled in five questionnaires: the FCB-TI (see section 5.2), the Pavlovian Temperament Survey (PTS; see section 2.3), the Revised Dimensions of Temperament Survey (DOTS-R; Windle & Lerner, 1986), the adult version of the Emotionality–Activity–Sociability Temperament Survey (EAS-TS; Buss & Plomin, 1984), and the Eysenck Personality Questionnaire–Revised (EPQ-R; Eysenck, Eysenck, & Barrett, 1985). The DOTS-R, which is derived from Thomas and Chess's theory of temperament (Thomas & Chess, 1977; see Strelau, 1998, for a description of the inventory), has ten scales: Activity Level-General, Activity Level-Sleep, Approach-Withdrawal, Flexibility-Rigidity, Mood, Rhythmicity-Sleep, Rhythmicity-Eating, Rhythmicity-Daily Habits, Distractability, and Persistence. The adult version of the EAS-TS measures the traits postulated by Buss and Plomin's (1975, 1984) behavior genetic theory of temperament and has five scales: Distress, Fearfulness, Anger, Activity, and Sociability. The EPQ-R scores will not be discussed here. A detailed analysis of the contribution of genetic and environmental factors to the variance of the phenotypic PEN factors postulated by Eysenck, based on self-report and rating, has been presented elsewhere (Wolf et al., 2004).

In the first step of the statistical data analysis, reliability of the temperament scales was assessed and correlations within the MZ and DZ twin pairs were calculated. In both the Polish and German samples, these calculations were conducted separately for the self-report data and rating data. A detailed account of these analyses is provided elsewhere (Oniszczenko et al., 2003). Here I will simply indicate that the mean alpha coefficients for all scales and two language versions ranged from 0.64 (EAS-TS) to 0.88 (PTS) for both self-report and rating. As predicted, the correlation coefficients (except for DOTS-R: Activity Level-Sleep, Polish sample) were higher for MZ twins than DZ twins in both the self-report measures and the ratings. On average the scores of the correlations between DZ twins were lower than half those between MZ twins. This suggests a moderate contribution of the additive genetic factor, a minor contribution of the nonadditive genetic factor, and a large contribution of the specific environment to the phenotypic variance of temperament traits.

Inferences concerning the respective contributions of genetic and environmental factors to the variance of temperament traits were made on the basis of the path model for MZ and DZ twins reared together (see Figure 8.2). This model was modified somewhat for the rating data; in this case twin phenotypes have the status of latent variables because the measure of temperament traits is the average of two independent assessments.

In order to identify any cultural differences in the contribution of genetic and environmental factors to the variance of temperament traits, two models were adopted. One model assumed that there is no difference between the Polish and German samples regarding genetic and environmental parameters (=); the other model assumed that there is a difference (≠). The chi^2 was used to determine the significance of the difference between the two samples. Goodness of fit of the two models was determined and the model with the better fit was selected. In this case between-sample inequality means that the Polish and German samples differ in the respective contributions of the genetic and environmental factors (regardless of which model was adopted for its goodness of fit).

Next we analyzed the structural equation data. All the one-way models typical for studies of MZ twins and DZ twins reared together (see section 8.1) were tested for goodness of fit. AE proved to be the best model for most temperament scales. This applies to both the Polish and German samples and to both the self-report and rating data (see Table 8.1).

As far as the self-report measures are concerned, goodness of fit was best for model DE for four scales (two DOTS-R scales and two EAS-TS scales) and model CE was best for one DOTS-R scale. As far as the ratings are concerned, once again model DE was found to be the best-fitting model (three FCB-TI scales and one DOTS-R scale). Model CE was the best for three DOTS-R scales and ADE, the full genetic model, had the best fit for one EAS-TS scale. It must be noted that goodness of fit was best in those cases where model AE was the best-fitting model. This applies to all the temperament scales and to both self-report and rating.

As far as self-report is concerned, differences emerged between the Polish and German samples with respect to the contribution of genetic and environmental factors to the variance of temperament traits in four cases. These were strength of excitation and mobility of the nervous processes (PTS), persistence (DOTS-R), and sociability (EAS-TS). As far as rating by other parties is concerned, differences between the two samples were found for four traits: perseveration (FCB-TI), strength of inhibition (PTS), persistence (DOTS-R), and activity and sociability (EAS-TS).

Finally, taking the best-fitting models (see Table 8.1) as our point of departure, we calculated the contribution of genetic variance (A and D) and environmental

Table 8.1 Goodness-of-fit parameters (chi^2) for best-fitting structural equation models: Fit indices of models with different parameters for Polish and German data are reported if these models yielded a significantly superior fit

	Self-report					Peer-report				
Trait	Model	E/U	df	chi^2	P	Model	E/U	df	chi^2	P
FCB-TI										
BR	AE	=	10	12.29	0.27	DE	=	14	17.63	0.22
PE	AE	=	10	6.51	0.77	DE	≠	14	12.92	0.07
SS	AE	=	10	17.52	0.06	AE	=	14	19.29	0.15
ER	AE	=	10	3.99	0.95	AE	=	14	19.68	0.14
EN	AE	=	10	10.24	0.42	AE	=	14	15.28	0.36
AC	AE	=	10	6.49	0.77	DE	=	14	16.90	0.26
PTS										
SE	AE	≠	8	8.47	0.39	AE	=	14	18.61	0.18
SI	AE	=	10	11.30	0.33	AE	≠	12	8.28	0.76
MO	AE	≠	8	13.59	0.09	AE	=	14	13.03	0.52
DOTS-R										
AcG	DE	=	10	3.07	0.98	AE	=	14	17.78	0.22
AcS	AE	=	10	4.39	0.93	CE	=	14	17.23	0.24
AW	AE	=	10	10.25	0.42	AE	=	14	10.16	0.75
FR	CE	=	10	9.26	0.51	AE	=	14	17.66	0.22
MQ	AE	=	10	8.23	0.61	AE	=	14	17.59	0.23
RS	AE	=	10	4.73	0.91	AE	=	14	15.07	0.37
RE	AE	=	10	4.74	0.91	CE	=	14	20.89	0.10
RD	AE	=	10	3.14	0.98	CE	=	14	8.88	0.84
DI	DE	=	10	5.77	0.83	AE	≠	12	11.33	0.50
PR	AE	≠	8	7.80	0.43	DE	=	14	18.26	0.19
EAS-TS										
DIS	AE	=	10	6.35	0.78	AE	=	14	8.24	0.88
FE	DE	=	10	4.99	0.89	AE	=	14	8.99	0.83
AN	DE	=	10	4.78	0.91	AE	=	14	12.62	0.56
ACT	AE	=	10	7.53	0.67	AE	≠	12	24.40	0.02
SO	AE	≠	8	7.58	0.47	ADE	≠	14	8.71	0.56

Note. FCB-TI = Formal Characteristics of Behavior–Temperament Inventory: BR = briskness, PE = perseveration, SS = sensory sensitivity, ER = emotional reactivity, EN = endurance, AC = activity; PTS = Pavlovian Temperament Survey: SE = strength of excitation, SI = strength of inhibition, MO = mobility of the nervous processes; DOTS-R = Revised Dimensions of Temperament Survey: AcG = activity level-general, AcS = activity level-sleep, AW = approach-withdrawal, FR = flexibility-rigidity, MQ = mood quality, RS = rythmicity-sleep, RE = rythmicity-eating, RD = rythmicity-daily habits, DI = distractibility, PR = persistence; EAS-TS = EAS Temperament Survey (for adults): DIS = distress, FE = fear, AN = anger, ACT = activity, SO = sociability; AE = additive genetic model, DE = nonadditive genetic model, ADE = full genetic model, E/U = equal (=) / unequal (≠) parameters. Adapted from "Genetic and Environmental Determinants of Temperament: A Comparative Study Based on Polish and German Samples" by W. Oniszczenko, B. Zawadzki, J. Strelau, R. Riemann, A. Angleitner, and F. Spinath, 2003, *European Journal of Personality, 17*, pp. 215–216. Copyright 2003 by John Wiley & Sons. Reprinted with permission.

variance (E and C) to the phenotypic variance of temperament traits. These data—with the exception of traits, for which we found differences between the two samples with respect to the contribution of the two factors—were combined for the Polish and German samples, as illustrated in Table 8.2.

The data in this table give rise to several important conclusions. First, contribution of the genetic factor to the variance of the measured traits is greater for the rating data than the self-report data (about 55 percent vs. about 40 percent). A similar pattern has been found in many studies including studies of other personality traits (see Riemann, Angleitner, & Strelau, 1997; Wolf et al., 2004). The difference in favor of rating can be attributed to the fact that rating based on two independent measures of temperament reduced the measurement error, which biases the variance of the specific environment in self-report.

Second, for the vast majority of temperament traits, no cultural specificity emerged in the contributions of genetic and environmental factors to the variance of the measured traits. The reason perhaps is that the two samples do not differ significantly in the contribution of the genetic factor. It is also possible that despite evident economic and social differences between Poland and Germany, the specific environments in the two countries have much in common and that genetic and environmental effects have similar covariance.

Third, with respect to those temperament traits for which differences were found in the contribution of genetic and environmental factors to the variance of these traits (i.e., traits mentioned in the discussion of Table 8.1), the genetic contribution is higher in the German sample. This in turn suggests that the environment is more homogeneous in the German sample, and this automatically increases the role of genetic variance (see Plomin et al., 2001). This pattern was found for the self-report data and for two rating instances, perseveration (FCB-TI) and activity (EAS-TS).

Fourth and finally, it is noteworthy that as far as the mean contribution of genetic variance to the traits postulated by the four temperament theories represented in this study is concerned, it is highest for RTT traits (46 percent) and lowest for the traits measured by the DOTS-R (30 percent)—a questionnaire representing the theory of Thomas and Chess (1977). These scores apply to self-report whereas they vary for rating, although their rank order remains basically the same. Once again, the mean contribution of genetic variance to the variance of the measured traits is highest for the FCB-TI (61 percent) and lowest for the DOTS-R and PTS (56 percent).

As far as RTT traits are concerned, we conducted a more refined analysis of the empirical data in order to compare the heritability of temperament traits in the two cultures as assessed by two different measurement approaches, self-report and rating. We applied Cholesky's bivariate genetic model (Neale & Cardon, 1992). This model not only allows the researcher to identify the genetic and environmental components of the variance of the trait assessed using each of these

Table 8.2 Proportion of variance explained by additive genetic (A), genetic dominance (D), shared environmental (C), and nonshared environmental (E) factors in the Polish and German samples for self-report and peer-report data

Trait	Self-report				Peer-report			
	A	**D**	**C**	**E**	**A**	**D**	**C**	**E**
FCB-TI								
BR	0.47			0.53	0.57			0.43
PE	0.40			0.60				
German					0.77			0.23
Polish					0.58			0.42
SS	0.45			0.55	0.72			0.28
ER	0.51			0.49	0.55			0.45
EN	0.47			0.53	0.63			0.37
AC	0.46			0.54			0.55	0.45
M	**0.46**			**0.54**	**0.61**			**0.38**
PTS								
SE					0.58			0.42
German	0.50			0.50				
Polish	0.38			0.62				
SI	0.38			0.62				
German					0.51			0.49
Polish					0.52			0.48
MO					0.59			0.41
German	0.54			0.46				
Polish	0.39			0.61				
M	**0.43**			**0.57**	**0.56**			**0.44**
DOTS-R								
AcG		0.35		0.65	0.50			0.50
AcS	0.18			0.82			0.36	0.64
AW	0.36			0.64	0.63			0.37
FR			0.30	0.70	0.49			0.51
MQ	0.31			0.69	0.60			0.40
RS	0.36			0.64	0.76			0.24
RE	0.32			0.68			0.55	0.45
RD	0.32			0.68			0.56	0.44
DI		0.31		0.69				
German					0.45			0.55
Polish					0.61			0.39
PR						0.64		0.36
German	0.36			0.64				
Polish	0.18			0.82				
M	**0.30**			**0.69**	**0.59**			**0.44**
EAS-TS								
DIS	0.37			0.63	0.58			0.42
FE		0.39		0.61	0.58			0.42
AN			0.31	0.69	0.60			0.40
ACT	0.37			0.63				
German								
Polish								
SO								
German	0.49			0.51	0.58			0.42
Polish	0.27			0.73	0.41			0.59
M				**0.36**	**0.64**		**0.56**	**0.44**

Note. For abbreviations see Table 8.1. Adapted from "Genetic and Environmental Determinants of Temperament: A Comparative Study Based on Polish and German Samples" by W. Oniszczenko, B. Zawadzki, J. Strelau, R. Riemann, A. Angleitner, and F. Spinath, 2003, *European Journal of Personality, 17*, pp. 215–216. Copyright 2003 by John Wiley & Sons. Reprinted with permission.

approaches, but also to estimate the contribution of the two factors to covariance between the methods. Assuming that all the genetic and environmental parameters are specific for the two cultures and the two methods of temperament assessment, we selected the model that fit the trait variance/covariance matrix for twins from the two samples, assessed by means of the two methods. This model was then employed to analyze the self-report and rating data, separately and combined. For the sake of cross-cultural comparison, two models—analogous to the models used to test the data in Table 8.1—were tested, one model assuming identity (=) and the other model assuming lack of identity (≠) of genetic and environmental parameters in the two samples. This analysis allowed us to estimate the heritability of temperament traits for the two methods: for each of them separately and for the two combined cultures.

This analysis based on the twin samples using the model of comparison of MZ and DZ twins reared together (see Zawadzki, Strelau, Oniszczenko, et al., 2002) was conducted in several steps that will not be presented here. Suffice it to say that the last step of this analysis involved assessment of goodness of fit between the covariance of temperament traits in Polish and German pairs of MZ and DZ twins and estimating the contribution of genetic and environmental variance to the latent phenotypic variance of these traits. In order to evaluate the cross-cultural differences in genetic and environmental determination, taking into consideration the relationships between self-report and rating, we included Cholesky's bivariate genetic model (Neale & Cardon, 1992) in this analysis for the two methods (self-report and rating) simultaneously. In other words, this model was expanded to include a psychometric model in which the phenotype is treated as a latent variable determining trait rating and self-report. The chi^2 statistics were used to test the differences. No significant differences were found, lending support to the conclusion that as far as the contribution of genetic and environmental variance to the covariance of the two methods is concerned, the two samples do not differ significantly. The self-report and rating data were therefore analyzed jointly.

The purpose of the heritability analysis, based on the two different assessment methods, was to isolate the environmental variance from the error variance. The results of this analysis illustrated that the differences in environmental variance between the German and Polish samples were not statistically significant as far as temperament traits are concerned. We were thus able to select the model that had identical parameters for the two samples and estimate the contribution of genotypic and environmental variance to the latent phenotypic variance of temperament traits. The results of this analysis, showing the separate estimates for the Polish and German samples, are presented in Table 8.3.

As we can see in this table, genetic factors (A, D) account for over 60 percent of the latent variance of RTT traits; this applies to the two samples treated jointly and to each sample treated separately. Table 8.3 also shows that dif-

Table 8.3 The contribution of genotypic and environmental variance to the latent phenotypic variance of temperament traits: Selection of models with best fit separately estimated for Polish and German samples and with identical parameters together for both samples

Trait	Model	$chi^2(p)$	Model	$chi^2(p)$	Polish A^2/d^2	e^2	German a^2/d^2	e^2	Total A^2/d^2	e^2
BR	DE≠[a]	41.09 (0.09)	DE=[b]	41.52 (0.12)	0.62	0.35	0.68	0.32	0.68	0.32
PE	AE≠[a]	36.08 (0.21)	AE=[b]	39.07 (0.18)	0.60	0.40	0.74	0.26	0.69	0.31
SS	AE≠[a]	78.82 (0.00)	AE=[b]	79.46 (0.00)	0.70	0.30	0.63	0.37	0.66	0.34
ER	AE≠[a]	28.90 (0.52)	AE=[b]	30.09 (0.56)	0.64	0.36	0.68	0.32	0.67	0.33
EN	AE≠[a]	34.63 (0.26)	AE=[b]	37.50 (0.23)	0.56	0.44	0.66	0.34	0.63	0.37
AC	DE≠[a]	43.85 (0.03)	DE=[b]	45.62 (0.06)	0.55	0.45	0.66	0.34	0.63	0.38
					0.62	0.38	0.68	0.32	0.66	0.34

Note. For abbreviations see Table 8.1. a – $df = 30$; b – $df = 32$; $chi^2 = 5.99$; $p < 0.05$; models based on diverse (≠) or identical (=) influence of genetic and environmental factors on latent phenotypic variance of temperament traits in both cultures; a^2 = variance explained by additive genetic factor; d^2 = variance explained by nonadditive genetic factor; e^2 = variance explained by nonshared environment. From "Genetyczne i środowiskowe uwarunkowania temperamentu. Polsko-niemiecka analiza porównawcza oparta na samoopisie i szacowaniu" [Genetic and Environmental Determinants of Temperament: A Polish-German Comparative Study Based on Self-Report and Peer-Rating Data] by B. Zawadzki, J. Strelau, W. Oniszczenko, R. Riemann, and A. Angleitner, 2002, *Psychologia–Etologia–Genetyka, 5*, p. 26. Copyright 2002 by Wydawnictwo Naukowe Scholar. Reprinted with permission.

ferences in heritability are largest for sensory sensitivity because the model we selected did not fit the data adequately. If we look at each temperament trait separately, we can see that the differences in heritability for the two combined samples are not large and range from 63 percent (endurance and activity) to 69 percent (perseveration). The results for each sample treated separately suggest that the differences in heritability are also small and range from 55 percent to 70 percent in the Polish sample and from 63 percent to 74 percent in the German sample.

These findings are yet another argument in support of the defining criteria of RTT traits, although it must also be pointed out that as far as the value of the heritability index is concerned, temperament is not any different than other personality traits (see Hofstee, 1994; Loehlin, 1992). Our data suggest that the heritability of temperament shows up regardless of the method used (self-report or rating), in line with findings from other studies (Riemann, Angleitner, & Strelau, 1997; Wolf et al., 2004). They also show that the contribution of genetic and environmental factors to the variance of the postulated RTT traits seems to be culturally universal, although this implication is somewhat weakened by the fact that only two culturally distinct samples were studied. If we assume that the two populations (the Polish and the German) do not differ significantly in their genotypic homogeneity, this would mean that the differences in environmental homogeneity are too small to have a significant effect on the variance of heritability (Zawadzki, Strelau, Oniszczenko, et al., 2002).

In addition to the twin studies, we were most curious about the role of temperament in difficult situations, ones in which the individual has to cope under stress. The next section takes a closer look at this problem from the behavior genetic perspective.

8.3
Genetic determinants of stress-related phenomena and their relationships with temperament

It follows from chapters 6 and 7 that the temperament traits measured by means of the FCB-TI correlate with various aspects of stress. This applies to stressors that are dependent on the individual and (above all) the psychological consequences of experienced states of stress. As I demonstrate in this section, these traits also correlate with coping styles. Taking as our point of departure the temperament-stress model presented in chapter 6 (see Figure 6.1), my collaborators and I launched a study to identify the degree to which the correlations that we had found between stressful phenomena and temperament traits can be attributed to genetic factors rather than environmental factors. But before we could answer this fundamental question as far as the RTT is concerned, we had to determine the degree to which the variance of the aspects of stress on which we had focused in our earlier research was due to hereditary and environmental factors. This research sequence is justified by the fact that it only makes sense to seek the genetic determinants of correlations between stress and temperament if the genetic factor accounts for at least some of the variance of stress-related phenomena, as it does for the variance of temperament traits. This section is devoted to this issue but first let me discuss the genetic determinants of stress-temperament relationships.

8.3.1. Stressors understood as life-changes and their relationships with temperament traits: A behavior genetic approach

It seems paradoxical to try to identify the genetic determination of environmentally generated stressors and therefore, in line with the temperament-stress model, our work is rooted in the assumption that certain stressors (e.g., disasters and catastrophes) are beyond human control and exist quite independently of the individuals who experience them (and these individuals' temperament). In such cases we can scarcely say that genes have an effect on phenomena over which the individual has no control. There are, however, certain environmental stressors that seem to be beyond human control but in fact are not completely independent. For example, high sensation seekers often face situations that are novel, highly stimulating, and even dangerous—that is, are intensely stressful (see, e.g., Hansen & Breivik, 2001; Zuckerman, 1994). This relationship between the situation (stressor) and individual attributes is an example of so-called active genotype-environment correlation and depends on individual genetic makeup. This makeup codetermines the individual's search for genotypically compatible environments (Plomin, DeFries, & Loehlin, 1977).

Ever since the pioneering work of Plomin, DeFries, and Loehlin (1977), numerous studies demonstrating environmental heritability have been conducted despite the deep-seated conviction that it is beyond the individual's control. Plomin and his collaborators (Plomin et al., 1994) found that certain characteristics of the family environment are codetermined by the genetic factors in individuals who live in this environment. The work on the heritability of stressors defined in terms of life-changes (see Rahe, 1987) has demonstrated that both environmental and genetic factors contribute to the variance of experienced life-changes and that the heritability of these changes is related to personality traits (Kendler et al., 1986). Other researchers have also found that the heritability of stressors understood in terms of life-changes depends on individual personality traits (Plomin et al., 1990; Saudino et al., 1997). Billing and collaborators (Billing et al., 1996) have pointed out that life-changes that are dependent on the individual (within the individual's control) are determined by the additive genetic factor and the specific environment.

These findings hardly exhaust the existing work on environmental heritability and its relationships with personality and encouraged us to launch several studies (see Sobolewski, Strelau, & Zawadzki, 2001), which are rooted in the hypothetical assumption that genotype and environment correlate. According to this assumption, temperament traits relating to the tendency to seek (avoid) highly stimulating environments correlate with individual-dependent stressors. And since previous work has shown that the variance of RTT traits is largely genetically determined, we assumed that correlation between these traits and environments that are (to some extent) under the individual's control will also be partly genetically determined.

In order to test the hypothesis, we launched a study using the MZ and DZ twins-reared-together method. The twins were recruited by mail and their zygoticity was determined by means of the Twin Physical Similarity Questionnaire (Oniszczenko & Rogucka, 1996; see section 8.2.2). The study was run on 464 pairs of twins, including 245 pairs of MZ twins aged 19–62 ($M = 34.0$; $SD =$

10.50) and 219 pairs of same-sex DZ twins aged 19–66 ($M = 34.5$; $SD = 11.40$). The sample was homogeneous in education and occupation.

Temperament traits were measured with the FCB-TI and stressors were assessed by means of the Recent Life Changes Questionnaire (RLCQ; Rahe, 1987) in Adam Sobolewski's (1996; Sobolewski, Strelau, & Zawadzki, 1999) Polish adaptation. (This questionnaire is presented in section 6.2). Taking the temperament-stress model (see Figure 6.1)—which includes both individual-dependent and individual-independent stressors—as our point of departure, we applied cluster analysis to identify individual-dependent and individual-independent stressors. This analysis was based on the RLCQ data that Sobolewski (2001) gathered for his doctoral dissertation. Three categories of individual-independent stressors were identified: death of a close relative, accidents, and serious illness requiring hospital treatment. Two classes of individual-dependent stressors were also identified taking emotional valence as their criterion: negative stressors (e.g., committed loss of job, major dental surgery) and challenges (e.g., change of lifestyle, expensive purchases, change of political orientation). Three basic categories of stressors were therefore included in the final analysis: individual-independent stressors, negative individual-dependent stressors, and individual-dependent challenges.

The data analysis was based on the five possible univariate models of structural equations postulated by the twin method (MZ and DZ twins reared together): ADE, AE, CE, E, and C (see section 8.1. for definitions). Two indices were applied, chi^2 and the Goodness-of-Fit Index. Model CE was the best-fitting model for individual-independent stressors (i.e., it explained the largest portion of the variance of this category of stressors). According to this model, the specific environment accounted for 88 percent of the variance of individual-independent stressors and the shared environment accounted for 12 percent of the variance of these stressors. The best-fitting model for the variance of negative individual-dependent stressors was model AE. According to this model, the specific environment accounted for 74 percent of the variance and the additive genetic factor accounted for 26 percent of the variance of these stressors. AE was also the best-fitting model for challenges. The specific environment accounted for 64 percent of the variance and the additive genetic factor accounted for 36 percent of the variance of these stressors. The details of the procedure applied to determine the goodness of fit for all three categories of stressors are discussed elsewhere (see Sobolewski, 2001; Sobolewski, Strelau, & Zawadzki, 2001). The results of this analysis confirmed our previous opinion that it is quite unjustified to try to identify relationships between individual independent stressors whose variance depends on neither genetic factors nor temperament.

In order to find out how strongly temperament traits are related to individual-dependent stressors whose variance (as we now knew) is partly determined by the additive genetic factor, we resorted to two-way analysis of goodness of fit. The path model on which this analysis was based is illustrated in Figure 8.4.

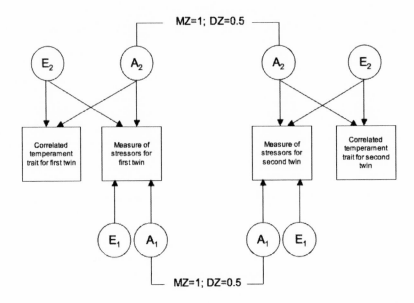

Figure 8.4. The path model for the two-way analysis that was used to explain the phenotypic correlation between temperament traits and individual-dependent stressors. Squares represent phenotypic variables. Circles represent latent variables. E_1 = specific environment relating to stressors; A_1 = additive genetic factor relating to stressors; E_2 = specific environment for correlated temperament trait; A_2 = additive genetic factor for correlated temperament trait. From "The Temperamental Determinants of Stressors as Life Changes: A Genetic Analysis" by A. Sobolewski, J. Strelau, and B. Zawadzki, 2001. *European Psychologist, 6*, p. 292. Copyright 2001 by Hogrefe & Huber Publishers. Reprinted with permission.

Three temperament traits—briskness, endurance, and activity—were selected for this analysis. These traits are believed to be particularly important regulators of the stimulating value of the environment (here stressors) and the two categories of individual-dependent stressors. Only model AE was considered in the two-way path analysis because we knew from the one-way analysis that this model had the best goodness of fit and most accurately accounted for the variance of individual-dependent stressors. In the two-way analysis, the phenotypic covariance between temperamental variables and the quantitative parameters of individual-dependent stressors was collapsed into covariance resulting from the effects of the specific environment and covariance resulting from the effects of the additive genetic factor. This analysis—that is, identification of the goodness of fit of models including the covariance between AE factors for the two types of individual-dependent stressors, separately for each of the three temperament traits—demonstrated that temperament traits account for about 10 percent of heritability, but this only applies to stressors that are challenges.

In addition to this analysis, we tested three pseudocausal models of relationships between stressors-cum-challenges and temperament. Two of these models apply to the effect of one variable on another variable (i.e., challenges on temperament and vice-versa); the third model applies to the reciprocal effects of these variables. When goodness-of-fit analysis was performed to explain the covariance between the AE factors, causality could only be determined for activity (see Table 8.4).

As we can see in this table, from which the data concerning the variance of measurement error that were included in the complete analysis (see Sobolewski, Strelau, & Zawadzki, 2001) have been omitted, the most adequate model shows the effect of activity on challenges. This model confirms the role of activity as a moderator that increases the chance of stressor occurrence (in the present study, however, this applies only to challenges). This partly genetically determined relationship between challenges and activity is easier to understand if we consider that the additive genetic factor is partially responsible for the variance of the two variables. We also know that, according to the RTT, activity as a temperament trait is expressed in behaviors and the search for environments that are sources of intensive stimulation. This fully corresponds to the category of stressors that have been identified as challenges.

The findings presented in section 7.2.2. clearly demonstrated that temperament traits, and particularly emotional reactivity, correlate above all with the consequences of trauma. These were usually assessed by means of the factorial version of the PTSD questionnaire (PTSD-F) regardless of when the assessment was made—that is, how much time had elapsed between the trauma and the assess-

Table 8.4 Results of model fitting of causal relationships between stressors dependent on individuals: Challenges and activity

Model	df	chi^2	p	GFI	Covariance	
AE x AE x covAE					β challenge-activity	β activity-challenge
Challenge → Activity	15	19.38	0.19	0.968	–	0.21
Challenge ← Activity	15	14.62*	0.47	0.973	0.23	–
Challenge ↔ Activity	14	11.96	0.61	0.979	0.48	-0.27
GBM	14	11.96	0.61	0.979		

Note. GFI = Goodness-of-Fit Index; GBM = genetic bivariate model; → / ← = unidirectional relationship between variable; ↔ = reciprocal relationship between variables. *Best-fitting model. Adapted from "The Temperamental Determinants of Stressors as Life Changes: A Genetic Analysis" by A. Sobolewski, J. Strelau, and B. Zawadzki, 2001, *European Psychologist*, 6, p. 293. Copyright 2001 by Hogrefe & Huber Publishers. Reprinted with permission.

ment). The next section presents research whose purpose was to identify the origins of the relationship between temperament and the consequences of trauma.

8.3.2. Genetic and environmental determinants of the consequences of trauma and their relationships with temperament traits: Family studies and studies based on the MZ and DZ twins-reared-together method

The review of the research on the role of individual differences in general and personality traits in particular in the moderation of the trauma-psychological consequences relationship (see section 7.2.1), as well as our own work that was presented in chapter 7, testify that these individual variables—in addition to trauma per se—significantly contribute to the variance of the consequences of trauma, which as a rule take the form of post-traumatic stress disorder.

Very little research has been done on the genetic foundations of PTSD, although studies using the twin study method (comparison of MZ and DZ twins reared together) suggest that the genetic factor contributes significantly to the variance of individual differences in PTSD symptoms (see Lyons et al., 1993; True et al., 1993). Studies of the genetic determinants of PTSD based on the biochemical correlates of this syndrome and conducted by means of the molecular genetic method do not unequivocally corroborate this pattern, however (see, e.g., Comings, Muhleman, & Gysin, 1996; Gelerntner et al., 1999; after Siwy & Kozak, 2004).

One of the studies conducted at our laboratory explored the heritability of the biochemical correlates of stress response. Level of state anxiety (measured by means of Spielberger's State–Trait Anxiety Inventory adapted by Wrześniewski & Sosnowski, 1987) during blood sampling was the indicator of the state of stress. This study was conducted using the twin method. In another study based on the family study method, we focused on the biochemical correlates of the psychological consequences of trauma caused by flooding (Oniszczenko, 2005; Oniszczenko et al., 2002).

The data were analyzed using one-way models based on structural equations typical for the MZ and DZ twins-reared-together method. Six biochemical correlates of stress response were analyzed (adrenalin, dopamine, cortisol, serotonin metabolite, noradrenalin, and serotonin). The genetic factor (AD) contributed significantly to the variance of two of these correlates, adrenalin and cortisol. The genetic factor accounted for 33 percent of the variance of adrenalin and 30 percent of the variance of cortisol. Because only 74 pairs of MZ and DZ twins aged 23–66 (including 42 pairs of same-sex DZ twins) were evaluated, this study should really be treated as a pilot study.

The family study was run on a group of flood victims consisting of biological families—parents (45 men and 90 women) and their children (69 sons and 61 daughters). Each family was represented by at least one parent and one child.

PTSD and biochemical correlates were assessed about two years after the trauma. The same biochemical correlates were measured as in the twin study presented above. Several patterns emerged from this work. Level of maternal serotonin correlated positively with the level of serotonin in the offspring (son or daughter). The same pattern was found for paternal and offspring serotonin levels; these correlations range from 0.62 to 0.92. A significant correlation also emerged for cortisol in all pair combinations except father-daughter, in which case the scores of the correlations ranged from 0.29 to 0.61. It is worth mentioning that the level of adrenalin, whose variance—as identified by means of the twin method—was accounted for by the significant contribution of the genetic factor, did not correlate with any parent-child configuration. The same applies to all the remaining biochemical correlates. These findings concerning the genetic determinants of the biochemical correlates of the state of stress, measured in terms of level of anxiety or the psychological consequences of this state only indirectly, shed some light on the problem of the genetic foundations of the studied variables.

The majority of our behavior genetic studies was concerned with the heritability of the consequences of disaster and their relationships with RTT traits. But from the very beginning of our work on flood victims, we wanted to identify the extent to which the genotype and the environment are responsible for the psychological consequences of this disaster and its relationships with temperament. This is why we had to study families (at least one parent and one child). This is also why all our studies of flood victims are based on the family study method.

Anna Siwy (2003; 2006; Siwy & Kozak, 2004) concentrated on this aspect of our work in her doctoral dissertation. She analyzed the heritability of the psychological consequences of disaster on a sample of victims of the 1997 Flood of the Century. This sample consisted of 81 families, 391 victims in all. Every family had two parents—mothers aged 35–67 ($M = 46.5$; $SD = 6.87$) and fathers aged 32–69 ($M = 48.9$; $SD = 7.21$). There were 41 male children and 40 female children aged 14–30 ($M = 19.8$; $SD = 3.72$).

PTSD was assessed by means of the PTSD-F, the two subscales (Intrusion-Hyperarousal and Avoidance-Numbing), and the General Scale (the total score for the two subscales). Temperament traits were measured with the FCB-TI. The data were analyzed by means of the path model for biological families (see Figure 8.3) using adequate structural equations. This analysis, which included such criteria as chi^2, AIC, and RMSEA (for a description of these criteria, see section 8.1), helped to identify one-way models that best fit the empirical data (see Table 8.5).

As we can see from this table, the variance of PTSD measured several weeks after the flood (retrospective data) is only slightly genetically determined (14 percent) and very strongly determined by the specific environment (86 percent). If we look at each of the two PTSD-F subscales for the same time period, we see that the contribution of the genetic factor to the variance of intrusion-hyperarousal is next to nil (3 percent) whereas the contribution of the specific environ-

Table 8.5 Contribution of genetic and environmental variance to the phenotypic variance of post-traumatic stress symptoms: Best-fitting one-way models based on family studies

Model	a^2	c^2	e^2	am	df	chi^2	P	AIC	RMSEA
Few weeks after flood									
PTSD									
AE	0.14	—	0.86	—	5	2.42	0.80	-7.58	0.00
Intrusion-Hyperarousal									
Aeam	0.03	—	0.97	-0.19	4	2.45	0.65	-5.55	0.00
Avoidance-Numbing									
Aeam	0.10	—	0.90	0.29	4	5.91	0.21	-2.10	0.08
2 years after flood									
PTSD									
Aeam	0.35	—	0.65	0.17	4	1.43	0.84	-6.57	0.00
Intrusion-Hyperarousal									
Aeam	0.26	—	0.74	0.16	4	1.35	0.85	-6.65	0.00
Avoidance-Numbing									
Aeam	0.16	—	0.84	0.40	4	2.35	0.67	-5.65	0.00

Note. a^2 = variance attributed to additive genetic factor; c^2 = variance attributed to shared environment; e^2 = variance attributed to nonshared environment; am = parental mating path; AIC = Akaike Information Criterion; RMSEA = Root Mean Squared Error Approximation; AE = additive genetic model; am = parental mating path. Adapted from "Zespół stresu pourazowego i style radzenia sobie ze stresem—uwarunkowania genetyczne i środowiskowe szacowane metodą studiów rodzinnych [PTSD and Coping Styles: Genetic and Environmental Determinants Assessed by Means of Family Studies] by A. Siwy and B. Kozak, 2004. In J. Strelau (Ed.), *Osobowość a ekstremalny stres*, p. 352. Copyright 2004 by Gdańskie Wydawnictwo Psychologiczne. Reprinted with permission.

ment is decisive (97 percent). The genetic factor contributes slightly more to the variance of avoidance-numbing. In this case the genetic factor accounts for 10 percent of the variance and the specific environment accounts for 90 percent of the variance.

A rather different picture emerges when we look at the results of the analysis based on PTSD measures taken about two years after the trauma. When we focus on the global PTSD score, we see that the genetic factor accounts for 35 percent of the variance of PTSD symptoms and the specific environment accounts for 65 percent of the variance. The contribution of the genetic factor is slightly smaller when we consider the variance of the intrusion-hyperarousal scores (26 percent and 74 percent, respectively, for the genetic factor and the specific environment). The contribution of the genetic factor is further reduced when we look at avoidance-numbing. In this case the genetic factor accounts for only 16 percent of the variance.

The role of the genetic factor in determining the variance of PTSD or its specific symptoms—presented here in the form of two factorial scales—hardly showed up when we measured PTSD within just a few weeks of the trauma, whereas it showed up very distinctly when we measured PTSD two years after the flood. The role of the genetic factor in particular was evident when we looked at all the symptoms of PTSD represented by the PTSD questionnaire general score. This pattern is quite obvious if we remember that the effect of the trauma itself, caused by so extreme a stressor as flooding, was more evident in the first phase of PTSD. Only later did individual differences, including personality, begin to have an effect. The nature of the stressors also evolved over time: objective stressors that accompany disasters (e.g., prolonged consequences of trauma due to loss of property) were replaced by a mix of objective and subjective stressors. As emphasized by Siwy and Kozak (2004), with the lapse of time since the trauma, stressors change into subjective cognitive representations of past events—which in turn are influenced, among other things, by perseveration and emotional reactivity.

In order to test the hypothesis that temperament traits may affect the variance of PTSD symptoms, especially when this syndrome is assessed long after the trauma, it was necessary to conduct another analysis. The purpose of this analysis was to identify the etiology of the relationship between temperament and PTSD symptoms, which we had demonstrated repeatedly in our earlier research (see section 7.2.2), and whether the genetic factor contributed to this relationship in any way. If it did, this would lend support to the hypothesis that PTSD symptoms depend on temperament to some extent.

In order to test this hypothesis, Siwy (2006) analyzed the data of the same flood victims once again. This time she applied Cholesky's two-way genetic model (Neale & Cardon, 1992). Basically this formula consists of searching for the model that best fits the empirical data by means of appropriate structural equations (see Neale et al., 1999). As opposed to one-way analysis, which is based on the "genotypic-environmental" variance of a single trait, this analysis includes the covariance between two traits. One issue needs to be pointed out here. The genetic correlation between compared variables (in this case temperament traits and PTSD symptoms) is independent of the level of heritability of each of these variables because the heritability of the compared variables may be accounted for either by genes that are partly shared by the two variables, or by genes that are quite distinct for each of these traits (see Plomin et al., 2001). Goodness of fit was estimated by means of such statistics as chi^2, AIC, and RMSEA. The two-way genetic correlations between general PTSD and the different temperament traits are presented in Table 8.6.

These findings show that PTSD symptoms correlate significantly with endurance, emotional reactivity, and perseveration (0.76, 0.54, and 0.49, respectively). Shared genetic variance between endurance, emotional reactivity, and

Table 8.6 Common genetic factors for PTSD and temperament: Bivariate model fitting (scores for best-fitting models)

Temperament trait	R	R^2
Activity	0.03	~0.01
Emotional reactivity	0.54*	0.29*
Endurance	0.76*	0.58*
Sensory sensitivity	0.16	0.03
Briskness	0.13	0.02
Perseveration	0.49*	0.24*

Note. *$p < 0.01$. R = multiple correlation; R^2 = explained variance. From "Genetic, Environmental, and Temperamental Correlates of Post-Traumatic Stress Disorder: Family Studies" by A. Siwy, 2006. In J. Strelau and T. Klonowicz (Eds.), *People Under Extreme Stress*, p. 201. Copyright 2006 by Nova Science Publishers. Reprinted with permission.

perseveration (on the one hand) and PTSD (on the other) is 0.58 percent, 29 percent, and 24 percent, respectively. These results, which have been comprehensively presented and interpreted by Siwy (2006), underscore that the relationship between selected temperament traits (here endurance, emotional reactivity, and perseveration) and PTSD is partly genetically determined, thus justifying the conclusion that temperament traits should be viewed as moderators that existed before the psychological consequences of trauma emerged. This finding is consistent with the findings of Jang and his collaborators (Jang et al., 2003), who found that personality variables based on the Big Five model are related to the consequences of trauma. By investigating the degree to which these correlations are genetically determined, it was possible to demonstrate that the genetic correlation coefficients were statistically significant and that the contribution of the genetic factor to the variance of this correlation ranged from 5 percent to 11 percent.

These results also suggest that the environment contributes most to the variance of PTSD symptoms. When we say environment, we mean almost exclusively the specific environment. This pattern emerged very distinctly from Siwy's analysis of PTSD shortly after the trauma. On the other hand, when PTSD was assessed again later, the genetic factor showed up distinctly and accounted for a considerable portion of the variance of PTSD—albeit not the dominant portion. Lyons and his collaborators (Lyons et al., 1993) obtained similar results using the twin method. They demonstrated that heritability of the consequences of war trauma falls in the 35–47 percent range and that only the specific environment is responsible for the remaining portion of the variance of these consequences.

Returning to the temperament-stress model discussed in chapters 7 and 8, we cannot ignore the relationship between temperament traits and styles of coping. This will be discussed in the next section.

8.3.3. Genetic and environmental determinants of coping styles and their relationships with temperament traits: Family studies and twin studies

Coping with stress, which I (Strelau, 1995b, p. 221) have defined as "a regulatory function that consists of maintaining the adequate balance between demands and capacities or reducing the discrepancy between demands and capacities," has been an object of our study for a long time, mainly in the context of temperament. It follows from the temperament-stress model presented in chapter 6 (see Figure 6.1) that temperament and coping are mutually related. *Nota bene*, coping generally had the status of style in this work. When we speak about coping in terms of style, as opposed to coping strategies, we mean the relatively stable tendency to use individually specific ways of coping with the purpose of removing or reducing the state of stress (Strelau, 2006).

Many studies investigating the relationships between coping styles and personality, particularly the three Eysenckian superfactors (Eysenck & Eysenck, 1985) or the Big Five (Costa & McCrae, 1992), have been reported in the literature. For example, Bolger (1990) and Costa, Somerfield, and McCrae (1996) found a positive correlation between neuroticism and emotion-oriented coping style. When extraversion—the other factor, in addition to neuroticism, that appears in the personality theories of both Eysenck and Costa and McCrae—was the focus of attention, it was found that it correlates with seeking social contact and task-oriented coping style (see, e.g., Nakano, 1992; O'Brien & DeLongis, 1996). Our own work (see Strelau et al., 2005; Szczepaniak, Strelau, & Wrześniewski, 1996) on the relationship between personality and coping style also found that neuroticism correlates with emotion-oriented coping style and that extraversion correlates with task-oriented and avoidance-oriented coping styles. This pattern emerged in studies using questionnaires measuring both PEN (EPQ-R) and the Big Five (NEO-FFI). Taking this and similar work as his point of departure, Ferguson (2001) concluded that in addition to elements shared by coping styles and selected personality traits, each of these constructs also introduced new elements.

Drawing from RTT traits and traits measured by the FCB-TI, we conducted a series of studies in which we measured the relationship between these traits and coping styles. We assessed coping styles by means of the Coping Inventory for Stressful Situations (CISS; Endler & Parker, 1990) in its authorized Polish adaptation (Strelau et al., 2005). The CISS has three scales: Task-Oriented Coping, Emotion-Oriented Coping, and Avoidance-Oriented Coping. The last coping style has two forms (subscales), Distraction and Social Diversity. We proposed the following hypotheses: the emotion-oriented style should correlate with emotional reactivity and perseveration; the task-oriented style should correlate with activity and briskness; and the avoidance-oriented style should correlate with activity, largely due to the tendency to seek social contact measured by the Social Diversity subscale.

Table 8.7 shows the median correlation coefficients from three independent studies illustrating the relationships between temperament traits and coping styles. More than two thousand individuals were examined, including a group of MZ and DZ twins from which only one twin per pair was included ($N = 1,327$, aged 19–81), flood victims tested two years after the flood ($N = 378$, aged 13–85), and flood victims examined fifteen months after the disaster ($N = 328$, aged 14–75). Their detailed demographic characteristics are presented elsewhere (Strelau et al., 2005).

A quick glance at the results in Table 8.7 reveals that our predictions concerning the relationships between temperament traits and coping styles were correct. The strongest correlation was found for emotion-oriented style on the one hand and emotional reactivity and perseveration on the other, and for social diversity and activity. Since endurance is negatively correlated with emotional reactivity (see Zawadzki & Strelau, 1997), the negative correlation between emotion-oriented coping style and endurance is quite understandable.

Our main goal, however, was to identify the etiology of the correlations that we found between coping style and temperament traits. To do this, we first had to determine the heritability of coping styles themselves because it would only make sense to seek the origins of the relationship between coping style and temperament if the variance of coping style was at least partly genetically determined, as is the case with temperament traits.

The first studies of the genetic etiology of individual differences in coping with stress were not conducted until the 1990s. We discussed them in one of our publications (see Kozak, Strelau, & Miles, 2005). For example, Kendler, and his collaborators (Kendler et al., 1991), who were probably the first to study coping style from a behavior genetic perspective, compared female MZ and DZ twins aged 21–37 and found that the genetic factor accounted for about 30 percent of the variance of coping styles. Mellins, Gatz, and Baker (1996) compared MZ and

Table 8.7 Medians of correlation coefficients between temperament traits and coping styles: Data from three independent studies ($N = 2,033$)

CISS Scales	BR	PE	SS	EN	ER	AC
Emotion-Oriented Coping style	0.25*	0.11*	0.22*	0.11	0.08	0.22*
Task-Oriented Coping style	-0.29*	0.49*	-0.11	-0.40*	0.60*	-0.16*
Avoidance-Oriented Coping style	0.06	0.13*	0.03	0.02	0.01	0.43*
Distraction	-0.07	0.11*	-0.06	-0.03	0.08	0.26*
Social Diversity	0.20*	0.08*	0.13*	0.08	-0.13*	0.50*

Note. *$p < 0.05$. BR = briskness; PE = perseveration; SS = sensory sensitivity; EN = endurance; ER = emotional reactivity; AC = activity.

DZ twins reared together (children aged 9–16) and found that five of the seven coping styles they investigated had some genetic contribution to the variance (from 18 percent to 99 percent), although the two remaining styles that are particularly important for us—that is, the emotion-oriented style and the task-oriented style—showed no genetic contribution. Busjahn and his collaborators (Busjahn et al., 1999) analyzed 19 coping styles and found some genetic contribution to the variance of each of these styles. This study was conducted on pairs of twins aged 20–48 using the twin method.

A study by Kato and Pedersen (2005) merits special attention. The authors examined Swedish twins within the framework of the Swedish Adoption/Twin Study of Aging (SATSA) program. They compared twins reared together and separately. This method of twin comparison is one of the most convincing sources of evidence supporting the role of various determinants of individual differences in the studied area (Plomin et al., 2001). The coping styles studied by them (problem solving, avoidance, and seeking contact with other people) are very similar to the ones that we assessed using the CISS. The Swedish researchers hypothesized that part of the variance of coping style is determined by personality dispositions and conducted a path analysis to determine the contribution of genetic factors to the phenotypic correlations between these coping style scales and personality scales. They included extraversion and neuroticism, which they measured with the Eysenck Personality Inventory (Eysenck & Eysenck, 1975), and openness to experience, which they measured with the NEO-FFI (Costa & McCrae, 1985).

The study, which was part of the longitudinal SATSA project, was run on 1,339 elderly and senile twins ($M = 58.0$; $SD = 12.80$). Structural analysis of the data, conducted separately for men and women, demonstrated that the genetic factor accounts for part of the variance of coping styles and that this contribution varies from 15 percent to 30 percent depending on the coping style. The authors also conducted a two-way path analysis of coping styles and personality traits and found that the specific environment contributes most to the phenotypic correlation between personality traits and coping styles, although the contribution of the genetic (additive) factor is also evident. The role of the latter factor is most pronounced in the correlation between the problem-solving coping style and openness to experience (27 percent in men and 23 percent in women) and least pronounced in the correlation between extraversion and seeking contact with other people (9 percent in men and 7 percent in women).

In a study that Beata Kozak undertook as part of the research for her doctoral dissertation (Kozak, 2000; Kozak, Strelau, & Miles, 2005), we analyzed the genetic relationship between coping style and RTT traits. But before we conducted this analysis, we had to determine the relative contributions of genetic factors and environmental factors to individual differences in coping style. A sample of 612 pairs of twins reared together—324 pairs of MZ twins (including 196 female pairs) and 288 pairs of same-sex DZ twins (including 165 female pairs)—was examined. The age of the entire sample ranged from 19 to 66 (M = 34.8; SD = 11.27). Zygoticity was assessed by means of the Twin Physical Similarity Questionnaire (see section 8.2.2) and coping styles were measured with the CISS. In order to determine the contribution of the genetic factor to individual differences in coping style, we conducted a one-way analysis based on structural models— typical for pairs of MZ and DZ twins reared together—applying the path model presented in Figure 8.2. The results of this analysis showing the best-fitting models are presented in Table 8.8. The global avoidance-oriented style is omitted and only its components (social diversity and distraction) are included.

As we can see from the table, model AE has the best fit for three coping styles whereas model DE has the best fit for social diversity. The contribution of the genetic factor to the variance of all the coping styles presented above ranges from 33 percent (distraction) to 39 percent (social diversity). As far as the variances of all four coping styles are concerned, the contribution of the specific environment is significantly greater than the contribution of the genetic factor, whereas the shared environment factor did not emerge at all. This outcome is consistent with the data presented earlier in the brief review (see Busjahn et al., 1999; Kendler et al., 1991; Mellins, Gatz, & Baker, 1996) where different coping styles were assessed in each case. Our other work based on the family study method (see the path model in Figure 8.3) and conducted by Siwy and Kozak (2004) has yielded similar results. These two researchers demonstrated that the best-fitting model includes the additive genetic factor (AE including the path for nonrandom parental mating) whose contribution to the variance of the same four coping

Table 8.8 Results of data fitting to univariate MZ and DZ twins, same-sex, reared-together models in coping styles

Model	a^2	d^2	e^2	c^2	df	chi^2	p	RMSEA	AIC
Emotion-oriented coping style									
AE	0.35		0.65		4	3.58	0.46	0.000	-4.42
Task-oriented coping style									
AE	0.34		0.66		4	2.61	0.62	0.000	-5.39
Distraction									
AE	0.33		0.67		4	5.36	0.25	0.024	-2.64
Social diversity									
DE		0.39	0.61		4	5.10	0.27	0.021	-2.90

Note. d^2 = variance attributed to nonadditive genetic factor; AE = additive genetic model; DE = nonadditive genetic model. For the remaining abbreviations, see Table 8.5. Adapted from "Genetic Determinants of Individual Differences in Coping Styles" by B. Kozak, J. Strelau, and J. N. V. Miles, 2005, *Anxiety, Stress, and Coping, 18*, p. 9. Copyright 2005 by Taylor & Francis Group. Reprinted with permission.

styles ranged from 22 percent (emotion-oriented style) to 28 percent (distraction). Here too the specific environment had the largest contribution to the variance of coping styles and the role of shared environment did not show up at all.

What interested us most was the degree to which the correlations we found between coping styles measured by the CISS and RTT traits (see Table 8.7) can be attributed to the genetic and environmental factors. Toward this end Kozak (2000) and Siwy (unpublished data) conducted two independent two-way analyses based on the goodness-of-fit method and using Cholesky's model (Neale & Cardon, 1992). They drew their data from the sample of MZ and DZ twins described above. Below I discuss the analysis that Anna Siwy conducted on 538 pairs of twins from the same sample; this sample included not only the two components of avoidance-oriented coping style, but also the avoidance style understood as the sum of these two components. The analysis demonstrated beyond doubt that the best-fitting model for all the correlations between coping styles and temperament traits is model AE, which takes the additive genetic factor into consideration.

The results of this analysis, whose final outcome is presented in Table 8.9, show that the contribution of the genetic factor—which accounts for the correlations between coping styles and temperament traits—varies considerably. The result for the correlation between emotional reactivity and the emotion-oriented coping style suggests that only the genetic factor is responsible for the relationship between these two variables. Presumably this variance can be attributed to the shared genetic factor. Another conclusion from this outcome, however, would be that the two variables have many common elements at the phenotypic level measured by means of self-rating. To test this hypothesis, we had to examine the two scales (emotion-oriented style and emotional reactivity) for item overlap. We found that the contribution of the genetic factor to the variance of the covariance between the two variables was also large for emotion-oriented coping and emotional reactivity (50 percent) and for social diversity-activity (51 percent). Genetic variance also contributed significantly to the relationships between emotion-oriented coping on the one hand and endurance and briskness on the other (27 percent and 28 percent, respectively). A similar pattern was found for the relationship between avoidance-oriented style and activity (29 percent). Surprisingly the genetic contribution to the variance of the remaining relationships between coping styles and temperament traits was either nonexistent or negligible (from < 0.01 percent to 0.09 percent).

I must point out that high coefficients of correlation between the variables (here the relationship between coping styles and temperament traits presented in Table 8.7) do not necessarily indicate that the genetic factor explains the covariance between these variables. It is also possible that a strong correlation between the variables may be caused by predominant responsibility of the environmental factor for the covariance. For example, the correlation between activity and

Table 8.9 Genetic variance common for correlations between temperament traits and style of coping with stress: Best-fitting models based on bivariate analysis for MZ and DZ twins reared together

Temperament trait	EOS		TOS		AV		SD		DI	
	R	R^2	R	R^2	R	R^2	R	R^2	R	R^2
Activity	-0.33	0.11	0.33	0.11	0.54	0.29	0.71	0.51	0.29	0.09
Emotional reactivity	1.00	1.00	-0.29	0.08	0.05	<0.01	-0.14	0.02	0.04	<0.01
Endurance	-0.52	0.27	0.02	<0.01	0.07	<0.01	0.14	0.02	0.01	<0.01
Sensory sensitivity	-0.15	0.02	0.53	0.28	-0.18	0.03	0.10	0.01	-0.34	0.12
Briskness	-0.53	0.28	0.38	0.14	0.12	0.01	0.33	0.11	-0.05	<0.01
Perseveration	0.71	0.50	0.16	0.02	0.10	0.01	0.20	0.04	-0.05	<0.01

Note. EOS = emotion-oriented coping style; TOS = task-oriented coping style; AV = avoidance-oriented coping style; SD = social diversity; DI = distraction; R = multiple correlation; R^2 = explained variance.

avoidance-oriented style is 0.43 (see Table 8.7), whereas the genetic contribution to the variance of this correlation is only 29 percent.

Our work on the etiology of the relationships between temperament traits and stress-related phenomena (stressors, the psychological consequences of state of stress, coping) has shown that the genetic factor is largely responsible for most of the correlations we have found. This is usually the case with the variance of the additive genetic factor. However, these correlations are largely attributable to the specific environmental factor, whereas the shared environment plays a very minor role or none at all. Our data also suggest that the stress-related phenomena we have studied share some of the shared genetic variance with temperament traits, although the molecular genetic paradigm would have to be adopted to test such hypotheses. This paradigm is becoming more popular in research on the foundations of intelligence and personality, including temperament. The last section presents the fledgling attempts to adopt this research approach in the study of the RTT.

8.3.4. Research on the genetic foundations of temperament traits conducted within the molecular genetic paradigm

Unlike many diseases whose etiology has been traced to single genes (e.g., Huntington's disease, phenylketonuria, or Folling's disease), resulting in the familiar saying "one gene, one disorder," behavior and behavior-inferred traits are determined by a larger pool of genes. These gene pools may have a minimal effect on the development of the trait in question and, just like traits, the multiple genes have a quantitative distribution (and hence are often presented in the form of a dimension). Polygenetic effects determine the genetic variance of these traits additively and interchangeably.

> Genes that contribute to genetic variance in quantitative traits are called quantitative trait loci (QTL). One implication of a multigene system is that genotypes are distributed quantitatively (dimensionally) even when traits are assessed phenotypically by dichotomous diagnoses. . . . The term QTL replaces the word "polygenic," which literally means "multiple genes" but has come to connote many genes of such infinitesimal effect size that they are unidentifiable. (Plomin, Owen, & McGuffin, 1994, pp. 1736–1737)

QTL research usually adopts the so-called allelic association strategy. This strategy is used to identify the relationship between an allele or alleles and a given trait. This approach, in which genetic differences at the gene level (DNA polymorphisms) apply to phenotypic individual differences, is frequently adopted in personality research (for a comprehensive review, see Plomin et al., 2001).

Psychological traits, including temperament traits, are not heritable per se; it is the physiological and biochemical mechanism underlying these traits that is genetically transmitted. Hence the best candidates among all the temperament traits for the search for allelic associations are those traits for which biological mechanisms have been identified or at least postulated. Research using the allelic association strategy has been conducted since the early 1990s, first on animals (for example, in studies of open field activity in mice; Flint et al., 1995) but subsequently on human beings. The volume edited by Benjamin, Ebstein, and Belmaker (2002; see also Oniszczenko, 2005) summarizes the findings of the work on allelic associations in the context of personality traits, including adult and child temperament.

In temperament research the most frequent candidates for QTL studies using allelic association techniques are the genes responsible for dopamine, serotonin, and noradrenalin receptors and transporters because their activity underlies several temperament traits (Strelau, 1998). Cloninger's theory (Cloninger, Przybeck, & Svrakic, 1991; Cloninger, Svrakic, & Przybeck, 1993) won particular acclaim in the search for allelic associations with temperament traits. This theory makes direct links between the author's postulated temperament traits and the level of functioning of the neurotransmitters. For example, harm avoidance is based on serotonin activity in the limbic system and novelty seeking is determined by the activity of dopaminergic paths in the *locus cinereus* (see Table 5.4).

Many studies in which temperament has been assessed by means of the Cloninger Tridimensional Personality Questionnaire (Cloninger, Przybeck, & Svrakic, 1991) or its expanded version, the Temperament and Character Questionnaire (Cloninger, Svrakic, & Przybeck, 1993), have sought the allelic associations between novelty seeking and polymorphism in the DRD4 dopamine receptor gene located in chromosome 11. This polymorphism applies to alleles of various lengths (numbers of repetitions). Individuals with "long" DRD4 gene alleles—whose receptor encodes low dopamine levels—have a greater tendency to pursue novelty than individuals with "shorter" DRD4 alleles, whose receptor encodes high dopamine levels. The results of the research on this relationship, which have been reviewed in several publications (Benjamin, Ebstein, & Belmaker, 2002; Munafo et al., 2003; Oniszczenko, 2005), are ambiguous. Therefore Paterson, Sunohara, and Kennedy (1999) are probably right when they say that the data concerning the relationship between novelty seeking and polymorphism of the DRD4 dopamine receptor gene have not been replicated.

Equally inconsistent are the findings concerning the relationship between level of serotonin activity and harm avoidance postulated by Cloninger. In this case the serotonin transporter gene (5-HTT) located in chromosome 17 was the object of study. This gene is responsible for removing serotonin from the synaptic cleft. The postulated relationship between polymorphism of this gene and harm avoidance was confirmed in some studies (e.g., Katsuragi et al., 1999; Samochowiec et al., 2001) but not in others (e.g., Ham et al., 2004; Kumakiri et al., 1999).

Many studies have been reported in the literature on the relationship between various personality traits, including temperament on the one hand and polymorphism of the DRD4 dopamine receptor gene and the 5-HTT serotonin transporter on the other, in both healthy and abnormal individuals (children as well as adults). Reviews of this work can be found in the publications cited above (see Benjamin, Ebstein, & Belmaker, 2002; Munafo et al., 2003; Oniszczenko (2005).

I am concentrating on Cloninger's theory here because this theory, more than any other theory of temperament, tries to relate its postulated traits to the level of activity of the aforementioned neurotransmitters. Because of the obvious correlations between RTT traits and the temperament traits postulated by Cloninger (see Table 5.6), this theory prompted Wojciech Dragan (2003, 2005) and his doctoral advisor Włodzimierz Oniszczenko (2005) to examine the relationship between the temperament traits measured by the FCB-TI on the one hand, and receptor gene polymorphism of the dopamine receptor and transporter and the serotonin transporter on the other. Two RTT traits were selected for this study: activity, the trait that correlated most strongly (0.45 and 0.33, respectively) with novelty seeking in two independent studies in Poland and Germany (see Table 5.6); and emotional reactivity, which correlated markedly with harm avoidance in these two studies (0.72 and 0.71, respectively). I cannot possibly discuss the expanded methodology underlying this work (for a detailed account, see Dragan & Oniszczenko, 2005; Oniszczenko & Dragan, 2005). Here let me say that the genotypes of the selected individuals were analyzed at the Institute of Biochemistry and Biophysics, Polish Academy of Sciences.

From a pool of 778 male students aged 18–27, 61 high scorers and 51 low scorers on the Emotional Reactivity scale, and 51 high scorers and 48 low scorers on the Activity scale, were selected. The differences between the groups were statistically significant for both these temperament traits. The procedure for sampling genetic material is discussed in detail in Oniszczenko (2005). A sample of the oral epithelium was taken from each individual and special kits were used to isolate the DNA genome, which was necessary to analyze polymorphism in the dopamine transporter gene (DAT-1), the D4 dopamine receptor gene (DRD4), and the serotonin transporter gene (5-HTT).

This analysis revealed no significant relationship between DRD4 gene polymorphism and activity or between activity and the dopamine transporter gene (DAT-1). On the other hand, a relationship was found between the dopamine receptor gene (DRD4) and emotional reactivity. When polymorphism of the serotonin transporter gene was analyzed, a significant relationship was found between the length of the allele of gene 5-HTT and activity, whereas no relationship was found between this allele and emotional reactivity.

It is still too early to draw any far-reaching conclusions from the results of this work. I am presenting these findings to show that a pivotal shift toward molecular genetics has taken place in research on the neurophysiological and biochemical mechanisms of RTT traits. A similar trend has been observed in personality and intelligence research within the last decade. In psychological (and psychopathological) research, however, molecular genetics is closely linked to behavior genetics. As I have indicated in the above examples, the findings obtained within the behavior genetic paradigm have provided molecular geneticists with a number of clues about those behaviors and traits that deserve closer scrutiny in an attempt to identify the genes responsible for their development. Research on the causal relationships between genetically determined level of neurotransmitter functioning and personality traits—including temperament—has encountered an almost insurmountable obstacle, however, as Von Knorring (1984) pointed out more than twenty years ago. Over thirty different neurotransmitter systems operate in the central nervous system and the extent of our current knowledge about the interactions among these systems is scant. Perhaps this partly explains why the work on the relationships between temperament traits and genetically determined neurotransmitter (receptor and transporter) activity has so far yielded ambiguous results.

The research findings summarized in this chapter suggest three major conclusions. First, individual differences in temperament traits measured by means of the FCB-TI are no less determined by the contribution of genetic variance than traits postulated by other theories of temperament. The existing data, scarce as they are, also suggest that the biochemical mechanisms underlying the temperament traits we have studied have genetic roots. These data lend support to Proposition 7 of the Regulative Theory of Temperament, which states that temperament (the result of biological evolution) is genetically determined to a considerable extent.

Second, this same research shows unequivocally that the variance of the specific environment plays a dominant role in shaping individual differences in the measured temperament traits. These data lend strong support to Proposition 8 of the Regulative Theory of Temperament, which accentuates the role of the environment in the ontogenetic development of temperament.

Finally, both the environment and the genetic factor account for the relationships we have found between stress-related phenomena such as stressors (but only individual-dependent stressors), the psychological consequences of stressors, and ways of coping with stress on the one hand and temperament traits on the other. When we say environment, we mainly mean specific environment; and when we say the genetic factor, we mainly mean the additive genetic factor (i.e., genes transmitted from generation to generation). This largely explains the origins of the temperament-stress relationships we have managed to identify and therefore lends support to Propositions 9 and 10 of the Regulative Theory of Temperament, which posit that the regulative functions of temperament are most obvious when the individual is confronted with extreme situations.

Postscript

The long-term studies of temperament that my coworkers, students, and I have conducted all had one major purpose in mind: to test the basic propositions of the Regulative Theory of Temperament (RTT) presented in chapter 3. Not all these propositions can be put to empirical test because some of them are assumptive by nature. If we define temperament as it is defined in the RTT (see chapter 4), which says that temperament refers to the formal characteristics of behavior, then the findings presented in this book lend credence to the conclusion that temperament traits thus understood play an important role in regulating the relationships between men and women and their surrounding reality. This regulative function is to modify (moderate) the stimulating (energetic) and temporal parameters of behaviors, reactions, and situations. As we have demonstrated in numerous studies, this function is most obvious in circumstances that we would call difficult or even extreme.

Although temperament is the principal variable in the presented research, its moderating or mediating role[1] has usually been examined in the context of other psychological and environmental variables—hence implementing a systemic approach in the study of the functional role of temperament traits. One example of this approach is the work of Korczyńska (see section 6.3.2.2) and Kaczmarek and Zawadzki (see section 7.2.2.4). Eliasz (1981, 1985) and his collaborators (See, e.g., Brandstätter & Eliasz, 2001; Zalewska, 2003) consistently adopted this approach in their temperament studies based on their Transactional Model of Temperament, a model rooted in the Regulative Theory of Temperament. This systemic approach allows the researcher to grasp the functional specificity of temperament traits in the context of many other individual (psychological and demographic) and environmental variables that codetermine human behavior.

Our own work conducted within the behavior genetic paradigm has produced

---

[1] Here I am using the terms "moderator" and "mediator" in a different sense than the one in which I have used them in this book (see the definition in chapter 3; that is, I am using them as they are defined in psychological research methodology. When I say moderator, I mean a variable (B) that affects the relationship between two other variables (A and C) that are related but only under certain contingencies of variable B. When I say mediator, I mean a variable (B) that enters the causal path between two other related variables (A and C). In other words, if A is significantly related to C, and A affects B, and B affects C, then B acts as a mediator between A and C (cf. Holmbeck, 1997).

powerful evidence regarding the origins of individual differences in temperament traits. It highlights the significance of genetic (i.e., biological) factors in the development of the variance of RTT traits. On the other hand, it also provides convincing arguments in favor of the role of the environment in the development of these individual differences—a role that I did not appreciate in the early stages of my temperament research (see Strelau, 1978). This work also offers an indirect answer to the question of stability versus changeability of temperament traits. It suggests that the environment can modify temperament traits. What we still do not know, however, is what must happen to trigger such change and what we mean when we say that temperament traits are stable (many researchers maintain that of all the personality traits, temperament traits are the most immutable; see Strelau, 1998). Because the stability-changeability of temperament has not yet been tested empirically, this is where the shortcomings of the RTT are most evident.

Throughout all the years of my temperament research, I have not managed to encourage any of my colleagues to undertake longitudinal studies of the RTT traits—the only research design that would allow us to convincingly resolve the issue of the stability-changeability of temperament traits throughout the life-span. Unfortunately graduate and postgraduate students usually study reality from a short-term perspective since that is the nature of research conducted within the university system. I must also confess that from the very beginning, my own work and the work of my colleagues and students (with just a few exceptions; see, e.g., Friedensberg, 1985) has focused on adults or adolescents. Only when Oniszczenko and Radomska (2002) developed their children's version of the FCB-TQ (which can be administered to 7- to 12-year-olds) was it possible to begin to study the functional role of temperament in children of early school age (see, e.g., Kaczmarek & Zawadzki, 2006), although the longitudinal approach is still absent in work conducted within the RTT paradigm.

If we review the longitudinal work on temperament that was conducted by Thomas and Chess (1986) for over thirty years—work that is quite unique on a worldwide scale—then we should repeat after these researchers that the stability of temperament traits is expressed in their definitional identity, whereas the changeability of these traits is expressed in the fact that as individuals develop, the manifestations and quality of performance of these (by definition) stable temperament traits change. In other words, to adopt the typology of the ancient Greeks, compared with her peers, the sanguine child will remain a sanguine type even in old age but the same temperament will be expressed quite differently in these two stages of life. Our own findings suggest, however, that environmental factors—especially extreme ones—may modify the physiological mechanisms that underlie temperament. So to return to Thomas and Chess's terminology, we may say that the definitional identity of temperament traits may change. The work of Eliasz (1981; see section 3.3.2) and Kaczmarek and Zawadzki, 2006; see section 7.2.2.4) suggests that this indeed may be so.

This rare focus on one phenomenon (i.e., temperament) throughout almost my entire academic career suggests that my research interests may be somewhat narrow, and in this sense I must agree. But on the other hand, this persistence shows that striving to gain insight into the nature and functional role of this human psychological quality (one of many) requires a complex and expanded approach, one that frequently branches into other research areas—and in this sense my perspective has really been quite broad. This is the kind of research my partners—my students and colleagues, who represent at least two new generations—and I have undertaken. We have studied RTT traits in adults and (less frequently) children, in humans and animals (see, e.g., Pisula, Ostaszewski, & Matysiak, 1992). We have crossed the boundaries into such fields as psychophysiology (see, e.g., chapter 1), neurophysiology (De Pascalis, Strelau, & Zawadzki, 1999), and biochemistry (see section 8.3.2) and, as illustrated in chapter 8, we have drawn abundantly from the behavior genetic paradigm in our studies of temperament and its relationships to stress. We have studied not only so-called normal individuals but also representative samples of the sick and disordered (see, e.g., Strelau & Zawadzki, 2005a). In addition to this, commencing in the early 1990s, we have studied temperament within the cross-cultural psychology paradigm (see, e.g., Strelau & Angleitner, 1994; Zawadzki, 2002).

I wish to argue rather immodestly that this complex and interdisciplinary approach to the study of temperament and its role is what distinguishes the Regulative Theory of Temperament from other concepts of this phenomenon. I must point out, however, that my own research and the work of my students and associates is originally rooted in the theory that we operationalized and then subjected to successive falsifications based on the incoming empirical data. This approach greatly distinguishes the RTT from work on the so-called Big Five personality traits. In the latter case, if theoretical considerations are present at all, they are the end point rather than the point of departure because the starting point has been the statistical analysis of empirical data gathered in lexical and psychometric studies (see, e.g., Costa & McCrae, 1988, 1992; Goldberg, 1990).

Although almost a half-century has elapsed since I published my first article on temperament, and even though the Regulative Theory of Temperament is a relatively narrow area of investigation, I must admit that many questions still remain to be answered. I sincerely hope that these questions will challenge younger scientists who will continue to do research convinced, as I am, that temperament plays a major role in the functioning of human beings.

References

Aleksandrowicz, J. W., Bierzyński, K., Filipiak, J., Kowalczyk, E., Martyniak, J., Mazoń, S., et al. (1981). Kwestionariusze objawowe "S" i "O"—Narzędzia służące do diagnozy i opisu zaburzeń nerwicowych [Symptomatic questionnaires: Tools aimed at diagnosing and describing neurotic disturbances]. *Psychoterapia, 37*, 11–27.

Allport, G. W. (1937). *Personality: A psychological interpretation.* New York: Holt.

Amelang, M. (1997). Using personality variables to predict cancer and heart disease. *European Journal of Personality, 11*, 319–342.

American Psychiatric Association (1980). *Diagnostic and statistical manual of mental disorders* (3rd ed.). Washington, DC: Author.

American Psychiatric Association (1987). *Diagnostic and statistical manual of mental disorders* (3rd rev. ed.). Washington, DC: Author.

American Psychiatric Association (1994). *Diagnostic and statistical manual of mental disorders* (4th ed.). Washington, DC: Author.

American Psychiatric Association (2000). *Diagnostic and statistical manual of mental disorders* (4th TR ed.). Washington, DC: Author.

Angleitner, A., & Riemann, R. (1991). What can we learn from the discussion of personality questionnaires for the construction of temperament inventories? In J. Strelau & A. Angleitner (Eds.), *Explorations in temperament: International perspectives on theory and measurement* (pp. 191–201). New York: Plenum Press.

Angleitner, A., Riemann, R., Spinath, F. M., & Borkenau, P. (2001). Genetic and environmental influences on Pavlovian oriented temperamental traits measured by laboratory methods, self-reports, and peer reports. In A. Eliasz & A. Angleitner (Eds.), *Advances in research on temperament* (pp. 60–82). Lengerich, Germany: Pabst Science Publishers.

Angleitner, A., Riemann, R., Spinath, F. M., Hempel, S., Thiel, W., & Strelau, J. (1995, July). *The Bielefeld-Warsaw Twin Project: First report on the Bielefeld samples.* Workshop on Genetic Studies on Temperament and Personality, Pułtusk, Poland.

Angleitner, A., & Spinath, F. M. (2003). Badania porównawcze koncepcji temperamentu Cloningera i Strelaua [Comparative studies based on Cloninger's and Strelau's theories of temperament]. In M. Marszał-Wiśniewska, T. Klonowicz, & M. Fajkowska-Stanik (Eds.), *Psychologia różnic indywidualnych. Wybrane zagadnienia* (pp. 115–129). Gdańsk: Gdańskie Wydawnictwo Psychologiczne.

Anokhin, P. K. (1978). *Collected works: Philosophical aspects of the functional system theory.* Moscow: Nauka (in Russian).

Anthony, J. L., Lonigan, C. L., & Hecht, S. A. (1999). Dimensionality of posttraumatic stress disorder symptoms in children exposed to disaster: Results from confirmatory factor analyses. *Journal of Abnormal Psychology, 108*, 326–336.

Bates, J. E., Freeland, C. A. B., & Lounsbury, M. L. (1979). Measurement of infant difficultness. *Child Development, 50*, 794–803.

Beer, J. M., & Rose, R. J. (1995). The five factors of personality: A study of twins. *Behavior Genetics, 25*, 254.

Beisert, M. (2000). Przejawy, mechanizmy, i przyczyny wypalania się pielęgniarek [Symptoms, mechanisms, and causes of burnout in nurses]. In H. Sęk (Ed.), *Wypalenie zawodowe. Przyczyny, mechanizmy, zapobieganie* (pp. 182–215). Warsaw: Wydawnictwo Naukowe PWN.

Bendien, J., & Groen, J. (1963). A psychological statistical study of neuroticism and extraversion in patients with myocardial infarction. *Journal of Psychosomatic Research, 7*, 11–14.

Benjamin, J., Ebstein, R. P., & Belmaker, R. H. (Eds.). (2002). *Molecular genetics and the human personality*. Washington, DC: American Psychiatric Publishing.

Bergeman, C. S., Chipuer, H. M., Plomin, R., Pedersen, N. L., McClearn, G. E., Nesselroade, J. R., et al. (1993). Genetic and environmental effects on openness to experience, agreeableness, and conscientiousness: An adoption/twin study. *Journal of Personality, 61*, 159–179.

Berlyne, D. E. (1960). *Conflict, arousal, curiosity*. New York: McGraw-Hill.

Berry, J. W. (1969). On cross-cultural comparability. *International Journal of Psychology, 4*, 119–128.

Berry, J. W. (1989). Imposed etics-emics-derived etics: The operationalization of a compelling idea. *International Journal of Psychology, 24*, 721–735.

Billing, J. P., Hershberger, S. L., Iacono, W. G., & McGue, M. (1996). Life events and personality in late adolescence: Genetic and environmental relations. *Behavior Genetics, 26*, 543–554.

Birman, B. N. (1951). An attempt for a clinical-physiological assessment of types of higher nervous activity. *Zhurnal Vysshei Nervnoi Deyatelnosti, 1*, 879–888 (in Russian).

Blake, R. R., & Mouton, J. S. (1964). *The managerial grid: Key orientation for achieving production through people*. Houston: Gulf Publishing.

Bobrowska, K. (1997). *Charakterystyka temperamentalna a sposób radzenia sobie ze stresem u osób z chorobą nowotworową* [Temperament characteristics and coping style in patients with cancer]. Unpublished master's thesis, Warsaw University, Warsaw.

Bodunov, M. V. (1993). Factor structure of the Pavlovian Temperament Survey in a Russian population: Comparison and preliminary findings. *Personality and Individual Differences, 14*, 557–563.

Bokszczanin, A. (2003). *Społeczne i psychiczne reakcje dzieci i młodzieży na powódź 1997 roku* [Social and psychological reactions in children and adolescents toward Flood 1997]. Warsaw: Wydawnictwo Instytutu Psychologii PAN i Szkoły Wyższej Psychologii Społecznej.

Bolger, N. (1990). Coping as a personality process: A prospective study. *Journal of Personality and Social Psychology, 59*, 525–537.

Bonanno, G. (2004). Loss, trauma, and human resilience. *American Psychologist, 59*, 20–28.

Bouchard, T. J., Jr. (1994). Genes, environment, and personality. *Science, 264*, 1700–1701.

Bouchard, T. J., Jr., & McGue, M. (1990). Genetic and rearing environmental influences on adult personality: An analysis of adopted twins reared apart. *Journal of Personality, 58*, 263–292.

Bouchard, T. J., Jr., Segal, N. L., Tellegen, A., McGue, M., Keyes, M., & Krueger, R. (2003). Evidence of the construct validity and heritability of the Wilson–Patterson Conservative Scale: A reared-apart twins study of social attitudes. *Personality and Individual Differences, 34*, 959–969.

Bouchard, T. J., Jr., Segal, N. L., Tellegen, A., McGue, M., Keyes, & M., Krueger, R. (2004). Genetic influences on social attitudes: Another challenge to psychology from behavior genetics. In L. F. DiLalla (Ed.), *Behavior genetics principles: Perspectives in development, personality, and psychopathology* (pp. 89–104). Washington, DC: American Psychological Association.

Brandstätter, H., & Eliasz, A. (Eds.). (2001). *Persons, situations, and emotions: An ecological approach.* Oxford: Oxford University Press.

Brett, E. A., & Ostroff, R. (1985). Imagery and post-traumatic stress disorder: An overview. *American Journal of Psychiatry, 142,* 417–424.

Brewin, C. R., Dalgleish, T., & Joseph, S. (1996). A dual representation theory of posttraumatic stress disorder. *Psychological Review, 103,* 670–686.

Broadhurst, P. L. (1975). The Maudsley reactive and non-reactive strains of rats: A survey. *Behavior Genetics, 5,* 299–319.

Broadhurst, P. L., & Levine, S. (1963). Behavioral consistency in strains of rats selectively bred for emotional elimination. *British Journal of Psychology, 56,* 121–125.

Brzeziński, J., & Stachowski, R. (1981). *Zastosowanie analizy wariancji w eksperymentalnych badaniach psychologicznych* [Application of the analysis of variance in experimental psychological research]. Warsaw: Państwowe Wydawnictwo Naukowe.

Brzozowski, P., & Drwal, R. Ł. (1995). *Kwestionariusz Osobowości Eysencka. Polska adaptacja EPQ-R. Podręcznik* [Eysenck Personality Questionnaire: Polish adaptation of the EPQ-R. Manual]. Warsaw: Pracowania Testów Psychologicznych PTP.

Burisch, M. (2002). A longitudinal study of burnout: The relative importance of dispositions and experiences. *Work & Stress, 16,* 1–17.

Busjahn, A., Faulhaber, H. D., Freier, K., & Luft, F. C. (1999). Genetic and environmental influences on coping styles: A twin study. *Psychosomatic Medicine, 4,* 469–475.

Buss, A. H., & Plomin, R. (1975). *A temperament theory of personality development.* New York: Wiley.

Buss, A. H., & Plomin, R. (1984). *Temperament: Early developing personality traits.* Hillsdale, NJ: Erlbaum.

Campbell, D. T., & Fiske, D. W. (1959). Convergent and discriminant validation by the multitrait-multimethod matrix. *Psychological Bulletin, 56,* 81–105.

Carey, W. B. (1986). The difficult child. *Pediatrics in Review, 8,* 39–45.

Carey, W. B., & McDevitt, S. C. (1978). Revision of the Infant Temperament Questionniare. *Pediatrics, 61,* 735–739.

Carlier, M. (1985). Factor analysis of Strelau's Questionnaire and an attempt to validate some of the factors. In J. Strelau, F. H. Farley, & A. Gale (Eds.), *The biological bases of personality and behavior: Vol. 1. Theories, measurement techniques, and development* (pp. 145–160). Washington, DC: Hemisphere.

Carroll, J. B. (1993). *Human cognitive abilities: A survey of factor-analytic studies.* New York: Cambridge University Press.

Cattell, R. B. (1965). *The scientific analysis of personality.* Baltimore: Penguin.

Cattell, R. B., & Warburton, F. W. (1967). *Objective personality and motivation tests: A theoretical introduction and practical compendium.* Urbana: University of Illinois Press.

Chen, E., Craske, M. G., Katz, E. R., Schwartz, E., & Zeltzer, L. (2000). Pain-sensitive temperament: Does it predict procedural distress and response to psychological treatment among children with cancer? *Journal of Pediatric Psychology, 25,* 269–278.

Chess, S., & Thomas, A. (1986). *Temperament in clinical practice.* New York: Guilford Press.

Choynowski, M. (1977). Podręcznik do "Inwentarza Osobowości" H. J. Eysencka [H. J. Eysenck's "Personality Inventory": Manual]. In M. Choynowski (Ed.), *Testy psychologiczne w poradnictwie wychowawczo-zawodowym* (pp. 493–536). Warsaw: Państwowe Wydawnictwo Naukowe.

Chudnovsky, V. E. (1963). Concerning the age approach to typological features. *Voprosy Psikhologii, 1,* 23–34 (in Russian).

Ciosek, M., & Oszmiańczuk, J. (1974). Właściwości procesów nerwowych a ekstrawersja i neurotyzm [Nervous system properties and extraversion and neuroticism]. *Przegląd Psychologiczny, 17,* 235–246.

Cloninger, C. R. (1986). A unified biosocial theory of personality and its role in the development of anxiety states. *Psychiatric Developments, 3,* 167–226.

Cloninger, C. R. (1997). A psychobiological model of personality and psychopathology. *Journal of Psychosomatic Medicine, 37,* 91–102.

Cloninger, C. R., Przybeck, T. R., & Svrakic, D. M. (1991). The Tridimensional Personality Questionnaire: U.S. normative data. *Psychological Reports, 69,* 1047–1057.

Cloninger, C. R., Przybeck, T. R., Svrakic, D. M., & Wetzel, R. D. (1994). *The Temperament and Character Inventory (TCI): A guide to its development and use.* St. Louis, MO: Center for Psychobiology of Personality.

Cloninger, C. R., Svrakic, D. M., & Przybeck T. R. (1993). A psychobiological model of temperament and character. *Archives of General Psychiatry, 50,* 975–990.

Comings, D. E., Muhleman, D., & Gysin, R. (1996). Dopamine D2 receptor (DRD2) gene and susceptibility to posttraumatic stress disorder: A study and replication. *Biological Psychiatry, 40,* 368–372.

Conrad, K. (1941). *Der Konstitutionstypus: Theoretische Grundlegung und praktische Bestimmung* [The constitutional type: Theoretical foundation and practical significance]. Berlin: Springer-Verlag.

Cooper, C. L., & Payne, R. (Eds.). (1979). *Stress at work.* New York: Wiley.

Cooper, H., Okamura, L., & McNeil, P. (1995). Situation and personality correlates of psychological well-being: Social activity and personal control. *Journal of Research in Personality, 29,* 395–417.

Coppen, A., & Metcalfe, M. (1963). Cancer and extraversion. *British Medical Journal, 6,* 18–19.

Cordova, M. J., Andrykowski, M. A., Kenady, D., McGrath, P., Sloan, D., & Redd, W. (1995). Frequency and correlates of posttraumatic-stress-disorder-like symptoms after treatment for breast cancer. *Journal of Consulting and Clinical Psychology, 63,* 981–986.

Costa, P. T., Jr., & McCrae, R. R. (1985). *The NEO Personality Inventory manual.* Odessa, FL: Psychological Assessment Resources.

Costa, P. T., Jr., & McCrae, R. R. (1988). Personality in adulthood: A six-year longitudinal study of self-reports and spouse ratings on the NEO Personality Inventory. *Journal of Personality and Social Psychology, 54,* 853–863.

Costa, P. T., Jr., & McCrae, R. R. (1989). *NEO-PI/FFI manual supplement.* Odessa, FL: Psychological Assessment Resources.

Costa, P. T., Jr., & McCrae, R. R. (1992). *Revised NEO Personality Inventory (NEO-PI-R) and NEO Five Factor Inventory (NEO-FFI): Professional manual.* Odessa FL: Psychological Assessment Resources.

Costa, P. T., Jr., Somerfield, M. R., Jr., & McCrae, R. R. (1996). Personality and coping:

A reconceptualization. In M. Zeidner & N. S. Endler (Eds.), *Handbook of coping: Theory, research, applications* (pp. 44–61). Toronto: Wiley.

Cupas, M. (1997) *Adaptacja Inwentarza Zdrowia Psychicznego MHI (Mental Health Inventory MHI) Clarice Veit i J. Ware do warunków polskich* [Adaptation of the Mental Heath Inventory (MHI), constructed by Clarice Veit and J. Ware, to Polish conditions]. Unpublished master's thesis, Warsaw University, Warsaw.

Cymes, I. (1974). *Reaktywność a indywidualny styl pracy umysłowej ucznia–na przykładzie uczenia się tekstu biologicznego* [Reactivity and individual style of mental activity: Exemplified by learning a biological text]. Unpublished master's thesis, Warsaw University, Warsaw.

Cytawa, J. (1959). Badanie typu układu nerwowego człowieka na podstawie wywiadu [Assesment of the human type of nervous system by means of interview]. *Annales Universitatis Mariae Curie-Skłodowska, 14*, 137–156.

Czyżkowska, A. M. (1974). *Wpływ poziomu reaktywności i rodzaju instrukcji na wykonywanie zadań* [The influence of reactivity level and kind of instruction on tasks performance]. Unpublished master's thesis, Warsaw Univeristy, Warsaw.

Danielak, M. (1972). *Reaktywność a wybór zawodów związanych z różnym stopniem stymulacji* [Reactivity and choice of professions characterized by different levels of stimulation]. Unpublished master's thesis, Warsaw University, Warsaw.

Daum, I., & Schugens, M. M. (1986). The Strelau Temperament Inventory (STI): Preliminary results in a West German sample. *Personality and Individual Differences, 7*, 509–517.

Davidson, J., Kudler, H., & Smith, R. (1987). Personality in chronic post-traumatic stress disorder: A study of the Eysenck inventory. *Journal of Anxiety Disorders, 1*, 295–300.

Davis, F. C. (1933). The measurement of aggressive behavior in laboratory rats. *Journal of Genetic Psychology, 43*, 213–217.

De Pascalis, V., Strelau, J., & Zawadzki, B. (1999). The effect of temperamental traits on event-related potentials, heart rate, and reaction time. *Personality and Individual Differences, 26*, 441–465.

Deary, I. J. (2000). *Looking down on human intelligence: From psychometrics to the brain.* Oxford: Oxford University Press.

Dekel, R., Solomon, Z., Ginzburg, K., Zakin, G., & Neria, Y. (2004). Radzenie sobie ze stresem w sytuacji niewoli wojennej. Wpływ osobowości na zespół stresu pourazowego [Coping with stress in a situation of war captivity: Influence of personality on PTSD]. In J. Strelau (Ed.), *Osobowość a ekstremalny stres* (pp. 264–280). Gdańsk, Poland: Gdańskie Wydawnictwo Psychologiczne.

Denollet, J. (1997). Personality, emotional distress, and coronary heart disease. *European Journal of Personality, 11*, 343–357.

Digman, J. M. (1989). Five robust trait dimensions: Development, stability, and utility. *Journal of Personality, 57*, 195–214.

Diamond, S. (1957). *Personality and temperament.* New York: Harper & Brothers.

Dragan, W. Ł. (2003). Genetycznie uwarunkowana zmienność w wychwycie zwrotnym serotoniny a cechy temperamentalne postulowane przez Regulacyjną Teorię Temperamentu Strelaua [Genetically driven variation in serotonin uptake and temperamental traits postulated by Strelau's Regulative Theory of Temperament]. *Psychologia–Etologia–Genetyka, 8*, 35–49.

Dragan, W. Ł. (2005). *Polimorfizm genu transportera serotoniny i polimorfizm genu transportera dopaminy a cechy temperamentalne postulowane przez Regulacyjną Teorię Temperamentu Jana Strelaua* [Polymorphism in the serotonin and dopamine gene tran-porters and temperamental traits postulated by Jan Strelau's Regulative Theory of Temperament]. Unpublished doctoral dissertation, Warsaw University, Warsaw.

Dragan, W. Ł., & Oniszczenko, W. (2005). Polymorphisms in the serotonin tranporter gene and their relationship to temperamental traits measured by the Formal Characteristics of Behavior–Temperament Inventory: Activity and emotional reactivity. *Neuropsychobiology, 51,* 269–274.

Duda, A. (1996). *Interakcja czynników osobowościowo-temperamentalnych i środowiskowych a występowanie nowotworu gruczołu piersi u kobiet* [The interaction between personality-temperament and environmental factors and the appearance of breast cancer in women]. Unpublished master's thesis, Silesian University, Katowice.

Dudek, B. (2003). *Zaburzenia po stresie traumatycznym* [Disturbances after traumatic stress]. Gdańsk: Gdańskie Wydawnictwo Psychologiczne.

Duffy, E. (1951). The concept of energy mobilization. *Psychological Review, 58,* 30–40.

Duffy, E. (1957). The psychological significance of the concept of "arousal" or "activation." *Psychological Review, 64,* 265–275.

Duffy, E. (1972). Activation. In N. S. Greenfield, & R. A. Sternbach (Eds.), *Handbook of psychophysiology* (pp. 577–622). New York: Holt, Rinehart & Winston.

Eaton, W. O., & Saudino, K. J. (1992). Prenatal activity level as a temperament dimension? Individual differences and developmental functions in fetal movement. *Infant Behavior and Development, 15,* 57–70.

Eaves, L. J., & Eysenck, H. J. (1975). The nature of extraversion: A genetical analysis. *Journal of Personality and Social Psychology, 32,* 102–112.

Eaves, L. J., & Eysenck, H. J. (1976). Genetical and environmental components of inconsistency and unrepeatability in twins' responses to a neuroticism questionnaire. *Behavior Genetics, 6,* 145–160.

Eaves, L. J., Eysenck, H. J., & Martin, N. G. (1989). *Genes, culture, and personality: An empirical approach.* New York: Academic Press.

Eliasz, A. (1974). *Temperament a osobowość* [Temperament and personality]. Wrocław, Poland: Ossolineum.

Eliasz, A. (1981). *Temperament a system regulacji stymulacji.* [Temperament and system of regulation of stimulation]. Warsaw: Państwowe Wydawnictwo Naukowe.

Eliasz, A. (1985). Transactional model of temperament. In J. Strelau (Ed.), *Temperamental bases of behavior: Warsaw studies on individual differences* (pp. 41–78). Lisse, The Netherlands: Swets & Zeitlinger.

Eliasz, A. (2001). Temperament, Type A, and motives: A time sampling study. In H. Brandstätter & A. Eliasz (Eds.), *Persons, situations, and emotions: An ecological approach* (pp. 55–73). Oxford: Oxford University Press.

Eliasz, A., & Marszał-Wiśniewska, M. (Eds.). (1992). *Temperament a rozwój człowieka* [Temperament and human development]. Warsaw: Instytut Psychologii PAN.

Eliasz, A., & Wrześniewski, K. (1988). *Ryzyko chorób psychosomatycznych. Środowisko i temperament a wzór zachowania A.* [Risk of psychosomatic diseases: Environment and temperament and Type A behavior]. Wrocław, Poland: Ossolineum.

Endler, N. S., & Parker, J. D. A. (1990). *Coping Inventory for Stressful Situations (CISS): Manual.* Toronto: Multi-Health Systems.

Epstein, S. (1979). The stability of behavior: On predicting most of the people much of the time. *Journal of Personality and Social Psychology, 37,* 1097–1126.

Epstein, S. (1984). The stability of behavior across time and situations. In R. Zucker, J.

Aronoff, & A. I. Rabin (Eds.), *Personality and the prediction of behavior* (pp. 209–268). San Diego: Academic Press.

Ewald, G. (1924). *Temperament und Charakter* [Temperament and character]. Berlin: Springer-Verlag.

Eysenck, H. J. (1957). *The dynamics of anxiety and hysteria.* London: Routledge & Kegan Paul.

Eysenck, H. J. (1965). Extraversion and the acquisition of eyeblink and GSR conditioned responses. *Psychological Bulletin, 63,* 258–270.

Eysenck, H. J. (1967). *The biological basis of personality.* Springfield, IL: Charles C. Thomas.

Eysenck, H. J. (1970). *The structure of human personality* (3rd ed.). London: Methuen.

Eysenck, H. J. (1972). Human typology, higher nervous activity, and factor analysis. In V. D. Nebylitsyn & J. A. Gray (Eds.), *Biological bases of individual behavior* (pp. 165–181). New York: Academic Press.

Eysenck, H. J. (1981). General features of the model. In H. J. Eysenck (Ed.), *A model for personality* (pp. 1–37). Berlin: Springer-Verlag.

Eysenck, H. J. (1983). Stress, disease, and personality: The "inoculation effect." In C. L. Cooper (Ed.), *Stress research* (pp. 121–131). London: Wiley.

Eysenck, H. J. (1988). Personality and stress as causal factors in cancer and coronary heart disease. In M. P. Janisse (Ed.), *Individual differences, stress, and health psychology* (pp. 129–145). New York: Springer-Verlag.

Eysenck, H. J. (1991). Dimensions of personality: The biosocial approach to personality. In J. Strelau & A. Angleitner (Eds.), *Explorations in temperament: International perspectives on theory and measurement* (pp. 87–103). New York: Plenum Press.

Eysenck, H. J. (1994). Cancer, personality, and stress: Prediction and prevention. *Advances in Behaviour Research and Therapy, 16,* 167–215.

Eysenck, H. J., & Eysenck, M. W. (1985). *Personality and individual differences: A natural science approach.* New York: Plenum Press.

Eysenck, H. J., & Eysenck, S. B. G. (1975). *Manual of the Eysenck Personality Questionnaire (Junior & Adult).* London: Hodder & Stoughton.

Eysenck, H. J., & Prell, D. B. (1951). The inheritance of neuroticism: An experimental study. *Journal of Mental Science, 97,* 441–465.

Eysenck, H. J., & Prell, D. B. (1956). The inheritance of introversion-extraversion. *Acta Psychologica, 12,* 95–110.

Eysenck, S. B. G., Eysenck, H. J., & Barrett, P. (1985). A revised version of the Psychoticism scale. *Personality and Individual Differences, 6,* 21–29.

Fahrenberg, J. (1987). Concepts of activation and arousal in the theory of emotionality (neuroticism): A multivariate conceptualization. In J. Strelau & H. J. Eysenck (Eds.), *Personality dimensions and arousal* (pp. 99–120). New York: Plenum Press.

Fahrenberg, J. (1992). Psychophysiology of neuroticism and anxiety. In A. Gale & M. W. Eysenck (Eds.), *Handbook of individual differences: Biological perspectives* (pp. 179–226). Chichester, UK: Wiley.

Fauerbach, J. A., Lawrence, J. W., Schmidt, C., Munster, A. M., & Costa, P. T. (2000). Personality predictors of injury-related posttraumatic stress disorder. *Journal of Nervous and Mental Disease, 188,* 510–517.

Fedorov, V. K. (1961). Comparison of results of different studies of basic properties of higher nervous activity in mice. *Zhurnal Vysshei Nervnoi Deyatelnosti, 11,* 746–752 (in Russian).

Ferguson, E. (2001). Personality and coping. *British Journal of Health Psychology, 6*, 311–325.

Fiske, D. W., & Maddi, S. R. (1961). *Functions of varied experience*. Homewood, IL: Dorsey Press.

Flint, J., Corley, R., DeFries, J. C., Fulker, D. W., Gray, J. A., Miller, S., et al. (1995). A simple genetic basis for a complex psychological trait in laboratory mice. *Science, 269*, 1432–1435.

Foa, E. B., Keane, T. M., & Friedman, M. J. (2000). Guidelines for treatment of PTSD. *Journal of Traumatic Stress, 13*, 539–599.

Folkman, S., & Lazarus, R. S. (1988). Coping as a mediator of emotion. *Journal of Personality and Social Psychology, 54*, 466–475.

Foy, D. W., & Goguen, C. A. (1998). Community violence related PTSD in children and adolescents. *PTSD Research Quarterly, 9*, 1–6.

Frankenfield, D. C., Rowe, W. A., Cooney, R. N., Smith, & J. S. Becker, D. (2001). Limits of body mass index to detect obesity and predict body composition. *Nutrition, 17*, 26–30.

Freedy, J. R., Kilpatrick, D. G., & Resnick, H. S. (1993). Natural disasters and mental health: Theory, assessment, and intervention. *Journal of Social Behavior and Personality, 8*, 49–103.

Freeman, G. L. (1948). *The energetics of human behavior*. Ithaca, NY: Cornell University Press.

Freudenberger, H. J. (1974). Staff burnout. *Journal of Social Issues, 30*, 159–165.

Freudenberger, H. J., & Richelson, G. (1980). *Burnout: The high cost of high achievement*. Garden City, NY: Doubleday.

Friedensberg, E. (1982). Skala ocen jako narzędzie do pomiaru reaktywnośc [Reactivity Rating Scale]. In J. Strelau (Ed.), *Regulacyjne funkcje temperamentu* (pp. 237–257). Wrocław, Poland: Ossolineum.

Friedensberg, E. (1985). Reactivity and individual style of work exemplified by constructional-type task performance: A developmental study. In J. Strelau, F. H. Farley, & A. Gale (Eds.), *The biological bases of personality and behavior: Vol. 1. Theories, measurement techniques, and development* (pp. 241–253). Washington, DC: Hemisphere.

Friedman, H. S., & Booth-Kewley, S. (1987). The "disease-prone personality": A meta-analytic view of the construct. *American Psychologist, 42*, 539–555.

Fulker, D. W., Eysenck, S. B. G., & Zuckerman, M. (1980). A genetic and environmental analysis of sensation seeking. *Journal of Research in Personality, 14*, 261–281.

Gabbay, F. H. (1992). Behavior-genetic strategies in the study of emotion. *Psychological Science, 3*, 50–55.

Galton, F. (1883). *Inquires into human faculty and its development*. London: Dent.

Garau, A., & Garcia-Sevilla, L. (1985). Drug postulate of Eysenck in the rat. *Personality and Individual Differences, 6*, 189–194.

Gartstein, M. A., & Rothbart, M. K. (2003). Studying infant temperament via the Revised Infant Behavior Questionnaire. *Infant Behavior and Development, 26*, 64–86.

Gelerntner, J., Southwick, S., Goodson, S., Morgan, A., Nagy, L., & Charney, D. S. (1999). No association between D2 dopamine receptor (DRD2) "A" system alleles, or DRD2 haplotypes, and posttraumatic stress disorder. *Biological Psychiatry, 45*, 620–625.

Gershenfeld, H. K., & Paul, S. M. (1998). Towards a genetics of anxious temperament: From mice to men. *Acta Psychiatrica Scandinavica, 98*, 56–65.

Gervai, J., Turner, P. J., & Hinde, R. A. (1993). Parents' and teachers' perceptions of personality traits of young children: Sex differences, cross-cultural comparisons, and relations with observed behaviour. *British Journal of Developmental Psychology, 11*, 343–358.

Gjone, H., & Stevenson, J. (1997). A longitudinal twin study of temperament and behavior problems: Common genetic or environmental influences? *Journal of the American Academy of Child and Adolescent Psychiatry, 36*, 1448–1456.

Gliszczyńska, X. (1990). Skala I-E w Pracy. *Technika pomiaru poczucia kontroli w sytuacji pracy* [I-E Scale at work: Assessment of sense of control in a work situation]. Warsaw: Pracownia Testów Psychologicznych PTP.

Goldberg, L. R. (1990). An alternative "description of personality": The Big-Five factor structure. *Journal of Personality and Social Psychology, 59*, 1216–1229.

Goldsmith, H. H. (1986). Heritability of temperament: Cautions and some empirical evidence. In G. A. Kohnstamm (Ed.), *Temperament discussed: Temperament and development in infancy and childhood* (pp. 83–96). Lisse, The Netherlands: Swets & Zeitlinger.

Goldsmith, H. H. (1989). Behavior-genetic approaches to temperament. In G. A. Kohnstamm, J. E. Bates, & M. K. Rothbart (Eds.), *Temperament in childhood* (pp. 111–132). Chichester, UK: Wiley.

Goldsmith, H. H. (1994). Genetics and emotional development. In N. Frijda (Ed.), *Proceeding of the International Society for Research on Emotion* (pp. 252–256). Storrs, CT: ISRE Publications.

Goldsmith, H. H., & Campos, J. J. (1982). Toward a theory of infant temperament. In R. N. Emde & R. J. Harmon (Eds.), *The development of attachment and affiliative systems* (pp. 161–193). New York: Plenum Press.

Goldsmith, H. H., & Campos, J. J. (1986). Fundamental issues in the study of early temperament: The Denver Twin Temperamental Study. In M. E. Lamb, A. L. Brown, & B. Rogoff (Eds.), *Advances in developmental psychology* (Vol. 4, pp. 231–283). Hillsdale, NJ: Erlbaum.

Goldsmith, H. H., & Campos, J. J. (1990). The structure of temperamental fear and pleasure in infants: A psychometric perspective. *Child Development, 61*, 1944–1964.

Golińska, L., & Świętochowski, W. (1998). Temperamentalne i osobowościowe determinanty wypalenia zawodowego u nauczycieli [Temperamental and personality determinants of professional burnout in teachers]. *Psychologia Wychowawcza, 5*, 385–398.

Gorbacheva, V. A. (1954). An attempt to study individual and typological features of 3-year-old children. *Izvestiya Academii Pedagogicheskikh Nauk RSFSR, 52*, 6–39 (in Russian).

Goryńska, E. (1982). Podstawowe cechy charakterystyki czasowej zachowania i ich pomiar metodą kwestionariusza [Basic traits of the temporal characteristics of behavior and their measurement by an inventory]. In J. Strelau (Ed.), *Regulacyjne funkcje temperamentu* (pp. 183–203). Wrocław, Poland: Ossolineum.

Goryńska, E., & Strelau, J. (1979). Basic traits of the temporal characteristics of behavior and their measurement by an inventory technique. *Polish Psychological Bulletin, 10*, 199–207.

Gosling, S. D., & John, O. P. (1999). Personality dimensions in nonhuman animals: A cross-species review. *Current Directions in Psychological Science, 8*, 69–75.

Gray, J. A. (1964). Strength of the nervous system and levels of arousal: A reinterpretation. In J. A. Gray (Ed.), *Pavlov's typology* (pp. 289–364). Oxford: Pergamon Press.

Gray, J. A. (1967). Disappointment and drugs in the rat. *Advancement of Science, 24,* 293–305.

Gray, J. A. (1972). The psychophysiological nature of introversion-extraversion: A modification of Eysenck's theory. In V. D. Nebylitsyn & J. A. Gray (Eds.), *Biological bases of individual behavior* (pp. 182–205). New York: Academic Press.

Gray, J. A. (1981). A critique of Eysenck's theory of personality. In H. J. Eysenck (Ed.), *A model for personality* (pp. 246–276). Berlin: Springer-Verlag.

Gray, J. A. (1982). *The neuropsychology of anxiety: An inquiry into the functions of the septo-hippocampal system.* Oxford: Oxford University Press.

Gray, J. A. (1991). The neuropsychology of temperament. In J. Strelau & A. Angleitner (Eds.), *Explorations in temperament: International perspectives on theory and measurement* (pp. 105–128). New York: Plenum Press.

Green, B. L., Friedman, M. J., de Jong, J. T. V. M., Solomon, S. D., Keane, T. M., Fairbank, J. A., et al. (Eds.). (2003). *Trauma interventions in war and peace: Prevention, practice, and policy.* New York: Kluwer Academic/Plenum Publishers.

Green, B. L., Goodman, L. A., Krupnik, J. L., Corcoran, C. B., Petty, R. M., Stockton, P., et al. (2000). Outcomes of single versus multiple trauma exposure in a screening sample. *Journal of Traumatic Stress, 13,* 271–286.

Green, B. L., Korol, M., Grace, M. C., Vary, M. G., Leonard, A. C., Gleser, G. C., et al. (1991). Children and disaster: Age, gender, and parental effects on PTSD symptoms. *Journal of the American Academy of Children and Adolescent Psychiatry, 30,* 945–951.

Grossarth-Maticek, R. (1980). Social psychotherapy and course of the disease. *Psychotherapy and Psychosomatics, 33,* 129–138.

Grossarth-Maticek, R., Bastiaans, J., & Kanazir, D. T. (1985). Psychosocial factors as strong predictors of mortality from cancer, ischaemic heart disease, and stroke: The Yugoslav prospective study. *Journal of Psychosomatic Research, 29,* 167–176.

Grossarth-Maticek, R., & Eysenck, H. J. (1991). Personality, stress, and motivational factors in drinking as determinants of risk for cancer and coronary heart disease. *Psychological Reports, 69,* 1027–1093.

Guerin, D. W., & Gottfried, A. W. (1994). Developmental stability and change in parent reports of temperament: A ten-year longitudinal investigation from infancy through preadolescence. *Merrill-Palmer Quarterly, 40,* 334–355.

Guilford, J. S., Zimmerman, W. S., & Guilford, J. P. (1976). *The Guilford–Zimmerman Temperament Survey handbook: Twenty-five years of research and application.* San Diego: EdiTS Publishers.

Habrat, E. (1997). *Reaktywność i zapotrzebowanie na stymulację w depresjach w przebiegu choroby afektywnej dwubiegunowej* [Reactivity and stimulation need in depression during bipolar affective disease]. Unpublished doctoral dissertation, Instytut Psychologii PAN, Warsaw.

Hall, C. S. (1941). Temperament: A survey of animal studies. *Psychological Bulletin, 38,* 909–943.

Ham, B. J., Kim, Y. H., Choi, M. J., Cha, J. H., Choi, Y. K., & Lee, M. S. (2004). Serotonergic genes and personality traits in the Korean population. *Neuroscience Letters, 354,* 2–5.

Hansen, E. B., & Breivik, G. (2001). Sensation seeking as a predictor of positive and negative risk behaviour among adolescents. *Personality and Individual Differences, 30,* 627–640.

Hartshorne, H., & May, M. A. (1928). *Studies in the nature of character: Vol. 1. Studies in deceit.* New York: Macmillan.

Haslam, D. R. (1972). Experimental pain. In V. D. Nebylitsyn & J. A. Gray (Eds.), *Biological bases of individual behavior* (pp. 242–253). New York: Academic Press.

Hayes, A. F., & Dunning, D. (1997). Construal processes and trait ambiguity: Implications for self-peer agreement in personality judgment. *Journal of Personality and Social Psychology, 72,* 664–677.

Heath, A. C., Neale, M. C., Hewitt, J. K., Eaves, L. J., & Fulker, D. W. (1989). Testing structural equation models for twin data using LISREL. *Behavior Genetics, 19,* 9–35.

Hebb, D. O. (1955). Drives and the C.N.S. (conceptual nervous system). *Psychological Review, 62,* 243–254.

Heitzman, J. (1998). PTSD jako następstwo klęski żywiołowej [PTSD as a consequence of disaster]. *Psychiatria Polska, 32,* 5–14.

Helson, H. (1964). *Adaptation-level theory: An experimental and systematic approach to behavior.* New York: Harper & Row.

Heszen, I. (2000). Teoria stresu psychologicznego i radzenia sobie [A theory of psychological stress and coping]. In J. Strelau (Ed.), *Psychologia. Podręcznik akademicki: Vol. 3. Jednostka w społeczeństwie i elementy psychologii stosowanej* (pp. 465–492). Gdańsk: Gdańskie Wydawnictwo Psychologiczne.

Heszen-Niejodek, I., & Sęk, H. (Eds.). (1997). *Psychologia zdrowia* [Health psychology]. Warsaw: Wydawnictwo Naukowe PWN.

Heymans, G. (1908). Über einige psychische Korrelationen [About some psychological correlations]. *Zeitschrift für angewandte Psychologie, 1,* 313–381.

Hobfoll, S. E. (1989). Conservation of resources: A new attempt at conceptualizing stress. *American Psychologist, 44,* 513–524.

Hobfoll, S. E. (1991). Conservation of resources in community intervention. *American Journal of Community Psychology, 19,* 111–121.

Hobfoll, S. E. (1998). *Stress, culture, and community: The psychology and philosophy of stress.* New York: Plenum Press.

Hobfoll, S. E., & de Vries, M. W. (Eds.). (1994). *Extreme stress and communities: Impact and intervention.* Dordrecht, The Netherlands: Kluwer Academic Publishers.

Hofstee, W. K. B. (1994). Who should own the definition of personality? *European Journal of Personality, 8, 149–162.*

Holmbeck, G. N. (1997). Toward terminological, conceptual, and statistical clarity in the study of mediators and moderators: Examples from the child-clinical and pediatric psychology literature. *Journal of Consulting and Clinical Psychology, 65,* 599–610.

Holmes, T. H., & Rahe, R. H. (1967). The Social Readjustment Rating Scale. *Journal of Psychosomatic Research, 11,* 213–218.

Holohan, C. J., & Moos, R. H. (1986). Personality, coping, and family resources in stress resistance: A longitudinal analysis. *Journal of Personality and Social Psychology, 51,* 389–395.

Hornowska, E. (2003). *Temperamentalne uwarunkowania zachowania. Badania z wykorzystaniem kwestionariusza TCI R. C. Cloningera* [Temperamental determinants of behavior: Study by making use of R. C. Cloninger's TCI questionnaire]. Poznań: Bogucki Wydawnictwo Naukowe.

Horowitz, M., Wilner, N., & Alvarez, W. (1979). Impact of Event Scale: A measure of subjective stress. *Psychosomatic Medicine, 41,* 209–218.

Hullin, C. L., Drasgow, F., & Parsons, C. K. (1983). Introduction to item response theory. In C. L. Hullin, F. Drasgow, & C. K. Parsons (Eds.), *Item response theory* (pp. 13–74). Homewood, IL: Dow Jones-Irwin.

Hur, J.-M., & Bouchard, T. J., Jr. (1997). The genetic correlation between impulsivity and sensation seeking traits. *Behavior Genetics, 27*, 455–463.

Hwang, J., & Rothbart, M. K. (2003). Behavior genetics studies of infant temperament: Findings vary across parent-report instruments. *Infant Behavior & Development, 26*, 112–114.

Ilin, E. P. (1978). *A study of nervous system properties*. Yaroslavl, USSR: Yaroslavl University Press (in Russian).

Ilina, A. I., & Paley, I. M. (1958). The method of anamnesis in the study of types of higher nervous activity. In V. S. Merlin (Ed.), *Problems of psychology of personality in relation to types of higher nervous activity* (pp. 47–75). Perm, USSR: Permskii Gosudarstvennyi Pedagogicheskii Institut (in Russian).

Jackson, D. N. (1967). *Manual for the Personality Research Form*. Goshen, CT: Research Psychologists Press.

Jachnis, A. (1996). Temperamentalne uwarunkowania efektywności zawodowej strażaków i sportowców [Temperamental determinants of professional efficiency in firemen and athletes]. *Przegląd Psychologiczny, 39*, 115–125.

Jang, K. L., Livesley, W. J., & Vernon, P. A. (1996). Heritability of the Big Five personality dimensions and their facets: A twin study. *Journal of Personality, 64*, 577–591.

Jang, K. L., Stein, M. B., Taylor, S., Asmundson, G. J., & Livesley, W. J. (2003). Exposure to traumatic events and experiences: Aetiological relationships with personality function. *Psychiatry Research, 120*, 61–69.

Janke, W., & Kallus, K. W. (1995). Reaktivität [Reactivity]. In M. Amelang (Ed.), *Enzyklopädie der Psychologie: Vol. 2. Verhaltens–und Leistungsunterschied* (pp. 1–89). Göttingen, Germany: Hogrefe & Huber.

Jeffery, R. W. (1989). Risk behaviors and health: Contrasting individual and population perspectives. *American Psychologist, 44*, 1194–1202.

Jerison, H. J. (1982). The evolution of biological intelligence. In R. J. Sternberg (Ed.), *Handbook of human intelligence* (pp. 723–791). New York: Cambridge University Press.

Jöreskog, K. G., & Sörbom, D. (1993). *LISREL 8: User's reference guide*. Chicago: SPSS.

Kaczmarek, M. (2004). *Środowiskowe i temperamentalne uwarunkowania nasilenia objawów zespołu stresu pourazowego u dzieci w wieku szkolnym w następstwie kataklizmu powodzi* [Environmental and temperamental determinants of the intensity of PTSD symptoms in children after a flood]. Unpublished doctoral dissertation, Warsaw School of Social Psychology, Warsaw.

Kaczmarek, M., Bieniek, A., Zawadzki, B., & Strelau, J. (2003). Zdarzenia traumatyczne a system cenionych wartości. Wyniki badań ofiar powodzi stulecia [A traumatic event and the system of values: The study of victims of the 1997 Polish Flood]. *Studia Psychologiczne, 41*, 2, 27–47.

Kaczmarek, M., & Zawadzki, B. (2006). Temperamental and environmental determinants of the intensity of PTSD symptoms in children two years after a flood. In J. Strelau & T. Klonowicz (Eds.), *People under extreme stress* (pp. 49–66). Hauppauge, NY: Nova Science Publishers.

Kagan, J. (1994). *Galen's prophecy: Temperament in human nature*. New York: Basic Books.

Kaniasty, K. (2003). *Klęska żywiołowa czy katastrofa społeczna? Psychospołeczne konsekwencje polskiej powodzi 1997 roku* [Natural disaster or social catastrophe? Psychosocial consequences of the 1997 Polish Flood]. Gdańsk, Poland: Gdańskie Wydawnictwo Psychologiczne.

Kant, I. ([1798] 1912). *Anthropologie in pragmatischer Hinsicht* (5th ed.) [Anthropology from a pragmatic point of view]. Leipzig: Verlag von Felix Meiner.

Karwowska-Szulkin, R. (1989). *Rola reaktywności w wyborze stylów kierowania o różnym obiektywnym i subiektywnym poziomie stymulacji* [The role of reactivity in choice of managerial style differing in objective and subjective level of stimulation]. Unpublished doctoral dissertation, Warsaw University, Warsaw.

Karwowska-Szulkin, R., & Strelau, J. (1990). Reactivity and the stimulative value of managerial styles. *Polish Psychological Bulletin, 21*, 49–60.

Kato, K., & Pedersen, N. L. (2005). Personality and coping: A study of twins reared apart and twins reared together. *Behavior Genetics, 35*, 147–158.

Katsuragi, S., Kunugi, H., Sano, A., Tsutsumi, T., Isogawa, K., Nanko, S., et al. (1999). Association between serotonin transporter gene polymorphism and anxiety-related traits. *Biological Psychiatry, 45*, 368–370.

Kendler, K. S., Kessler, R. C., Heath, A. C., Neale, M. C., & Eaves, L. J. (1991). Coping: A genetic epidemiological investigation. *Psychological Medicine, 21*, 337–346.

Kendler, K. S., Neale, M. C., Kessler, R., Heath, A., & Eaves, L. J. (1986). A twin study of recent life events and difficulties. *Archives of General Psychiatry, 50*, 789–796.

Kerr, M. (2001). Culture as a context for temperament: Suggestions from the life courses of shy Swedes and Americans. In T. D. Wachs & G. A. Kohnstamm (Eds.), *Temperament in context* (pp. 139–152). Mahawah, NJ: Erlbaum.

Khilchenko, A. E. (1958). Methods of studying mobility of basic nervous processes in man. *Zhurnal Vysshei Nervnoi Deyatielnosti, 8*, 945–948 (in Russian).

King, L. A., King, D. W., Fairbank, J. A., Keane, T. M., & Adams, G. A. (1998). Resilience-recovery factors in post-traumatic stress disorder among female and male Vietnam veterans: Hardiness, postwar social support, and additional stressful life events. *Journal of Personality and Social Psychology, 74*, 420–434.

Kissen, D. M. (1964). Relationship between lung cancer, cigarette smoking, inhalation, and personality. *British Journal of Medical Psychology, 37*, 203–216.

Kissen, D. M., & Eysenck, H. J. (1962). Personality in male lung cancer patients. *Journal of Psychosomatic Research, 6*, 123–137.

Kliś, M., & Kossewska, J. (1998). Cechy osobowości nauczycieli a syndrom wypalenia zawodowego [Teachers' personality traits and the burnout syndrome]. *Psychologia Wychowawcza, 2*, 125–140.

Klonowicz, T. (1974). Wpływ poziomu reaktywności i rodzaju instrukcji na wykonywanie prostych zadań konstrukcyjnych [The effect of reactivity level and type of instruction on performance in simple constuction tasks]. In J. Strelau (Ed.), *Rola cech temperamentalnych w działaniu* (pp. 143–152). Wrocław, Poland: Ossolineum.

Klonowicz, T. (1984). *Reaktywność a funkcjonowanie człowieka w różnych warunkach stymulacyjnych* [Reactivity, level of performance, and adaptation costs under varied stimulation load]. Wrocław, Poland: Ossolineum.

Klonowicz, T. (1985). Temperament and performance. In J. Strelau (Ed.), *Temperamental bases of behavior: Warsaw studies on individual differences* (pp. 79–115). Lisse, The Netherlands: Swets & Zeitlinger.

Klonowicz, T. (1987a). *Reactivity, experience, and capacity*. Warsaw: Wydawnictwa Uniwersytetu Warszawskiego.

Klonowicz, T. (1987b). Reactivity and the control of arousal. In J. Strelau & H. J. Eysenck (Eds.), *Personality dimensions and arousal* (pp. 183–196). New York: Plenum Press.

Klonowicz, T. (1992). *Stres w Wieży Babel. Różnice indywidualne a wysiłek inwestowany w trudną pracę umysłową* [Stress in the Tower of Babel: Individual differences and allocation of effort during difficult mental work]. Wrocław, Poland: Ossolineum.

Klonowicz, T. (2000). Konsekwencje katastrof dla funkcjonowania człowieka. Przegląd literatury [Psychological sequele of traumatic events: Review]. *Psychologia–Etologia–Genetyka, 2*, 69–103.

Klonowicz, T. (2001a). *Stres bezrobocia* [Stress of unemployment]. Warsaw: Wydawnictwo IP PAN i SWPS.

Klonowicz, T. (2001b). Personal resources and organizational well-being. In H. Brandstätter & A. Eliasz (Eds.), *Persons, situations, and emotions: An ecological approach* (pp. 55–73). Oxford: Oxford University Press.

Klonowicz, T., & Eliasz, A., (2004). Traumatyczny stres w zawodowym doświadczeniu pracowników pogotowia. Rola niedopasowania osobowościowych regulatorów zachowania [Traumatic stress in professional experience of ambulance workers: The role of poor fitness-of-personality regulators of behavior]. In J. Strelau (Ed.), *Osobowośc a ekstremalny stres* (pp. 167–182). Gdańsk, Poland: Gdańskie Wydawnictwo Psychologiczne.

Konorski, J. (1967). *Integrative activity of the brain*. Chicago: University of Chicago Press.

Koopmans, J. R., Boomsma, D. I., Heath, A. C., & van Doornen, L. J. P. (1995). A multivariate genetic analysis of sensation seeking. *Behavior Genetics, 25*, 349–356.

Kopytova, L. A. (1963). Expression of typological properties of the nervous system in the activity of machine operators when machines are idle. *Voprosy Psikhologii, 4*, 59–72 (in Russian).

Korczyńska, J. (2001). *Temperantalny czynnik ryzyka wypalenia zawodowego na przykładzie pracowników służby więziennej.* [Temperament risk factor of professional burnout in prison service personnel]. Unpublished doctoral dissertation, Silesian University, Katowice, Poland.

Korczyńska, J. (2004). Temperamentalny czynnik ryzyka wypalenia zawodowego na przykładzie pracowników służby więziennej [Temperament risk factor of professional burnout in prison service personnel]. In J. Strelau (Ed.), *Osobowość a ekstremalny stres* (pp. 317–342). Gdańsk, Poland: Gdańskie Wydawnictwo Psychologiczne.

Kowalczyk, A. (2000). *Stres pourazowy jako konsekwencja przeżycia wypadku górniczego i jego korelaty* [Traumatic stress and its symptoms as a consequence of experiencing a coalmining accident]. Unpublished master's thesis, Silesian University, Katowice, Poland.

Kozak, B. (2000). *Genetyczne uwarunkowania różnic indywidualnych w stylach radzenia sobie ze stresem i ich związku z temperamentem* [Genetic determinants of individual differences in coping styles and their relationship with temperament]. Unpublished doctoral dissertation, Silesian University, Katowice, Poland.

Kozak, B., Strelau, J., & Miles, J. N. V. (2005). Genetic determinants of individual differences in coping styles. *Anxiety, Stress, and Coping, 18*, 1–15.

Koženy, K., & Šulcová, E. (1994). Neonatal Temperament Questionnaire (NTQ): Psychometric characteristic. *International Journal of Prenatal and Perinatal Psychology and Medicine, 6*, 221–231.

Krasusky, V. K. (1971). On some additional criteria of assessment of higher nervous activity properties. In V. K. Krasusky & V. K. Fedorov (Eds.), *Methods of assessment of higher nervous activity properties* (pp. 64–72). Leningrad: Nauka (in Russian).

Kretschmer, E. (1944). *Körperbau and Charakter: Untersuchungen zum Konstitutionsproblem and zur Lehre von den Temperamenten* [Physique and character: Research concerning problems of constitution and knowledge on temperament] (17th–18th ed.). Berlin: Springer-Verlag.

Krohne, H. W., & Laux, L. (Eds.). (1982). *Achievement, stress, and anxiety.* Washington, DC: Hemisphere.

Kulka, R. A., Schlenger, W. E., Fairbank, J. A., Hough, R. L., Jordan, B. K., Marmar, C. R., et al. (1990). *Trauma and the Vietnam War generation: Report of findings from the National Vietnam Veterans Readjustment Study.* New York: Brunner/Mazel.

Kumakiri, C., Kodama, K., Shimizu, E., Yamanouchi, N., Okada, S., Noda, S., et al. (1999). Study of the association between the serotonin transporter gene regulatory region polymorphism and personality traits in a Japanese population. *Neuroscience Letters, 263,* 205–207.

Kurcz, I., & Kądzielawa, D. (Eds.). (2002). *Psychologia czynności. Nowe perspektywy* [Psychology of action: New perspectives]. Warsaw: Wydawnictwo Naukowe Scholar.

Kurcz, I., & Reykowski, J. (Eds.). (1975). *Studia nad teorią czynności* [Studies on a theory of action]. Warsaw: Państwowe Wydawnictwo Naukowe.

Kyrios. M., & Prior, M. (1990). Temperament, stress, and family factors in behavioural adjustment of 3–5-year-old children. *International Journal of Behavioral Development, 13,* 67–93.

Lauterbach, D. (2006). Personality, trauma exposure, and posttraumatic stress disorder severity: Moving beyond the monovariable predictor model. In J. Strelau & T. Klonowicz (Eds.), *People under extreme stress* (pp. 15–30). Hauppauge, NY: Nova Science Publishers.

Lauterbach, D., & Vrana, S. (2001). The relationship among personality variables, exposure to traumatic events, and severity of posttraumatic stress symptoms. *Journal of Traumatic Stress, 14,* 29–45.

Lazarus, R. S. (1966). *Psychological stress and the coping process.* New York: McGraw-Hill.

Lazarus, R. S. (1991). *Emotion and adaptation.* New York: Oxford University Press.

Lazarus, R. S. (1993). From psychological stress to the emotions: A history of changing outlooks. *Annual Review of Psychology, 44,* 1–21.

Lazarus, R. S., & Folkman, S. (1984). *Stress, appraisal, and coping.* New York: Springer Publishing.

Lee, K. A., Vaillant, G. E., Torrey, W. C., & Elder, G. H. (1995). A 50-year prospective study of the psychological sequelae of World War II combat. *American Journal of Psychiatry, 152,* 516–522.

Leiter, M. P. (1993). Burnout as a developmental process: Considerations of models. In W. B. Schaufeli, C. Maslach, & T. Marek (Eds.), *Professional burnout: Recent developments in theory and research* (pp. 237–250). Washington, DC: Taylor & Francis.

Leiter, M. P., & Maslach, C. (1988). The impact of interpersonal environment on burnout and organizational commitment. *Journal of Organizational Behavior, 9,* 297–308.

Leites, N. S. (1956). An attempt to give a psychological description of temperaments. In B. M. Teplov (Ed.), *Typological features of higher nervous activity in man.* (Vol. 1, pp. 267–303). Moscow: Akademiya Pedagogicheskikh Nauk RSFSR (in Russian).

Lemery, K. S., Goldsmith, H. H., Klinnert, M. D., & Mrazek, D. A. (1999). Developmental models of infant and childhood temperament. *Developmental Psychology, 35*, 189–204.

Leuba, C. (1955). Toward some integration of learning theories: The concept of optimal stimulation. *Psychological Reports, 1*, 27–33.

Leung, K. (1989). Cross-cultural differences: Individual-level vs. culture-level analysis. *International Journal of Psychology, 24*, 703–719.

Levinson, D. J. (1990). A theory of life structure development in adulthood. In N. C. Alexander & E. J. Langer (Eds.), *Higher stages of human development* (pp. 35–54). New York: Oxford University Press.

Loehlin, J. C. (1986) Heredity, environment, and the Thurstone Temperament Schedule. *Behavior Genetics, 16*, 61–73.

Loehlin, J. C. (1992). *Genes and environment in personality development*. Newbury Park, CA: Sage.

Loehlin, J. C., & Martin, N. G. (2001). Age changes in personality traits and their heritabilities during the adult years: Evidence from Australian twin registry samples. *Personality and Individual Differences, 30*, 1147–1160.

Lunenburg, F. C., & Cadavid, V. (1992). Locus of control, pupil control ideology, and dimensions of teacher burnout. *Journal of Instructional Psychology, 19*, 13–22.

Lynn, R. (1981). Cross-cultural differences in neuroticism, extraversion, and psychoticism. In R. Lynn (Ed.), *Dimensions of personality: Papers in honour of H. J. Eysenck* (pp. 263–286). Oxford: Pergamon Press.

Lynn, R., & Martin, T. (1995). National differences for thirty-seven nations in extraversion, neuroticism, psychoticism, and economic, demographic, and other correlates. *Personality and Individual Differences, 19*, 40.

Lyons, M. J., Goldberg, J., Eisen, S. A., True, W., Tsuang, M. T., Meyer, J. M., et al. (1993). Do genes influence exposure to trauma? A twin study of combat. *American Journal of Medical Genetics, 48*, 22–27.

Łukaszewski, W. (1974). *Osobowość—struktura i funkcje regulacyjne*. [Personality: Structure and regulatory functions]. Warsaw: Państwowe Wydawnictwo Naukowe.

Maciejczyk, J. (1974). Reaktywność a podejmowanie decyzji w sytuacji trudnej u pilotów [Reactivity and decision making in difficult situations in pilots]. In J. Strelau (Ed.), *Rola cech temperamentalnych w działaniu* (pp. 201–215). Wrocław, Poland: Ossolineum.

Malina, R. M., & Katzmarzyk, P. T. (1999). Validity of the body mass index as an indicator of the risk and presence of overweight in adolescents. *American Journal of Clinical Nutrition, 70*, 131S–136S.

Malmo, R. B. (1959). Activation: A neuropsychological dimension. *Psychological Review, 66*, 367–386.

Mangan, G. L. (1982). *The biology of human conduct: East-West models of temperament and personality*. Oxford: Pergamon Press.

Maslach, C. (1976). Burnet-out. *Human Behavior, 5*, 16–22.

Maslach, C. (1982). Understanding burnout: Definitional issues in analyzing a complex phenomenon. In W. S. Paine (Ed.), *Job stress and burnout* (pp. 29–40). Beverly Hills, CA: Sage.

Maslach, C. (1993). Burnout: A multidimensional perspective. In W. B. Schaufeli, C. Maslach, & T. Marek (Eds.), *Professional burnout: Recent developments in theory and research* (pp. 19–32). Washington, DC: Taylor & Francis.

Maslach, C., & Jackson, S. E. (1981). *The Maslach Burnout Inventory: Research edition*. Palo Alto, CA: Consulting Psychologists Press.

Maslach, C., & Jackson, S. E. (1986). *The Maslach Burnout Inventory: Manual* (2nd ed.). Palo Alto, CA: Consulting Psychologists Press.

Maslach, C., Jackson, S. E., & Leiter, M. P. (1996). *Maslach Burnout Inventory manual* (3rd ed.). Palo Alto, CA: Consulting Psychologists Press.

Maslach, C., & Leiter, M. P. (1997). *The truth about burnout*. San Francisco: Jossey-Bass.

Materska, M. (1978). Programowanie ludzkiej działalności zadaniowej w świetle badań nad strukturą i efektywnością czynności wykonawczych [Programming human task activities in light of studies on structure and effectiveness of performance]. *Przegląd Psychologiczny, 21*, 425–443.

Matysiak, J. (1993). *Głód stymulacji*. [Need for stimulation]. Warsaw: Faculty of Psychology, Warsaw University.

Maziade, M. (1988). Child temperament as a developmental or an epidemiological concept: A methodological point of view. *Psychiatric Developments, 3*, 195–211.

McCrae, R. R., & Costa, P. T., Jr. (1987). Validation of the five-factor model of personality across instruments and observers. *Journal of Personality and Social Psychology, 54*, 853–863.

McCrae, R. R., Yik, M. S. M., Trapnell, P. D., Bond, M. H., & Paulhus, D. L. (1998). Interpreting personality profiles across cultures: Bilingual, acculturation, and peer rating studies of Chinese undergraduates. *Journal of Personality and Social Psychology, 74*, 1041–1055.

McCranie, E. W., Lambert, V. A., & Lambert, C. A. (1987). Work stress, hardiness, and burnout among hospital staff nurses. *Nursing Research, 36*, 374–378.

McFarlane, A. C. (1986). Posttraumatic morbidity of a disaster: A study of cases presenting for psychiatric treatment. *Journal of Nervous and Mental Disease, 174*, 4–14.

McFarlane, A. C. (1989). The aetiology of post-traumatic morbidity: Predisposing, precipitating, and perpetuating factors. *British Journal of Psychiatry, 154*, 221–228.

McFarlane, A. C. (1992). Avoidance and intrusion in posttraumatic stress disorder. *Journal of Nervous and Mental Disease, 180*, 439–445.

McFarlane, A. C. (2006). The relationship between personality and post traumatic stress disorder. In J. Strelau & T. Klonowicz (Eds.), *People under extreme stress* (pp. 1–14). Hauppauge, NY: Nova Science Publishers.

McFarlane, A. C., Clayer, J. R., & Bookless, C. L. (1997). Psychiatric morbidity following a natural disaster: An Australian bushfire. *Social Psychiatry and Psychiatric Epidemiology, 32*, 261–268.

McGee, R., Williams, S., & Elwood, M. (1994). Depression and the development of cancer: A meta-analysis. *Social Sciences and Medicine, 38*, 187–192.

McGrath, J. E. (Ed.). (1970). *Social and psychological factors in stress*. New York: Holt, Rinehart & Winston.

Medoff-Cooper, B., Carey, W. B., & McDevitt, S. C. (1993). The Early Infancy Temperament Questionnaire. *Journal of Developmental and Behavioral Pediatrics, 14*, 230–235.

Mehrabian, A. (1991). Outline of a general emotion-based theory of temperament. In J. Strelau & A. Angleitner (Eds.), *Explorations in temperament: International perspectives on theory and measurement* (pp. 75–86). New York: Plenum Press.

Mellins, C. A., Gatz, M., & Baker, L. (1996). Children's methods of coping with stress: A twin study of genetic and environmental influences. *Journal of Child Psychology and Psychiatry and Allied Disciplines, 37*, 721–730.

Merlin, V. S. (1958). A method of testing the properties of the general type of higher nervous activity in man using GSR. *Voprosy Psikhologii, 5*, 159–162 (in Russian).

Merlin, V. S. (Ed.). (1973). *Outline of the theory of temperament* (2nd ed.). Perm, USSR: Permskoye Knizhnoye Izdatelstvo (in Russian).

Merlin, V. S. (1986). *Outline of integral research on individuality.* Moscow: Pedagogika (in Russian).

Miazga, K. (2001). *Związek zespołu stresu pourazowego ze wsparciem społecznym u powodzian* [The relationship between post-traumatic stress disorder and social support in flood victims]. Unpublished master's thesis, Silesian University, Katowice, Poland.

Michałowska, K. (2001). *Rola wsparcia społecznego jako mediatora w przeżywaniu stresu pourazowego—analiza konsekwencji kataklizmu u ofiar powodzi z 1997 roku* [The role of social suport as a mediator in experiencing traumatic stress: Analysis of disaster consequences in victims of Flood 1997]. Unpublished master's thesis, Silesian University, Katowice, Poland.

Miller, T., Smith, T. W., & Turner, C. (1996). A meta-analytic review of research on hostility and physical health. *Psychological Bulletin, 119*, 322–348.

Mintzberg, H. (1980). *The nature of managerial work.* Englewood Cliffs, NJ: Prentice-Hall.

Mischel, W. (1968). *Personality and assessment.* New York: Wiley.

Moos, R. H., & Moos, B. S. (1994). *Family Environment Scale manual.* Palo Alto, CA: Consulting Psychologists Press.

Munafo, M. R., Clark, T. G., Moore, L. R., Payne, E., Walton, R., & Flint, J. (2003). Genetic polymorphisms and personality in healthy adults: A systematic review and meta-analysis. *Molecular Psychiatry, 8*, 471–484.

Murray, H. A. (1938). *Explorations in personality.* New York: Oxford University Press.

Mündelein, H. (1982). *Simulierte Arbeitssituation an Bildschirmterminals: Ein Beitrag zu einer ökologisch orientierten Psychologie.* [Simulated job situation at computer terminals: A contribution to ecological-oriented psychology]. Frankfurt/Main: Fischer Verlag.

Nakano, K. (1992). Role of personality characteristics in coping behaviors. *Psychological Reports, 71*, 687–690.

Neale, M. C., Boker, S. M., Xie, G., & Maes, H. H. (1999). *Statistical modeling: Manual* (5th ed.). Richmond, VA: Virginia Commonwealth University.

Neale, M. C., & Cardon, L. R. (1992). *Methodology for genetic studies of twins and families.* Dordrecht, The Netherlands: Kluwer Academic Publishers.

Nebylitsyn, V. D. (1957). Individual differences in strength-sensitivity in the visual and auditory analyzers. *Voprosy Psikhologii, 3*, 53–69 (in Russian).

Nebylitsyn, V. D. (1972). *Fundamental properties of the human nervous system.* New York: Plenum Press.

Nebylitsyn, V. D. (1976). *Psychophysiological studies on individual differences.* Moscow: Nauka (in Russian).

Norris, F., Friedman, M. J., & Watson, P. J. (2002a). 60,000 disaster victims speak: Part II. Summary and implications of the disaster mental health research. *Psychiatry, 65*, 240–260.

Norris, F., Friedman, M. J., Watson, P. J., Byrne, C. M., Diaz, E., & Kaniasty, K. (2002b). 60,000 disaster victims speak: Part I. An empirical review of the empirical literature, 1981–2001. *Psychiatry, 65*, 207–239.

Norris, F., & Perilla, J. (1996). The revised Civilian Mississippi Scale for PTSD: Reliability, validity, and cross-language stability. *Journal of Traumatic Stress, 9*, 285–298.

Nosarzewski, J. (1997). Analogiczny transfer w rozwiązywaniu zadań [Analogical transfer in tasks solving]. *Czasopismo Psychologiczne, 3*, 113–120.

Nowack, K. M. (1991). Psychosocial predictors of health status. *Work & Stress, 5*, 117–131.

Noworol, C. (1998). Zespół wypalenia zawodowego u pielęgniarek pracujących na zmiany [Burnout symptoms in nurses' shift work]. In I. Iskra-Golec, G. Costa, S. Folkard, T. Marek, J. Pokorski, & L. Smith (Eds.), *Stres w pracy zmianowej. Przyczyny, skutki, strategie przeciwdziałania* (pp. 213–226). Warsaw: TAiWPN Universitas.

Noworol, C., & Marek, T. (1993). Typology of burnout: Methodology modeling of the syndrome. *Polish Psychological Bulletin, 24*, 319–326.

O'Brien, T. B., & DeLongis, A. (1996). The interactional context of problem-, emotion-, and relationship-focused coping: The role of the big five personality factors. *Journal of Personality, 64*, 775–813.

Oleszkiewicz-Zsurzs, E. (1986). Zapotrzebowanie na stymulację a preferencje do wyboru zawodu. [Demand for stimulation and vocational preferences]. *Przegląd Psychologiczny, 29*, 509–525.

Oniszczenko, W. (1997). *Kwestionariusz Temperamentu EAS Arnolda Bussa i Roberta Plomina. Wersje dla dorosłych i dla dzieci. Adaptacja polska. Podręcznik* [Arnold Buss and Robert Plomin's EAS Temperament Survey for adults and children: Polish adaptation. Manual]. Warsaw: Pracownia Testów Psychologicznych PTP.

Oniszczenko, W. (2005). *Genetyczne podstawy ludzkich zachowań. Przegląd badań w populacji polskiej* [Genetic foundations of human behavior: A review of data obtained in the Polish population]. Gdańsk, Poland: Gdańskie Wydawnictwo Psychologiczne.

Oniszczenko, W., & Dragan, W. Ł. (2005). Association between dopamine D4 receptor exon III polymorphism and emotional reactivity as a temperamental trait. *Twin Research and Human Genetics, 6*, 633–637.

Oniszczenko, W., & Radomska, A. (2002). Kwestionariusz Temperamentu dla Dzieci (KTD) oparty na Regulacyjnej Teorii Temperamentu—wersja eksperymentalna [Temperament Inventory for Children (TIC) based on the Regulative Theory of Temperament: Experimental version]. *Psychologia–Etologia–Genetyka, 5*, 85–98.

Oniszczenko, W., & Rogucka, E. (1996). Diagnoza zygotyczności bliźniąt na podstawie Kwestionariusza Fizycznego Podobieństwa Bliźniąt [The twins zygosity diagnosis by means of the Questionnaire of Twins Physical Resemblance]. *Przegląd Psychologiczny, 39*, 151–160.

Oniszczenko, W., Strelau, J., Fogel, A., Zawadzki B., & Siwy, A. (2002). Reakcja na ostry stres. Udział czynników genetycznych i środowiskowych [Reaction to acute stress: The contribution of genetic and environmental factors]. *Psychologia–Etologia–Genetyka, 5*, 35–50.

Oniszczenko, W., Zawadzki, B., Strelau, J., Riemann, R., Angleitner, A., & Spinath, F. M. (2003). Genetic and environmental determinants of temperament: A comparative study based on Polish and German samples. *European Journal of Personality, 17*, 207–220.

Oniszczenko, W., & Ziółkowska, H. (2004). Polska wersja Skali Środowiska Rodzinnego (FES) Rudolfa H. Moosa i Bernice S. Moos—harakterystyka psychometryczna [Polish version of the Moos and Moos Family Environment Scale (FES): Psychometric characteristics]. *Przegląd Psychologiczny, 47*, 131–145.

Ormel, J., & Schaufeli, W. B. (1991). Stability and change in psychological distress and their relationship with self-esteem and locus of control: A dynamic equilibrium model. *Journal of Personality and Social Psychology, 60*, 288–299.

Ostendorf, F., & Angleitner, A. (1994). A comparison of different instruments proposed to measure the Big Five. *European Review of Applied Psychology, 44*, 45–53.

Osterman, K., Bjorkqvist, K., Lagerpsetz, K. M. J., Kaukianine, A., Huesmann, L. R., & Frączek, A. (1994). Peer and self-estimated aggression and victimization in 8-year-old children from five ethnic groups. *Aggressive Behavior, 20*, 411–428.

Ozer, E. J., Best, S. R., Lipsey, T. L., & Weiss, D. S. (2003). Predictors of posttraumatic stress disorder and symptoms in adults: A meta-analysis. *Psychological Bulletin, 129*, 52–73.

Paisey, T. J. H., & Mangan, G. L. (1980). The relationship of extraversion, neuroticism, and sensation seeking to questionnaire-derived measures of nervous system properties. *Pavlovian Journal of Biological Science, 15*, 123–130.

Parkes, K. R. (1984). Locus of control, cognitive appraisal, and coping in stressful episodes. *Journal of Personality and Social Psychology, 46*, 655–668.

Pasikowski, T. (2000). Polska adaptacja kwestionariusza Maslach Burnout Inventory [Polish adaptation of the Maslach Burnout Inventory]. In H. Sęk (Ed.), *Wypalenie zawodowe. Przyczyny, mechanizmy, zapobieganie* (pp. 135–148). Warsaw: Wydawnictwo Naukowe PWN.

Paterson, A. D., Sunohara, G. A., & Kennedy, J. L. (1999). Dopamine D4 receptor gene: Novelty or nonsense? *Neuropsychopharmacology, 21*, 3–16.

Pavlov, I. P. (1928). *Lectures on conditioned reflexes: Twenty-five years of objective study of the higher nervous activity (behaviour) of animals*. New York: Liveright Publishing.

Pavlov, I. P. (1938). *Twenty-five years of objective study of the higher nervous activity (behavior) of animals*. Moscow-Leningrad: Narkomzdraw SSSR (in Russian).

Pavot, W., Fujita, F., & Diener, E. (1997). The relationship between self-aspect congruence, personality, and subjective well-being. *Personality and Individual Differences, 22*, 183–191.

Pedersen, N. L., Plomin, R., McClearn, G. E., & Frisberg, L. (1988). Neuroticism, extraversion, and related traits in adult twins reared apart and reared together. *Journal of Personality and Social Psychology, 55*, 950–957.

Pedhazur, E. J., & Pedhazur-Schmelkin, L. (1991). *Measurement, design, and analysis: An integrated approach*. Hillsdale, NJ: Erlbaum.

Pellegrini, D. S. (1990). Psychosocial risk and protective factors in childhood. *Journal of Developmental and Behavioral Pediatrics, 11*, 201–209.

Pengilly, J. W., & Dowd, E. T. (2000). Hardiness and social support as moderators of stress. *Journal of Clinical Psychology, 56*, 813–820.

Perlman, B., & Hartman, A. E. (1982). Burnout: Summary and future research. *Human Relations, 35*, 283–305.

Petrie, A. (1967). *Individuality in pain and suffering*. Chicago: University of Chicago Press.

Pines, A. M., Aronson, & E., Kafry, D. (1981). *Burnout*. New York: Free Press.

Pisula, W. (1994). Sequential analysis of rat behavior in the open field. *International Journal of Comparative Psychology, 7*, 194–201.

Pisula, W., Ostaszewski, P. M., & Matysiak, J. (1992). Effects of physical environment and social experience on stimulus seeking behavior and emotionality in rats. *International Journal of Comparative Psychology, 5*, 124–137.

Plomin, R. (2001). CNS "temperamental" functioning and "g." In A. Eliasz & A. Angleitner (Eds.), *Advances in research on temperament* (pp. 84–96). Lengerich, Germany: Pabst Science Publishers.

Plomin, R., DeFries, J. C., & Loehlin, J. (1977). Genotype-environment interaction and correlation in the analysis of human behavior. *Psychological Bulletin, 84*, 309–322.

Plomin, R., DeFries, J. C., McClearn, G. E., & McGuffin, P. (2001). *Behavioral genetics* (4th ed.). New York: Worth Publishers.

Plomin, R., Kagan, J., Emde, R. N., Reznick, J. S., Braungart, J. M., Robinson, J., et al. (1993). Genetic change and continuity from fourteen to twenty months: The MacArthur Longitudinal Twin Study. *Child Development, 64*, 1354–1376.

Plomin, R., Lichtenstein, P., Pedersen, N. L., McClearn, G. E., & Nesselroade, J. R. (1990). Genetic influence on life events: During the last half of the life span. *Psychology and Aging, 5*, 25–30.

Plomin, R., Owen, M. J., & McGuffin, P. (1994). The genetic basis of complex human behaviors. *Science, 264*, 1733–1739.

Plomin, R., Reiss, D., Hetherington, M., & Howe, G. W. (1994). Nature and nurture: Genetic contribution to measures of the family environment. *Developmental Psychology, 30*, 32–43.

Poortinga, Y. H. (1989). Equivalence of cross-cultural data: An overview of basic issues. *International Journal of Psychology, 24*, 737–756.

Popielarska, M. (1972). *Poziom reaktywności a udział w sytuacjach o różnym stopniu natężenia stymulacji* [Level of reactivity and participation in situations of different stimulative value]. Unpublished master's thesis, Warsaw University, Warsaw.

Rahe, R. H. (1987). Recent life changes, emotions, and behaviors in coronary heart disease. In A. Baum & J. E. Singer (Eds.), *Handbook of psychology and health* (Vol. 5, pp. 229–254). Hillsdale, NJ: Erlbaum.

Richter, J., Eisemann, M., Richter, G., & Cloninger, C. R. (1999). *Das Temperament–und Charakter–Inventar (TCI). Ein Leitfaden über seine Entwicklung und Anwendung* [The Temperament and Character Inventory (TCI): Development and application]. Frankfurt/M: Swets Test Services.

Riemann, R., Angleitner, A., & Strelau, J. (1997). Genetic and environmental influences on personality: A study of twins reared together using the self- and peer report NEO-FFI scales. *Journal of Personality, 65*, 449–475.

Roberts, B. W., & DelVecchio, W. F. (2000). The rank-order consistency of personality traits from childhood to old age: A quantitative review of longitudinal studies. *Psychological Bulletin, 126*, 3–25.

Robinson, J. L., Kagan, J., Reznick, J. S., & Corley, R. (1992). The heritability of inhibited and uninhibited behavior: A twin study. *Developmental Psychology, 28*, 1030–1037.

Rothbart, M. K. (1981). Measurement of temperament in infancy. *Child Development, 52*, 569–578.

Rothbart, M. K. (1989). Temperament in childhood: A framework. In G. A. Kohnstamm, J. E. Bates, & M. K. Rothbart (Eds.), *Temperament in childhood* (pp. 59–73). Chichester, UK: Wiley.

Rothbart, M. K. (1991). Temperament: A developmental framework. In J. Strelau & A. Angleitner (Eds.), *Explorations in temperament: International perspectives on theory and measurement* (pp. 61–74). New York: Plenum Press.

Rothbart, M. K., Ahadi, S. A., & Evans, D. E. (2000). Temperament and personality: Origins and outcomes. *Journal of Personality and Social Psychology, 78*, 122–135.

Rothbart, M. K., & Derryberry, D. (1981). Development of individual differences in temperament. In M. E. Lamb & A. L. Brown (Eds.), *Advances in developmental psychology* (Vol. 1, pp. 37–86). Hillsdale, NJ: Erlbaum.

Rothbart, M. K., Derryberry, & D., Posner, M. I. (1994). A psychobiological approach to the development of temperament. In J. E. Bates & T. D. Wachs (Eds.), *Temperament: Individual differences at the interface of biology and behavior* (pp. 83–116). Washington, DC: American Psychological Association.

Rothbart, M. K., & Posner, M. I. (1985). Temperament and the development of self-regulation. In L. C. Hartlage & C. F. Telzrow (Eds.), *The neuropsychology of individual differences: A developmental perspective* (pp. 93–123). New York: Plenum Press.

Roussis, P. & Wells, A. (2006). Post-traumatic stress symptoms: Tests of relationships with thought control strategies and beliefs as predicted by the metacognitive model. *Personality and Individual Differences, 40*, 111–122.

Rowe, M. M. (1997). Hardiness, stress, temperament, coping, and burnout in health professionals. *American Journal of Health Behavior, 21*, 163–171.

Rozhdestvenskaya, V. I. (1955). An attempt to measure the strength of excitatory processes through aspects of its irradiation and concentration in the visual analyzer. *Voprosy Psikhologii, 1*, 90–98 (in Russian).

Rozhdestvenskaya, V. I., Golubeva, E. A., & Yermolayeva-Tomina, L. B. (1969). On general and partial factors of the strength of the nervous system. In V. D. Nebylitsyn (Ed.), *Problems of differential psychophysiology* (Vol. 6, pp. 3–14). Moscow: Proswieszczenije (in Russian).

Rundquist, E. A. (1933). Inheritance of spontaneous activity in rats. *Journal of Comparative Psychology, 16*, 415–438.

Rusalov, V. M. (1979). *Biological bases of individual-psychological differences*. Moscow: Nauka (in Russian).

Ruscio, A. M., Ruscio, J., & Keane, T. M. (2002). The latent structure of posttraumatic stress disorder: A taxonomic investigation of reactions to extreme stress. *Journal of Abnormal Psychology, 111*, 290–301.

Ryan, R. M., & Frederick, C. M. (1997). On energy, personality, and health: Subjective validity as a dynamic reflection of well-being. *Journal of Personality, 65*, 529–565.

Samochowiec, J. Rybakowski, F., Czerski, P., Zakrzewska, M., Stępień, G., Pełka-Wysiecka, J., et al. (2001). Polymorphisms in the dopamine, serotonin, and norepinephrine transporter genes and their relationship to temperamental dimensions measured by the Temperament and Character Inventory in healthy volunteers. *Neuropsychobiology, 4*, 248–253.

Sanson, A., Prior, M., Garino, E. Oberklaid, F., & Sewell, J. (1987). The structure of infant temperament: Factor analysis of the Revised Infant Temperament Questionnarie. *Infant Behavior and Development, 10*, 97–104.

Saudino, K. J., McGuire, S., Reiss, D., Hetherington, E. M., & Plomin, R. (1995). Parent ratings of EAS temperaments in twins, full siblings, half siblings, and step siblings. *Journal of Personality and Social Psychology, 68*, 723–733.

Saudino, K. J., Pedersen, N. L., Lichtenstein, P., & McClearn, G. E. (1997). Can personality explain genetic influences on life events? *Journal of Personality and Social Psychology, 72*, 196–206.

Schaufeli, W. B., Maslach, C., & Marek, T. (Eds.). (1993). *Professional burnout: Recent developments in theory and research*. Washington, DC: Taylor & Francis.

Schmitz, P. G. (1992). Personality, stress-reactions, and disease. *Personality and Individual Differences, 13*, 683–691.

Schmitz, P. G. (1993). Personality, stress-reactions, and psychosomatic complaints. In G.

L. Van Heck, P. Bonaiuto, I. J. Deary, & W. Nowack (Eds.), *Personality Psychology in Europe* (Vol. 4, pp. 321–343). Tilburg, The Netherlands: Tilburg University Press.

Schmitz, S., Saudino, K. J., Plomin, R., Fulker, D. W., & DeFries, J. C. (1996). Genetic and environmental influences on temperament in middle childhood: Analyses of teacher and tester ratings. *Child Development, 6,* 409–422.

Schnurr, P. P., & Vielhauer, M. J. (2000). Personality as a risk factor for PTSD. In R. Yehuda (Ed.), *Risk factors for posttraumatic stress disorder* (pp. 191–222). Washington, DC: American Psychiatric Publishing.

Schönpflug, W. (1993). Effort regulation and individual differences in effort expenditure. In G. R. J. Hockey, A. W. K. Gaillard, & M. G. H. Coles (Eds.), *Energetics and human information processing* (pp. 271–283). Dordrecht, The Netherlands: Martinus Nijhoff Publishers.

Schulz, P., & Schönpflug, W. (1982). Regulatory activity during states of stress. In H. W. Krohne & L. Laux (Eds.), *Achievement, stress, and anxiety* (pp. 51–73). Washington, DC: Hemisphere.

Selye, H. (1956). *The stress of life.* New York: McGraw-Hill.

Selye, H. (1975). *Stress without distress.* New York: New American Library.

Sęk, H. (Ed.). (1996). *Wypalenie zawodowe—psychologiczne mechanizmy i uwarunkowania* [Professional burnout: Psychological mechanisms and determinants]. Poznań, Poland: K. Domke.

Sęk, H. (2000). Uwarunkowania i mechanizmy wypalenia zawodowego w modelu społecznej psychologii poznawczej [Determinants and mechanisms of professional burnout in a model of social cognitive psychology]. In H. Sęk (Ed.), *Wypalenie zawodowe. Przyczyny, mechanizmy, zapobieganie* (pp. 83–112). Warsaw: Wydawnictwo Naukowe PWN.

Sheldon, W. H., & Stevens, S. S. (1942). *The varieties of temperament: A psychology of constitutional differences.* New York: Harper & Brothers.

Sheridan, C. L., & Radmacher, S. A. (1998). *Psychologia zdrowia* [Health psychology]. Warsaw: Instytut Psychologii Zdrowia.

Shinn, M., Rosaris, M., Morch, H., & Chestnut, D. E. (1984). Coping with job stress and burnout in the human services. *Journal of Personality and Social Psychology, 46,* 864–876.

Shvarts, L. A. (1965). Speed of restoration of visual sensitivity after visual fatigue and after light exposure as indices of lability of nervous processes. In B. M. Teplov (Ed.), *Typological features of higher nervous activity in man* (Vol. 4, pp. 141–146). Moscow: Prosveshcheniye (in Russian).

Simonov, P. V. (1987). Individual characteristics of brain limbic structures interactions as the basis of Pavlovian/Eysenckian typology. In J. Strelau & H. J. Eysenck (Eds.), *Personality dimensions and arousal* (pp. 123–132). New York: Plenum Press.

Siwak, K. (1999). *Interakcja cech temperamentalnych i stylów radzenia sobie ze stresem u kobiet z nowotworem piersi* [The interaction between temperament and coping styles in women with breast cancer]. Unpublished master's thesis, Silesian University, Katowice, Poland.

Siwy, A. (2003). *Uwarunkowania genetyczne i środowiskowe wystąpienia zespołu stresu pourazowego u powodzian. Studia rodzinne* [Genetic and environmental determinants of post-traumatic symptoms in flood victims: Family studies]. Unpublished doctoral dissertation. Warsaw School of Social Psychology, Warsaw.

Siwy, A. (2006). Genetic, environmental, and temperamental correlates of post-traumatic stress disorder: Family studies. In J. Strelau & T. Klonowicz (Eds.), *People under extreme stress* (pp. 189–208). Hauppauge, NY: Nova Science Publishers.

Siwy, A., & Kozak, B. (2004). Zespół stresu pourazowego i style radzenia sobie ze stresem—uwarunkowania genetyczne i środowiskowe szacowane metodą studiów rodzinnych [PTSD and coping styles: Genetic and environmental determinants assessed by means of family studies]. In J. Strelau (Ed.), *Osobowość a ekstremalny stres* (pp. 343–357). Gdańsk, Poland: Gdańskie Wydawnictwo Psychologiczne.

Słabach, E., Morrow, J., & Wachs, T. D. (1991). Questionnaire measurement of infant and child. In J. Strelau & A. Angleitner (Eds.), *Explorations in temperament: International perspectives on theory and measurement* (pp. 205–234). New York: Plenum Press.

Smedslund, G. (1995). Personality and vulnerability to cancer and heart disease: Relations to demographic and life-style variables. *Personality and Individual Differences, 19*, 691–697.

Sobolewski, A. (1996). *Adaptacja Kwestionariusza Zmian Życiowych do warunków polskich (Recent Life Changes Questionnaire—R. H. Rahe'a). Pomiar stresorów w aspekcie normatywnym i indywidualnym* [Polish adaptation of the Recent Life Changes Questionnaire by R. H. Rahe: The measurement of normative and individual stressors]. Unpublished master's thesis, Warsaw University, Warsaw.

Sobolewski, A. (2001). *Specyfika stresorów zależnych versus niezależnych od jednostki. Podejście genetyczne* [The specificity of dependent versus independent stressors: A genetic approach]. Unpublished doctoral dissertation, Warsaw University, Warsaw.

Sobolewski, A., Strelau, J., & Zawadzki, B. (1999). Kwestionariusz Zmian Życiowych (KZŻ): Polska adaptacja kwestionariusza "Recent Life Changes Questionnaire" (RLCQ). R. H. Rahe'a [Rahe's Recent Life Changes Questionnaire (RLCQ): Polish adaptation]. *Przegląd Psychologiczny, 42*, 27–49.

Sobolewski, A., Strelau, J., & Zawadzki, B. (2001). The temperamental determinants of stressors as life changes: A genetic analysis. *European Psychologist, 6*, 287–295.

Sokolov, E. N. (1963). *Perception and the conditioned reflex*. New York: Macmillan.

Somasundaram, D., Norris, F., Asukai, N., & Murthy, R. S. (2003). Natural and technological disasters. In B. L. Green,, M. J. Friedman, J. T. V. M. de Jong, S. D. Solomon, T. M. Keane, J. A. Fairbank, et al. (Eds.), *Trauma interventions in war and peace: Prevention, practice, and policy* (pp. 291–318). New York: Kluwer Academic/Plenum Publishers.

Sosnowski T., & Zimmer, K. (Eds.). (1993). *Metody psychofizjologiczne w badaniach psychologicznych* [Psychophysiological methods in psychological research]. Warsaw: Wydawnictwo Naukowe PWN.

Spence, K. W. (1956). *Behavior theory and conditioning*. New Haven, CT: Yale University Press.

Spence, K. W., & Taylor, J. A. (1951). Anxiety and strength of UCS as determinants of amount of eyelid conditioning. *Journal of Experimental Psychology, 42*, 183–188.

Spielberger, C. D. (1979). *Preliminary manual for the State–Trait Personality Inventory (STPI)*. Odessa, FL: Psychological Assessment Resources.

Spielberger, C. D., Gorsuch, R. L., & Lushene, R. E. (1970). *Manual for the State–Trait Anxiety Inventory*. Palo Alto, CA: Consulting Psychologists Press.

Spielberger, C. D., Sarason, I. G., & Strelau, J. (Eds.). (1989). *Stress and anxiety* (Vol. 12). New York: Hemisphere.

Spurrell, M. T., & McFarlane, A. C. (1993). Post-traumatic stress disorder and coping after a natural disaster. *Social Psychiatry and Psychiatric Epidemiology, 28,* 1–7.

Stagner, R. (1984). Trait psychology. In N. E. Endler & J. McV. Hunt (Eds.), *Personality and the behavioral disorders* (pp. 3–38). New York: Wiley.

Stawowska, L. (1973). *Diagnoza typów osobowości* [The diagnosis of personality types]. Kielce, Poland: Wydawnictwo Uniwersytetu Śląskiego.

Steimer, T., la Fleur, S., & Schulz, P. E. (1997). Neuroendocrine correlates of emotional reactivity and coping in male rats from the Roman high (RHA/Verh)– and low (RLA/Verh)–avoidance lines. *Behavior Genetics, 27,* 503–512.

Stelmack, R. M., Kruidenier, B. G., & Anthony, S. B. (1985). A factor analysis of the Eysenck Personality Questionnaire and the Strelau Temperament Inventory. *Personality and Individual Differences, 6,* 657–659.

Stern, W. (1921). *Differentielle Psychologie* [Differential psychology] (3rd ed.). Leipzig: Johann Ambrosius Barth.

Strelau, J. (1958). Problem parcjalnych typów wyższej czynności nerwowej [Problems of partial types of higher nervous activity]. *Psychologia Wychowawcza, 1,* 244–251.

Strelau, J. (1960). Przewaga ruchliwości analizatora wzrokowego nad słuchowym u człowieka [The prevalence of mobility of the visual analyzer over the auditory one in man]. *Studia Psychologiczne, 3,* 181–198.

Strelau, J. (1964). The dependence of the diagnosis of the type of higher nervous activity on the kind of UCS in CR procedure. *Voprosy Psikhologii, 6,* 37–44 (in Russian).

Strelau, J. (1965a). *Problemy i metody badań typów układu nerwowego człowieka* [Problems and methods of research into types of nervous system]. Wrocław, Poland: Ossolineum.

Strelau, J. (1965b). *O temperamencie i jego poznawaniu* [How to diagnose temperament]. Warsaw: Nasza Księgarnia.

Strelau, J. (1969). *Temperament i typ układu nerwowego* [Temperament and type of nervous system]. Warsaw: Państwowe Wydawnictwo Naukowe.

Strelau, J. (1970). Indywidualny styl pracy ucznia a cechy temperamentalny [The pupil's individual style of work and temperament traits]. *Kwartalnik Pedagogiczny, 15,* 59–77.

Strelau, J. (1972a). The general and partial nervous system types: Data and theory. In V. D. Nebylitsyn & J. A. Gray (Eds.), *Biological bases of individual behavior* (pp. 62–73). New York: Academic Press.

Strelau, J. (1972b). A diagnosis of temperament by nonexperimental techniques. *Polish Psychological Bulletin, 3,* 97–105.

Strelau, J. (1974a). Temperament as an expression of energy level and temporal features of behavior. *Polish Psychological Bulletin, 5,* 119–127.

Strelau, J. (Ed.). (1974b). *Rola cech temperamentalnych w działaniu* [The role of temperamental traits in action]. Wrocław, Poland: Ossolineum.

Strelau, J. (1978). *Rola temperamentu w rozwoju psychicznym* [The role of temperament in mental development]. Warsaw: Wydawnictwa Szkolne i Pedagogiczne.

Strelau, J. (Ed.). (1982). *Regulacyjne funkcje temperamentu* [The regulating functions of temperament]. Wrocław, Poland: Ossolineum.

Strelau, J. (1983). *Temperament, personality, activity.* London: Academic Press.

Strelau, J. (1984). Temperament and personality. In H. Bonarius, G. van Heck, & N. Smid (Eds.), *Personality psychology in Europe: Theoretical and empirical developments* (pp. 303–315). Lisse, The Netherlands: Swets & Zeitlinger.

Strelau, J. (Ed.). (1985). *Temperamental bases of behavior: Warsaw studies on individual differences.* Lisse, The Netherlands: Swets & Zeitlinger.

Strelau, J. (1986). Stability does not mean stability. In G. A. Kohnstamm (Ed.), *Temperament discussed: Temperament and development in infancy and childhood* (pp. 59–62). Lisse, The Netherlands: Swets & Zeitlinger.

Strelau, J. (1987a). The concept of temperament in personality research. *European Journal of Personality, 1*, 107–117.

Strelau, J. (1987b). Emotion as a key concept in temperament research. *Journal of Research in Personality, 21*, 510–528.

Strelau, J. (1988). Temperamental dimensions as co-determinants of resistance to stress. In M. P. Janisse (Ed.), *Individual differences, stress, and health psychology* (pp. 146–169). New York: Springer-Verlag.

Strelau, J. (1991). Are psychophysiological/psychophysical scores good candidates for diagnosing temperament/personality traits and for a demonstration of the construct validity of psychometrically measured traits? *European Journal of Personality, 5*, 323–342.

Strelau, J. (1993). The location of the regulative theory of temperament (RTT) among other temperament theories. In J. Hettema & I. J. Deary (Eds.), *Foundations of personality* (pp. 113–132). Dordrecht, The Netherlands: Kluwer Academic Publishers.

Strelau, J. (1994). The concepts of arousal and arousability as used in temperament studies. In J. E. Bates & T. D. Wachs (Eds.), *Temperament: Individual differences at the interface of biology and behavior* (pp. 117–141). Washington, DC: American Psychological Association.

Strelau, J. (1995a). Autobiografia naukowa [Autobiography of academic activity]. In T. Rzepa (Ed.), *Historia polskiej psychologii w autobiografiach* (Part II, pp. 79–163). Szczecin, Poland: Uniwersytet Szczeciński, Ośrodek Badań Biograficznych.

Strelau, J. (1995b). Temperament and stress: Temperament as a moderator of stressors, emotional states, coping, and costs. In C. D. Spielberger & I. G. Sarason (Eds.), *Stress and emotion: Anxiety, anger, and curiosity* (Vol. 15, pp. 215–254). Washington, DC: Hemisphere.

Strelau, J. (Ed.). (1995c). Narzędzia do diagnozy cech temperamentu i wybranych charakterystyk osobowościowych (tom tematyczny) [Instruments for assessing temperament traits and selected personality characteristics (Special issue)]. *Studia Psychologiczne, 44* (1, 2).

Strelau, J. (1996). Temperament as a moderator of coping with stress. In W. Battmann & S. Dutke (Eds.), *Processes of the molar regulation of behavior* (pp. 205–217). Lengerich, Germany: Pabst Science Publishers.

Strelau, J. (1998). *Temperament: A psychological perspective.* New York: Plenum Press.

Strelau, J. (2000). Temperament [Temperament]. In J. Strelau (Ed.), *Psychologia. Podręcznik akademicki. Vol. 2. Psychologia ogólna* (pp. 683–719). Gdańsk, Poland: Gdańskie Wydawnictwo Psychologiczne.

Strelau, J. (2001a). *Psychologia temperamentu* [Psychology of temperament] (2nd ed.). Warsaw: Wydawnictwo Naukowe PWN.

Strelau, J. (2001b). The place of the construct of arousal in temperament research. In R. Riemann, F. M. Spinath, & F. Ostendorf (Eds.), *Personality and temperament: Genetics, evolution, and structure* (pp. 105–128). Lengerich, Germany: Pabst Science Publishers.

Strelau, J. (2001c). The concept and status of trait in research on temperament. *European Journal of Personality, 15*, 311–325.

Strelau, J. (2001d). The role of temperament as a moderator of stress. In T. D. Wachs & G. A. Kohnstamm (Eds.), *Temperament in context* (pp. 153–172). Mahawah: NJ: Erlbaum.

Strelau, J. (2002). Od teorii regulacji Tadeusza Tomaszewskiego do regulacyjnej teorii temperamentu [From the regulative theory by Tadeusz Tomaszewski to the Regulative Theory of Temperament]. In I. Kurcz & D. Kądzielawa (Eds.), *Psychologia czynności. Nowe perspektywy* (pp. 34–44). Warsaw: Wydawnictwo Naukowe Scholar.

Strelau, J. (2006). *Psychologia różnic indywidualnych* [Psychology of individual differences]. Warsaw: Wydawnictwo Naukowe Scholar.

Strelau, J., & Angleitner, A. (1994). Cross-cultural studies on temperament: Theoretical considerations and empirical studies based on the Pavlovian Temperament Survey (PTS). *Personality and Individual Differences, 16*, 331–342.

Strelau, J., Angleitner, A., & Newberry, B. H. (1999). *Pavlovian Temperament Survey (PTS): An international handbook.* Göttingen, Germany: Hogrefe & Huber.

Strelau, J., Angleitner, A., & Ruch, W. (1990). Strelau Temperament Inventory (STI): General review and studies based on German samples. In J. N. Butcher & C. D. Spielberger (Eds.), *Advances in personality assessment* (Vol. 8, pp. 187–241). Hillsdale, NJ: Erlbaum.

Strelau, J., & Eliasz, A. (1994). Temperament risk factors for Type A behavior patterns in adolescents. In W. B. Carey & S. C. McDevitt (Eds.), *Prevention and early intervention: Individual differences as risk factors for the mental health of children* (pp. 42–49). New York: Brunner/Mazel.

Strelau, J., & Eysenck, H. J. (Eds.). (1987). *Personality dimensions and arousal.* New York: Plenum Press.

Strelau, J., Farley, F. H., & Gale, A. (Eds.). (1985). *The biological bases of personality and behavior: Vol. 1. Theories measurement techniques, and development.* Washington, DC: Hemisphere.

Strelau, J., Farley, F. H., & Gale, A. (Eds.). (1986). *The biological bases of personality and behavior: Vol. 2. Psychophysiology, performance, and applications.* Washington, DC: Hemisphere.

Strelau, J., Jaworowska, A., Wrześniewski, K., & Szczepaniak, P. (2005). *Kwestionariusz Radzenia Sobie w Sytuacjach Stresowych CISS. Podręcznik* [Questionnaire of Coping in Stressful Situations CISS: Manual]. Warsaw: Pracownia Testów Psychologicznych PTP.

Strelau, J., & Kaczmarek, M. (2004). Warsaw studies on sensation seeking. In R. M. Stelmack (Ed.), *On the psychobiology of personality: Essays in honor of Marvin Zuckerman* (pp. 29–45). Amsterdam: Elsevier.

Strelau, J., Kaczmarek, M., & Zawadzki, B. (2006). Temperament as predictor of maladaptive behavior under extreme stress: The Polish studies of natural disasters. In Q. Jing, M. R. Rosenzweig, G. d'Ydewalle, H. Zhang, H.-C. Chen, & K. Zhang (Eds.), *Progress in psychological sciences around the world: Vol. 2. Social and applied issues* (pp. 139–158). Hove, UK: Psychology Press.

Strelau, J., & Klonowicz, T. (Eds.). (2006). *People under extreme stress.* Hauppauge, NY: Nova Science Publishers.

Strelau, J. Klonowicz, T., & Eliasz, A. (1972). Fizjologiczne mechanizmy cech temperamentalnych [Physiological mechanisms of temperamental traits]. *Przegląd Psychologiczny, 15*, 25–51.

Strelau, J., & Krajewski, A. (1974). Individual style of activity and strength of the nervous system. In K. M. Gurevich (Ed.), *Psychophysiological problems of higher level professional experience* (pp. 176–186). Moscow: Sovetskaja Rossija (in Russian).

Strelau, J., Oniszczenko, W., & Zawadzki, B. (1994). *Genetyczne uwarunkowanie i struktura temperamentu młodzieży i dorosłych* [Genetic determination and the structure of temperament in adolescents and adults]. (KBN, Report No. 1.1108.91.02). Warsaw: Warsaw University, Faculty of Psychology.

Strelau, J. Oniszczenko, W., Zawadzki, B., Bodunov, M., & Angleitner, A. (1995). Temperamental traits postulated by RTT viewed from a behavior-genetic perspective: Self-report twin data. *Polish Psychological Bulletin, 26*, 283–295.

Strelau, J., & Zawadzki, B. (1993). The Formal Characteristics of Behaviour–Temperament Inventory (FCB-TI): Theoretical assumptions and scale construction. *European Journal of Personality, 7*, 313–336.

Strelau, J., & Zawadzki, B. (1995). The Formal Characteristics of Behaviour–Temperament Inventory (FCB-TI): Validity studies. *European Journal of Personality, 9*, 207–229.

Strelau, J., & Zawadzki, B. (1996). Temperament dimensions as related to the Giant Three and the Big Five factors: A psychometric approach. In A. Brushlinsky & T. Ushakova (Eds.), *V. D. Nebylitsyn: Life and scientific creativity* (pp. 260–281). Moscow: Publishing House Ladomir.

Strelau, J., & Zawadzki, B. (1997). Temperament and personality: Eysenck's three superfactors as related to temperamental dimensions. In H. Nyborg (Ed.), *The scientific study of human nature: Tribute to Hans J. Eysenck at eighty* (pp. 68–91). Oxford: Pergamon Press.

Strelau, J., & Zawadzki, B. (1998). *Kwestionariusz Temperamentu PTS. Podręcznik.* [Temperament Questionnaire PTS: Manual]. Warsaw: Pracowania Testów Psychologicznych PTP.

Strelau, J., & Zawadzki, B. (2004). Trauma and temperament as predictors of posttraumatic stress disorder and its dimensions 3, 15 months, and two years after experiencing flood. *Polish Psychological Bulletin, 35*, 5–13.

Strelau, J., & Zawadzki, B. (2005a). The functional significance of temperament empirically tested: Data based on hypotheses derived from the regulative theory of temperament. In A. Eliasz, S. Hampson, & B. de Raad, (Eds.), *Advances in personality psychology* (Vol. 2, pp. 19–46). Hove, UK: Psychology Press.

Strelau, J., & Zawadzki, B. (2005b). Trauma and temperament as predictors of intensity of posttraumatic stress disorder symptoms after disaster. *European Psychologist, 10*, 124–135.

Strelau, J., & Zawadzki, B. (2006). Individual differences as moderators of posttraumatic stress symptoms experienced after flood: The role of temperament and coping styles. In J. Strelau & T. Klonowicz (Eds.), *People under extreme stress* (pp. 67–82). Hauppauge, NY: Nova Science Publishers.

Strelau, J., Zawadzki B., Oniszczenko, W., & Sobolewski, A. (2002). Kwestionariusz PTSD–wersja czynnikowa (PTSD-C). Konstrukcja narzędzia do diagnozy głównych wymiarów zespołu stresu pourazowego [The factorial version of the PTSD Inventory (PTSD-F): The development of a questionnaire aimed at assessing basic dimensions of post-traumatic stress disorder]. *Przegląd Psychologiczny, 45*, 149–176.

Strelau, J., Zawadzki, B., Oniszczenko, W., Sobolewski, & A., Pawłowski, P. (2004). Temperament i style radzenia sobie ze stresem jako moderatory zespołu stresu pourazowego w następstwie przeżytej katastrofy [Temperament and style of coping with stress as a moderator of PTSD resulting from experienced disaster]. In J. Strelau (Ed.), *Osobowość a ekstremalny stres* (pp. 48–64). Gdańsk, Poland: Gdańskie Wydawnictwo Psychologiczne.

Strzałecki, A. (2003). *Psychologia twórczości. Między tradycją a ponowoczesnością.* [Psychology of creativity: Between tradition and postmodernism]. Warsaw: Wydawnictwo Uniwersytetu Kardynała Stefana Wyszyńskiego.

Super, C. M., & Harkness, S. (1986). Temperament, development, and culture. In R. Plomin & J. Dunn (Eds.), *The study of temperament: Changes, continuities, and challenges* (pp. 131–149). Hillsdale, NJ: Erlbaum.

Szczepaniak, P., Strelau, J., & Wrześniewski, K. (1996). Diagnoza stylów radzenia sobie ze stresem za pomocą polskiej wersji kwestionariusza CISS Endlera i Parkera [Assessment of styles of coping with stress by means of Endler and Parker's CISS: Polish version]. *Przegląd Psychologiczny, 39,* 187–210.

Szczerbicka, M. (1996). *Interakcja czynników temperamentalno-środowiskowych w etiologii choroby wieńcowej* [The interaction between temperamental and environmental factors in the etiology of coronary disease]. Unpublished master's thesis, Silesian University, Katowice, Poland.

Szlachta, M. (1996). *Interakcja czynników temperamentalno-osobowościowych w etiologii raka piersi u kobiet* [The interaction between temperamental and environmental factors in the etiology of breast cancer in women]. Unpublished master's thesis, Silesian University, Katowice, Poland.

Śliwińska, M., Zawadzki, B., & Strelau, J. (1995). Adaptacja "Zmodyfikowanego Kwestionariusza Wymiarów Temperamentu" W. Windle'a i R. M. Lernera do warunków polskich. Zastosowanie do diagnozy temperamentu młodzieży i osób dorosłych [Polish adaptation of the "Revised Dimensions of Temperament Survey": The application for assessing temperament in adolescents and adults]. *Studia Psychologiczne, 33,* 113–145.

Talbot, N. L., Duberstein, P. R., King, D. A., Cox, C., & Giles, D. E. (2000). Personality traits of women with a history of childhood sexual abuse. *Comprehensive Psychiatry, 41,* 130–136.

Taylor, S., Kuch, K., Koch, W. J., Crockett, D. J., & Passey, G. (1998). The structure of posttraumatic stress symptoms. *Journal of Abnormal Psychology, 107,* 154–160.

Temoshok, L., & Dreher, H. (1992). *The Type C connection.* New York: Random House.

Teplov, B. M. (1956). Problems in the study of general types of higher nervous activity in man and animals. In B. M. Teplov (Ed.), *Typological features of higher nervous activity in man* (Vol. 1, pp. 5–123). Moscow: Akademiya Pedagogicheskikh Nauk RSFSR (in Russian).

Teplov, B. M. (1972). The problem of types of human higher nervous activity and methods of determining them. In V. D. Nebylitsyn & J. A. Gray (Eds.), *Biological bases of individual behavior* (pp. 1–10). New York: Academic Press.

Teplov, B. M. (1985). *Selected works* (Vols. 1–2). Moscow: Pedagogika (in Russian).

Teplov, B. M., & Nebylitsyn, V. D. (1963). Experimental study of properties of the nervous system in man. *Zhurnal Vysshei Nervnoi Deyatelnosti, 13,* 789–797 (in Russian).

Terelak, J. (1974). Reaktywność mierzona indeksem alfa a cechy temperamentalne [Reactivity measured by means of alpha index and temperamental traits]. In J. Strelau (Ed.), *Rola cech temperamentalnych w działaniu* (pp. 45–70). Wrocław, Poland: Ossolineum.

Terelak, J. (1982). *Człowiek w sytuacjach ekstremalnych. Izolacja antarktyczna* [Man under extreme situations: Antarctic isolation]. Warsaw: Wydawnictwo MON.

Tesser, A. (1993). The importance of heritability in psychological research: The case of attitudes. *Psychological Review, 100,* 129–142.

Thomas, A., & Chess, S. (1957). An approach to the study of sources of individual differences in child behavior. *Journal of Clinical and Experimental Psychopathology and Quarterly Review of Psychiatry and Neurology, 18,* 347–357.

Thomas, A., & Chess, S. (1977). *Temperament and development.* New York: Brunner/Mazel.

Thomas, A., & Chess, S. (1986). The New York Longitudinal Study: From infancy to early adult life. In R. Plomin & J. Dunn (Eds.), *The study of temperament: Changes, continuities, and challenges* (pp. 39–52). Hillsdale, NJ: Erlbaum.

Thurstone, L. L. (1951). The dimensions of temperament. *Psychometrica, 16,* 11–20.

Tomaszewski, T. (1963). *Wstęp do psychologii* [Introduction to psychology]. Warsaw: Państwowe Wydawnictwo Naukowe.

Tomaszewski, T. (1967). Aktywność człowieka [Man's activity]. In M. Maruszewski, J. Reykowski, & T. Tomaszewski (Eds.), *Psychologia jako nauka o człowieku* (pp. 219–278). Warsaw: Książka i Wiedza.

Tomaszewski, T. (1975). Człowiek w sytuacji [Man in situation]. In T. Tomaszewski (Ed.), *Psychologia* (pp. 13–36). Warsaw: Państwowe Wydawnictwo Naukowe.

Tomaszewski, T. (1978). *Tätigkeit und Bewusstsein: Beiträge zur Einführung in die polnische Tätigkeitspsychologie* [Action and consciousness: Contribution to the introduction to the Polish theory of action]. Weinheim, Germany: Beltz Verlag.

Tomaszewski, T. (1984). *Ślady i wzorce* [Tracks and patterns]. Warsaw: Wydawnictwa Szkolne i Pedagogiczne.

Topf, M. (1989). Personality, hardiness, occupational stress, and burnout in critical care nurses. *Research Nursing Health, 12,* 179–186.

Troshikhin, V. A., Moldavskaya, S. I., & Kolchenko, N. V. (1978). *Functional mobility of nervous process and professional selection.* Kiev, Ukraine: Naukova Dumka (in Russian).

True, W. R., Rice, J., Eisen, S. A., Heath, A. C., Goldberg, J., Lyons, M. J., et al. (1993). A twin study of genetic and environmental contributions to liability for posttraumatic stress symptoms. *Archives of General Psychiatry, 50,* 257–264.

Trzcińska, M. (1996) *Wpływ temperamentu i stresu na stan zdrowia. Adaptacja Inwentarza Zdrowia GHQ (General Health Questionnaire–D. Goldberga).* [The influence of temperament and stress on health status: Adaptation of D. Goldberg's General Health Questionnaire]. Unpublished master's thesis, Warsaw University, Warsaw.

Turovskaya, Z. G. (1963). The relation between some indices of strength and mobility of the nervous system. In B. M. Teplov (Ed.), *Typological features of higher nervous activity in man* (Vol. 3, pp. 248–261). Moscow: Akademiya Pedagogicheskikh Nauk RSFSR (in Russian).

Ursano, R. J., Fullerton, C. S., & Norwood, A. E. (Eds.). (2003). *Terrorism and disaster: Individual and community mental health interventions.* Cambridge, UK: Cambridge University Press.

Ursin, H. (1980). Personality, activation, and somatic health: A new psychosomatic theory. In S. Levine & H. Ursin (Eds.), *Coping and health* (pp. 259–279). New York: Plenum Press.

Uszyńska, Z. (1971). *Cechy temperamentalne a styl pracy produkcyjnej* [Temperamental traits and productive work]. Unpublished master's thesis, Warsaw University, Warsaw.

van de Vijver, F., & Hambleton, R. (1996). Translating tests: Some practical guidelines. *European Psychologist, 1*, 89–99.

Van der Staay, F. J., Kerbusch, S., & Raaijmakers, W. (1990). Genetic correlation in validating emotionality. *Behavior Genetics, 20*, 51–62.

Van Heck, G. L. (1987). *Temperament and coping strategies.* Unpublished manuscript, Tilburg University, Tilburg, The Netherlands.

Vatsuro, E. G. (1945). The investigation of the comparative lability of the processes of higher nervous activity as applied to the functioning of the separate analyzers. *Trudy Fiziologicheskikh Laboratorii im. I. P. Pavlowa, 12*, 33–57 (in Russian).

Veisaeth, L. (1995). Preventive psychosocial intervention after disaster. In S. E. Hobfoll & M. W. de Vries (Eds.), *Extreme stress and communities: Impact and intervention* (pp. 401–419). Dordrecht, The Netherlands: Kluwer Academic Publishers.

Veit, C. T., & Ware, J. E., Jr. (1983). The structure of psychological distress and wellbeing in general populations. *Journal of Consulting and Clinical Psychology, 51*, 730–742.

Von Knorring, L. (1984). The biochemical basis of sensation-seeking behavior. *Behavioral and Brain Sciences, 7*, 443–445.

Wachs, T. D., & Kohnstamm, G. A. (Eds.). (2001). *Temperament in context.* Mahwah, NJ: Erlbaum.

Wachs, T. D., & Plomin, R. (1991). *Conceptualization and measurement of organism-environment interaction.* Washington, DC: American Psychological Association.

Waller, N. G., Kojetin, B. A., Bouchard, T. J., Jr., Lykken, D. T., & Tellegen, A. (1990). Genetic and environmental influences on religious interests, attitudes, and values: A study of twins reared apart and together. *Psychological Science, 1*, 138–142.

Watten, R. G., Vassend, O., Myhrer, T., & Syversen, J.-L. (1997). Personality factors and somatic symptoms. *European Journal of Personality, 11*, 57–68.

Wenglorz, D. (1996). *Interakcja czynnków temperamentalno-osobowościowych i środowiskowych w etiologii choroby wieńcowej, ze szczególnym uwzględnieniem zawału serca* [The interaction between temperament-personality and environmental factors in the etiology of coronary disease, especially with myocardial infarction]. Unpublished master's thesis, Silesian University, Katowice, Poland.

Whiteman, M. C., Deary, I. J., & Fowkes, F. G. R. (2000). Personality and health: Cardiovascular disease. In W. S. E. Hampson (Ed.), *Advances in personality psychology* (Vol. 1, pp. 157–198). Hove, UK: Psychology Press.

Williams, R. B., & Barefoot, J. C. (1988). Coronary-prone behavior: The emerging role of the hostility complex. In B. K. Houston & C. R. Snyder (Eds.), *Type A behavior pattern: Research, theory, and intervention* (pp. 189–211). New York: Wiley.

Williams, R. J. (1956). *Biochemical individuality: The basis for the genetotrophic concept.* New York: Wiley.

Windle, M. (1989). Predicting temperament-mental health relationships: A covariance structure latent variable analysis. *Journal of Research in Personality, 23*, 118–144.

Windle, M., & Lerner, R. M. (1986). Reassessing the dimensions of temperamental individuality across the life-span: The Revised Dimensions of Temperament Survey (DOTS-R). *Journal of Adolescent Research, 1*, 213–230.

Wolf, H., Angleitner, A., Spinath, F. M., Riemann, R., & Strelau, J. (2004). Genetic and environmental influences on the EPQ-RS scales: A twin study using self- and peer reports. *Personality and Individual Differences, 37*, 579–590.

Wróbel, B. (2001). *Związek temperamentu ze spostrzeganiem wsparcia społecznego w sytu-*

acji stresu [The relationship between temperament and perceived social support in a stressful situation]. Unpublished master's thesis, Silelsian University, Katowice.

Wrześniewski, K. (1984). Development of the Polish form of the State–Trait Personality Inventory. In H. M. Van der Ploeg, R. Schwarzer, & C. D. Spielberger (Eds.), *Advances in test anxiety research* (pp. 265–275). Hillsdale, NJ: Erlbaum.

Wrześniewski, K., & Sosnowski, T. (1987). *Inwentarz Stanu i Cechy Lęku (ISCL). Polska adaptacja STAI* [State– and Trait–Anxiety Inventory (STAI): Polish adaptation]. Warsaw: Polskie Towarzystwo Psychologiczne.

Wundt, W. (1887). *Grundzüge der physiologischen Psychologie* [Outlines of physiological psychology] (Vol. 2, 3rd ed.). Leipzig: Verlag von Wilhelm Engelmann.

Zakrzewska, M. (1994). *Analiza czynnikowa w budowaniu i sprawdzaniu modeli psychologicznych* [Factor analysis in bulding and verification of psychological models]. Poznań: Wydawnictwo Naukowe UAM.

Zalewska, A. (2003). *Dwa światy. Emocjonalne i poznawcze oceny jakości życia i ich uwarunkowania u osób o wysokiej i niskiej reaktywności* [Two worlds: Emotional and cognitive assessments of quality of life and their determinants in persons with high and low reactivity]. Warsaw: Academica.

Zarzycka, M. (1980). *Rola cech temperamentu i osobowości w powodowaniu wypadków przez maszynistów PKP* [The role of temperament and personality in causing accidents by railroad engineers]. Unpublished doctoral dissertation, Warsaw University, Warsaw.

Zawadzki, B. (1992). *Cechy temperamentu w ujęciu Regulacyjnej Teorii Temperamentu i ich pomiar metodą kwestionariusza* [Temperament traits according to the Regulative Theory of Temperament and their measurement by means of a questionnaire]. Unpublished doctoral dissertation, Warsaw University, Warsaw.

Zawadzki, B. (2001). Temperamentalny czynnik ryzyka chorób somatycznych—raka płuca i zawału serca [Temperament as a risk factor of somatic diseases: Lung cancer and myocardial infarction]. In W. Ciarkowska & A. Matczak (Eds.), *Różnice indywidualne. Wybrane badania inspirowane Regulacyjną Teorią Temperamentu Profesora Jana Strelaua.* (pp. 27–52). Warsaw: Interdisciplinary Center for Behavior Genetic Research, Warsaw University.

Zawadzki, B. (2002). *Temperament—geny i środowisko. Porównania wewnątrz–i międzypopulacyjne* [Temperament—genes and environment: Intrapopulation and interpopulation comparisons]. Gdańsk: Gdańskie Wydawnictwo Psychologiczne.

Zawadzki, B., & Strelau, J. (1995). Podstawy teoretyczne, konstrukcja i własności psychometryczne inwentarza "Formalna Charakterystyka Zachowania–Kwestionariusz Temperamentu" [Theoretical basis, construction, and psychometric properties of the questionnaire: "Formal Characteristics of Behavior–Temperament Inventory"]. *Studia Psychologiczne, 33,* 49–96.

Zawadzki B., & Strelau J. (1997). *Formalna Charakterystyka Zachowania–Kwestionariusz Temperamentu (FCZ-KT). Podręcznik* [Formal Characteristics of Behavior–Temperament Inventory (FCB-TI): Manual]. Warsaw: Pracownia Testów Psychologicznych PTP.

Zawadzki, B., Strelau, J., Bieniek. A., Sobolewski, & A., Oniszczenko, W. (2002). Kwestionariusz PTSD–wersja kliniczna (PTSD-K). Konstrukcja narzędzia do diagnozy zespołu stresu pourazowego [PTSD Inventory–Clinical version (PTSD-C): The development of a questionnaire aimed at assessing post-traumatic stress disorder]. *Przegląd Psychologiczny, 45,* 289–315.

Zawadzki, B., Strelau, J., Kobyłka, E., Oniszczenko, W., Pawłowski, P., & Sobolewski, A.

(2002). Współwystępowanie objawów zespołu stresu pourazowego (PTSD) w rodzinach powodzian. Trauma, temperament i indukowanie rodzinne [The coexistence of post-traumatic stress disorder (PTSD) symptoms in flood victims' families: Trauma, temperament, and within-family contamination]. *Psychologia–Etologia–Genetyka, 6,* 7–34.

Zawadzki, B., Strelau, J., Oniszczenko, W., Riemann, R., & Angleitner, A. (2002). Genetyczne i środowiskowe uwarunnkowania temperamentu. Polsko-niemiecka analiza porównawcza oparta na samoopisie i szacowaniu [Genetic and environmental determinants of temperament: A Polish-German comparative study based on self-report and peer-rating data]. *Psychologia–Etologia–Genetyka, 5,* 7–33.

Zawadzki, B., Strelau, J., Oniszczenko, W., Sobolewski, A., & Bieniek, A. (2004). Diagnoza zespołu stresu pourazowego. Charakterystyka psychometryczna wersji czynnikowej i wersji klinicznej kwestionariusza PTSD [The diagnosis of PTSD: Psychometric characteristics of the factorial and clinical version of the PTSD inventory]. In J. Strelau (Ed.), *Osobowość a ekstremalny stres* (pp. 220–237). Gdańsk: Gdańskie Wydawnictwo Psychologiczne.

Zawadzki, B., Strelau, J., Szczepaniak, P., & Śliwińska, M. (1988). *Inwentarz Osobowości NEO-FFI Costy i McCrae—adaptacja polska. Podręcznik.* [Personality Inventory NEO-FFI by Costa and McCrae: Polish adaptation. Manual]. Warsaw: Pracowania Testów Psychologicznych PTP.

Zawadzki, B., van de Vijver, F. J. R., Angleitner, A., de Pascalis, V., Newberry, B., Clark, W., et al. (2001). The comparison of two basic approaches of cross-cultural assessment of Strelau's temperament dimensions in eight countries. *Polish Psychological Bulletin, 32,* 133–141.

Zianowicz, A. (1998). *Specyfika strategii radzenia sobie ze stresem u kobiet z nowotworem piersi i jej związek z charakterystyką temperamentalną* [Temperament-related specificity of the strategy of coping in women with breast cancer]. Unpublished master's thesis, Warsaw University, Warsaw.

Zuckerman, M. (1979). *Sensation seeking: Beyond the optimal level of arousal.* Hillsdale, NJ: Erlbaum.

Zuckerman, M. (1991). *Psychobiology of personality.* New York: Cambridge University Press.

Zuckerman, M. (1994). *Behavioral expressions and biosocial bases of sensation seeking.* New York: Cambridge University Press.

Zuckerman, M. (2005). Genetics of sensation seeking. In J. Benjamin, R. P. Ebstein, & R. H. Belmaker (Eds.), *Molecular genetics and the personality* (pp. 193–210). Washington, DC: American Psychiatric Publishing.

Żmudzki, A. (1986). *Poziom reaktywności a powodzenie w trakcie startu u zawodników w podnoszeniu ciężarów.* [Level of reactivity and success during competition in weightlifters]. Warsaw: Wydawnictwa Instytutu Sportu.

Index